# THE ABC-CLIO WORLD HISTORY COMPANION TO

# Utopian Movements

# THE
# ABC-CLIO
# WORLD HISTORY
## COMPANION TO

# *Utopian Movements*

*Daniel W. Hollis III*

**ABC-CLIO**

Library of Congress Cataloging-in-Publication Data

Hollis, Daniel Webster, 1941–   .
The ABC-CLIO world history companion to utopian movements
/ Daniel Webster Hollis III
     p.     cm.
Includes bibliographical references and index.
ISBN 0-87436-882-0 (hardbound)  (alk. paper)
ISBN 57697-122-7 (paperback)
1. Utopias—history.  2. Utopian socialism—history.
   3. Collective settlements—history. 4. Collectivism—history.
   I. Title.  II. Series
   HX626.H65   1998
   335´.02—dc2198-16577

02   01   00   99   98          10   9   8   7   6   5   4   3   2   1

ABC-CLIO, Inc.
130 Cremona Drive, P.O. Box 1911
Santa Barbara, California 93116-1911


This book is printed on acid-free paper ∞ .
Manufactured in the United States of America.

*For my mentor and friend Paul H. Hardacre,*
*and to the memory of Robert R. Rea*

# Contents

# Preface

Because of Western civilization's fascination with the subject, the amount of writing on utopias is staggering and includes both original literary schemes and critical commentaries. There exist a number of excellent surveys as well as specialized works covering periods since the Renaissance and including Europe and the Americas. However, there is no reference-type work on the subject. Further, existing works usually have not included non-Western utopias. Therefore, in the tradition of the ABC-CLIO Companion series, the present volume seeks to fill an important void. It is not intended to be encyclopedic in covering every utopian movement, whether theoretical/literary or practical/applied experiments. However, it does include all of the major utopian movements since 1450, including those in Asia, Africa, the Pacific, and the Americas as well as Europe.

Although the study of utopias is not a required course in secondary and postsecondary schools, utopian theories, theorists, and activities occupy a prominent place in world, European, and U.S. survey courses in both history and literature, not to mention specialized courses on social, cultural, and intellectual history, literature, philosophy, sociology, and architecture. Moreover, general readers often seek the assistance of a reference source to become familiar with utopian subjects. Hence the potential audience and usefulness of such a reference work is obvious.

The volume's entries are tied to the utopian literary and historical movements, but they include thereby significant utopian thinkers, various sects, settlements, and communes. The primary aim of the entries has been to outline the utopian ideas and the main ingredients in utopian experiments rather than to provide exhaustive summaries of the literature or details of the communities. Because the utopian phenomenon has been uniquely Western, the coverage naturally concentrates upon Western sources. However, because Western ideas spread during the modern era to all other parts of the globe, various hybrid utopian movements—combining Western thought with native traditions—appeared in other continents and cultures. Entries are cross-indexed in the text with "See" and "See also" notes as well as being cited in the general index. Appropriate illustrations have been selected to enhance the textual information. A chronology of utopian movements is located in an appendix. Each entry includes at least one reference that the reader can use as a starting point for more detailed research or reading, and a general bibliography includes complete citations of the sources referenced in the text, as well as general reference sources, anthologies, and bibliographies.

My gratitude for the assistance and cooperation of many people extends to my editors at ABC-CLIO: Todd Hallman, Alicia Merritt, Liz Kincaid, and Allan Sutton. The copy editor, Kathy Delfosse, saved me from many errors and made the text more readable. My colleagues in the History Department at Jacksonville State University offered many helpful suggestions, and David T. Childress read and critiqued a number of entries in draft form. Likewise, Gene Blanton and Rufus Kinney in the English Department critically reviewed draft entries. History Department secretary Audrey Smelley provided constant technical aid. The library staff at Jacksonville State University graciously aided my search for material, especially Debra Thompson, Linda Cain, George Whitesel, and Harry Nuttall. Also, the library personnel at the University of North Carolina, Chapel Hill, showed me many courtesies. My wife, Lynda, endured with equanimity my long hours of research and writing. Whatever the shortcomings of this product, the author accepts the responsibility.

# Introduction

Because utopian schemes aim to improve existing conditions, utopian ideas have been in many respects the essence of Western civilization, which continually projects the present into the future. Indeed, the very search for order and harmony in a future-perfect (or even past-perfect) society became part and parcel of the meaning of Western civilization. Even though other civilizations may devise an image of the perfect society, they have not been as consumed by concerns for future well-being as has the West, mostly because they focused either upon the past or upon a next life beyond the present physical existence. Despite its forward-looking, progressive intent, utopian thought has more often been viewed in the negative because it is grounded in fantasy and thus is mostly unconnected with reality. For example, rarely do utopists describe the practical means to move from the present to a utopian future condition. Also, in their very creation to solve existing problems, the utopias presented new, usually unforeseen, dilemmas. Indeed, many if not most utopian thinkers did not actually conceive that their proposals could be literally applied. They merely hoped that discussion of possibilities for improvement might create a climate of opinion

that would permit reforms. Yet the more profound and serious utopian thinkers preferred to think of their ideas as a vision of the future inextricably linked to the present. Certainly, even the most superficial utopian schemes were tied to their contemporary environment in some fashion. A utopian could not know what to propose in the way of change unless it could be known what was wrong with the extant society. The utopian proclivity can be found in almost every area of modern thought and institutions, from reform movements to revolutions, from literature to architecture, from political theory to economic systems, from science to psychology.

Scholarly disputations about the definition of utopia have occupied almost as much space as descriptions of the utopias themselves. Though the present work will consider utopian movements in both the theoretical (that is, literary) and applied forms, it is important to understand the varied approaches to definition. The fundamental question has revolved around whether to use a comprehensive or narrowly based definition. J. C. Davis has offered the most persuasive case for a narrow definition in his *Utopia and the Ideal Society*. Beginning with the premise that utopia is simply one of many types of ideal society, Davis separates from the utopian category such modes as millennium, Arcadia, Land of Cockaygne, and the perfect moral commonwealth. Frank and Fritzie Manuel in their tour de force, *Utopian Thought in the Western World*, feature various utopian "constellations": pre-utopias (ancient-medieval), early modern Christian utopias (humanism and pansophism), post-Christian utopias (euchronias, communes, socialism, positivism), and dystopias. Some scholars have trouble using the term "utopia" to describe applied experiments. Others would distinguish between the literary and the applied utopias. Glenn Negley and J. Max Patrick argue that using the utopian label requires that the work be fictional and describe a particular human community primarily in terms of its political structure. The science fiction scholar Darko Suvin insists that a utopia is a description of an alternative society organized with sociopolitical structures that are intended to be superior to those that currently exist. Northrop Frye sees the essential ingredient in utopias to be romanticism, a technique of wishful thinking that seeks either the replacement or the transformation of the existing social system.

In addition to the application of sociopolitical frameworks to utopias, ideology has played a large part in shaping the ideal worlds since the beginning of the nineteenth century. Yet the relationship was not much noticed until the second quarter of the twentieth century. Near the end of the long era of dominance by ideologies, Karl Mannheim's famous 1929 treatise *Ideology and Utopia* argued that though both ideology and utopia are unreal, ideology seeks to maintain the status quo whereas utopia proposes to change it through social engineering. Analyzing Mannheim's thesis, Paul Ricouer in *Lectures on Ideology and Utopia* believes Mannheim should have stressed utopia's dual destructive-creative role as well as the potential congruence of utopia and reality. Thus, whereas Mannheim argued that utopia was becoming reality by 1929, Ricouer feared that the end of utopia would also signal the end of society because utopian projections gave society a necessary goal to pursue, a raison d'être. Examining utopia's confrontation with power and authority, Ricouer grappled with the apparent requirement that one must stimulate irrational passions in order to move along the utopian agenda.

Although utopian tendencies may be found in the writings of several ancient peoples, the Greeks were the first to compose full-fledged utopias. The themes found in ancient works recur with regularity among modern utopias. Those topics include stressing the common rather than the diverse elements of humanity, opposition to inhumane government while supporting the power of the state over the individual, the necessity for universal education, the ideals of justice and tolerance, peaceful and natural religion, gender equality, a fascination with eugenics and social engineering, and the elimination of private property rights. Almost all utopias, ancient and modern, do not allow an excess of material possessions and stress, while reforming, the role of work. Iambulus's island utopia of the sun emphasized the harmony of nature with humanity. Plato composed his ideal society, the *Republic*, in the era following Athens' fall from greatness and defeat in the Peloponnesian War when greed and pleasure seeking became the dominant traits. The social system was composed of philosopher-kings (who held all the political and social authority), the military, and laborers. Plato included communal ownership of property, gender equality, and strict censorship of outside influences in his republic. The paramount virtue of the philosopher-king is selfless wisdom, which allows him to pursue and apply the Good, a trait characteristic of all the authoritarian rulers of future utopias. Since utopias possess an absolute authority, utopists such as Plato prefer to portray the residents of their utopias as "subjects" rather than "citizens." There is no need for individual freedoms when the utopian residents have all of their material needs provided as well as a guarantee of justice and security. The ethics of utopia becomes the duty and responsibility of the individual to the whole community instead of self. Moral authority in utopia is embodied in the political authority of the all-knowing, guileless utopian governments.

When Thomas More coined the word "utopia" in 1516, he deliberately combined two similar Greek words into a single meaning: Utopia was both "outopos," meaning no place, and "eutopos," meaning an ideal place. Though there were definite ancient and medieval roots to the notion of an ideal society in descriptions of a golden age, Arcadia, or Land of Cockaygne, utopia as it has been understood in the modern era really had its beginning in More's creation of Utopia. The earlier ideal societies lacked any definite connection with reality. Though the modern utopia may sometimes possess certain golden age, Arcadian, or Cockaygne qualities, it is distinguished from the ancient-medieval versions by its juxtaposition with the society from which it springs. The modern utopia also has links to religion, especially Judeo-Christian traditions, in its incorporation of religious language and symbols. Both religion and utopia are focused on the perfect society and how humanity can reach it. Yet because utopia by definition is man-made, it cannot be a true utopia if transcendent elements predominate. Hence, movements such as millenarianism or messianism are not genuine utopias, although they usually possess some utopian ingredients.

Utopias have been created in various places, but the remodeled city and some geographical entity isolated from the real world have been constant choices for utopian locales because of the need to maintain the tension between the ideal and reality. More popularized the island setting for an ideal society because it was easier to contrast the isolated utopian society with existing society. Other early modern utopists preferred the city since it was an excitingly new and modern demographic and architectural phenomenon. Those who advocated locating their utopias in a different place obviously thought in terms of either eutopia or outopia. Generally, utopists like More who opted for an island thought in terms of outopia, or no place, whereas thinkers who dreamed of a new city conceived of it as a eutopia, or good place. Yet all of the urban eutopias envisioned a reform of humanity as well as a reconstruction of the natural environment. Thus even the secular orientation of these eutopists sprang from a moral-religious sensibility. From the seventeenth century forward, the notion of an extraterrestrial location such as the moon also became popular. By the twentieth century, due to the rapid urbanization spurred by the Industrial Revolution, city planners abounded among architects, and many used the opportunity to frame utopian redesigns of cities. The new eutopians, such as Lewis Mumford, Ebenezer Howard, Le Corbusier, and Frank Lloyd Wright, thought of city design and planning as part of a comprehensive reform of society that would organically unite nature with humanity.

Another vehicle for the utopists was escape in time, either to a remote past or, increasingly after the seventeenth century, to a future time. The emergence of the idea of progress from the Renaissance to the Enlightenment tended to project everything into future time, whether near future or distant future. Those who believed in the idea of progress were convinced that almost any future time would be better than the present or the past. The idea of progress also changed the older notion that utopias were merely fanciful dreams to a recognition that utopias could actually be achieved. Hence, experiments to apply utopian ideas in action became quite fashionable by the nineteenth century. For utopists, therefore, setting the ideal society in the future merely recognized the reality of change and encouraged them to draw blueprints to ensure that the changes would follow rational planning. The advance of science and technology went hand in hand with the pervasive popularity for the idea of progress. The obstacles to progress presented by the natural environment could be altered with the use of such scientific-technological knowledge. Even when the dystopia emerged to crowd out the utopian tradition in the twentieth century, it invariably relied upon a future-time setting to express fears about idealistic dream worlds gone awry.

The modern utopia has gone through several stages since the sixteenth century. Historians have attempted from two to two dozen various organizational typologies. Utopias in the early modern period resembled More's model to one extent or another. That is, the utopias were usually located on islands or in cities seemingly isolated from the rest of the world. They retained religion, but it was a remodeled ecumenical Christianity with a subordinated role. Early modern utopian societies were communist, with no private property permitted. Yet they were also hierarchical, being governed by a benevolent prince and some type of aristocracy, since representative governments had not yet been proven viable. Most of these early modern utopias also tended to be ascetic, providing adequately for needs but without excessive indulgences. Thus they usually possessed certain Arcadian qualities. The daily routines of life seemed utterly boring and static, yet the utopian residents were fully satisfied.

The pansophists of the seventeenth century added the element of science in their constructions while retaining the powerful Christian dynamic. Indeed, their contribution seems fascinating today because of the effort to unite science and Christianity behind the goal of remodeling society. Certainly, the pansophists proved marvelous translators of the practical implications of the Scientific Revolution. The full-fledged introduction of science and technology to utopian designs also began the transformation of utopias from mere dreams to actual potential. Previously, utopists could not conceive of a successful means to produce a reform of

humanity, but science and technology offered a concrete method that could alter the physical environment. Thus utopists after the seventeenth century seized upon environmental, and eventually genetic, engineering as the best avenue of social reform. If mankind's living conditions could be improved, many if not most of the obstacles to social reform could be removed. Seventeenth-century utopists also became acutely aware of a world beyond Europe. The new worlds of other continents and cultures allowed comparisons that provided grist for the utopian mills. Genres such as the Robinsonade and noble savage utopias from the late seventeenth century through the nineteenth century gave rise to utopian critiques of human and institutional corruptions via contrasts with uncorrupted native societies and customs.

By giving definition and structure to the idea of progress, the era of the Enlightenment in the eighteenth century paved the way for the practical utopias of the next century. The utopian philosophers of the Enlightenment outlined the euchronia, or future-time utopia, as a new vehicle to express the anticipated realization of the ideal society. They also laid the foundations for the age of ideology, which allowed utopists to focus upon a specific reform program. Further, the Enlightenment became purely secular in its orientation, largely leaving behind the Christian framework in utopian constructions.

By the time of the Industrial Revolution and the French Revolution in the late eighteenth and early nineteenth centuries, virtually all utopian schemes reflected the different orientation that had emerged in the Enlightenment. The application of science and technology in a secular framework gave utopian thinkers the hope that schemes for reform could be translated from myth into reality. Human attitudes changed from a focus upon needs in a world of scarcity to one of wants in a world of abundance, which recalled the late medieval quasi-utopian setting, the Land of Cockaygne. The old ascetic approach did not die altogether, however, as some nineteenth-century utopian thinkers, such as the utopian socialists, continued to orient themselves more from the Arcadian than the Land of Cockaygne perspective. Nonetheless, a definite new direction emerged with the prospect of social engineering guided by science, making what was once impractical or impossible seem practical. The nineteenth-century model of utopia also reflected an infatuation with egalitarian ideals, which replaced the hierarchical mind-set of an earlier era. The people, disdained as lacking the ability to be self-governing in the early modern era and thus needing disciplined direction, could now make their own collective decisions thanks to an expansion of freedoms and education. Whereas the early modern utopian projectors found it easier for a single authority to institute reforms (More was an important exception), the later planners felt compelled to incorporate the philosophical underpinnings of participatory politics in their ideal societies. Egalitarian thought thus opened the door for groups like the working class and women to entertain utopian schemata to improve their conditions.

Another nineteenth-century response to industrialism was the socialist ideal. The utopian socialists were the first to systematically dissect the social effects of the Industrial Revolution upon the working classes. However, their egalitarian solutions of utopian communities, most often agrarian, proved unable to stop the inexorable tide of industrialism and urbanism. Thus Marxian socialism assumed the mainstream position for the remainder of the nineteenth and the twentieth centuries. Despite Marx's critique of utopias as fantasies, he was unable to completely disconnect utopian elements from his own schemes, particularly the concept of a historical classless society. Marx was evidence of the lineage of utopias from one era to another; each generation of utopian thinkers was profoundly aware of and influenced by their predecessors.

By the twentieth century another stage of utopian thinking was reached with the anti-utopia or dystopia, a bad place. Major twentieth-century philosophers such as José Ortega y Gasset and Karl Popper criticized utopian thinking as not only fatuous but dangerous. The anti-utopians were convinced that naive utopian concepts created a mental frame of reference amenable to authoritarian systems because utopias sought to mute or eliminate individualism. By World War I, the welfare state had emerged as a practicing utopia dependent upon mass rather than individual appeal. The fact that totalitarianism was born in and dominated much of the twentieth century had a profound impact on dystopian writers such as Aldous Huxley and George Orwell, who desired a resurrection of the self-sufficient individual. The fracturing of the liberal tradition after World War I led to an intellectual and cultural void. The most influential postwar philosophy, existentialism, actually was no philosophy at all since it condemned all system making and advocated complete independence of thought and action by individuals. Further, existentialism fostered the growth of relativism, a latter-day revival of sophistry that argued that no fundamental truths existed in the universe or that if such truths existed mankind did not have the capacity to know them. Finally, science and technology, which had been the foundation stones of the liberal tradition, were themselves being called into question because of the development of weapons of mass destruction and by creating the means for greater interference with individual freedom.

The popularity of dystopias among twentieth-century thinkers did not necessarily mean that utopias were no longer possible, even though skepticism about creating an ideal society was greater than ever. Mankind's ability in the twentieth century to control the environment and social conditions came to be regarded as a danger to human freedom rather than as a means to establish an ideal society. Moreover, utopian theorists seemed unable to visualize a small-scale utopia; only massive structures, programs, and governments were considered feasible. Even new problems, which were the motivation for another sequence of utopian proposals, usually treated one or a few aspects of society rather than providing a universal format. Solving problems such as environ-mental pollution seemed to require authoritarian methods that would compromise individual freedom. Yet some of the most recent schemes resurrected certain early modern frameworks, such as the ideal city.

Virtually all of the non-Western utopias emerge because of the impact of Western ideas upon the attitudes toward fate or fortune and personal salvation. As mentioned above, most cultures in Africa, Asia, or Native America were rooted in ancient customs and philosophies that centered upon either the past or eternity and were passive in accepting a personal fate, without recourse to human effort to alter the course. Non-Western cultures showed an even greater reluctance than Western cultures to challenge those traditions and advocate change. The resulting fusion of native culture and traditions with Western utopian concepts has produced many curious hybrids. The most enduring Western influences among non-Western peoples have been Christianity and socialism.

Thus many utopias in Africa, Asia, the Pacific and the Americas can be connected either to millennialism or messianism. Whenever socialism impinged upon non-Western societies, it was refashioned to suit the local conditions. Nonetheless, the non-Western utopias are both fascinating and instructive about the evolution of those societies, and they demonstrate that the ideal of utopia is not limited ultimately by place or peoples.

It would be difficult to encompass all of the ancillary trends that may possess certain utopian elements. Thus no attempt is made to incorporate the category of "fantasies," which would include products such as Lewis Carroll's Alice books, Richard Adams's *Watership Down*, L. Frank Baum's *Wizard of Oz*, or James Barrie's *Peter Pan*. These works are surveyed in Mary Ellen Snodgrass's *Encyclopedia of Utopian Literature*. Further, the celluloid world of fantasy produced by Walt Disney's studios in the twentieth century has not been included. Likewise this work does not survey all of the voluminous science fiction literature, although utopian projects that utilize science fiction formulas are included.

## Alberti, Leon Battista
*See* Renaissance City-State Utopias.

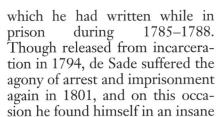

## *Aline et Valcour* (1795)

Noted for his bizarre sexual practices during the era of the French Revolution, the Marquis de Sade also penned a notable utopia, *Aline et Valcour*, partly based upon his freethinking. De Sade seemed in many ways to be in friendly company with the blatant secular nature of utopian constructions by the end of the eighteenth century. He added a peculiar sexual interpretation to the expanding ideas and political constructions of utopia. De Sade, better than early modern utopists, understood the relationship between the sensual and the ideal of happiness.

The Marquis Donatien-Alphonse-François de Sade (1740–1814) was born in Paris to an aristocratic family that had connections with the Bourbon royal family. De Sade was educated by his uncle before entering a Jesuit college. He moved quickly into military service as a cavalry officer, seeing his first action at age fifteen in the Seven Years War (1756–1763). After the war, de Sade married, and the couple had three children, but his domestic life was littered with legal entanglements stemming from his illicit sexual escapades. Indeed, he had served ten years in prison before being liberated in 1790, during which time he contemplated utopian schemes. He published *The School for Libertinism* in 1785, a story of innocent males and females imprisoned in a chateau by a secret society to serve the sensual pleasures of the society's members. In 1790 de Sade became a minor functionary to the revolutionary governments before being arrested again in 1793. In that same year he completed the manuscript for *Aline et Valcour, ou Le Roman philosophique*, most of which he had written while in prison during 1785–1788. Though released from incarceration in 1794, de Sade suffered the agony of arrest and imprisonment again in 1801, and on this occasion he found himself in an insane asylum. By the time of his death in 1814, the Marquis de Sade had endured 34 of his 74 years in prison.

The story of *Aline et Valcour* follows Sainville's search for his kidnapped wife, Leonore, who was carried off by a Venetian aristocrat. Ultimately, Sainville travels widely through Europe, Africa, and parts of Asia. In the course of his travels, he encounters two societies that de Sade described in detail and compared with Europe. Whereas the land of Butua, de Sade's version of Europe, was ruled by a repressive prince, Ben Maacoro, the idyllic island of Tamoe seemed to be the complete opposite, a veritable Arcadia. In stereotypical utopian Tamoe, residents enjoy ample but not excessive fruits for existence, wear plain clothing, suppress passions, and have no fear of crime, which is virtually nonexistent. Although de Sade included Tamoe as a kind of sop to the traditional contemporary utopian ideal, he draws the reader more intently to the picture of the troubling society of Butua. Sainville encountered in Butua the king's Portuguese counselor, Sarmiento, who explained that cannibalism practiced by the Butuans was simply the natural consequence of enjoying the reward of dominion over their natural enemy neighbors, the Jagians. De Sade suggests in the account of Butua that despite its cruelties and despite the absence of either pity or fear of death, Butua existed as a society without hypocrisy and hence possessed a certain innate virtue. The Butuans lived for the moment and showed little concern about the past or the future.

De Sade used the Butuans to promote his belief that the state should exist almost solely to defend the territory against aggressor enemies and not to enforce social rules that limited the individual expression of passions. Liberty of the passions must coexist with liberty of the press or conscience. De Sade would eliminate virtually all criminal laws. For example, he argued that theft of property occurred because of the lack of vigilance by the owner, and in the event theft had the consequence of distributing property more equally. Even murder is compelled, de Sade concluded, by an urge of nature that should not be punished since human life was no more sacred than animal or plant life. Christianity's Golden Rule of loving one's neighbor was irrational since it went against the innate characteristic selfishness. Sainville defended, rather ineffectively, Sarmiento's assault upon many of the tenets of Enlightenment thought that de Sade decried. De Sade was fond of turning Enlightenment principles inside out. In another semi-utopian work, *The Philosophy of the Boudoir* (1795), de Sade carried the Enlightenment's egalitarian theme to the extreme—even while advocating female equality—by arranging sexual orgies for groups including all social classes. De Sade enjoyed mocking the established sexual order as a motif for advocating extreme egalitarianism. Known in his own time simply as a pornographer, de Sade may have influenced the ideas of future egalitarians such as Charles Fourier and John Humphrey Noyes about sexual freedom. Yet in the twentieth century Aldous Huxley dismissed de Sade's bizarre revolutionary notions as a "peculiar brand of insanity."

**Reference** Favre, Pierre. *Sade, utopiste: Sexualité, pouvoir et L'Etat dans le roman* Aline et Valcour (1967).

## *Altneuland* (1902)

Although he was not the founder of Zionism, Theodor Herzl moved the discussion of a national Jewish state from Jewish circles to the world stage. His utopian future-time projection of a Zionist state in *Altneu-land* became the most coherent structure for the realization of a Jewish dream. Herzl borrowed from many nineteenth-century utopists, especially from Theodor Hertzka's *Freeland*, the framework for his own utopia. He showed great insight into the future prospects for Zionism and the Jewish state, so his utopia proved to be not only realistic but achievable.

Theodor Herzl (1860–1904) was born into a secular, middle-class Jewish family in Budapest, Hungary. The family later moved to Vienna, Austria, when Theodor was a child. Through his educational preparation in the law, Herzl adopted a bourgeois liberal philosophy typical of late-nineteenth-century Europe. Herzl had heard about the idea of a Jewish state while in his youth and gradually embraced it as a practical solution to the problem of anti-Semitism. Exchanging a law practice for journalism, Herzl proved his writing skills while working for the Vienna *New Free Press*. He sought to impress upon his Gentile readers as well as on Jews the importance of establishing a Jewish nation. As the *New Free Press*'s Paris correspondent after 1891, he quickly gauged the depth of European anti-Semitism while covering the internationally known Dreyfus Affair. After immersing himself in the Jewish problem through a play called *The New Ghetto* (1894), Herzl produced the major outline of a solution in *The Jewish State* (1896). In the latter, he concluded that international anti-Semitism forced the Jews to seek a haven in a nation-state as the only practical solution to repression and discrimination. He summarized all of the issues affecting Jews and surveyed the various Jewish organizations and the idea of a nation-state in either Argentina or Palestine. Herzl then launched the first Zionist Congress at Basel, Switzerland, in 1897, which led to the founding of the World Zionist Organization. Thereafter he focused almost exclusively upon the dream of a Zionist state.

In *Altneuland* (Old-new land), Herzl used the utopian technique to imagine a Jewish state, the New Society, in 1923 Palestine. The name for Herzl's utopia was probably derived from a Jewish synagogue in Prague called *Altneuschul* (Old-new synagogue). He chose Palestine as the site because it was the location of ancient Israel. In addition to using a utopian setting to describe the hoped-for Jewish state, Herzl also made *Altneuland* a society that achieved social justice and that therefore was similar to those found in many other utopian writings. Thus, Herzl sought in *Altneuland* to create a Jewish society different from the traditions of the past. He understood that though most Jews were middle class, all classes must be comprehended in the Jewish state. Herzl's idea for his social reorganization, or *gemeinschaftlich*, was derived from nineteenth-century utopian socialist ideas. One of the economic means to his social goal was the public ownership of land first outlined in *The Jewish State*. The state's National Fund would lease plots of land to individual farmers. The state would also operate public housing and social welfare agencies and supervise a seven-hour workday. Herzl's theory suggested that although the principle of cooperation pervades the economy and society, individual initiative will be rewarded.

Herzl's chief character, David Littwak, in a town meeting at Neudorf in Galilee explained the principles behind the New Society. Littwak implied that the idea for this type of society derived from the common experiences of Jews in all corners of the world before they arrived in Palestine. He mentioned the French socialist Charles Fourier's phalansteries, Etienne Cabet's Icarie, Theodor Hertzka's Freeland, and Edward Bellamy's communist society as inspirations for the New Society. No doubt Herzl understood that a Jewish state established from scratch had a much greater opportunity to implement an abstract economic and social structure. Another liberal innovation in *Altneuland* involved granting women full political rights, including the franchise. The New Society would provide free education to children through postsecondary schools. Every citizen of the Jewish state would be required to give two years' national service. Moreover, Herzl did not envision males satisfying their obligation in military service. Rather, both men and women would serve in institutions such as hospitals, orphanages, retirement homes, and youth camps. Through such an arrangement, much of the social welfare system would be staffed by those young people fulfilling their national service rather than by bureaucrats. The state would supervise careful urban planning in laying out cities and constructing the infrastructure. Herzl conceived of a mass transportation system within and between urban centers. Further, the New Society would utilize fully all the contemporary technology to make the economy and society run smoothly.

Herzl knew that one of the thorniest problems facing a Zionist utopia located in Palestine would be relations with the majority Arab population. The local Arabs would be allowed to join the New Society on an equal standing with Jews. Herzl introduced an Arab character, Reschid Bey, to project the problem of Arabs relating to Jews. Of course, Herzl favored toleration toward Arab and Islamic traditions so that if Muslim women preferred not to assume the political roles of Jewish women in the New Society, there would be no coercion or penalties upon them. In the story, Littwak leads a moderate effort to block a campaign to limit civil and political rights to Jews only, but the inclusion of the episode demonstrated Herzl's awareness of the potential dangers of fanatical national or religious movements. However, because at the time Herzl wrote *Altneuland* the Arabs were subjects of the Turks, he could not have anticipated the intensity of future Arab nationalism.

*See also* Kibbutzim.

*Reference* Avineri, Shlomo. *The Making of Modern Zionism: The Intellectual Origins of the Jewish State* (1981).

## Altruria

The prolific American novelist of realism William Dean Howells sought to make a fictional utopia seem realistic and attractive to his own time in *A Traveler from Altruria* (1894) and its sequel, *Through the Eye of the Needle: A Romance* (1907). After reading Edward Bellamy's famous altruistic utopian treatise *Looking Backward* (1887), Howells chose to depart from his typical fictional stories to create his own utopia. Howells had initiated the utopian project with 23 essays entitled "Letters of an Altrurian Traveler," which were published in *Cosmopolitan* magazine between 1892 and 1894. He later reissued the first 12 essays in book form as *A Traveler from Altruria* and used 6 of the remaining essays as the first part of *Through the Eye of the Needle*. Altruria was located in the near future partly to allow an interchange between Howells's contemporaneous United States and Altruria. Howells clearly hoped that the United States would learn to imitate the ways of Altruria.

Born in Ohio, William Dean Howells (1837–1920) learned to set type in his father's printing office and later entered the newspaper business as an editor. However, he quickly launched a literary career, publishing a book of poems at age 23. He served as the U.S. consul at Venice, Italy, during the Civil War and wrote for the *Nation* and *Atlantic Monthly* following the war. In later years, Howells also wrote for *Century Magazine* and *Harper's Monthly*. By the 1870s, Howells began to produce novels on a regular basis. The 1886 Haymarket Square labor riot in Chicago seemed to trigger Howells's serious thought about contemporary social problems. Howells's utopian thinking also was influenced by reading Laurence Gronlund's *Cooperative Commonwealth* (1884), which pointed out both the flaws and the potential for reform in the U.S. tradition. Thus Howells became a leader in the development of realism in late-nineteenth-century U.S. literature.

Howells's fictional South Seas island nation of Altruria had established an ideal society in the first century from Hellenic roots, but in more recent times it had been overwhelmed and corrupted by neighboring American capitalist imperialists. Thus the Altrurian era of degradation, the "Period of Accumulation," corresponded to the United States of Howells's day. Yet the Altrurians had ultimately rejected the corrupting lifestyle in favor of a pastoral utopia that operated on the principles of equality and cooperation. Altruria was something of a compromise between an advanced capitalist, technological, urban society and a pastoral agrarian society. The classless Altrurians enjoyed universal education and had no crime, in part because Howells had followed the inspiration of Leo Tolstoy and banished money and thus avarice from Altruria. The Altrurians lived simple rather than ostentatious lives and because of their cooperative spirit worked only three hours per day. After laboring in the fields, the Altrurians, both male and female, found time to perform happily other household work and to pursue their avocations. Yet even this idyllic heaven-on-earth society maintained worship of God and belief in an afterlife owing to an early conversion of the Altrurians by a Christian missionary. Hence Howells portrayed a type of Christian socialist utopia similar to Bellamy's, but he added a mythology about an agrarian pastoral life, which Howells may have envisioned as part of America's early colonial history.

Howells allowed the real world to confront the utopia of Altruria through the visit of Aristedes Homos to New England. The politically incorrect Homos quickly understands that the United States and his acquaintance and guide Mr. Twelvemough are the complete antithesis of Altruria and Altrurians. A later visit to New York City confirms Homos's analysis that U.S. social injustices are caused by a greedy plutocracy. Yet Howells hopes to show through Homos and Altruria that America and Americans, especially the middle class, can embrace the utopian ideal and achieve social justice. Homos discovers in a nearby village both the degradation of capitalism and the hope for a link with Altruria. The local farmers are suffering from the effects of monopolistic practices and have adopted a populist political outlook. Homos tells the

Americans that Altrurian society missed but did not seek a return to their previously opulent lifestyle. Indeed, Homos meets and marries an American woman who agrees to return with Homos to Altruria to learn the enjoyment of utopian felicities. Yet because they seemed unsure of their society's contribution, the native Altrurians did not seek to spread their system elsewhere or to compare their ideal society favorably with others. Howells does not deal directly with politics, war, or disease because all were absent in Altruria. Thus Altruria appears quite romantic in comparison to all of Howells's portrayals of realism in his other novels. Moreover, Altruria becomes a statement of Howells's idealism about the importance of morals and his faith in the problem-solving capacity of political democracy.

Howells seems most concerned to bring U.S. practices more into line with what he sees as its historic ideals through the vehicle of Altruria. By comparing the ideal with the practice, Howells hoped to demonstrate to Americans the real potential of applying utopian ideas to improve society. The primary problem with the United States, according to Howells, was that its democratic (that is, utopian) political principles clashed with its aristocratic social system. Altruria's history stands as a model of how developments such as Christianity, representative government, and capitalism could be blended effectively into the society in an equitable fashion. Howells's use of utopia as a reform instrument appears to be a more classical than modern technique. He saw utopia as simply a means of providing proper perspective on the ills of the present rather than as a blueprint for specific reforms. Howells also departed from virtually all modern secular utopists in providing a significant role for Christianity in his model. Thus Altrurians possess a set of unambiguous values, which gives Howells's utopia an easy justification for reforms. Unlike Bellamy's technologically advanced utopia, Howells preferred the radical simplicity of the pastoral utopia, which offered fewer obstacles to reform.

On the other hand, Howells's utopia met with much less public fanfare than Bellamy's in 1890s America, though the term "Altruria" was borrowed often by other utopists. The issue for contemporary liberals like Howells was how to make the ideal of social justice conform to the unequal social structure without arbitrarily abolishing property rights and redistributing wealth. He did not seek to found a movement, although his socialist ideas found renewed interest during the depression years of the 1930s.

*Reference* Bennett, George N. *The Realism of William Dean Howells, 1889–1920* (1973).

## Amana Society

Beginning in Germany as the Society of True Inspiration, the Pietist sect immigrated to the United States in 1842 to establish a utopian community in New York. It later moved to the Iowa frontier and flourished there, as the Amana Society, on a small scale for decades. The Amana communities adopted a limited communism that they applied to their real property but less to personal property. The communitarian features of the experiment focused upon their development of skilled crafts, which became their livelihood. Their craftsmanship was most notable in the distinctive furniture they produced. The society lasted until 1932, when its communal features were terminated.

Pietists had originated in eighteenth-century Germany but had experienced a variety of difficulties. Most of their members were skilled tradesmen who attempted to maintain the unity of their communities without sacrificing their religious practices. By the 1840s, Pietists were subject to persecution by the state owing to their refusal to take oaths and serve in the military. Led by Christian Metz (1794–1867), a carpenter, a group of Pietists who believed in divine and specific inspiration as a guide to life determined to leave Germany for the United States. With three companions, Metz sailed from Bremen to New York in 1842 and purchased 5,000 acres of land from the

*A bell tower stands outside an Amana Colony church in Homestead, Iowa.*

Seneca Indians near Buffalo. The Inspirationists organized themselves under the name Ebenezer Society, complete with a constitution, and by 1846 about 800 immigrants, mostly from Hesse, had established several communities. Metz proposed a temporary two-year system of communal ownership of property (except personal property), but it soon became permanent. Since most of the settlers had been craftsmen rather than farmers in Germany, their U.S. economy was oriented around manufacturing. Although they had not conceived that communal ownership of property would be necessary back in Germany, they found that it worked best for the U.S. experiment. When land prices skyrocketed around Buffalo, the community decided to sell their New York estates and move to Iowa, where they could expand at less cost.

The move began in 1855, with the first Iowa village constructed at Amana in east central Iowa near the Iowa River. Five other communities followed, and the six settlements were completed by 1862. In 1859 the settlement was incorporated as the Amana Society. The six villages, covering about 25,000 acres, were situated about one and one-half miles apart. Later a seventh village was established at Homestead on the rail line. Each village had a school, general store, and various workshops. The operations also included communal barns and mills. Families possessed their own houses, but they utilized common eating and meeting facilities. Because the villages were small, they were managed collectively and independently.

The government at Amana consisted of 13 elders elected each year by the adult males. The only female leader was an early German émigré, Barbara Heinemann, a former servant who worked closely with Metz. The 13 leaders elected a president as presiding officer. The central government primarily assisted the villages to acquire what they needed whenever shortages occurred. The society was held together by the close internal relationships carried on in both political and religious convocations. Women were required to wear nondistinct clothing, including black caps to keep their hair above their necks, without ornamentation. In meetings women were either segregated from the men or excused. There was even a segregation of sexes among the children. Like other Pietist sects the Amana Society honored celibacy, but it did not entirely discourage marriage, though men could not marry until age 24. The prospective bride and groom had to remain apart for a year prior to the marriage vows to demonstrate their sincerity. Both of the society's long-time leaders, Metz and Heinemann, were married. Admission to the society by outsiders was carefully scrutinized. In other respects the society was not as ascetic as the Shakers. They had a full diet, which included beer and wine. They often read materials such as newspapers from outside the community that might offer means of improving their economy. The education of children included religious instruction but also music along with the rudiments of language and math skills.

In their religious services the members read the Bible and their own special writings. The Amana Society recognized Saturday as the Sabbath when their principal worship services were held, usually led by Metz. Following Metz's death in 1867, Heinemann became more active as a leader until her own death in 1883. The Amana Society celebrated the traditional Christian holy days and placed great emphasis upon the observance of communion, and the elders conducted an annual religious examination that included confession of sins and healing of personal disputes. The society also published a variety of religious literature including hymns and histories.

The Amana system remained largely intact until 1932, when the society was incorporated as a capitalist entity. A religious board continued to govern the society's members, but a separate secular business agency handled the manufacturing side, which produced the famous furniture. The original villages retained their social and religious traditions after 1932. The population of the settlements did not vary greatly over the decades because of the strict requirements for joining the society and the limited birthrate.

*Reference* Barthel, Diane L. *Amana: From Pietist Sect to American Community* (1984).


## Anarchism

As the third stage of nineteenth-century socialism, anarchism offered less structure for the future than did either of its predecessors, the utopian and scientific socialism. Because of its coincidental attach-ment to real-world conditions and unreal descriptions of a future postcapitalist age, anarchism has been associated with both utopian and anti-utopian themes. The intellectual founders of anarchism were a diverse group and included William Godwin in England, Pierre-Joseph Proudhon in France, and Mikhail Bakunin in Russia. The anarchists agreed with the Marxists that capitalist private property should be abolished and redistributed. However, they rejected the Marxist dictatorship of the proletariat as a scheme to empower socialist intellectuals and to continue the historical oppression of the underclasses. Thus the anarchists wanted the immediate destruction of capitalism and property, followed by the spontaneous creation of a moral society without government or laws.

William Godwin (1756–1836), in his *Enquiry Concerning Political Justice* (1793), reflected a tradition in England that hearkened back to an anarchic period in the civil war (1640s). He proposed a society without either private ownership of property or formal government. In the process, Godwin assailed the Enlightenment social contract theory by arguing that society must re-create literally the theoretical state of nature in which man was absolutely free and sovereign. Thomas Hobbes, John Locke, and Jean-Jacques Rousseau had used the theory of the state of nature as a starting point for their social contract theories. Drawing from his religious training, Godwin believed in the basic goodness of humanity

*The Russian revolutionary and writer Michael Alexandrowitsch Bakunin (1820–1910), photographed in Paris by Gaspard Félix Nadar, 1865.*

and like Rousseau saw sociopolitical institutions as the source of inequality and corruption. If absolute freedom could be established, humans would live in peace and harmony by voluntarily forming groups of individuals united by common interests. Godwin's state of anarchy would also ensure gender equality, one of his favorite themes. Godwin understood that for a philosophy of anarchy to be accepted, most traditional attitudes would have to be reformed. His system of discipline included psychological techniques, such as shaming, to reform antisocial conduct. Godwin's influence was felt most immediately among the romantic poets in England. Robert Southey and Samuel Taylor Coleridge proposed the creation of an anarchic settlement called a Pantisocracy in western Pennsylvania in 1794, but it never developed beyond the conceptual stage.

Decades after Godwin's outline of anarchism, the French printer Pierre-Joseph Proudhon (1809–1865) penned the gospel according to anarchism in the pamphlet *What Is Property?* (1840). Proudhon's purely intellectual attack upon the concept of private property appealed to only a few followers in an era dominated by the utopian socialists. Seeking to redefine work in terms of human creativity and dignity, Proudhon thought in terms of the moral values of human labor. Proudhon was suspicious of Marx's notion of revolution, seeing it as merely a vehicle for exchanging one exploiter class for another. He moralized against the capitalist system but saw in the socialist replacement another system potentially ripe for corruption. He felt that even the liberal slogans about liberty, equality, and justice were pipe dreams since they depended upon a system for their implementation. Instead, Proudhon proposed independent mutual associations of affiliated free individuals to be formed after the revolutionary overthrow of capitalism. With the abolition of the state, property, and capital, an equal redistribution of property combined with elimination of the temptations of accumulation and legal manipulation would produce a truly free society operated by individuals. Proudhon, unlike the utopian socialists, admired the traditional patriarchal family and envisioned an anarchist society dominated by males.

Anarchism found its greatest following under the leadership of two alienated Russian aristocrats, Mikhail Bakunin (1814–1876) and Petr Kropotkin (1842–1921), both of whom spent time in prison for their political views. The Russian socialists initially joined the Marxist First International (founded in 1864), where they soon dominated the organization. Like their intellectual heirs, the Russian anarchists became suspicious of Marx's doctrine of the dictatorship of the proletariat, believing it to be merely a technique to allow socialist intellectuals to become the new oppressor class. Bakunin was contemptuous of Marx's controlled revolutionary stages and confident in the immediate action of the proletariat. Fearing an anarchist takeover,

Marx dissolved the First International in 1872, and the anarchists became a distinct socialist movement thereafter. While Bakunin disdained intellectual theory, Kropotkin sought to embrace science and history as tools to explain the anarchist prospects. Through his study of zoology Kropotkin, in *Mutual Aid: A Factor of Evolution* (1902), assailed the social Darwinist view of human struggle and argued that mankind could and would work together for its common good. Kropotkin later joined with the Bolsheviks in overturning the czarist regime in Russia because he believed anarchism and communism were essentially compatible. Anarchism rejected middle-class values, including representative government, so that they rarely formed political parties to promote their programs in legislative form. Rather, the anarchist plan of action, through rather loose organizations, included violent acts against capitalist institutions and representative leaders: physical sabotage and assassinations. The list of their assassination victims was impressive: France's president, Spain's premier, Italy's king, Austria's empress, and a U.S. president.

Undoubtedly the earliest precursor to modern anarchism can be found in ancient Chinese Taoism and the "doctrine of the absence of princes" (*wu-chun-lun*). Taoism taught that anarchism existed in the world of the dead and also in certain countries far beyond the boundaries of China. Over the centuries, anarchism in China was nurtured by various disappointments with the existing order. When the Chinese considered the possibility of changing the existing system, they thought more in terms of the restoration of a natural order than in terms of liberation or freedom for the individual. Certainly, in China the foundations for anarchism in the modern era had been established centuries earlier.

The emergence of anarchism in China in the modern era can be traced to a group of Chinese students studying in Paris who formed an organization in 1907 led by former journalist Wu Chih-hui (1864–1954). They were drawn to the theories of

Bakunin and Kropotkin and began publishing an anarchist journal, *New Century*, which blended modern concepts of social Darwinism and libertarianism with ancient Taoist teachings. Wu and his fellow anarchists became acquainted with Sun Yat-sen and conceived of anarchism as the means of salvation for China. Evolution and especially the advance of technology indicated to the Chinese anarchists that a progressive anarchist state could be created in China. However, Wu and his disciples also believed that the evolutionary process meant that the chasm between good and evil would increase over time, so that the ideal society would not inevitably develop. Without question, Wu Chih-hui represented a break with the traditions in China, such as Taoism and Confucianism, wherein utopian concepts were conceived in terms of a return to a primitive past. For Wu, the future was not in the past but in the possibilities of growth and development from the present. The Chinese anarchists also departed from their intellectual heritage by their focus upon the individual rather than on society as a whole. Wu Chih-hui's ideas were supplemented by those of another Chinese anarchist living in Japan, Liu Shih-p'ei (1884–1919), editor of the journal *Natural Justice*. Liu's agrarian utopianism argued that labor should not be compartmentalized but, rather, should integrate its theoretical (moral imperative) and practical (necessary for survival) aspects. He also argued strongly that women should be at the forefront of the anarchist revolution. After the overthrow of the Manchu monarchy in 1911, the anarchists emerged in China itself, initially concentrating on establishing a universal language. There was a brief experiment outlined by Liu called the New Village Movement, a quasi-anarchist concept during 1918–1919. However, Chinese anarchism never fully developed because it was overwhelmed by the movement of nationalism and eventually merged into the developing communist organization led by Mao Ze-dong.

The most profound illustration of anarchism as anti-utopia was the thinking of the

French engineer Georges Sorel (1847–1922), who used the term "utopia" as an epithet against liberal schemes of reform. Seeking to completely overturn and replace the existing establishment, Sorel's syncretism drew from a variety of sources, including the works of Marx, pragmatists, and antirationalists such as Friedrich Nietzsche. Inspired by Nietzsche's "superman," Sorel constructed a Romantic, antihero, model socialist symbolized by the working-class leaders of the revolutionary French Commune of the early 1870s. Sorel urged socialists not to participate in the Commune's successor, the French Third Republic, since cooperation with liberalism would compromise anarchism's ideals and goals. In his *Reflections on Violence* (1906), Sorel argued that mankind, especially the proletariat, rose to its highest potential throughout history in heroically resisting selfish materialism while embracing an ascetic lifestyle. Since Sorel did not consider historical myths to be utopian, he wanted to create his own peculiar heroic myth of collective, selfless individuals without elite controls or legal institutions. The technique of voluntarist organization advocated by Sorel, the syndicate of workers, existed without formal structure and would help to bring down the capitalist system via the general strike, which would cause capitalists to surrender the means of production to the heroic proletariat. The most infamous anarchist workers' group was the International Workers of the World, founded in the United States in 1905 and spearheaded by "Wild Bill" Haywood. The first time the general strike was attempted in Britain in 1926, it failed miserably to achieve the aims of workers. Yet the 1968 French student uprising employed a more successful general strike, and the 1991 general strike in Albania won major government concessions to workers. Sorel's anarchosyndicalism continues to garner support from contemporary intellectuals such as Noam Chomsky.

Twentieth-century anarchist theorists have become more diverse, some questioning the real possibility of a totally voluntary, nonauthoritarian society. The German Jewish anarchist Gustav Landauer (1870–1919) sought to blend romantic themes of the *volk* (the people) with anarchist individualism. Robert Nozick's *Anarchy, State, and Utopia* (1974) argues that anarchism is compatible with both a "minimal state" and utopia. He believes it is impossible to re-create the ideal state of nature described by early anarchists. Other theorists have suggested that anarchism is not antithetical to every form of authority. Antigovernment movements and the growing breakdown of law in Western societies are also cited as evidence of anarchism's viability at the end of the twentieth century. The establishment and growth of the quasi-anarchist Libertarian Party in the United States since the 1970s is cited by anarchist thinkers as evidence of its present and future influence. Among the anti-system existentialists, there have also been anarchist thinkers including Landauer's disciple Martin Buber and Nikolay Berdyayev. Ecotopian Murray Bookchin likewise reflects a kind of communitarian anarchism in his *Post-Scarcity Anarchism* (1971) and *The Ecology of Freedom* (1982). Finally, anarchism attracted its share of female leaders who combined elements of the feminist critique (for example, birth control) with their socialism. Federica Montseny in Spain and Emma Goldman in the United States promoted anarchist-model schools (especially the so-called Ferrer schools) to root out vestiges of antifemale biases and stereotypes. Sometimes they were also willing to compromise the anarchist opposition to government. In the early stages of the Spanish civil war of the 1930s, Montseny became the first woman to hold cabinet rank in Spain as minister of health. Hence, although there has been less agreement in recent years about the meaning of anarchism, it retains resilience and influence as a utopian idea.

*See also* Ecotopia; Kibbutzim; Marxism.

*Reference* Sonn, Richard D. *Anarchism* (1992).

## *Anatomy of Melancholy* (1621)

Although primarily concerned with the subject of melancholia, Robert Burton's

*Anatomy of Melancholy* included a section suggesting a utopian solution. Because melancholia—defined by Burton's contemporaries to be a mental disease—was regarded as a universal human affliction, Burton sought a method of distinguishing it from sanity. After considering other ideal society alternatives—Arcadia, the millennium, ideal commonwealth—Burton settled upon a utopian solution despite some misgivings about aspects of earlier utopias. Burton also demonstrated the difficulty that early modern utopian writers found in attempting to divorce their schemes entirely from the Christian milieu. The attitude reflected Burton's admiration for both the model of utopia set forth by Sir Thomas More and the Christian humanist tradition that included More.

Born into a large Leicestershire family, Robert Burton (1577–1640) was educated at Oxford University, although he changed colleges and his university tenure was longer than average. He became a fellow of Christ Church College about 1600 and also held a couple of clerical posts to ensure a comfortable life. As an academician Burton penned poems and plays, but his most famous work was the *Anatomy of Melancholy*, written under the pseudonym of Democritus Junior. Because of its success, Burton spent the remainder of his life revising and reissuing the work, five editions appearing before his death. During the nineteenth century, the *Anatomy* experienced renewed attention and went through another 60 editions. Burton's success stemmed in part from the interest in his subject, but it was also due to his excellent prose. Burton treated melancholy not merely as a disease afflicting a few but as a general condition of almost all men. His description of the malady in effect became a survey of the nature of mankind, of mankind's physical and spiritual condition.

Burton began his examination of the human condition with the biblical Fall in the Garden of Eden. Hence, his analysis revolved around his view of original sin and its consequences; he saw melancholia as an inherent function of human nature. Melancholia caused humanity to act against reason in a self-destructive manner. Although mankind could rely upon reason to respond to the pitfalls of nature, reason was not effective against the passions of self-destruction—hatred, selfishness, covetousness, aggression, malice. Burton utilized contemporary social examples to support his argument. Evil was spawned by religious disputes, wars, legal arguments, ambition, and political divisions. Society respected fame, wealth, and greed while despising virtue, poverty, and charity. The culture had turned genuine justice on its head and made history senseless.

In his search for a remedy to the condition of society, Burton explored several possible ideal societies—Arcadia, the millennium, and the ideal commonwealth—before settling upon a utopia. One reason was Burton's belief that melancholia was nurtured by the existing environment, which must be removed. Thus, like most early modern utopian writers, he envisioned a land isolated from Europe. It must have a salubrious climate (bad air could aggravate melancholia) and a state divided into a dozen provinces, each with a central city. The cities, located along streams of water, would be laid out carefully and became the source of material exchange for the province. Planning included symmetrical avenues and uniform houses and structures. Burton cited a long list of "public" buildings including churches, markets, courts, hospitals, and even "public housing." In short, Burton's cities, like other early modern utopian cities, featured ordered structure and sameness. Since the author provided the utopian system with all the necessary rules, there is little discussion of laws or political systems in the *Anatomy*. Each city had a governor who was assisted by an array of bureaucrats, drawn from the aristocratic classes. Burton viewed social equality as desirable but impractical, although his social hierarchy was based upon merit rather than birthright. Burton demonstrated not only that he was a man of his time in endorsing a social hierarchy but also that he was typical of Renaissance humanists in rewarding virtuous and competent behavior.

The central government was headed by a monarch, but his powers were mostly ceremonial and paled in comparison to the authority of absolute monarchs actually ruling European states at the time. The chief role of the central government was to ensure that the economy operated effectively. The state would subsidize scientific research through a system of public laboratories. Though Burton mentioned Francis Bacon a few times in the *Anatomy*, he wrote much more admiringly of the Paracelsian science of alchemy. State regulation occurred in areas such as finances, management of land, and trade—including elements such as a state bank, weights and measures, and price controls—with the byword being the efficient use of resources. Although inheritance of property was permitted, profits from the land were controlled by the state in order to preclude egregious fortunes. Each city would become specialized in a particular product. Thus Burton proposed to effectively eliminate the power of the private landlord in contemporary Europe, a rather radical proposition. The central government would maintain a defensive military establishment. Despite his criticism of contemporary wars, Burton followed More in allowing defensive measures in his utopia.

Social policy in the *Anatomy* reflected many of the contemporary concerns in Burton's England and anticipated the welfare state. Wages, hours, and prices were regulated by the state. Able-bodied poor were expected to work to receive relief, while those unable to maintain themselves would be cared for by the state. Thus hospitals, orphanages, and insane asylums would be maintained by the state. There were even provisions for health insurance and old-age pensions. The professions of medicine and law were to be provided through the state rather than private sources. The religious arrangements called for the least changes from the real world of the seventeenth century. The church contained an episcopal governing body, and parish clergy were to be qualified by education and training. Education in Burton's utopia was made available to all classes by the state. It did not include universities, which he singled out for criticism; higher education existed in the form of specialized colleges for various disciplines. The maintenance of social order emphasized crime prevention more than punishment—citizens could not keep weapons on their persons—although firm punishments existed for drunkenness, debt, bankruptcy, perjury, and theft. Because citizens wore the same attire, dress could not become a measure of social distinction. Marriage was not permitted until age 25 for men and 20 for women, apparently a means of population control. Burton would not allow individuals with mental defects to marry and reproduce, since he felt that the multiplication of inferior species endangered social stability.

Since Robert Burton began with the premise that melancholia was a universal problem of man, he set about to devise a corrective. He examined other ideal societies but settled upon a utopia since it allowed easier management through its creator. A utopia could establish a planned economy, a regulated society, and functional institutions that would guarantee a peaceful, productive society. The utopian framework could eliminate external factors such as *fortuna* that had plagued all Renaissance reform formulas, including the most secular ones, such as the one conceived by Niccolò Machiavelli. Burton's utopia acted like a sanatorium for afflicted humans, who could not depend upon either divine intervention or human reason to resolve their dilemma. Burton's simplistic scheme of eliminating vices from society provided another small step away from the medieval problem solving based upon reliance on the metaphysical toward the modern obsession with overcoming the limitations of the physical world.

**Reference** Patrick, J. Max. "Robert Burton's Utopianism" (1948).

## Andreae, Johann Valentin

*See* Christianopolis.

## *Anthem* (1937)

Following the dystopian models of Yevgeny Zamyatin's *We* and Aldous Huxley's *Brave New World*, Ayn Rand's novel *Anthem* reflects an even more bitter appraisal of utopian dreams than did its predecessors. *Anthem* represents a vigorous condemnation of collectivist methods, especially totalitarianism, which stifle individualism and freedom. People have become mere objects of manipulation and almost totally dehumanized in *Anthem*. Yet Rand does not propose recourse to either religious faith or love as an escape from such repression. *Anthem* favors a purely existential response to the dehumanization and depersonalization represented by the system's attempt to exterminate the word "I" from society's vocabulary. Since her death in 1982, Rand's following and the maturing of the philosophy of objectivism have grown steadily.

Born Alissa Zinovievna Rosenbaum in St. Petersburg to a middle-class family, Ayn Rand (1905–1982) studied history and came under the influence of the neo-idealists, chiefly N. O. Lossky, at Petrograd University. Lossky's philosophy hearkened back to Leibniz's monadology with its view of an organic universe made up of intricately interrelated parts. As Stalinist repression advanced in the Soviet Union, Rand strongly rejected communism and fled to safety in the United States in the 1930s. Initially, she worked in Hollywood for several years as a scriptwriter before turning to serious writing projects. Her most successful work, *The Fountainhead* (1943), fictionalized the life of innovative utopian architect Frank Lloyd Wright and became

a motion picture in 1949. Following a move to New York City, Rand in 1957 published perhaps her most profound statement of individualism, *Atlas Shrugged*. Altogether, Rand's books have sold more than 30 million copies. Rand exhibited a unique philosophy—objectivism—oddly combining her emotional antitotalitarianism with both capitalism and atheism. Rand coedited the journal *The Objectivist* from 1966 to 1968 with her longtime friend Nathaniel Branden and then, following her break with Branden, by herself from 1968 to 1971. Evidence of her influence since her death can be seen in the existence of the Ayn Rand Institute (1985), the Ayn Rand Society (1989), and the Institute for Objectivist Studies (1990).

Rand's dystopian polemic, *Anthem*, was among her earliest full-length works, yet it reflects almost all aspects of her philosophy. Unquestionably, the most powerful influence upon Rand's dystopian thinking was Zamyatin's *We*, which she had read during her university education. However, in *Anthem*, Rand portrays the future dystopia in a primitive state unlike the advanced technology of *We*, since she believed that pursuit of the collective-totalitarian ideal would lead to a decline of industrialization as well as of humanitarianism. The names of the characters have numbers attached to them to remind the reader of the dehumanizing aspects of the dystopia. The setting is a rural barracks of workers who have been conditioned to follow orders like robots. Yet despite all the indoctrination, the chief character, Equality 7-2521, seeks to free his mind from his regimented environment. As he puts it: "I am. I think. I will." Thus Rand follows Huxley and Orwell in focusing upon a solitary dissident voice hopelessly fighting against the system in the name of freedom and individualism.

Equality 7-2521's mental ruminations, which run counter to state indoctrination, are also shared by other inmates, the young boy Solidarity 9-6347 and Fraternity 2-5503. The control of the population originates with the Council of Vocations, which directs a program of eugenics as well as education. The authority has attempted to banish knowledge of the previous historical era, the Unmentionable Times. Desperately attempting "to know the meaning of things," Equality 7-2521 begins keeping a diary of his thoughts, which gradually reveal a rediscovery of the self that the totalitarian regime sought to eliminate. Even as a child, Equality 7-2521 confesses, he could not easily conform to the regimented system. Working in secret, Equality 7-2521 establishes a workshop to pursue more-advanced technical knowledge, and finally he adopts the Greek mythical name of Prometheus. In the process of seeking liberation, Equality 7-2521 becomes involved with the captivating female Liberty 5-300. Upon inventing an electrical generator, Equality 7-2521 is determined to convince the Council of Scholars of its value to enhance life through the production of electricity. Yet the authorities reject his invention, forcing Equality 7-2521 to flee, followed closely by Liberty 5-300, with his generator to the Uncharted Forest. The newly freed couple pursue knowledge without restraint, discover the pronoun "I" as a replacement of the collective "we," and produce an offspring.

Rand's unwillingness to admit different points of view from her own and determination to stress both her hatred of totalitarianism and love of individual freedom often meant that she was ostracized from existing intellectual movements. Undismayed, Rand simply created her own small following among her friends such as the Brandens. Hence her philosophy of objectivism gradually grew to occupy an independent status even while Rand herself continued to confound the intellectual establishment. *Anthem* mirrored the fear of totalitarian repression of individualism found in *We, Brave New World*, and *1984*. Yet Rand's primitive, postindustrial setting contrasted with the technologically advanced environments in the other major dystopias. Rand believed that there was no possible compromise with human freedom. Because of her atheism and secular approaches, she did not entertain any spiritual framework of escape or encouragement for her characters in *Anthem*. On the other hand, Rand believed that pursuit of pure capitalism was the surest method of nurturing individualism. Certainly, her other works, such as *The Fountainhead* and *Atlas Shrugged*, also reflect her obsession with individualism and opposition to collective systems.

*Reference* Sciabarra, Chris Matthew. *Ayn Rand: The Russian Radical* (1995).

## Arcadia

Unlike the medieval "Land of Cockaygne" tradition, which sought to relieve the lower classes of drudgery through the pure satisfaction of sensual pleasures, the Renaissance revived the ancient Arcadian tradition in which the desire for satisfaction is tempered through moderation. Arcadia referred in ancient times to a specific place in Greece that became the source of numerous utopian stories of an idyllic lifestyle. The Arcadian theme emphasized a congenial, if simple, harmony between humans and nature. Though nature is bountiful in Arcadia, humans do not indulge themselves beyond their needs. The human qualities of selfishness and greed simply do not exist in Arcadia; hence its utopian quality. Arcadia became popular again as a theme of the Renaissance humanists seeking to restrain the selfish tendencies of the rich and powerful classes. For the humanists Arcadia was preferable to the popular medieval theme of the Land of Cockaygne. After the early modern period, Arcadian themes reappear in a variety of utopian works. Yet despite its incorporation of certain utopian features, Arcadia properly has been distinguished from pure utopias. Rather than simply positing a harmony between mankind and nature, utopias require humanity to dominate and use nature to help produce the ideal society.

*Claude Lorraine*, Landscape with Mercury, *mid-seventeenth century. (Galleria Doria Pamphili, Rome)*

The Arcadian writers, including Hebrew prophets and ancient Greek authors such as Hesiod, believed that if an ample supply of the necessities of life (especially food) were provided, humans would live peacefully and happily. Arcadia was not a place of excess like the "golden age" milieu, another ideal society originating in the ancient era. Thus in Arcadia residents willingly restrained their desires by conforming to laws and customs in an ordered society. Yet the Arcadians did have fun and found happiness in sober singing, dancing, and recreation. Also, unlike the residents of the updated golden age in the Land of Cockaygne, Arcadians engaged in work and lived to a ripe old age. Indeed, death itself became a peculiar ideal, since it resembled the ultimate state of rest.

Arcadias as a literary genre disappeared for about a thousand years after the Roman era. They were reborn in the Italian Renaissance beginning with Jacopo Sannazaro (1456–1530), whose *Arcadia* (1504) reestablished the standard that would become part and parcel of many modern utopian constructions. Sannazaro's principal character, Sincero, was a disillusioned Neopolitan courtier who left the war-torn city of Naples and his romantic love for a bucolic Arcadian retreat. Though Sannazaro showed some contempt for the aristocratic lifestyle, his *Arcadia* resembled a medieval romance rather than a modern utopia. The model re-created by Sannazaro found many imitators over the next 200 years. In Spain, Jorge de Montemayor's *Diana* blended Neoplatonism with the pastoral utopia, but it still featured a discontented hero, Sireno, who romantically pursued a married woman. There was no attempt to elaborate the concept of an ideal society contrasted with the courtly life. France's Honoré d'Urfé, in *L'Astrée*, replicated the theme with the character of Sireine, but the work was largely a romance.

Following the pattern of Sannazaro's *Arcadia*, two Elizabethan poets, Edmund Spenser (1552–1599) and Sir Philip Sidney (1554–1586), utilized the pastoral Arcadian settings for their major literary works. Spenser's *The Shepheardes Calendar* (1579) tells a love story of Colin and Rosalind through fables in Arcadian settings. Selfishness and greed are eliminated by both the purity of the subjects and their ideal surroundings. Sidney's *Arcadia* (1580) was written during a period of withdrawal from public life at his sister's estate of Wilton.

Sidney expanded Sannazaro's theme only slightly in the sonnet. The narrative follows courtly episodes in 77 poems, again using a backdrop of a pastoral Arcadia in which simple human needs are provided by nature. Sidney's romance did lead to a virtuous rebellion against the political system, that is, authority, but his ambivalence about rebellion prevented him from sketching an alternative system to replace the existing arrangements. The stories also feature autobiographical elements that parallel Sidney's own stormy relationship with Queen Elizabeth. Both William Shakespeare and John Milton also resorted to Arcadian settings for some of their major works. The notion that a favorable environment could somehow alter or eliminate certain harmful human tendencies certainly reflects a utopian sensibility as well as the fact that early modern utopists did not really believe that their ideal societies could actually exist.

The sixteenth-century French writer Michel de Montaigne (1533–1592) exhibited the Arcadian form in his essay "Of Cannibals" (1580). In his youth, the well-educated Montaigne had recoiled at the selfish intrigue of church, state, and commerce. Following a career in government and the military, Montaigne spent his mature years studying and writing literature. Intrigued by the simple life discovered by European voyagers to the New World, Montaigne depicted primitive savages frolicking in a temperate climate with an ample supply of food. Yet their desires were not insatiable but, rather, naturally moderate, fulfilling only basic needs. The natives' languages did not have words in their vocabulary for Montaigne's great fears: lies, envy, greed, and so on. The natives willingly performed their share of work and taught the equal worth of all people, male or female, young or old. Their only serious vice was their cannibalism, which resulted from wars with their hostile neighbors. Exhibiting a cultural tolerance for primitive naturalism, Montaigne insisted that "barbarism" was in the eye of the beholder. The opening of the New World to other European nations by the seventeenth century led to further depictions of primitive settings and peoples living happily in ignorance of Europe's materialism. Arcadians lived close to nature yet were able to integrate their restrained lifestyle with their natural environment. Their limited appetites were satisfied by the provision of their unexploited, unspoiled environment.

The seventeenth-century English writer Henry Neville (1620–1694) advanced the Arcadian theme to a more complicated level in his *Isle of Pines* (1668). The story was based on an account from a Dutch sea captain's journal of a voyage to Madagascar. Several foreign-language editions appeared within the first six months after Neville's English edition appeared, testifying to the popularity of voyage literature and presaging the Robinsonade, wherein a castaway was forced to subdue nature in order to survive. The isle described by Neville was a remote place populated by English-speaking primitives, the progeny of a man named George Pine and four women, all survivors of a shipwreck. Pine and his heirs adapted their lifestyle to the circumstances, especially the practice of polygamy. The Isle of Pines was an Arcadian paradise with sufficient food and a temperate climate. Yet Neville's implicit warning noted that the practice of polygamy and other violations of social conventions caused an uncontrolled population growth and licentiousness. Hence later generations found their idyllic lifestyle on the Isle of Pines endangered. Neville's suggestion was that human immoderation could indeed spoil an idyllic life by taxing the natural resources so that Arcadia could not survive.

Another seventeenth-century tribute to Arcadian frugality and simplicity came from François de Salignac de la Mothe-Fénelon (1651–1715) in his *Adventures of Telemachus* (1699). An impoverished noble ordained into the Catholic clergy, Fénelon worked as a tutor to young women and wrote a treatise on female education. Eventually, Fénelon's reputation led to an appointment as archbishop of Cambrai (1695), but he lost the post a few years later by defending the mystical Quietist movement. Although the purpose of *Telemachus* was both to criticize certain methods of France's Louis XIV and to serve as a handbook for Louis's successor, it utilized a utopian anecdote to make the author's points. Fénelon introduces two utopian ideal societies, Boetica and Salentum. Boetica was a society discovered by a shipwrecked Phoenician adventurer, a society that closely resembles the golden-age utopias of ancient writers with its excess of resources. Salentum, on the other hand, mimics the Arcadian version of a society without excesses but sufficiently provisioned for its needs. Also following an Arcadian tenet, Salentum placed more emphasis upon the necessity and desirability of work than did Boetica. Fénelon's character Mentor warns against excesses such as wine, debt, and taxes while championing public education for children. Most of the problems in Salentum, it appears, would be solved by redistributing the excess urban population into the uncultivated countryside. The sovereign is only as strong as his subjects are contented and productive. In the event, although Fénelon's purpose was not to compose a utopia, he anticipated Rousseau in his descriptions of an ideal society.

In order to arrive at his own reconstruction of society based on the social contract, Jean-Jacques Rousseau (1712–1778) considered the origins of social inequality in his *Discourse on the Origin of Inequality* (1755). In his digression into the past, Rousseau claimed that he had discovered the existence of an early Arcadian society in which equality thrived. In Germany Salomon Gessner's *Idyllen* (1756) adeptly blended the Arcadian tradition with the Enlightenment emphasis upon nature. Gessner proposed that all social and political structures be eliminated to allow humanity to be guided solely by nature, establishing at once a symbiotic and didactic relationship. Like other Age of Reason philosophers, Gessner thought mostly in terms of a moral reconstruction of society rather than the guise of a social engineer. Unlike most contemporary philosophers, Gessner viewed nature in malleable organic rather than inflexible static terms. Arcadia was no longer simply the background for romantic escapades; it was a dynamic, compatible environment for humanity and nature.

With the gradual advent in the nineteenth century of a post-scarcity economy, the Arcadian theme appeared less frequently in utopian works. Yet it remained viable. Romantic writers, repulsed by the negative effects of the Industrial Revolution, often resorted to the Arcadian model more as a vehicle of escapism than a design for an ideal society. Arcadian themes appear in the poems of William Wordsworth and John Keats in England and Henry David Thoreau and the Transcendentalists in America. Some modern utopias, such as William Morris's "Nowhere," showed a distinct influence from the Arcadian tradition. Reacting to the sordid side of nineteenth-century urbanization and industrialization, W. H. Hudson's *A Crystal Age* (1887) projected a future-time Arcadia that followed a global natural disaster. Small family groups inhabited an earth restored to its natural primitive form. A harmonious blend of humanity and nature had been restored, but only after returning historically to a preindustrial pastoral era. The ideal society of Arcadia sought a compatibility between the abundance of nature and the limited needs of humanity, but it was portrayed as a society that required certain preconditions that had only limited existence in reality. Nonetheless, the notion of an idealized earthly paradise in Arcadia shares many common features with the utopian tradition.

*See also* Noble Savage Utopias; Robinsonades.

*References* Davis, Walter R., and Richard A. Lanham. *Sidney's Arcadia* (1965); Grimm, Reinhold, and Jost Herman, eds. *From the Greeks to the Greens: Images of the Simple Life* (1989).

## Arcologies

The late-twentieth-century architect Paolo Soleri introduced the integrated designs known as arcologies as a utopian vision. The primary concern behind the arcologies was to make architecture compatible with local ecology as well as to make efficient use of limited space for urban communities. Arcologies would also help solve urban transportation problems of congestion and pollution. Soleri's designs focused upon urban construction, especially the massive structures popular with other "megastructure" architects of the 1960s, who often used the term "utopian" to describe their creations. Megastructurists such as Soleri wanted to impose architectural, though not necessarily economic, order upon the cities. In short, megastructure architects would substitute cohesive unity for unplanned growth.

Born in Turin, Italy, and recipient of a Ph.D. there, Paolo Soleri (b. 1919) came to the United States and from 1947 to 1949 was apprenticed as an architect under the tutelage of Frank Lloyd Wright. He became concerned that in the second half of the twentieth century the city had become a megalopolis that spread in concentric circles of ill-designed suburban sprawl away from the city center. The suburbanites depended upon the automobile to bring them into the center of the city, thus polluting the air. The expansion of residential and commercial buildings into suburbia occurred without regard to protecting the local environment. The spread of cities also divided and isolated their populations, thereby eroding civic consciousness. All of these conditions inspired Soleri to rely upon arcology to recentralize the urban populations through huge structures that could efficiently accommodate thousands of people per square mile. His original model was the ocean liner with its defined yet functional limits on size. Indeed, Soleri's fascination with miniaturization tends to separate him from other megastructure architects. Soleri thought that applying arcologies would both solve the majority of environmental problems and restore civic unity. Concentrated arcologies would facilitate solutions to problems such as the waste of natural resources or the expensive maintenance of infrastructures.

Soleri's arcologies were very large symmetrical buildings designed to create a sense of unified community while preserving individual freedoms. Because of the concentration of structures into a relatively small area, residents would be able to walk almost anywhere they wanted to go rather than resorting to automobiles or mass transit. The construction of massive arcologies in the inner cities would allow more land use in the rural areas for both crops and leisure without the damaging environmental results of urban sprawl. Soleri expected that scientific and technological advances would allow society to become increasingly miniaturized through reliance upon computers and cybernetics.

During the 1960s Soleri crafted about 30 models of arcologies. One of Soleri's first projects in the Southwest, Mesa City (1959), showed the influence of his mentor Frank Lloyd Wright. In the "Babelnoah" project (1964), Soleri's urban design showed his plan to locate residential, industrial, and cultural areas in distinct zones. The plan featured a favorite Soleri structure, the spool-shaped high-rises. The most obvious contribution to architecture and ecology was Soleri's "Veladiga" (1964), in which human residences would be contained within a massive dam, thus blending into the environment and avoiding large-scale land use. The "Astermo" (1967) featured an orbiting space-station city, the ultimate ecological conservation of earth space. In all of Soleri's arcologies, the focus was more upon the form than the function of his compressed cities. Little thought was given to how his designs would affect actual living conditions in the densely populated arcologies or to how uncalculated factors such as energy use would fit the ideal design.

The nonprofit Cosanti Foundation offered financial backing to Soleri in 1970 to construct a community for 3,000 residents called "Arcosanti" in the Arizona desert. Arcosanti was built on 10 acres surrounded by an 860-acre greenbelt buffer. The structures built there demonstrate the distinctiveness of Soleri's designs, and he moved to Arcosanti himself. Despite the fact that students who helped construct Arcosanti used primitive hand tools, Soleri envisioned a utopia that relied upon advanced technology that did not threaten the ecological surroundings and also would not pander to hedonistic desires. Indeed, Soleri predicted the eventual extinction of the automobile and frowned upon mass-production industries. Yet Soleri believed his designs could resolve not only structural issues but human and environmental concerns as well.

**Reference** Soleri, Paolo. *Arcology: The City in the Image of Man* (1969).

## Atwood, Margaret
*See The Handmaid's Tale.*

### Back to Methuselah (1921)

The Irish playwright George Bernard Shaw made his contribution to utopian literature in the 1921 five-act play *Back to Methuselah*. Although the play includes some utopian themes, it tends to reflect a dystopian viewpoint. The primary reason for composing the play was Shaw's desire to express his views about Darwinian evolutionary theory. He used a broad time frame, starting with the Garden of Eden and ending in the late thirty-second millennium. Shaw expressed his belief that human will can overcome deterministic schemes because of the ability to change to meet the varied circumstances of life. He stated his conviction that the mind, the most creative element of evolution, was as important as matter and expressed that view in his own theory, which he called creative evolution.

George Bernard Shaw (1856–1950) was born in Ireland, the son of a merchant who later deserted the family. Forced to work at a young age, Shaw moved to London with his mother and soon entered journalism, which allowed him to write essays on current issues as well as serving as art and drama critic. His early plays relied upon satire to lampoon traditions and institutions. Shaw also became enamored of both Freudian psychology and Darwinian biology. He drew from both those sources to evaluate the "life force" and evolution in his play *Back to Methuselah*. Shaw rejected the conclusion of Darwinian natural selection, which suggested that species developed in a deterministic fashion that only considered the preservation of life. For Shaw human development in Darwin's theory proved singularly limited. In *Pygmalion* (1913), perhaps his most famous play, Shaw experimented humorously with his theory of creative evolution by delving into both social conventions and male-female relations. Shaw was awarded the Nobel Prize

for Literature in 1925. *Back to Methuselah* relied upon the biblical account of the Garden of Eden as the framework for each of the five parts of the play. In the first part, which deals with Adam and Eve, Shaw introduced into the utopian paradise the theme of life versus death in Adam and Eve's exchanges with the Devil. Shaw suggests that death was a necessary development in order to ensure the continuation of life. The post-Edenic period allowed Shaw to comment upon his view of the social Darwinist theme of "survival of the fittest" in the story of Cain murdering his brother Abel. Shaw introduced his theory of the "life force," which held that each individual life has the opportunity to contribute in a creative or destructive manner to the ongoing life force through life's continuing existence through progeny. The life force can only be manifested through the actions of individuals since it does not have an independent nature of its own. Though Eve felt dismay about the destructive acts of Cain, she placed her hopes for a better future in her remaining sons, who were dreamers and had the will to be creative in a positive way.

In part two, Shaw jumps forward to the present, presenting a group of men discussing World War I and giving their views about life, death, and longevity. The contemporary individuals sympathized with the dilemma of Adam and Eve, that they had to choose between everlasting life and their death, which would spell the end of human history. The third part of the play moves forward to the twenty-second century to show the scientific advances that permitted greater longevity of human life. Likewise, part four, set in the year 3000, dwells on the ability of humans to live as long as Methuselah owing to their evolutionary creativity. Then in the final section of the play, the time frame extends to the thirty-second millennium in a setting reminiscent of Hesiod's ancient Greek Golden Age. Food is bountiful and requires no labor to produce, the surroundings are peaceful and healthy, diseases have been eliminated, and a kind of bliss has overtaken the population, whose members live to the age of 800. Each mutated life-form must function as an artist for four years during childhood. Children spring from eggs rather than from normal human birth, but Pygmalion has re-created male and female life-forms from the earlier evolutionary stage, people full of vanity and selfishness. The anachronistic life-forms show not only the fear of death but, like Cain in the Garden of Eden, the capacity to kill. Shaw thus concluded that although thought is superior to the body, the mind cannot exist without the corruptible body. Thus, the story has come full circle back to the beginning, but Shaw does not dismiss the positive possibilities of evolutionary creationism. So although the play contains certain anti-utopian forays, in the end it expresses Shaw's optimism about the human capacity to create an ideal society.

Shaw therefore feared that embracing Darwin's evolutionary theory would destroy human hope and create an utterly pessimistic outlook. Indeed, Shaw saw modern science as tending to lack direction and purpose and contributing to the cynicism of the modern age. Shaw's evolutionary theory stated his emphatic belief that "living organisms change because they want to." Thus, to him human capacities were not limited by biology but were open to the energy of will and imagination to create a society that could change the future. The mind conceives, and the body creates according to the mind's direction. Shaw borrowed from Friedrich Nietzsche the notion of elitism in the evolutionary process, an elitism that exists since only a select group would be able to overcome the natural selection process to alter the agenda of change. Indeed, it would take a kind of heroic life-force effort against the deterministic forces. In the mutated form of human life from the third part of *Back to Methuselah* forward, Shaw seems to state his argument that long life ensures greater wisdom. Hence when humanity has successfully extended life, people can find ways to avoid what seems to be inevitable. Of course, Shaw suggested that the supermen of his creative evolution would resemble artists rather than scientists because only artists possessed the ability to project a vision of the future. Thus for Shaw utopia is an artistic creation by visionary minds. They alone hold the hopes of humanity's future.

**Reference** Tanzy, Eugene. "Contrasting Views of Man and the Evolutionary Process: *Back to Methuselah* and *Childhood's End*" (1977).

**Bacon, Francis**
*See New Atlantis.*

**Bakunin, Mikhail**
*See* Anarchism.

**Beilhart, Jacob**
*See* Spirit Fruit Society.

**Bellamy, Edward**
*See Looking Backward: 2000–1887.*

**Bend Sinister (1947)**
The prolific Russian novelist Vladimir Nabokov, best known for his scandalous novel *Lolita*, ventured into utopian writing with his second novel published in the United States, *Bend Sinister.* The elements of disdain for totalitarian systems reflected the view enunciated in 1940 by Arthur Koestler in *Darkness at Noon.* In many respects, *Bend Sinister* also anticipated George Orwell's assault on totalitarian nightmares since it was based on Nabokov's own knowledge of the Soviet system. Perhaps Nabokov tells the story even better than Orwell of the individual versus the repressive modern state.

Vladimir Nabokov (1899–1977) was born in St. Petersburg, and he published his first book of poetry in 1916 on the eve of the Russian Revolution. His father was a founder of the liberal Cadet political party. Fearing reprisals by the Bolsheviks, the Nabokov family fled Russia in 1919 for England, where Vladimir entered Cambridge University. Following his graduation in 1923, Nabokov moved to Berlin, where his father had been murdered by Russian dissidents the previous year. His first novel appeared in print under a nom de plume in 1926. Nabokov continued to publish novels in German with regularity until he moved to Paris in 1938 fleeing the Nazi regime. He was forced to leave France again in 1940 to escape the German invaders; the United States became his home for the next 20 years. Nabokov taught in several U.S. universities and published *Bend Sinister* in 1947, soon after becoming a U.S. citizen. He moved to Switzerland in 1960 but continued to publish novels with dependable regularity.

In *Bend Sinister*, Nabokov dealt with politics in a way different from his treatment in his other works. The story delineates the spell of melancholy that can affect individuals and whole societies. The principal character is an academic philosopher named Adam Krug who contrasts the separate worlds of the university and political realities. In the unnamed eastern European nation, a revolution led by a charismatic figure named Paduk—former leader of the Party of the Average Man—overthrows the existing republican government. Paduk institutes a propaganda doctrine known as Ekwilism that aims to standardize the thought and actions of the state's subjects and stifle individualism. Nabokov clearly believed that the worst aspect of totalitarian systems was the killing of the heart through the state's "spiritual uniformity." Indeed, Nabokov was one of the first intellectuals to recognize that modern authoritarian systems were all similar, whether structured as fascist or communist or even capitalist. Nonsense in the repressive regime becomes habitual and logical to those trained to conform to an imposed mind-set. Krug is a former classmate of Paduk's, who seeks his favor to give the regime some

credibility. Yet Krug, whose wife has just died, rejects political involvement and refuses to endorse Paduk's authority. Moreover, Krug apparently feels that his own reputation and determination will protect him from Paduk. Determined to win Krug's approval, Paduk tortures Krug's acquaintances and even his son, causing Krug to give in. When Krug's son is killed in a state medical experiment gone awry, Krug has a breakdown, condemns Paduk, and is killed himself.

Nabokov sought in *Bend Sinister* to glaringly contrast the philosophies of the artist and the politician. He meticulously blended structure, images, and style to produce the desired effect in all of his novels. His favorite references were to Shakespeare; indeed, Krug works with a colleague to secretly transcribe Shakespeare's works. In times of despair, humans need a diversion and a method of escape from the present. Shakespeare became that outlet for Krug and his associate. Krug finds in some of the Shakespearean characters the strength and courage that he needs himself to face Paduk. Shakespearean language is also contrasted to the empty if terrifying language of totalitarianism. The word "Krug" in Russian means "circle," an image that fascinated Nabokov throughout his career. The circle symbolized more than one concept: completeness, complexity, and sameness. The word "Paduk" is said to mean "toad," a term of foreboding in Shakespeare's idiom. Some critics viewed *Bend Sinister* as farcical, yet such a view misses Nabokov's instinctive fears about the impact of totalitarian systems upon civilization and humanity. Nabokov's work was a tragedy, not a comedy.

*Reference* Steiner, Page. *Escape into Aesthetics: The Art of Vladimir Nabokov* (1966).

## Bernal, John Desmond
*See* Science and Society Movement.

## Blavatsky, Helena
*See* Theosophy.

## Bloch, Ernst
*See* Concrete Utopia.

## Bolshevism

Revolutionary contexts serve as breeding grounds for experimental social concepts. The prospect of new beginnings inspires many ideal blueprints that seem feasible momentarily. Because it incorporated many indigenous utopian modes, Russia's 1917 Revolution was more than just another facet of Marxist socialism. The revolt against czarist oppression unleashed various pent-up forces in Russia. Bolshevism initially attracted a variety of utopian elements that sought to dominate policy decisions. For a time after the Bolshevik takeover, the utopian dreams flourished, only to be consumed by the single-minded Stalinist repression beginning in the late 1920s.

The reaction against absolutism and repression in czarist Russia grew broader and deeper as the nineteenth century progressed. The reforms of the 1860s merely whetted the appetites of Russian liberals and socialists for greater freedoms. Yet whenever such reforms occurred, as in the Revolution of 1905, they were expedient and lacked genuine support from either the czars or the nobility. Attacks by the intellectuals upon the antiquated czarist system mounted in the decades before World War I. Often those critiques took the form of utopian constructions, both literary and applied. Socialism, both the Marxist and anarchist versions, appealed to many Russian intellectuals in the late nineteenth century. Yet fundamental dichotomies long part of the Russian landscape continued to play a major role in shaping utopian dreams. Foremost among these elements was the urban-rural dichotomy. Peasant utopias tended to focus upon a Land of Cockaygne or communal model, whereas the urban bourgeoisie and intellectuals preferred a modern, industrial paradigm utilizing science and technology. The Bolsheviks belonged to the latter group and initially allowed an experiment that would combine the utopian elements of late-czarist Russia

with their revolutionary aims. Ultimately, however, Bolshevism's fundamental totalitarian impulse overwhelmed the idealistic utopian aspects.

Prior to the 1917 Revolution, essentially three strands of utopian influence had emerged in Russia. The bureaucratic mentality of an ordered society dated from the Westernization program of Peter the Great in the early eighteenth century. Thereafter, many government (czarist) bureaucrats thought in terms of a Western and thus non-Russian model that reflected utopian, that is, unreal, expectations. A second element was the popular, that is, peasant, mind-set. Repressed peasants (mostly serfs) desperately sought to escape the clutches of seignorial authority, and so developed a self-contained cultural fantasy. When the reforms of the 1860s abolished serfdom and offered a modicum of relief, the peasants were merely encouraged to think in terms of even better conditions that did not materialize before the 1917 Revolution. The third strand of utopian thought was socialist. It had remained almost the exclusive possession of the intelligentsia, which sought to establish social justice but was forced by the reality of the political-social system to frame those aims in utopian formats. The Marxists (and thus Bolsheviks) eventually shifted their appeal from the rural peasants to the urban proletariat.

In the years immediately after the revolution, a struggle began within Bolshevism between, on the one hand, those utopian advocates who desired a psychological facilitation of a proletarian mentality that would lead to a socioeconomic restructuring to achieve a classless society and, on the other, pragmatists who preferred a methodical construction of a modern socialist economy. Among the theoretical antagonists were Alexander Rodchenko, representing the pragmatists, mostly Leninists, and El Lissitzky, championing the esoteric approach favored by orthodox Marxists led by Leon Trotsky. The question of whether the revolution should pursue a cultural or an economic reform program would of course finally be determined by a totalitarian dicta-

*Executive committee of soldiers and workers' deputies at a Bolshevik demonstration, St. Petersburg, Russia, January 1919.*

Leon Trotsky. The question of whether the revolution should pursue a cultural or an economic reform program would of course finally be determined by a totalitarian dictator rather than intellectual elites. Because he was unsure of the precise direction the revolution should take, Lenin allowed the exploration of various conceptual options during his tenure as dictator. Thus rival Bolshevik factions led by Trotsky and Josef Stalin debated the means of achieving the new society.

Despite his basic pragmatism, Lenin demonstrated a capacity to fantasize about an experimental new society without regard to the impact upon the Russian people. He had been profoundly influenced by reading Nikolay Chernyshevsky's *What Is to Be Done?* in his youth. Lenin understood that the revolution was driven by the mass participation of the proletariat, but he refused to predict what would be the final outcome of the revolution in the future. Thus Lenin did not have a preconceived blueprint of the new society because it would evolve from trial and error. Certainly Lenin believed that the new society required a vigorous work ethic, involving both men and women, who would be treated equally. The improved technology gradually would allow a lessening of the work burden and the greater opportunity for free time, although Lenin thought in terms of communal play as well as work. Lenin remained true in his theoretical thinking to the Marxist ideal of the withering away of the state, that is, the movement from imperfect socialism to perfected communism. Ordinary people would assume the role of administrators from state bureaucrats, although technical expertise must remain a ready resource for decision making.

The problem of Bolshevism and its utopian options thus became one of debate over the means to the goal of pure communism. The rational side of Lenin recognized that utopian fantasies could not alone achieve either socialism or communism. It would take struggle and sacrifice as well as experimentation. The revolutionary state would serve as a teacher to indoctrinate the people in the new system once it was articulated. Lenin remained suspicious of abstract utopian ventures such as the Vladimir Mayakovsky–led futurist and Alexander Bogdanov–led Proletarian Cul-

war, and revolutionary upheaval. In the end, Lenin had to scrap the Marxist (and utopian) War Communism policy in exchange for a limited return to capitalism in the utterly expedient but revolution-saving New Economic Policy. The more distant utopian dreams simply could not be considered in such circumstances, even though some were devised by various Bolshevik intellectuals. The ideal of utopian experimentation met the realities of economic disaster, and it was the latter force that drove policy rather than the former.

The first requirement of constructing a new society was to clear away the manifestations, especially the symbols, of the old establishment, and the Bolsheviks proved efficient in incorporating such methods in the new political, social, economic, and cultural system. Fearing a self-generated popular culture and ever mindful of the necessity for order, Bolsheviks replaced old symbols with new ones featuring a revised mythology replete with festivals celebrating the end of czarist repression and honoring martyrs to the revolution. Communist flags, banners, and songs appeared in the new tradition, the May Day parade. Because God and the Orthodox church had been equated with czarism, the Bolsheviks exerted a determined effort to scourge Christianity from the thought and actions of the Soviet population. The attempt, including Bolshevik substitutes for Christmas and Easter, ultimately failed because official atheism was not truly a replacement religion. Likewise, the new Bolshevik morality stressed loyalty and obedience to the state and the revolution—all conduct would be measured against those standards. Eventually, the cult of personality, especially with Stalin, would be the closest the Bolsheviks came to a secularized form of religion.

Bolshevism certainly borrowed from utopian ideas the concept of egalitarianism, which was preached thoroughly in propaganda, although in practice the state relied upon loyalty to enhance efficiency and productivity. This was especially true with women, who were granted theoretical equality with men while being vigorously exploited as both reproductive machines and workers. Stalin eventually scrapped even the pretense of egalitarianism, and with it died another element of utopianism. Indeed, in many respects egalitarianism was supplanted by the higher good of the cult of machines, so crucial to advancing Soviet industrial and military technology. Bolshevik planners admired the schemes of U.S. industrial thinkers Frederick Winslow Taylor and Henry Ford. The prospect of constructing an ideal society driven by the machine evolved from the older bureaucratic and urban utopian models as well as from the Marxist notion of social justice. Machines would make life easier and better for everyone. No human cost, and it was greater than any society had ever known, seemed too much to achieve efficient technological progress.

Bolshevism began in the flush of revolutionary success with a commitment to orthodox Marxism, but the traditional forms of utopianism erected in the past played a brief role in seeking to revise Marxism along a visionary ideal. More rooted in the past than he might admit, Lenin allowed virtual free play to the varied utopian notions among Bolshevik intelligentsia because he actually had no fixed conception of what the final format of the ideal society might be. Nonetheless, Lenin was directed more by circumstances than by utopian schemes. The practical necessity of economic recovery following war, revolution, and civil war required sacrificing most utopian ideas. Stalin then proceeded to complete the dismantling of utopian dreams, which he replaced with unrelenting totalitarian terror.

**References** Stites, Richard. *Revolutionary Dreams: Utopian Vision and Experimental Life in the Russian Revolution* (1989); McClelland, James. "Utopianism versus Revolutionary Heroism in Bolshevik Policy: The Proletarian Culture Debate" (1980).

## *The Book of the Courtier* (1528)

Considered perhaps the greatest "handbook" of the Renaissance, creating an idealized guide for aristocratic life, Baldassare

Castiglione's *Il Libro del Cortegiano (The Book of the Courtier)* also possesses a distinctive utopian quality that has been compared with that of Thomas More's contemporaneous *Utopia*. Castiglione discussed the noble and scholar community of Urbino, not as it existed but as it should function. *The Book of the Courtier* also responds to themes found in Francesco Patrizi's aristocratic utopia, *Città felice*. Hence it contains qualities that reflect Renaissance Italian aristocratic society while also projecting ideal aesthetic reforms. Scholars continue to debate the question of whether the author created a utopian ideal in *The Book of the Courtier* or mirrored the real world of his day.

Baldassare Castiglione (1478–1529) almost seemed out of step with contemporary intellectuals in Italy, such as Niccolò Machiavelli, who cynically examined real-world trends. Born into a noble family on the outskirts of Mantua, Castiglione received an excellent humanist education at universities in Mantua and Milan. After marrying into the aristocratic d'Este family, Castiglione served as both soldier and diplomat for major political rulers: the Sforza in Milan and the Gonzaga in Mantua. Yet it was Castiglione's service for the Duke of Urbino (1504–1516) that inspired the composition of *The Book of the Courtier*. Castiglione began writing the *Book* about 1513, and it went through numerous revisions and additions before its publication in 1528. After acting as ambassador to the papacy for the princes of Mantua and Urbino, Castiglione served Pope Clement VII as a special diplomatic envoy to Spain. *The Book of the Courtier* proved to be an enormously popular work, and it was quickly translated into other languages.

Castiglione used a familiar classical device, the dialogue, as the format for *The Book of the Courtier*. It involved a series of imaginary discussions amid the ideal court life of Urbino. Indeed, it was Duchess Elisabetta Gonzaga (1471–1526) who presided over the circle of nobles and scholars. Castiglione desired to guide the development of the whole person, well rounded and suited to every conceivable aristocratic endeavor and obligation. The ideal male courtier should become skilled in various games as well as in handling swords. He should be proficient in Latin and Greek as well as the vernacular literature and should be talented in the fine arts and music. Courtiers must be honest, diplomatic, and especially polite and discreet with women. Court women should look to Duchess Elisabetta as their example. They must possess a good sense of humor, be able to engage in literate conversation, and always remain virtuous. Yet women should utilize all available means, including the use of cosmetics, to enhance their natural beauty. In the last section of *The Book of the Courtier*, Castiglione digresses into a statement of the Neoplatonic philosophy that was immensely popular in the late Italian Renaissance. Neoplatonism emphasized proper decorum combined with gracefulness and equanimity.

In many respects, *The Book of the Courtier* reflected a utopian view that was the opposite of that in Thomas More's *Utopia*. Castiglione argued that form, or style, was actually more important than substance in reforming a society. More agreed that an intellectual structure for society would be good, but he did not see it as necessary; Castiglione went farther by actually creating such a structure in the ideal society of the courtier. It is the framework of society and not its innate ideology that provides stability. In the midst of dramatic changes ushered in by the Renaissance, many thoughtful aristocrats like Castiglione worried about social stability, in large part—consciously or subconsciously—because of a fear of chaos and threats to their position and fortunes. Even though, as some scholars have pointed out, Castiglione treats the creation of the stylized society of the courtier as a game, playing with several different utopias, he concludes after his survey that the society at Urbino is the best utopia since it promotes an aristocratic value system. Castiglione's playfulness has the serious purpose of attempting to reconcile human nature with a suitable social system.

Castiglione's distinctiveness can be seen in the terminology he used to describe society. His concept of *sprezzatura*, a kind of natural artifice, is an example; it expressed the author's view of human contrasts and contradictions, the conflict between social theory and practice. *Sprezzatura* meant that an individual's social existence must be related to the actual society rather than a theoretical one. Thought is expressed in behavior rather than vice versa. Thus the courtier must skillfully avoid direct, explicit acts if he is to develop the proper graceful style. In this regard *The Book of the Courtier* also contrasts with More's *Utopia* because Castiglione viewed society as being diverse rather than uniform. Castiglione opposed a society that was bound rigidly by rules of behavior. Rigid rules, as in More's *Utopia*, do not allow for a sense of humor or playfulness, which were essential in Castiglione's ideal society. *The Book of the Courtier* advocated a system in which both style and purpose could be blended to create a flexible social order that could explore differences and consider change as normal. Thus Castiglione offered a sharp contrast to Thomas More in the evolving framework of Renaissance utopias. *The Book of the Courtier* argued for more individualism, self-consciousness, and style than was allowed by *Utopia*. Castiglione may have anticipated the late-nineteenth-century utopists, who grappled with a "new man" as created by Darwin's theories. Yet More's utopia of purpose dominated Castiglione's utopia of style in the interim.

*Reference Castiglione: The Ideal and the Real in Renaissance Culture*, edited by Robert W. Hanning and David Rosand (1983).

## Bookchin, Murray
*See* Ecotopia.

## Borges, Jorge Luis
*See* "Tlön, Uqbar, Orbis Tertius."

## Bradbury, Ray
*See* Science Fiction Anti-Utopias.

## *Brave New World* (1932)

In the wake of the collapsing liberal paradigm after World War I, utopias had become passé. Yet a new twist on the old idea emerged to create new interest from a different perspective, the dystopia. None of the twentieth-century dystopias was more influential than Aldous Huxley's *Brave New World*. Totalitarianism seemed to manifest all of the images portrayed in dystopias, making the literary images all the more engaging. Huxley did not see the necessity for projecting utopia into a disconnected future since the present was pregnant with the shape of future societies. The present system of the 1920s was bankrupt, from the fraudulent claims of democracy to the philosophical myth of the rule of reason. *Brave New World* was Huxley's method of critiquing the present contained in the future.

Aldous Leonard Huxley (1894–1963) was the grandson of Thomas Henry Huxley (d. 1895), the Darwinian publicist and mentor to the modern utopist H. G. Wells. It is certain that Aldous Huxley wrote in response to Wells's admiration for utopian possibilities. In his first work, *Crome Yellow* (1921), Huxley's chief character mimics Wells's adoration of science and technology. Later, upon the publication of *Brave New World*, in 1932, Huxley stated bluntly that it was a revolt against the "Wellsian Utopia." Yet after writing *Brave New World* Huxley evolved back toward being a utopian, and his last work, *The Island* (1962), represented the culmination of that transformation from antiutopian to utopian. Huxley became interested in the dystopian technique after reading the Russian Yevgeny Zamyatin's *We* (1921), which first depicted the dangerous consequences of a Wellsian one-world state. Further, Huxley became alarmed at the hubris demonstrated in the Science and Society movement in England, led by John Desmond Bernal, which equated scientists with God.

In *Brave New World*, Huxley turned the adoration of science on its head, suggesting that the scientifically grounded idea of progress had been an unmitigated destructive illusion. The Scientific Revolution of the seventeenth century, the Enlightenment of the eighteenth century, and the Industrial Revolution of the nineteenth century had produced by the twentieth century a hell rather than the heaven on earth promised by the utopians. It is rather easy to identify the historical models for Huxley's characters, including Mustapha Mond (Kemal Atatürk), Lenina Crowne (Lenin), and Bernard Marx (Karl Marx). Other minor characters refer to Rousseau, Wells, Shaw, Engels, Mussolini, and Darwin. Henry Ford is represented as the epitome of the new scientific-industrial self-assurance, with its mass-production mentality that demeans and exploits humanity as well as rejects the past. Huxley visited the United States in 1926 and saw firsthand the technologically advanced industrial system and the social hedonism of the Roaring Twenties. The United States represented the future of the world more than Europe for Huxley. Indeed, Huxley elevated the assembly line to the production of humans through the Central London Hatchery and Conditioning Centre with its human cloning process. Humanity itself has become artificial and purely utilitarian in *Brave New World*.

Huxley thought that the cornerstone of the liberal tradition, democracy, had also become an empty promise. As prophesied by the early-nineteenth-century liberals, democracy had succumbed to demagoguery since the masses were essentially ignorant and gullible about their own self-interest as well as society's. Only rarely did the masses become politically engaged, leaving control of the instruments of power in the hands of corrupt or incompetent leaders. Liberal education had surrendered the goal of teaching ideas to that of acquiring skills and produced one-dimensional ignoramuses. The secular liberal tradition attempted to substitute institutional values for religion and thereby contributed to the degeneration of morals and the advent of a regressive barbarism. Even the expansion of leisure time had only made mankind

slaves to amusement and frivolity. The mass production–consumption mentality even pervaded the arts, which also had been consumed with the worship of the machine and technique. Huxley was careful to attack not science per se but, rather, the worship of science because he saw value in the products of science.

The chief characters in the story include some nonconformists such as the technician Bernard Marx, who seems discomfited by the controlling elements of the World State. A like-minded professor, Helmholtz Watson, shares some of Marx's concerns. Marx's conformist sexual liaison, Lenina Crowne, accompanies Marx to an American Reservation outside of utopia where they meet Linda, a former resident of utopia accidentally displaced, and her son, John the Savage, who represents the Rousseauian noble savage. Linda and John agree to return to utopia with Marx, but John is repelled by the vapid culture and Linda imbibes an overdose of the mind-numbing drug *soma*, which is freely used to coordinate the conditioning in *Brave New World*. John leads a small-scale rebellion against the state, and he, Bernard Marx, and Helmholtz Watson are arrested. Marx and Watson are sent into exile, while John attempts to isolate himself to purge the utopian culture from his system. Instead, after being kidnapped and forced to endure the typical pleasures of *Brave New World*, John commits suicide.

The new society of *Brave New World* reflects the totalitarian system in many respects. The traditional family does not exist since the state has taken over its function, especially regarding the role of children. Individual development is also completely conditioned by the artificial human production. Each human has a specific function and role in the society and will not seek to deviate from it because his or her very creation has been orchestrated. Indeed, the genetic engineering in *Brave New World* creates a society of castes, with the Alphas occupying the highest level in the hierarchy as administrators and scientists. The lower castes become the objects of the Alphas' benevolence, yet they can never mature to a higher level and must remain as children conforming to the dictates of the Alphas' parental authority. The people are controlled in every realm of activity, especially through the banal state aphorisms that they learn to live by. The principal byword of the society is "stability," as embodied in the World State's motto of "Community, Identity, Stability." The Controller Mustapha Mond's dictum is plain: "No civilization without stability. No social stability without individual stability." Not only is there no freedom in this brave new world, but there is also no social interaction since everything is carefully rehearsed and actions become mere reflexes to the proper stimulus. The hapless automatons are told that the alternatives to control and stability are chaos and destruction. They confirm their adherence to the system through participation in Solidarity Rites. The educational system stresses the behavioral "operant" conditioning, popular with psychologists in Huxley's time, complete with the *soma* drug therapy. In contradiction to Marx's dictum that religion is the opiate of the people, in *Brave New World* it is *soma* that serves as a literal opiate to calm people and prevent them from becoming ill-adjusted to their controlled existence. Education also involves the suppression of knowledge of the irrelevant past—which includes closing museums and destroying books—and the elimination of hope for the future. There is only the present, a stifling, regulated, boring existence.

Politics also does not exist in any traditional form in *Brave New World* since all of the choices about the future are in the hands of the World State's ten benevolent Controllers, who maintain equilibrium. However, there is no repression in *Brave New World* to enforce the Controllers' will. Since the subjects are provided with their basic necessities and live in a pleasant environment, not to mention functioning in a drugged stupor, there is no necessity for force. Bread and circuses provide ample entertainment and diversion, and self-denial is unnecessary and discouraged. World State subjects are even conditioned to reject the pain and separation caused by death. Of course, there are those rare occurrences of rebellion, but even captured rebels are treated mildly by being exiled to a place of isolation. Huxley succeeds where other utopists have met nothing but frustration, finding a way to persuade the utopians to live as they are supposed to without coercion. Certainly, Huxley understood as well as had others before him the basic tension between reason and desire, between the conscience and lust. He solved the problem by positing a conditioning process that artificially harmonizes mind and body. Human happiness was achieved, and even the loss of human freedom didn't diminish the result. In order to emphasize the strength and power of the centralized regime, Huxley introduced some dissidents who pathetically challenge the rules and are easily overwhelmed. The rebel John the Savage's response to the set piece of *Brave New World* seems ungrateful: He still wants the freedom to be "unhappy." The best that the Savage can offer in response to the Controller is to quote Shakespeare. That type of refrain is irrational for someone who is offered a perfect utopia. The World State's antagonists such as the Savage (and, even more, Bernard Marx and Helmholtz Watson) also appear weak because Huxley did not conceive of an adequate alternative to the system of totalitarianism.

Obviously, for Huxley the worship of science produces a society of negative outcomes, secular, materialist, utilitarian, nonhistorical. Not only has modern society sold its soul to the machine, but it has rejected all past civilizations, whether Western or non-Western. With remarkable clarity, Huxley proved prophetic about a late-twentieth-century society that worships the cult of youth and beauty and that resorts to aberrant behavior, free love, and drugs to escape the stilted, impersonal welfare state. As long as the body's desires can be satiated, why should the individual care if the government is totalitarian and he lacks genuine freedom? Huxley's prophesy about a post-scarcity affluent society is all the more noteworthy since it was conceived in the depths of the Great Depression. It was not until the 1950s that other intellectuals embraced Huxley's model for purposes of social criticism. Certainly, Huxley understood that whenever rapid technological change occurs, it is accompanied by an increase in the powers of government. Moreover, Huxley also knew that the post-scarcity form of totalitarianism would not necessarily resemble the Nazi or Bolshevik systems but could easily be acclimated to a pseudo-democratic framework. Political totalitarianism would be complemented by the economic efficiencies that would be described in terms such as "the managerial revolution" and "the organization man." *Brave New World* also anticipated the impact of the mass media upon postmodern society in preventing the populace from focusing upon reality. It would be perception, particularly guided by feelings, rather than reality grounded in reason with a cynical methodology, that would mark the emerging era of mass communications. Hence the era of Big Government, Big Business, and Big Media would all combine to create the "brave new world" of the postmodern era.

*See also* Ecotopia.

*References* Firchow, Peter Edgerly. *The End of Utopia: A Study of Aldous Huxley's "Brave New World"* (1984); Rose, Steven. "The Fear of Utopia" (1974).

## Broadacre City

Among several utopian architectural schemes in the early twentieth century, Frank Lloyd Wright's Broadacre City assumed a prominent place. As Ebenezer Howard did in his Garden City concept, Wright sought to decentralize the urban environment backward toward an older rural paradigm and to create a symbiotic relationship between humanity and nature. Wright's scheme deliberately clashed directly with Le Corbusier's megascale

metropolis concept. Wright's plan did not even provide for a city center, which was a part of all other designs, including Howard's. Wright did not propose an alternative to the industrial Machine Age in the manner of the utopian socialists, however. Rather, he wanted to take full advantage of the latest technological developments in designing his ideal settlements. Thus, like Le Corbusier, he included advanced transportation systems and labor-saving devices. Yet Broadacre City was more than an architectural project; it embodied Wright's dream of a thorough remodeling of the entire nation, a true utopia.

Born in rural Wisconsin, Frank Lloyd Wright (1867–1959) ultimately sought to return to his roots as a mature architect. Wright's father, a Baptist minister, moved the family to suburban Massachusetts, but young Wright returned in the summers to his grandfather's Wisconsin farm. Wright's mother, who provided the inspiration for his profession as an architect, returned to Wisconsin with her son in 1885 after her divorce from her husband. Wright enrolled at the University of Wisconsin in engineering since there was no architecture school, but he dropped out of school after little more than a year. The main architectural influence upon Wright came from Louis Sullivan and his Chicago school, which specialized in designing the early skyscrapers. Wright began working for Sullivan at age 19 and learned from his mentor that the architect should be the agent for creativity to preserve civilization. Ultimately, Wright felt that architecture should assume the dominant role in society that it had held during the Middle Ages. Like the great Gothic cathedrals, buildings should also reflect a balance between mass and space. Rejecting the socialist theories of John Ruskin and William Morris, Wright embraced the Machine Age and technology as not an obstacle to but an opportunity for social reform and the preservation of beauty. However, Wright agreed with social critics that the city needed a complete overhaul and admired Edward Bellamy's utopian novel *Looking Backward*. After a brief period designing homes in suburban Oak Park, Illinois, Wright left the United States for Europe in 1909. Upon his return to the United States in 1911, Wright once more directed his efforts toward house plans. But in 1916 he left again for a six-year sojourn in Japan to design various projects for the government.

Not long after returning to the United States from Japan in the 1920s, Wright began to focus his efforts upon creating Broadacre City. No doubt Wright had been contemplating for some time the dream of designing a total living environment that would encompass the operations of government, the economy, the home, and education. The scheme for Broadacre City was unveiled initially in lectures that Wright gave at Princeton University in 1930 and published in *The Disappearing City* in 1932. In Wright's view the megascale urban cities had become obstacles to progress because they were inefficient and unnecessary for the accomplishment of the needed social functions. Aesthetically appealing buildings would complement the beauty of the natural surroundings. By decentralizing the population, land could be more effectively utilized with the help of technology. Moreover, a decentralized arrangement would encourage the development of greater individuality, in the fashion of the ideals of Jeffersonian democracy. Broadacre City was indeed a complete vision of society and not just an architectural plan.

Wright focused upon the role of rent in the reconstruction of society. Rent allowed control of land, money, and entrepreneurship, all of which were centered in the city. Productive and cooperative work thus became the victim of the greedy quest for gain. Hence in Broadacre City there is no rent. Following the theories of Henry George, Wright wanted to end the conflict between capital and labor by eliminating the unequal ownership of land, which could only be effectively accomplished through a planned design. In essence, Wright wanted to allow individuals or families to own as much land as they could

feasibly improve, but no more. Broadacre City would contain 1,400 families occupying 16 square miles. Compared to other more compact urban designs, including Howard's Garden City, the broad expanse of Broadacre City would be interconnected primarily through an efficient transportation network for automobiles and trains. Moreover, there was no designated city center in Broadacre City's "open plan." Whereas Howard hoped to blend the elements of town and country, Wright wanted to eliminate the distinctions altogether. In particular, Wright hoped to integrate private housing into the total natural environment and make the family the essential economic unit once more. Wright viewed the economic infrastructure as subservient to the family unit rather than vice versa. Commodity exchange centers, the Roadside Market, would replace commercial department stores. Moreover, government (almost entirely local) should not be involved in any regulatory capacity in the economy. Wright used the terms "democracy" and "utopia" interchangeably in the tradition of Walt Whitman. Viewing large educational bureaucracies with great skepticism, Wright wanted smaller-scale schools for Broadacre City and very specialized higher-education units emphasizing practical functions and skills.

Because the political and economic structures implied by Broadacre City were impractical, Wright's concept of a decentralized design gathered few followers, and his opportunity to put his ideas into practice was limited. He was hired to design a Broadacre-type settlement outside Detroit in 1940, but the project never moved forward. He presented a working model of Broadacre City in Pittsburgh in 1940 but was soon distracted by World War II and his involvement in an isolationist campaign. Wright continued to design individual houses and buildings in the 1930s and 1940s, but despite his abiding hope for a realization of his Broadacre City dream, expressed again in his last work, *The Living City* (1958), it failed to materialize before his death in 1959. Wright's quest for a new urban design that allowed both stability and security for the individual struggled against the more powerful tradition of megascale urban centers designed more for economic than human progress.

*References* Collins, George R. "Broadacre City: Wright's Utopia Reconsidered" (1970); Menocal, Narciso G. "The Sources of Frank Lloyd Wright's Architectural Utopia: Variations on a Theme of Nature," in Berghahn, Klaus L., and Reinhold Grimm, eds., *Utopian Vision, Technological Innovation, and Poetic Imagination* (1990).

## Brüderhof
*See* Hutterites.

## Bruno, Giordano
*See The Expulsion of the Triumphant Beast.*

## Buddhism
*See* Messianism.

## Bulwer-Lytton, Edward
*See The Coming Race.*

## Burgess, Anthony
*See* Science Fiction Anti-Utopias.

## Burton, Robert
*See Anatomy of Melancholy.*

## Butler, Samuel
*See Erewhon.*

**Cabet, Etienne**
*See* Utopian Socialism.


**Callenbach, Ernest**
*See* Ecotopia.


**Campanella, Tommaso**
*See City of the Sun.*


**Cargo Cults**
*See* Millennialism.


**Castiglione, Baldassare**
*See The Book of the Courtier.*


**Cervantes, Miguel de**
*See Don Quixote.*


**Chernyshevski, Nikolay**
*See* Utopian Socialism.


**Chesterton, G. K.**
*See The Napoleon of Notting Hill.*


## *Childhood's End* (1953)

Architect of numerous postmodern science fiction anti-utopias, Arthur C. Clarke's most important early work helped to shape the model of the period. Inspired by the macrocosmic evolutionism of William Olaf Stapledon, Clarke used a popular vehicle to express a form of atavism, that is, primitivism, in the nostalgia of childhood. The individual mind coalesces into the group mind via the world's children, who in turn merge with a universal spirit. *Childhood's End* was the first part of a trilogy by Clarke, followed much later by *Rendezvous with*

*Rama* (1973) and *Imperial Earth* (1976). Clarke was not averse to mingling science fiction with myth and eschatology, as he did in *Childhood's End*, because he was clearly fascinated by what the future might be. He was also fond of debunking the notion that science is the answer to all human issues. Although the utopian elements are not central to Clarke's aim in *Childhood's End*, they nonetheless reflect a tendency in modern science fiction to incorporate utopian constructions. Moreover, Clarke's utopia exists without relation to history or philosophical formulations and claims no superior values as a system.

Arthur C. Clarke (b. 1917) became fascinated by science fiction as he learned to write. He was fascinated by Stapledon's free play with the theory of evolution and sought to experiment with the concept in his own science fiction utopias. Clarke became convinced after reading Stapledon that Darwin's theory of evolution as understood by previous generations was incomplete and that it could be applied to nonmaterial substances as well as matter. Like Pierre Teilhard de Chardin, Clarke sought a reconciliation between science and the mystical. Certainly, Clarke utilized a variety of science fiction technologies for both the humans and the disembodied Overlords. Yet it was not the science and technology that dominated *Childhood's End* but, rather, the quest for human solutions to existence and survival.

*Childhood's End* begins with the world in a state of crisis and on the brink of self-destruction. Space aliens known as Overlords arrive on the scene to try to salvage humanity and the planet, principally by preventing global war. Led by Karellen, the Overlords fault the human limitation of science to material subjects, especially its omission of metaphysical phenomena such as mental telepathy and spiritual forces. Because the Overlords force humanity to turn from making and fearing the machines of war, over time earth becomes a utopia where leisure is as important as work. Crime is reduced, though not eliminated, and sexual freedom is expanded. Religion has all but disappeared since the Overlords have preempted God's role in the extension of life. The Overlords descend to the utopian island of New Athens to supervise the transformation of children under ten who will be the first to move from the material to the mental state. Clarke used the supposed superior psychic powers of the Overlords to address his concerns about the limits of conventional evolutionary theory. Although humans represented the ultimate physical evolutionary stage of living creatures, there was yet another stage beyond the physical that was yet to be reached on earth. The benevolent dictatorial Overlords and their superior, the Overmind, forge a kinship with humans through the common heritage of psychic awareness. The Overlords, like those at the advanced levels of evolution in Stapledon's *Last and First Men*, possess the capacity for mental telepathy and extrasensory perception. Hence the concern exhibited by the Overlord visitors about the condition of earthlings and their desire to assist humanity to achieve the next level of evolution. Karellen tells the earthlings that they could not have achieved the movement from matter to mind without a catastrophe.

There are clear parallels to theism and Christianity in Clarke's depiction of the Overmind. It is a sort of mental version of the God-spirit, yet it is not all-powerful because it is subject to the laws of nature. Unlike most skeptics, Clarke does not give humans the chance to save themselves; he says they cannot. There must be a saving external intervention from a power superior to humans. The Overlords possess demonic powers to command human obedience to their plan of universal salvation. Humans must live in a communal society governed by a one-world state system for a

millennium as preparation for their journey through space to merge with the Overmind. During the millennium, the humans in New Athens will enjoy the benefits of advanced technology and effectively live in a new golden age. Further, Clarke's description of the destruction of the earth remarkably resembles that found in 2 Pet. 3:10. And the last judgment allows only the children of mankind to make the transition from the physical to the metaphysical realm.

Perhaps Arthur Clarke felt that if humans believed that superior alien beings existed, then earthlings would agree to end petty disputes and work together for the mutual improvement of the earth. In a sequel to *Childhood's End* written in the 1970s, Clarke introduced the possibility of cloning humans to perfect the species. Yet Clarke continually returned to the basics, that humans are nurtured by their hopes, their beliefs, and their love of self and others. Some critics have suggested that Clarke intended his work to be not a utopia but, rather, a criticism of utopian aims. For all of the uses of technological gadgets, Clarke's fascination with the spiritual and mystical tends to dominate the meanings of *Childhood's End*. Given his reliance upon a science fiction framework, Clarke seems almost conventional in his symbols and imagery. Structurally flawed in its details and with a disjointed plot and character development, *Childhood's End* disappointed many science fiction critics. Yet Clarke obviously preferred to concentrate on the large themes instead, in part because he intended for *Childhood's End* to be more than just a science fiction story—it was an experiment in utopian fantasy. It certainly has proven popular with young readers; the paperback edition has gone through about 60 printings and many more than a million copies are in print.

*See also* Science Fiction Anti-Utopias.

*References* Abash, Merritt. "Utopia Subverted: Unstated Messages in *Childhood's End*" (1989); Tanzy, Eugene. "Contrasting Views of Man and the Evolutionary Process: *Back to Methuselah* and *Childhood's End*" (1977).

# Christianopolis (1619)

The German Lutheran pastor Johann Valentin Andreae was inspired by Tommaso Campanella's *City of the Sun* (1602) to create a nonmillennial Christian utopia in *The Description of a Christian Republic* (1619). Andreae lived toward the end of the Reformation era and had seen considerable upheaval and violence justified by religious belief. He was not alone among seventeenth-century thinkers in seeking an end to unrest in a viable utopia.

Johann Valentin Andreae (1586–1654) was clearly influenced in his youth by the mystical Rosicrucian movement. A secret society, the Rosicrucians believed in alchemy, psychic healing, and hermeticism among a variety of controversial positions that were at odds with the new science of the seventeenth century. Questioning their adherence to Christian principles, Andreae eventually broke with the Rosicrucians and embraced the more orthodox science of the pansophists and their leading thinker, Johann Comenius. Andreae also traveled widely outside of his native Germany, to France, Italy, Spain, and elsewhere, including a visit to John Calvin's Geneva, which may have inspired some elements in Christianopolis. During his university education, Andreae read some of the Italian Catholic Campanella's manuscripts while retaining rather different political and religious views. Thus the influences upon Johann Andreae were wide and diverse, yet his concept of the ideal society seemed rather typical of those of other utopians writing in the seventeenth century.

The narrator in *The Description of a Christian Republic*, Cosmoxenus Christianus, fled an immoral, ungodly land seeking a more perfect commonwealth. Upon sailing on the good ship *Fantasy*, Christianus shipwrecks on the island of Caphar Salama, which contains bountiful harvests and beautiful streams and landscapes. After passing a moral examination, Christianus is allowed to enter the walled city of the pristine Christianopolis, where planning has ensured that all material needs, without excess, will be satisfied. Significantly, Christianopolis's primary landmark is its library, which happens to contain all of the world's writings previously lost or destroyed. The economic arrangements, which include guilds, seem rather medieval since all work—agriculture, commerce, and manufacturing—is carefully structured. There is no private property in Christianopolis; indeed, no luxuries either. Its residents direct their efforts toward work, education, and the practice of morals.

All of these activities are predicated on a knowledge and implementation of Christianity. Residents are required to attend public prayers three times daily, and the spiritual leaders become the superior class in Christianopolis because they possess special, secret knowledge. There is even a prescribed age for males and females to marry. Women are allowed an education but do not enjoy political rights. The priests provide examples and correct misbehavior (never serious violations), although there are no jails or prisons.

It is striking to modern scholars to observe the ease with which a Christian system embraces modern science in Christianopolis. Far from encountering a clash between theology and science, Christianopolis effortlessly combines the two into a Christian science. Ordinary workers and craftsmen employ scientific knowledge to make their labors easier as well as meaningful. Significantly, the educational system eschews Scholastic logic and philosophy as imprecise and tending to foster muddled intellectual ideas. Near the center of Christianopolis is a laboratory where cutting-edge scientific experiments, especially in chemistry and pharmacology, yield practical knowledge for the effective use of the residents. Even so, science is neither a panacea for all human ills nor a guarantor of an extended life span. It is simply useful.

Some readers might think of Christianopolis as a modern-day structured theocracy with limited repression. Clearly, Andreae believed, with many of his contemporaries, that the needs of society were few: good morals, effective learning, and a guarantee of justice for all citizens. Like many early modern secular utopias, Christianopolis was a place devoid of injustice, serious crime, disease, selfishness, and political repression. For Andreae, Christianity offered the most certain plan for achieving an idyllic system. A Christian utopia would ensure the best ideal society. In his insistence upon strict adherence to Christian principles, Andreae's Christianopolis does not compare closely to most sixteenth- and seventeenth-century utopias—for example, those of Thomas More, Francis Bacon, or Tommaso Campanella—which, though containing Christian elements, were more secular. Still, Andreae represented a practical theologian at the end of the Reformation era who sought a common basis for all Christians to work together for social unity and the solution of human problems. And although Andreae probably recognized that Christianopolis would remain myth rather than fact, it could be the instrument for focusing society's attention upon serious reforms.

*See also* Nova Solyma; Pansophism.

*Reference* Montgomery, John Warwick. *Cross and Crucible: Johann Valentin Andreae (1586–1654), Phoenix of the Theologians* (1973).

## Città felice
*See* Renaissance City-State Utopias.

## City of the Sun (1602)
Like his contemporaneous utopists Francis Bacon and Johann Valentin Andreae, the Italian philosopher Tommaso Campanella composed a utopia that happily combined the elements of Christianity and the new science. Known for his polemics and distaste for Aristotle, Campanella ran afoul of the authorities and spent many years in prison. It was there that he first composed *La città del sole* in 1602, though many years of revisions followed before it appeared in print. Campanella softened his strident preimprisonment tone in the final version, yet it remained faithful to his vision of a unified Christian theocracy implementing the advances of knowledge, especially science.

Born into poverty at Calabria, Italy, Tommaso Campanella (1568–1639) entered a Dominican monastery at age 14. From the beginning of his training, however, Campanella was attracted to the controversial writings of the anti-Aristotelian Italian Bernardino Telesio and a Jewish astrologist, Abraham. Campanella also showed contempt for the learning of his fellow monks. Despite accepting all of the basic orthodoxies of the Catholic church, Campanella seemed determined to dispute the influence of Aristotle, whom he regarded as a pagan Greek with untenable scientific theories. With the publication of his first philosophical treatise in 1591 defending Telesio's philosophy, Campanella began a lengthy confrontation with religious authorities, who tried him for heresy or demonic practices. He escaped punishment after his first trial in 1592, but a second trial relating to criticism of church doctrine led to a brief imprisonment at Padua in 1594. Other questions of heretical tendencies pursued Campanella until he was arrested on charges of instigating an anti-Spanish conspiracy in Calabria in 1599. At his trial in Naples, he was charged with both heresy and inciting a political insurrection against Spain by aiding the Turks. After considerable torture, he was sentenced in 1602 to life imprisonment and spent the next 27 years as a prisoner. Finally, soon after his release by the pope in 1629 and in his despair at persuading Spain to lead his utopian revival, Campanella made his way out of Italy to France, where he spent his remaining years befriending French political leaders and scientists.

Campanella began work on *La città del sole* in 1602 near the outset of his longest prison term. After numerous revisions, it was published in Latin in Frankfurt in 1623 and Paris in 1637. Campanella had entertained the idea for constructing a comprehensive utopia for several years prior to 1603. Some contemporaries believed that he devised the ideal society to replace the Spanish rule in Italy, whereas later critics argued that Campanella dreamed of a papal revival to lead an ecumenical Christianity that would even convert Jews and Muslims. Typical of other intellectuals of his day, Campanella effectively harmonized his Hermeticism, including alchemy and astrology, with Christian traditions. English writers of his day compared Campanella to Machiavelli, and modern scholars have agreed that the seventeenth-century Italian promoted the ideals of *raison d'état*. In seventeenth-century Germany Campanella was deemed to be a precursor of the pansophist dreams of a scientific utopia. Campanella's writings after his imprisonment seemed less radical and more compromising than those of his youth.

The setting for *La città del sole* was the routine one for early modern utopias: an island separated geographically from Europe. A Genoese commercial sailor enters a Lucian dialogue with a member of a defunct Crusading order. The captain recounts a trip to the island of Taprobane in the South Seas ruled by an all-powerful and virtuous monarch, the Sole (or metaphysician), who was assisted by three wise lieutenants (Power, Wisdom, Love) controlling the three functional divisions of the City of the Sun (military, education, reproduction). The Sole possessed superior knowledge of everything except foreign languages; he was a philosopher, prophet, and scientist as well as ruler. The Sole even held the exclusive privilege of naming children. Other subdivisions of authority descended in groups of threes for a total of 40 magistrates, with all but the top 4 elected.

The most interesting division of the city was the one dealing with the sciences, headed by Sapienza (i.e., Wisdom). Thus scientists comprised at least one-third of the ruling body in the City of the Sun. The scientific knowledge was dispersed into the society by means of visual representations on the seven concentric walls in the circular city, each ring representing a different aspect of knowledge and a logical progression suitable for instruction. Each picture had only a brief caption describing the particular element of knowledge, making it easy for small children to learn as they played. The illustrations included a world map and the Solarian alphabet. At the center of the city was the Solarian temple, with seven golden lamps permanently lighted, each named for one of the planets, providing a magical protection for the city. The mechanistic universe ensured that everything, including humans, served a precise and complementary purpose.

It was not the primacy of science and scientists that made Campanella's City of the Sun controversial, however. Instead, it was the elimination of the traditional family and private property that caused concern. Because the Solarians genuinely adored their country, they agreed to allow the state to control their property. The love of country also ensured that the residents would work for the common good. Meanwhile, friendship replaced familial ties as the social cement for the City of the Sun, and children lived in communal residences. Women had equal rights with men and performed the same duties including military service, although women tended to migrate to household work and music more than men. All residents wore white garments which they changed with the rotation of the seasons. Solarians were full of mirth, enjoyed recreation and games, and avoided both gluttony and poor nutrition. Though there were no prisons in the City of the Sun for criminals, the magistrates could mete out punishments ranging from loss of privileges to exile or execution. Magistrates also assisted in disciplining children to keep their education focused upon morals and development of a specialized talent. At least four hours a day were spent studying the sciences, including physical and biological as well as mathematics. Campanella trumpeted the fact that Solarians learned much more and much faster than real-world Europeans. The granting of honors for excellent achievement in either work or study demonstrates Campanella's belief in motivation. He did not tolerate either idleness or idle luxury in his City of the Sun. Indeed, the Solarians frequently compared their egalitarian society with its strong work ethic to neighboring peoples' sloth and greed. Since there were four other states on the island with the Solarians, they maintained constant military defensive readiness. Whenever they engaged in war, the Solarians destroyed the enemy fortifications and executed their rulers but attempted to persuade the conquered peoples to adopt their system. Cowardice on the battlefield was punished, whereas courage and self-discipline were rewarded and praised in poetry. What had begun as Campanella's call to arms and revolution in the earliest versions of *La città del sole* became in later editions more of a prophecy for the future. Still, it is likely that Campanella continued to believe in the viability of his ideal society in the corporeal world. As he wrote: "The whole world is paradise for men who use to a virtuous purpose the marvelous works of God."

Campanella's City of the Sun not only resembled aspects of Bacon's New Atlantis and Andreae's Christianopolis but also incorporated many elements from More's Utopia, which Campanella admired. Both More's and Campanella's societies were isolated from the real world on islands and were centered in carefully planned cities. The Utopians and Solarians mocked the reverence for gold and fought defensive wars while maintaining commercial contact with the outside world. Both More, writing before the Reformation, and Campanella, writing at the end of the Reformation, favored a type of universal Christianity that required substantive papal reform. But both portrayed their fictional utopias as pre-Christian yet joyful for the residents. Of course, there were differences, chief of which was Campanella's hostility toward Aristotelianism and embracing of the Hermetic tradition.

Despite recondite contradictions and inconsistencies in Campanella's utopia, it remains a society ordered around an all-powerful state. Campanella seemed to anticipate the future power of central governments over people's lives, whether by an absolute monarchy, widespread in the seventeenth century, or by a welfare state, of the sort dominating the twentieth century. He was adept at reconciling the various inconsistencies, such as Christianity, with his pre-Christian Solarian society. Campanella also assumed that knowledge was the basis of political authority. Attributing the great divisions of his own society to the selfish desires of the individual and states, Campanella determined that extensions of the person such as individual rights, private property, and the traditional family must be sacrificed in his utopia in favor of a collective body. Competition and diversity were unnecessary and would undermine unity. The Solarian state much better than Campanella's current society could ensure that merit would be rewarded without bias.

**Reference** Calomino, Salvatore. "Mechanism, Diversity, and Social Progress: Emblems of Scientific Reality in Campanella's *La città del sole*," in Berghahn, Klaus L., and Reinhold Grimm, eds., *Utopian Vision, Technological Innovation, and Poetic Imagination* (1990).

## Clan Communism
*See* Neo-Confucian Utopias.

## Clarke, Arthur C.
*See* Science Fiction Anti-Utopias.

## Cockaygne
A medieval English poem, "The Land of Cockaygne," summarized an ancient tradition about a golden age of happiness portrayed in Hesiod's Greek "Age of Kronos" and Virgil's Roman "Age of Saturn." The Cockaygne tradition was nurtured primarily by the lower classes, who often endured unbearable burdens of harsh life and work with no social justice and with precious little time for relaxation and amusement. Cockaygne served as a con-

*Pieter Brueghel the Elder,* The Land of Cockaygne. *(Alte Pinakothek, Munich)*

tributing element to the modern utopia, though it should be carefully distinguished from true utopias.

The origins of the idea of an escapist, nonhistorical golden age go back at least to the Gilgamesh epic poem from ancient Mesopotamia. It started with the concept of the Land of Dilmun, a happy confluence of man and nature in an earthly paradise with abundant resources and aesthetically appealing surroundings. The people of Dilmun did not have to work and were thus able to enjoy the bounty of nature and social tranquillity. In later centuries, from ancient times to the medieval period, the golden age formula reappeared most often during times of dearth, plagues, or wars. The idea of a golden age was also satirized by Greek and Roman writers in a collected dystopia entitled *Deipnosophistai* (Feast of the intellectuals), which included 30 stories. Classical writers such as Lucian in the *True History* poked fun at the notion of elaborate social reforms and gastronomic indulgences.

By the Middle Ages, the classical dystopias critical of the golden age were in fact the main sources for the Cockaygne tradition. Lucian's writings, for example, reappeared in Europe during the fifteenth century. In addition to classical sources, Celtic myths of an abundant earthly paradise circulated in England. The poem "The Land of Cockaygne" appeared in various forms in fourteenth-century France and England. It recited the satisfaction of physical appetites in the word "cockaygne," which meant "small cakes." A cruder form, "*Schlaraffendland*" (glutton's paradise), appeared in the sixteenth-century poem by German writer Hans Sachs (1494–1576). Moreover, an element of revulsive scorn toward Cockaygne remained in the early seventeenth century. In Ben Jonson's *Bartholomew Fair*, the Land of Cockaygne became "Lubberland," a place inhabited by indolent louts. Joseph Hall, bishop of Norwich, attacked Cockaygne in a passage of his *Mundus Alter et Idem* (translated as *Discovery of a*

*New World*). The voyage happened upon the repellent Crapulia, a land of excess. Crapulia had five regions populated respectively by gluttons, drunkards, women, fools, and rogues. Finally, William Shakespeare briefly described the golden age in *The Tempest* (1611).

The main ingredient in the Cockaygne literature was an excess of food and drink. Cockaygne also featured an eternally youthful, peaceful, idle peasantry who were not restrained by traditional social customs or laws. They lived in an ideal climate and enjoyed perfect health. Cockaygne did not recognize private property rights, guaranteed social justice, and was essentially a classless society. Cockaygne also featured an anticlerical and even pagan tendency among its members.

The Cockaygne utopia, virtually pure fantasy, was not grounded in specific or realistic social reforms as most utopian literature proposed. Yet its influence was important: A hint of Cockaygne appeared in many utopian concepts. Nineteenth-century U.S. folk songs such as "Big Rock Candy Mountain" and "Poor Man's Heaven" evoked the Land of Cockaygne symbols. Bernard Suits's *The Grasshopper* (1978) presented a conscious attempt to frame the Cockaygne utopia in modern dress. Cockaygne was a dream world for the laboring classes, allowing them to conceive of a paradisaical retreat into a land of physical, as opposed to spiritual or intellectual, pleasures. Hence it also does not correspond well to the hedonism that evolved from ancient Epicureanism. Imaginary people in the Land of Cockaygne were not masters of their destiny but simply accepted their good fortune in the same way that real peasants endured misfortune in medieval Europe. Yet by the fourteenth century, peasants felt that serfdom was not just to be endured but, rather, needed to be reformed. Cockaygne offered a glimmer of hope, albeit in unreal terms, that serfdom could be dismantled. The fact that work was not required in Cockaygne reflected peasant hatred of serfdom's labor for masters instead of for themselves.

The Cockaygne literary tradition found its greatest connection to reality in the various medieval festivals or carnivals, which also had their origins in the classical era. These festivals included the Saturnalia, the Feast of Fools, and the Lord of Misrule. At the French Feast of Fools and English Lord of Misrule in March, the peasants would turn social conventions upside down celebrating the new year (old-style calendar). They elected as "lord of revels" a member of the lower clergy, who was styled the Pope of Fools. The feast included earthy talk and songs, gambling, dining on the church altar, bouts of drinking and dancing, and an uproarious burlesque parade through the village. The idea of turning society on its head was not unique to Europe or the classical age. The Apo annual celebration among the Ashanti tribes of West Africa allowed the lower classes to criticize and satirize tribal leaders.

**Reference** Morton, A. L. *The English Utopia* (1952).

## *Code of Nature* (1754)

The anonymous eighteenth-century French writer known as Morelly (contemporaries attributed the authorship to Denis Diderot) produced a transitional communism that bridged the gap between the early versions mimicking More's *Utopia* and the mature nineteenth-century system. Morelly sought to deal with the twin evils of property and marital rules in his *Code de la nature, ou le véritable Esprit de ses Loix, de tout tems négligé ou méconnu*. By prohibiting the private ownership of property, most crimes of violence would be eliminated. By restricting formal gender relationships in marriage, issues such as adultery and prostitution would be ended. Morelly's interpretation of humanity as basically good rather than evil fit the philosophy of the Enlightenment perfectly. Following Rousseau, Morelly argued that human institutions, not human nature, had corrupted society. The *Code* was published in late 1754, although the date listed was 1755; a second edition appeared in 1757 and a third in 1760. It was not printed again in its entirety until 1841.

In Morelly's *Code* there were only three fundamental laws: no personal ownership of real estate (although personal property possession was permitted), public maintenance of the needs of all residents of the state (an extreme version of the welfare state), and individual contributions to (and expectations from) society would be based on abilities. The feature that most distinguished Morelly's utopia from previous early modern versions was its totally secular nature, even though he justified the common ownership of property as being based upon early Christian practices. The French Enlightenment's hostility toward the Catholic church and Christianity undoubtedly determined the strident secularism of the eighteenth-century utopias. Morelly, however, did not anticipate the impact of industrialization; his society was totally agrarian, and not for the reasons pursued by the utopian socialists of the nineteenth century. Morelly did not view his code as purely ideal, for he expected that it could be applied in his own time. Indeed, the *Code* directly influenced Gracchus Babeuf's attempt to establish a communist utopia a few decades later; Babeuf quoted the *Code* at his 1797 trial. However, the work alienated all but the most radical fringe, including intellectuals, nobility, and bourgeoisie. For example, the revolutionary chronicler La Harpe viciously attacked the *Code* (though he assumed the author was Diderot) in his 19-volume *Lycée*, which was issued following 1799 and devoted 125 pages to the *Code*. Among other things, La Harpe pointed out the *Code*'s false analogy between a moral system and physical mechanisms. Etienne Cabet wrote admiringly of the *Code* in his *Journey to Icaria* (1840), showing Morelly's influence upon the utopian socialists. Morelly was also favorably viewed by Marxist and anarchist intellectuals.

The agricultural communes described by Morelly maintained rigid rules regarding work schedules and gender relations.

He proposed that marriages, required by the *Code*'s laws, be indissoluble for a period of ten years, after which divorce would be allowed. The strict regulation of marital relations was intended to forestall disruptive practices such as adultery. The society frowned strongly upon crime, which was punished severely. Participants were limited in the pursuit of unnecessary goods that might be deemed luxuries. Even the slightest unequal distribution of goods would upset the delicate balance of communal unity, especially the closeness of the family. Indeed, Morelly even insisted that unequal property undermined marital relations. The absence of temptation, whether someone else's property or wife, would tend to make the populace moral. Hence, though Morelly accepted the same virtues that Thomas More might admit, he imposed them through a different social structure. By creating the proper environment, humans would become virtuous without having to be told to be virtuous— they would be perfect. Society rather than the individual conscience would determine what is moral. The state rather than the individual had the moral responsibility to assist those in poverty and to provide schools for education. Morelly conceived his rules to be applicable universally, not just for France. Although Morelly looked forward to his plan's implementation, his communism as well as the static nature of his ideal society were more reminiscent of early modern utopias than of later, modern versions. Perhaps Morelly's most novel concept was the link between morals and economics.

*Reference* Coe, Richard N. *Morelly: Ein Rationalist auf dem Wege zum Sozialismus* (1961).

## Comenius, Johann Amos
*See Macaria*; Pansophism.

## *The Coming Race* (1871)
Fascinated by the dramatic discoveries of science and technology in his own era, Edward Bulwer-Lytton wrote a novel, *The*

*Coming Race*, in which he utilized a utopian framework to convey his message. He incorporated the contemporary adoration of science—that is, positivism—as the basis for projecting his ideal society into the future. Like many of his contemporaries, Bulwer-Lytton was fascinated by Darwin's theory of evolution and, especially, by Herbert Spencer's attempt to apply the theory to social engineering through his environmental determinism. Bulwer-Lytton thought in more radical terms than Spencer, and wrote in *The Coming Race* of a great evolutionary leap forward for mankind. Bulwer-Lytton's effort is often compared to Samuel Butler's *Erewhon*, though Bulwer-Lytton's utopia sold much better. Liberal England was gradually moving beyond its fixation with bourgeois values to consider the plight of the working man and woman. Bulwer-Lytton anticipated in the "coming race" of America the breakdown of the family, with impotent parents and rebellious children.

Edward Bulwer-Lytton (1803–1873) was born into a wealthy English family and attended Cambridge University, where he was influenced by the English Romantics. He sold plays and novels for his livelihood and also served two terms in Parliament, once in the 1830s and again in the 1850s. His best-known work was *The Last Days of Pompeii* (1834). Raised to the peerage in 1866, Bulwer-Lytton composed the brief utopia, *The Coming Race*, in 1871 following his retirement and just two years before his death.

Scholars have debated whether *The Coming Race* should be classified as a utopia or a dystopia, but it definitely possesses Swiftian overtones. The story begins with a well-to-do American descending into a mine shaft in an anonymous country. He stumbles upon a world beneath the earth's surface known as An and consisting of attractive landscapes and a salubrious climate. The structures remind the visitor of ancient Egypt, though they are more ornate, yet art has acquired a purely utilitarian function. The residents of this other world, who possess technical knowledge

greatly advanced over that of humans, are tall and have wings, almost godlike. The seven-foot-tall liberated women in An are more intelligent than the men. The families, in the form of extended social units, in the underworld exist along traditional lines. The residents of this strange world employ "vril," an awesome power consisting of something like an electrical charge that can be used either for restoration or destruction. Because vril was so widely available, it served as a deterrent against war and violent crime (similar to nuclear weapons of the mid-twentieth century). The existence of vril, the absence of crime or poverty, and the hereditary capacity of restraint meant that laws and traditional government were unnecessary. The only offices are those related to provision of services, and they are held by children. The residents are served by robots that do most of the manual labor, so that the older members become totally indolent after passing from their youth. This superior, disease-free society conceives of death as simply a normal passage to another realm. Thus, because the visitor has created a competition for affection among several of the females, a child is ordered to kill him as a defensive measure. Nonetheless, a sympathetic female resident rescues the visitor and sends him back through the mine shaft to his own world.

Undoubtedly, Bulwer-Lytton used satire particularly to assail modern U.S. society, the emergence of women's liberation, and increased reliance upon technology. Further, it is possible to interpret the visitor's journey to the underworld as revealing a society lacking individual incentives and satisfied with mediocrity. Thus some scholars have considered *The Coming Race* as a dystopia. Indeed, some see Bulwer-Lytton as the father of the modern dystopia, following Swift's precursor, *Gulliver's Travels*. Others, however, have pointed out that even the flawed utopia of the underground world was definitely superior to the visitor's society and that Bulwer-Lytton has thus taken an overall positive view of utopian potential, while qualifying that perspective by suggesting that the striving for an ideal society could go awry. There is little debate that Bulwer-Lytton believed that scientific knowledge was superior to and must precede social systems. The underground residents had developed their utopia through careful planning rather than by natural selection. Francis Bacon's seventeenth-century *New Atlantis* first relied upon experimental science as the basis for a utopia. Bulwer-Lytton expanded that tradition and influenced not only George Bernard Shaw's plays but also H. G. Wells's *A Modern Utopia*.

*See also* Positivism.

*Reference* Wagner, Geoffrey. "A Forgotten Satire: Bulwer-Lytton's *The Coming Race*" (1965).

## *The Commonwealth of Oceana* (1656)

The wealthy English landowner James Harrington composed *The Commonwealth of Oceana* in 1656 in response to the English civil war and the temporary end to monarchy. The purpose of *Oceana* was to explain both how the monarchy had failed and why a republic was the only realistic substitute for monarchy in seventeenth-century England. Harrington represented a group of "republicans" who hoped that Oliver Cromwell would adopt his perfect "equal commonwealth" form of government. In *Oceana*, Harrington based political power upon ownership of property. Since the feudal powers of crown, church, and nobles had seen their historic control of property lost to a rising middle class, the new basis of political power would be vested in a much larger segment of the population.

Harrington's views provided the basis for a lengthy "commonwealth" tradition in English political history, even though his abstract system proved impractical in an England mired in tradition. More important, perhaps, the commonwealth ideas found more fertile ground in America, where a Harringtonian republic was established at the end of the eighteenth century. The tension between the real-world republican and theoretical utopian traditions was nowhere more clearly outlined that in Harrington's stimulating treatise.

James Harrington (1611–1677) came from a wealthy landed family in Rutland. He briefly attended Cambridge and spent even less time at one of the Inns of Court studying the law. It was on his tour of Europe in 1632 that he became fascinated by the quasi-republican government of Venice, which became a model for his *Oceana*. Although sympathetic toward Parliament in the civil war, Harrington took an office in the king's household toward the end of the conflict. Shocked by Charles I's execution, Harrington withdrew from public affairs and began working on *Oceana* in 1654. Harrington believed that England needed a government grounded in a realistic theory and complete with a detailed operating system. Although the work was dedicated to Oliver Cromwell (called Olphaus Megaletor in *Oceana*), the lord protector ordered the publication seized and never considered adopting Harrington's republican ideas. In 1659, Harrington founded the Rota Club in London to promote his theories and wrote additional tracts outlining his philosophy. Membership in the club was open to all comers, and their meetings in coffee houses attracted large audiences. Upon the Restoration of King Charles II, Harrington was arrested and imprisoned briefly because of his republican views. Harrington always believed that his critics had misconstrued his theories by extracting parts to criticize without looking at the whole system. Even some admirers thought that portions of Harrington's thought could be implemented, but the author always conceived of *Oceana* as a package that would only work if adopted in its entirety.

Undoubtedly the chaotic upheaval in England caused Harrington to contemplate the perfect government. He used the term "political architecture" to describe the methods of constructing a new republican system. Like Thomas More in the previous century, Harrington had little faith in the human capacity to act virtuously by following the dictates of reason and conscience alone. Though a perfect commonwealth would not make men virtuous, it could restrain and correct their tendency toward selfish and antisocial acts. Harrington realistically faced the most difficult problem of utopian thinkers who wanted their ideas to be realized in a world peopled by imperfect humans: the danger of corruption. The government of Oceana was structured so that corruption would not even be possible. Harrington saw in the collapse of the agents that disciplined society, the crown and the church, the necessity to create a new structure to fill the need. Like Machiavelli, Harrington only offered a secular solution; there would be no divine or millennial intervention. Though God had ordained human government, he had not ordained the proper form of that government, so man was free to fashion it himself.

Relying upon political architecture, Harrington believed that a commonwealth system was the best type of government to enforce a moral code of conduct. Moreover, a commonwealth system had the best chance of establishing a permanent and comprehensive social organization that could forestall future upheavals such as the civil war. Certainly, Harrington was familiar with two other alternative systems proposed in the civil war era: Gerrard Winstanley's communism and the Levellers' expanded franchise. Not surprisingly, since he was a large landowner, Harrington rejected communism. Yet his ideas about which subjects should participate in government resembled those of the Levellers. Harrington's political theory still relied upon a patriarchical construct and was not ready to embrace the method of social contract, another alternative introduced in this era by Thomas Hobbes. Thus, although Harrington's system moved closer to the ideas of a social contract than to absolute monarchy, it remained loosely attached to a patriarchal system.

The structure of Harrington's government in Oceana was not greatly dissimilar from the existing parliamentary system. Indeed, the history of Oceana up to the 1650s was essentially the history of England, and even Harrington's pseudonyms for English leaders and place-names are easily identifiable. He cited four critical features necessary to sustain the "equal commonwealth": (1) the "equal agrarian," which consisted of 5,000 landowners who would control the reins of government; (2) a secret ballot; (3) a bicameral legislature with a 300-member senate, which would exhibit wisdom in their debates of legislation, and a popular assembly (Prerogative Tribe) of 450 members representing the interests of the people, which would enact laws; (4) rotation of office (with legislators limited to three-year terms). The executive officials would be appointed by the senate and served only one year. Although both legislators and executives could serve more than one term, they could not serve consecutive terms. One executive council supervised religion; there was a national religion, but liberty of conscience was also guaranteed. Harrington did not allow a powerful role for the clergy: Since the clergy in Oceana did not own property they could not participate in politics. The utopian features of Harrington's equal commonwealth resided in the structure of government rather than in the broad distribution of property, although the agrarian law aimed to prevent the growth of massive fortunes. The laws and institutions of Oceana, based upon the interest of the whole nation, must be able to restrain the ambition and avarice of individuals. Thus private initiative must defer to the public interest.

Another feature of Oceana was its emphasis upon local government, almost nonexistent in most other utopias. England's county system would be replaced in Oceana by an organization of 50 tribes, each composed of 20 hundreds, and each hundred had 10 parishes, for a total of 10,000 parishes. There was no separate municipal government in Oceana. Moreover, local officials answered to their local institutions rather than to national authority, a situation that already existed with sheriffs and justices of the peace. Education in Oceana, organized by the tribes, consisted of six divisions: grammar schools, universities, law schools, tradecraft schools, travel, and the military education for males in the local militia. Attendance was compulsory up to age 15, and free education was provided to poor children. *Oceana* did not specify a criminal code or a social welfare system, probably because Harrington was so consumed with the problem of political stability.

Perhaps no theorist since Plato had attempted to integrate theory and reality in the manner of Harrington's *Oceana*. The most serious unresolved question in Harrington's thought was the tension between the ideal of the classical republic and utopia. Harrington could not specify how a popularly based government that was essentially led by the landed aristocracy could prevent anarchy on the one hand or oligarchy on the other. Most other utopists opted for an authoritarian system in order to remove the question of individual choice about the rules in utopia. Harrington favored creating the ideal society through institutional changes rather than individual acts. Thus the removal of choice for the subject would be imposed by constitutional-institutional restraints. Harrington's influence was felt from the late seventeenth to the nineteenth centuries. He endorsed Cromwell's ideas of religious toleration, which were legislated by Parliament in 1689.

One of the many responses to Harrington's *Oceana* was the anonymous *Free State of Noland*, published in 1690. It located a utopia in the South Seas that resembled England in most physical respects, that is, soil, climate, religion, laws, government, language, and so on. Like Oceana, Noland was divided into geographical sectors including hundreds, counties, free cities, and provinces. A Grand Council of 600 representatives made up a bicameral legislature. The upper house was called a Senate and the elected lower house limited members to three-year terms and paid them a salary. Even the colonies had representatives in the Grand Council. Revenues were derived from a 5 percent income tax. The author of Noland sought to resolve the potential problem of giving too much power to bureaucrats, which he deemed to be a weakness in Oceana. Despite his disparagement of utopias in general, David Hume, in *The Idea of the Perfect Commonwealth* (1752), admired Harrington's republican scheme and offered emendations. Harrington argued for the extension of the voting franchise and the use of the secret ballot, both of which were adopted in the nineteenth century. In the history of utopian political thought, Harrington marks the beginning of a new school of utopists who attempted to translate theory into practice. His failure to achieve implementation should not diminish the importance of Harrington's contribution.

*References* Patrick, J. Max. "The Free State of Noland: A Neglected Utopia from the Age of Queen Anne" (1946); Pocock, J. G. A. "James Harrington and the Good Old Cause: A Study of the Ideological Context of His Writings" (1970); Blitzer, Charles. *An Immortal Commonwealth: The Political Thought of James Harrington* (1960).

## Concrete Utopia

The German neo-Marxist Ernst Bloch believed that he was the first socialist utopist to make the transition from the theory to the practice of utopia, sometimes called the concrete utopia. Although theory is clearly a part of the concrete utopia, it also contains the expectation of actual application in the real world. Bloch argued that the utopian sensibility was an essential instrument for progressive change in Western civilization because it allowed an unfettered examination of possible reforms of society. Unlike the best-known post–World War II neo-Marxist, Herbert Marcuse, Bloch was unwilling to abandon the dream of a proletarian revival. True to the perception of German inscrutability, Bloch's writings have been interpreted as the work of anything from a mystic to a revolutionary philosopher. Yet his most profound influence may well be in the arena of utopia.

Ernst Bloch (1885–1977) was educated in his native Germany in a period that displayed wide support for and debate over socialism. When he moved to Heidelberg before World War I, Bloch befriended a fellow Marxist, György Lukács, and both came under the influence of the sociologist Max Weber. Bloch's first major work on utopias, *Geist der Utopie* (Spirit of Utopia), was published in 1918. Very much influenced by German expressionism's utopian possibilities, Bloch developed an unfettered willingness to challenge existing systems, including classical Marxism. Seeking to discover a positive application of utopia, Bloch's *Geist* presented an in-depth study of the Reformation-era German radical Thomas Münzer. Bloch's work in turn became a major influence upon Karl Mannheim's seminal exposition on the distinction between utopias and ideology, *Ideologie und Utopie* (1929). Increasingly, Bloch found himself focused upon reconstructing Marxism as a revolutionary liberation movement, retaining the class conflict framework but jettisoning the familiar Marxist doctrine of alienation.

Bloch's politics proved less consistent than his philosophy. During the 1930s, Bloch became an apologist for Stalinism, including the bloody purges. Because of his Jewish heritage Bloch fled Nazi Germany to live briefly in Switzerland, France, Austria, and Czechoslovakia. He later spent the years from 1938 to 1948 in the United States, during which time his writing ended while he researched his major work. He returned to communist East Germany in 1948 as professor of philosophy at the University of Leipzig, hoping to find support for his ideas about revised socialism. Later, in 1961, Bloch moved to West Germany and took a position at the University of Tübingen, but he continued to participate in reform campaigns, opposing the spread of nuclear weapons and the Vietnam War. During this period Bloch published his magnum opus, a three-volume summary of utopian thought, *Das Prinzip Hoffnung* (*The Principle of Hope*). The elements of Bloch's phi-losophy were derived from the idealism of Hegel, Marxist socialism, and expressionist art. He developed a "philosophy of hope" based upon those nineteenth-century ideas, though he desired to rid Marxism of its sense of alienation.

Ernst Bloch's philosophy of history proved somewhat at variance with Marx's. For Bloch, humanity continuously struggled against the obstacles to self-realized completeness with the conscious aim of establishing nonalienating relationships. Thus the past (especially the cultural), with its varied possible outcomes, must be analyzed to elucidate the present, which can prepare the way for the future. History did involve class conflict, but the goal was not victory of one class, the proletariat, over another, the bourgeoisie. The individual seeks to become part of the whole classless community, which is a natural condition usually thwarted by social and institutional barriers. Further, Bloch insisted that humanity seeks through its hopes and dreams to become one with nature in a kind of mystical symbiosis. Expressionism had convinced Bloch that the primary avenues of the movement toward genuine social community and human communion with nature include art, music, literature, philosophy, and religion. However, Bloch's philosophy of religion was simply a socialist utopia, that is, self-realization, rather than a body of doctrine, dogma, and ritual. According to Bloch, blind obedience to ideology is a faulty method of achieving human aims. Rather, for Bloch it was in the criticism and analysis of ideologies, including Marxism, that the possibilities for more positive means to the end may be discovered.

*The Principle of Hope* contained a descriptive catalog of previous utopian schemes preparatory to placing Bloch's unique ideas in the proper context. His primary concept was that human beings have a natural tendency to imagine another better world (most effectively through daydreams), which includes elements of both fantasy (abstract) and reality (concrete). Bloch developed a technique known as the *Vor-*

*schein* (emergence) by which a writer could project the application of a theoretical idea in reality beginning with simple dreams and progressing to realistic images. The concrete utopia required that theorists understand precisely how a particular notion could become real. Bloch believed that there had been occasions, albeit few, in past history—present in contemporary consciousness—when theory was put literally into practice, especially the ideal of egalitarian societies. Thus, since utopias must project from the present, the utopian theorist must be in tune with the times in which the ideas will be placed, which required not merely an acquaintance with contemporary conditions but the ability to understand how a new method can work in the context of the times. Bloch's method of evaluating the possible was put in terms of the "not yet conscious" and the "not yet become." Influenced by Sigmund Freud's dichotomy of the conscious and unconscious mind, Bloch nevertheless rejected Freud's notion that the unconscious realm was the domain of the irrational. Instead, Bloch argued that the unconscious realm was a creative place of preparation for ideas that would soon enter the conscious mind. Since reality was in a constant condition of becoming, it was in the dynamic relationship of the creative unconscious and conscious realms that the "not yet conscious" merged with the "not yet become" to produce the possible.

Bloch therefore spent much of his effort attempting to illustrate the distinction between abstract, theoretical utopias and real, concrete utopias. A concrete utopia, such as Marxism, thus becomes a new reality in the making because it shows what is in the process of becoming a reality, that utopia—that is, a classless society with an absence of alienation—is indeed possible. Obviously, Bloch did not accept Marx's own dictum regarding the unreal nature of utopias. He redefined Marxism as embodying two elements, the "cold stream" of reason and the "warm stream" of passion. Thus a concrete utopia required not only a cold calculating analysis of the means of production but also the applica-tion of the ideal of freedom from oppression and alienation. Bloch hoped that a concrete Marxist utopia could emerge, primarily thinking in his lifetime of the East German state or the Soviet Union. However, Bloch did not elucidate the structure or plan of a utopia as most utopian writers did. He discussed the four functions of utopia: the cognitive (that is, reason), the educational (that is, the idea of progress), the anticipatory (that is, a possible future), and the causal (that is, actual changes). Indeed, Bloch argued that humanity cannot influence or shape the future without the vehicle of the utopia.

Bloch also carefully dissected the function of dreaming. He suggested that there were two distinctive types of dreams: daydreams and night dreams. The daydream was the key because it, rather than the night dream—rooted in the past—anticipated the future. Some of Bloch's disciples—Christa Wolf, Irmtraud Morgner, Peter Hacks—have used his "philosophy of hope" in writing science fiction. Thinking in terms of life as an art form, Bloch perceived utopian techniques as illuminating the proper path to realization of individual and societal emancipation. In such an approach, Bloch believed that the potential could become the actual and the ethical ideal could become the live model. However Bloch's schemes could be challenged, his utopian thought represented a movement away from detailed planning of utopia to the "education" of the passions, as Bloch labeled the shift. The transition from the abstract to the concrete was a gradual one that allowed the future to drive the present. By educating desires, humanity could transform itself within rather than outside of reality.

*See also* Expressionism; Frankfurt School; Marxism.

*References* Kellner, Douglas, and Harry O'Hara. "Utopia and Marxism in Ernst Bloch" (1976); Levitas, Ruth. "Marxism, Romanticism, and Utopia: Ernst Bloch and William Morris" (1989).

## Condorcet, Marquis de
*See* Future-Time Utopias.

*Sir Sagramoe le Desirous, a pen-and-ink drawing by Danile Carter Beard in Mark Twain's* A Connecticut Yankee in King Arthur's Court *(1889)*

## *A Connecticut Yankee in King Arthur's Court* (1889)

The storyteller and wit Mark Twain remained true to his tradition of utilizing humor in the only serious utopian scheme in his many works. He took his contemporary character Hank Morgan backward in time to the mythical era of Camelot in sixth-century Britain. Twain shows how modern ideas and technology might play in a foreign environment and the conclusion seems to suggest that he was not fond of modernism.

Mark Twain was the nom de plume of Samuel Langhorne Clemens (1835–1910), the son of a Missouri lawyer. Twain grew up along the Mississippi River at Hannibal, and his first job as a printer's devil indelibly ingrained the written word upon his future. Spinning his famous stories based upon boyhood experiences and as a river pilot, Twain lived and wrote in an era of change and expansion in the United States. After a brief enlistment in the Confederate Army early in the Civil War, Twain struck out for the frontier of Nevada and California to work as a journalist and develop his writing skills. Afterward he traveled around the Mediterranean and described his trip in *The Innocents Abroad.* Thus Twain was well acquainted with the concept behind the adventurous utopian voyage literature that became the framework for *A Connecticut Yankee.* Upon his marriage in 1870, Twain moved to Connecticut, where he resided during the height of his writing career. Injecting humor in almost all of his serious works—*Huckleberry Finn, Tom Sawyer,* and even *The Gilded Age*—did not prevent Twain from portraying life with a definite realism. Hence the use of utopian ideals in *A Connecticut Yankee* represented a departure from realism, although the book retained a humorous element.

Although some critics have challenged the suggestion that Twain's piece was utopian, Twain himself stated that he wanted to show how superior modern society was by comparing it with a primitive society. Twain begins his experiment by linking the new industrial era to the ideal of republican government. Merely because the attempted remodeling of primitive society failed does not make the effort any less utopian. The setting for *A Connecticut Yankee* allowed Twain to use a common utopian formula, the clash of the primitive and the modern, to examine human responses to foreign ideas and environments. Thus it resembles other utopian voyages into strange worlds, such as those created by Jonathan Swift and Daniel Defoe. The nineteenth-century visitor from Hartford, Connecticut, Hank Morgan, must either conform to the primitive society of the ancient Britons or persuade and teach them to accept his modern methods. Morgan chose the latter, but the effort ultimately failed, in large measure because Morgan's approach was utopian in the setting where he worked. The methods of the future simply cannot work in the conditions of the past, according to Twain, even when those modern ways are palpably superior. Knowledge became power to Morgan, but that power also required an oppressive framework in order to be implemented. Twain came to realize what almost all utopists discovered: Utopias must rely upon authoritarian methods, even when the oppression is not intended. For Twain as for dozens of other literary utopists, the creation of a fictional utopia requires that it be physically separated from the real world as well as being a different society.

When Hank Morgan arrives in Camelot, he finds that the local population—savages in Twain's image—marvels at him. Yet Morgan quickly determines that he does not want to be merely an object of fascination. He presumes that because they are backward, the people can be convinced to discard their primitive and superstitious ways. Indeed, Morgan compares himself to other conquerors—Columbus, Cortés—who invaded and subdued primitive lands and peoples. Lacking military resources to enforce his will, Morgan attempts to make himself a part of the society rather than remaining aloof from it. Only by becoming one of the members of the group can he hope to persuade them to implement Morgan's version of civilization. Much like Defoe, Twain thinks in terms of the practical application of utopian ideas, that is, what Morgan proposes is indeed capable of being actualized. Morgan's power derives largely from the fact that modern knowledge gives him an apparent advantage over the primitives. That Morgan comes from a different world makes him superior to others in the ancient British society. Although Twain used the term "Boss" to describe Morgan's relationship to the residents of Camelot, actually he operated more like a father figure to the childlike population. Indeed, Morgan seeks to replace King Arthur as the father figure to his people.

Hank Morgan decides that, rather than conform to the ways of the Britons, he will try to make them adhere to his nineteenth-century ways. There is always only one worldview in utopias since the utopia must remain pure and undiluted if it is to remain true to its nature. Utopias cannot exist as compromise amalgamations of different elements, which makes Twain's story of the clash of the civilized and the primitive problematic. In fact, Morgan wants to destroy the system of knight-errantry operating in Camelot. One of the modern methods that Morgan relies on is a newspaper, operated by a local convert, Clarence. Twain shows how important propaganda through the printed word can be to persuade people and produce change. Thus Morgan uses not only his superior technological skills but also the weapon of rhetoric. Morgan dreams of instituting modern ideas such as universal suffrage, which did not even exist in his own world. Oddly, Morgan relies upon a desire to assimilate the primitive culture into a modern one but also realizes the necessity of excluding those traditions, such as suffrage, that did not fit the author's ideal. Sometimes, Twain realizes, an idea that makes sense in theory does not necessarily work effectively in practice. Debates about the protective tariff, perhaps the major issue in the United States of Twain's day, simply lacked relevance to Morgan's situation in Camelot. Moreover, what would happen if Morgan changed history? Would the future of Twain's present be altered if the past was modified? Twain seems to be suggesting that utopian impulses to reform society should be approached carefully, anticipating as far as possible all of the consequences, intended and unintended. Naive, quixotic reforms may be harmless, but Twain apparently believed that utopian schemes should be practical, since he wanted results and not just fantasy.

*Reference* Sewell, David R. "Hank Morgan and the Colonization of Utopia" (1989).

## Crichton, Michael
*See* Science Fiction Anti-Utopias.

**de Bergerac, Cyrano**
*See* Lunar Utopias.


**de Quiroga, Vasco**
*See* Noble Savage Utopias.


**Delany, Samuel**
*See* Lunar Utopias.


# Diggers

The seventeenth-century English Digger community was small and lasted only a brief time, yet it has attracted extensive scholarly attention. Fewer than 100 people participated in the digging of the common fields at St. George's Hill. Their leader was Gerrard Winstanley, who left a compact corpus of writing, including *The Law of Freedom in a Platform*, which proposed a utopian community based partly upon the experiences of the common digging at St. George's Hill. It is for his writing rather than his social experiment that Winstanley has garnered historical attention. The Diggers are often regarded as the first genuine communist experiment in the modern era.

The English civil war (1642–1648) left some devastation and much social disruption in its wake. Following the war a series of bad harvests led to increased food prices that further hurt the common classes. Gerrard Winstanley (1609–1676) was a native of Lancashire who came to London in 1630 as an apprentice to a clothier. After failing in his occupation as a merchant tailor between 1637 and 1643, Winstanley took up residence in Surrey with a group known as the Seekers, millennialists conforming to a spiritual inner light rather than an outward religion. Upon the disruption by the military of local church services at Walton, Surrey, in April 1649,

many of the locals protested conditions by leaving the estates of their employers and digging the common fields at St. George's Hill. The common folk viewed the action as a symbolic gesture of their discontent, particularly of their discontent at laboring for a master instead of for themselves. Because of St. George's Hill's close proximity to London, other poor refugees, including some ex-soldiers, migrated to Surrey to join the Diggers. Local landlords complained to the Commonwealth government about the Digger activity in 1649. Thus the Diggers were forced to withdraw to Cobham Heath, but their settlements were destroyed and the participants removed by April 1650. Other Digger settlements in Bedfordshire, Buckinghamshire, Gloucestershire, Hertfordshire, Kent, Leicestershire, Middlesex, and Northamptonshire also lasted only a short time.

The brief episode of the Diggers, or as they called themselves, the True Levellers, would not have attracted much attention if Winstanley had not used the events as the basis for his 90-page treatise *The Law of Freedom in a Platform or True Magistracy Restored* (1652). The brief plan contained all the elements—social, economic, and political—for a utopian community, and it was addressed to Oliver Cromwell, the most important force for change in the post–civil war years. Winstanley's treatise was not intended to be merely a literary exercise. He expected Cromwell to implement his plans. Prior to this one, almost all of Winstanley's works could be classified as millenarian. Winstanley was among many who saw the civil war era as a portent of the biblical millennia, the 1,000-year reign of Christ on earth. Thus his transition from the mystical, religious millennialist in his earlier writings to the secular utopian of *The Law of Freedom* was probably the result of his experience with the Diggers, which had resulted from economic necessity.

Winstanley's outline of the new society in *The Law of Freedom* included all aspects of organization. There was no private ownership of property, and work and repasts occurred in a communal setting. Buying and selling was illegal, so money was nonexistent; if any member of the community had needs, he or she could obtain the necessities from the community storehouse without charge. Winstanley also had a particular aversion to lawyers and clergy, who, he felt, had created a self-serving and unjust system. The strongest element of the desire for change was the withdrawal of laborers from the estates of the wealthy to the cultivation of the common fields. By digging in the common fields, Winstanley demonstrated his disdain for the system of property and its control by the rich. However, he did not advocate the seizure of privately held property, so his communism was not as rigorous as some have argued. Oddly, Karl Marx and Friedrich Engels completely overlooked Winstanley in their study of the English civil war period. Also, Winstanley was less an anarchist in his attitude toward government and laws than he was an idealist, a believer in the perfect moral commonwealth. He certainly showed that he was a supporter of patriarchy, which was the basis of authority in his utopia. As for religion, Winstanley trusted that all men would be saved by God, even those dead whose souls were in hell. He wrote two pamphlets specifically dissociating the Diggers from the amoral Ranters.

Although Winstanley was far from being a modern anarchist or communist, his *Law of Freedom* fascinates because of its clarity and thoroughness. Moving away from his early religious attitude of the dependence of mankind upon God, Winstanley recognized the need for discipline and laws to organize a new society. Yet there was no conception of natural rights; only economic necessity dictated the basis of social reorganization. There were 62 specific laws in the utopia's constitution. The law would be enforced to the letter, but no one could profit from enforcement of the law. Citizens were to be taught the law and have it repeated on a regular basis. Officials were elected annually by the adult males, but only those 40 years old or older could hold office. State officials were bound to enforce the laws uniformly, and they could call upon citizens for assistance where needed. Punishments included servitude or bondage for specific periods. There was no state church and thus no clergy paid by the state. Marriage involved a civil ceremony only. The highest authority in the utopia was a parliament, the only agency allowed to interpret the spirit of the law to ensure justice.

Winstanley's vision of utopia was fashioned from real-life experiences and a puritanical frame of reference. The resulting proposal seemed harsher than most literary utopias of the age, whose appeal often lay in abundance and licentiousness. The state, according to Winstanley, must wage a vigilant contest against mankind's base instincts. Winstanley expected his citizens to be well educated, well trained, and hardworking. He hoped that his utopia would eliminate the two most dreaded aspects of contemporary society: poverty and economic injustice. Thus, when he spoke of freedom, he meant primarily freedom from want. Though his utopian concepts were colored to some extent by his previous religious orientation—particularly his Puritan upbringing—Winstanley's ideal society was remarkably secular.

**Reference** Petegorsky, David W. *Left-Wing Democracy in the English Civil War: A Study of the Social Philosophy of Gerrard Winstanley* (1940).

## *Don Quixote* (1605–1615)

Miguel de Cervantes's timeless seventeenth-century story of knight-errantry, *Don Quixote*, contains significant elements of both utopian and dystopian thought. Cervantes's tale focused upon how the impact of modernity in Renaissance Spain intruded upon the medieval practice of chivalry. In his attempt to reestablish the rural and pastoral traditions of the past, Quixote represented seventeenth-century disillusionment with modernity and the advent of the utopia of evasion or dystopia. Thus Cervantes offered a caveat about the consequences of pursuing fantasy.

Miguel de Cervantes (1547–1616) had only a limited education but was widely traveled. He put his strong Christian beliefs into action by serving in the military and being wounded in the great Christian victory over the Turks at the Battle of Lepanto (1571). Yet his valor was unrewarded and even frustrated during a five-year imprisonment by Mediterranean pirates. Cervantes remained in financial trouble the remainder of his life. His composition *Don Quixote de la Mancha* appeared in two parts, the first in 1605 and the second nearly a decade later in 1615. The first part treated the character and his misadventures in a comic fashion; the second installment concentrated on the tragic elements. *Don Quixote* has remained one of the most popular and influential pieces of literature ever written. Major historical figures from Sigmund Freud to William Faulkner have testified to their fascination with the story. Fyodor Dostoyevsky claimed that *Don Quixote*'s influence in history was second only to that of Jesus Christ.

Cervantes begins his story with the introduction of a middle-aged dreamer caught up in the images of medieval chivalry. He sells his land, dons an old suit of armor, takes on a noble title, and pursues a series of romantic quests, including the search for the elusive maiden Dulcinea. Consistently in all his adventures, Don Quixote refuses to allow reality to impinge upon his illusions. Nonetheless, at the end of his exploits, in the second part, Don Quixote finally renounces his optimistic faith in chivalry and returns home a broken man.

The principal utopian episode in *Don Quixote* concerns the award by Quixote of

Don Quixote illustré, *a nineteenth-century lithograph by J. J. Du Lochet depicting Don Quixote and his squire, Sancho Panza.*

the isle of Barataria to his down-to-earth squire, Sancho Panza, to establish an ordered society. Cervantes indicated through irony Don Quixote's intention of restoring the age of chivalry as well as the golden age of ancient writers. The real world, after all, was full of injustice, poverty, and class prejudice. The methods of strict obedience to tradition, which was part of the code of the medieval knight, would in fact usher in the golden age. Yet through his recounting of Sancho Panza's plans for the governance of the island of Barataria, Cervantes concluded that the notion of an ideal natural society was impractical and probably unachievable. For example, Sancho stated that there were too many nobles who did not contribute to the necessary work of the society. Yet Don Quixote himself claimed membership in that privileged class. Even so, the task of the knight was not merely to be a symbol of the golden age but, rather, to re-create it, a more daunting task.

Quixote must help Sancho establish a government based on reason, not a scientific utopia but a society grounded on respect for nature. There need not be formal laws in Cervantes's utopia, only a general reverence for natural conditions. Quixote warns Sancho that as governor he will have to demonstrate ability and courage to both discipline his subjects and defend against invaders. Sancho thinks that his observance of the chivalric methods of Quixote will be sufficient to guide him as governor. In the event, Sancho believes that qualifications for governance require neither training nor aristocratic lineage since the ruler must only conform to the precepts of nature. Quixote agrees that neither much ability nor education is necessary for governors as long as their rule is directed by good intentions. For his government, Sancho states that he will rely upon the maxims of the people as the basis of laws. Hence Cervantes suggested that popular traditions were the best foundation of law because they both originated with the common people and could be understood by them. Don Quixote also expresses his fondness for proverbial, thus ancient, wisdom of the people.

Cervantes sought both to restore the commonsense, natural golden age and to warn against reliance upon extravagant ideals. He also cited the historical examples of paternalism that became absolutist. Cervantes realized that the Renaissance humanist ideal of a government like Solomon's was impossible and that to speak of such a utopian society was to exist in a dream world, a utopia of evasion. In short, Cervantes concluded that a utopian construct—to dream the impossible dream—was appropriate as a guide for social reform but not as a form of escape from reality. The encroachment of modernity must be faced, not evaded. *Don Quixote* became Cervantes's warning to his age not to indulge in flights of fantasy.

**Reference** Maravall, Jose Antonio. *Utopia and Counterutopia in the "Quixote"* (1991).

## Ecotopia

The 1960s, another era in which technological abuses were criticized, led to a utopian vision of reduced and controlled growth designed to protect and conserve the earth's ecological balance. The  "ecotopia" was perhaps the first hint of a reaction to the industrial era and the beginning of the postindustrial age. Concern emanated initially from a troubling 1954 treatise by Jacques Ellul called *The Technological Society*. Ellul outlined the prospect of an emerging nonhuman technological totalitarianism that would adversely affect humanity by undermining freedom. The reemergence of the problem of scarcity also aided the ecotopian arguments. In the 1970s, events such as the petroleum shortage and the consequent increase in the price of oil reversed the prior belief in unlimited technological growth and caused ecological advocates to focus upon the need for more carefully regulated and even reduced technological applications. Paul Ehrlich's *The Population Bomb* (1968) heightened ecological concerns through its dire predictions about the exponential growth of world populations.

Many descriptions of the 1970s ecotopia genre hearkened back to the writings of the Russian anarchist Petr Kropotkin, especially his *Fields, Factories, and Workshops* (1899). Anarchic revival first appeared in Paul Goodman's *Communitas* (1960), which offered potential answers to the question of how industry (that is, the economy) could be reorganized to allow a rational development of communities (that is, society). The concern for thoughtful organization was motivated by a desire for efficiency and was also an attempt to inculcate a moral ethos. The "alternative" technique of the ecotopians was meant to replace the megascale centralized bureaucratic and corporate methods. Such "alternative" technologies were first outlined by British economist E. F. Schumacher in his work *Small Is Beautiful* (1973). Schumacher's pragmatic scientific method was wedded to a philosophical moralism derived from Buddhism's and Christianity's admonitions about nurturing the earth's resources.

Because of the oil shortage and increases in the price of oil after 1973, the alternative technology advocates espoused new sources of cleaner energy such as wind and solar power as well as a return to an earlier reliance on water power. *The Ecologist* magazine helped to educate readers and to popularize the various alternative concepts. The primary thrust of *The Ecologist* was to convince governments and corporations that unrestrained growth was no longer possible. Far from being anti-technology, the ecotopia movement sought to utilize the emerging computer technology to assist in new designs. The ecotopians tended to be specific rather than general and scientific rather than literary when making their proposals.

Yet the utopian feature of ecotopia became evident as early as 1962 in the final work of Aldous Huxley, *Island*. Ironically relying upon his own critique of utopia in *Brave New World* (1932), the biologist Huxley created the ecologically conscious society of Pala. The Palanese were always ecologically correct, restricting not only the growth of technology and industry but also of population. The education of the Palanese was weighted heavily toward knowledge of sciences related to ecology so as to instill a respect for nature. There was therefore more concern to infuse an ethical tone into scientific research. The Palanese were opposed by the growth-conscious, resource-wasting, corporate-oriented people of neighboring Rendang, who eventually, at the end of *Island*, conquered the

Palanese, ending their experiment in ecological survival. Huxley's *Island* appeared a little ahead of ecotopia's emergence but came to be noticed a decade later.

Ursula Le Guin's *The Dispossessed* (1974) offered the most complex ecotopian treatise utilizing a science fiction format. The story revolved around a scientist who moved between two planets, one a utopia founded on ecological anarchism and the other representing earth's direction: an anti-utopia of unregulated economic expansion. On the utopian planet of Anarres, cutting-edge technology allowed for a decentralized, balanced, and small-scale society with the utmost respect for the environment. All scientific knowledge was geared to pro-ecological uses on Anarres. Yet the planet was no Eden, the soil yielding more dust than food. Moreover, there was a certain regimentation and authoritarian control on Anarres not apparent on the anti-utopian planet. Le Guin seemed to suggest that the price for ecological regulation was the loss of personal freedom, thus blurring the lines between utopia and anti-utopia.

The American Ernest Callenbach, who first coined the term "ecotopia," described in *Ecotopia* (1975) a near-future maternalistic utopian state located in the Pacific Northwest that seceded from and felt threatened by the anti-ecological United States. Sovereign Ecotopia, with its capital at San Francisco, did not allow private ownership of property, and all economic units were kept small in an effort to eliminate class consciousness. In Ecotopia there was less influence by government bureaucracies, but there was also no great influence by technology. The workload for residents remained light, allowing for much leisure time to enjoy the beauty of the environment, although there was greater emphasis upon ecological education than pursuing pleasure. Female dominance in Ecotopia meant extensive reliance on contraceptives and abortion to control population growth. The closest resemblance to religion in Ecotopia was the near-worship of trees. Ecotopians

believed they would be recycled at death. The Ecotopians showed keen interest in Native Americans' traditional reverence for the environment.

Perhaps the most outspoken and widely read ecotopia enthusiast has been Murray Bookchin, onetime director of the Institute for Social Ecology, whose *Remaking Society: Pathways to a Green Future* (1990) summarized his anarchocommunitarian perspective and propositions for the ecological health of the globe. Bookchin decries "liberal environmentalists" who rely upon cooperation with government and corporations to protect natural resources by continuing past policies with only slight modifications. True to his anarchist beliefs, Bookchin advocates a staunchly libertarian approach of educating citizens for collective action to eliminate harmful hierarchies (political, social, and economic). His Nietzschean attitude can be summarized by the statement: "The moment human beings fall to their knees before any thing that is 'higher' than themselves, hierarchy will have made its first triumph over freedom."

A veteran of the counterculture movement during the 1960s, Theodore Roszak also entered the ecotopia debate in 1972 with the publication of *Where the Wasteland Ends*. Whereas most ecotopians showed a respect for the positive potential of science, Roszak was openly antiscience in his pronouncements, resulting in a deconstruction of even the possible positive uses of technology in preserving the environment. Roszak not only would halt technological growth, he would transform the whole contemporary urban society itself into a rural arrangement. Roszak's open criticism of science and technology was not typical of the ecotopian movement, however.

Except for Roszak, the ecotopian writers have resisted the tendency to become antitechnology, to move the postindustrial society back to the preindustrial era. Even with the general emphasis on making proper and controlled use of technology to protect and preserve the environment and its resources, ecotopia's most distinguishing trait has been its moral tone. Like Thomas More and his heirs, the ecotopians have been as concerned about the human qualities as about the scientific factors in their utopian vision. The ecotopian influence has manifested itself among various "green" organizations, both political and service oriented, established in most Western nations. Rejecting the traditional leftist agenda, green movements have jettisoned the Marxist version of the idea of progress for the theme of survival. Their platform stresses not only drastic ecological measures but also social reform, grassroots democratic participation, and nonviolence. The neo-Marxist Rudolf Bahro, author of *Building the Green Movement* (1986), briefly became the spiritual father of the West German Green Party (founded in 1980), only to leave it in disgust over compromises with the establishment. Ecotopian enthusiasts tend to be most similar to anarchists in their political philosophy, but there is considerable diversity and disagreement among its various articulations.

*See also* Anarchism.

*References* Bookchin, Murray. *Toward an Ecological Society* (1980); Brockmann, Stephen, Julia Hell, and Reinhilde Wiegmann. "The Greens: Images of Survival in the Early 1980s" (1989).

## Edger, Henry
*See* Positivism.

## *Erewhon* (1872)
Strongly influenced by Jonathan Swift's *Gulliver's Travels*, Samuel Butler's *Erewhon, or Over the Range* (1872) has been difficult to categorize, being labeled both a utopian romance and a dystopia. Unquestionably Butler anticipated, probably inadvertently, the great antitechnology dystopias of the twentieth century by Zamyatin, Huxley, and Orwell. Butler sought a format to critique Victorian English society and opted for an imaginary though not ideal society. The satirical novel depicts a shepherd who discovers a land known as

*Samuel Butler, the English satirist and author of* Erewhon.

Erewhon (that is, nowhere). The description of Erewhon's society allowed Butler to critically examine his contemporary Victorian mores, from religion and science to crime and disease, but especially the increasing role of technology. Butler displays the future of Victorian England in an unfavorable light through his distinctive vision.

The grandson of a famous English bishop and reared in a strict religious atmosphere, Samuel Butler (1835–1902) attended Cambridge University (1854–1858) in preparation for a clerical career in the Church of England. Yet his skepticism caused him to depart from that plan, to the dismay of his father; indeed, Butler later became known to many as a rebellious atheist. Though he grew up in an era when Charles Darwin's theories found great popularity among intellectuals, Butler believed that Darwin's ideas had been misapplied. Darwinism had produced a social system of reward and punishment aimed at ordering human behavior, a determinism from which Butler recoiled. He ultimately rejected many Darwinian elements and even proposed an alternative system in *Life and Habit* (1878). Much of the setting for

*Erewhon* resulted from a four-year residence (1860–1864) in New Zealand as a sheep farmer, during which time he also published essays in the local newspaper. Several articles about Darwin published in New Zealand anticipate Butler's views in *Erewhon*. Butler's manuscript for *Erewhon* was turned down by the first publisher who considered it, and the first edition did not include his name. Yet *Erewhon* proved to be the most popular of Butler's many writings, and before his death it went through eight editions and one major revision that added a chapter on ancient (and later irrelevant) "rights" of animals and vegetables (that is, banning eating them). He also penned a sequel, *Erewhon Revisited* (1901).

The story is told by a visitor, a shepherd later identified in *Erewhon Revisited* as George Higgs, who arrives to survey the society of Erewhon. Higgs discovers ten statues at the entrance to the land of Erewhon, prompting the assumption that he had discovered the ten lost tribes of Israel. The symbols thereby parodied the Ten Commandments, which Butler had by then cast as obstacles rather than gates to human development. Butler suggested that his own struggle to move beyond the Christian influences of his youth proved difficult. Once past the gates, that is, "over the range," Higgs finds the Erewhonians to be peaceful and happy, an obvious parallel to Lewis Carroll's fantasy *Alice's Adventures in Wonderland* (1865). Butler explored the relative status of moral and ethical codes through a variety of satirical devices.

One of these is the "Book of the Machines," which invokes a Darwinian principle, that machines would evolve to the capacity of humans in reasoning and decision making; hence they were to be avoided. Erewhon banned all future machines some 500 years before Higgs's visit following a war over the issue of technology. Butler intimated that the Erewhonians were a throwback to the Middle Ages in terms of their technology; they feared that given the opportunity to evolve, machines would displace humanity since

machine evolution was more rapid than human. As Butler put it, the machines "serve that they may rule." Thus, by their opposition to the advance of technology, Butler showed that the Erewhonians endorsed an absurd argument. The Erewhonians sensed the danger of human greed, which Butler viewed as the source of the quest for continuous technological advancements. Moreover, the banning of machines would prevent undesirable consequences such as industrial pollution, more efficient weapons of war, and drastic fluctuations in employment. Following the trail of inconsistencies, Butler also introduced a counter philosophy to the Book of Machines that argued that mankind was already "machine-like" in function, a cyborg. Many seventeenth-century scientists had used the analogy of nature working like a clock, though they generally did not apply the image to mankind. Such Butlerian dichotomies heighten the utopian-dystopian confusion often cited by critics. Which voice speaks for Butler? Because of the confusion in the first edition, Butler made it plain in the second edition that he was not attempting to be critical of Darwin. Nonetheless, the conflicting picture remains.

The residents of Erewhon, an isolated pastoral isle, were a polite and optimistic people who showed only casual dedication to matters such as religion. Reflecting again his own views, Butler had the character Higgs remark in the 1901 edition that he had known many people who "had a great knowledge of divinity, but no sense of the divine." The Musical Banks in Erewhon reflect a bankrupt Victorian church, a seeming necessity without any validity. The Erewhonians were more serious about their cheerful, unhurried pursuit of pleasure and thus rejected the concept of immortality. Hedonism and the prospect of death do not mix well. Openly disdainful of Victorian mores, the Erewhonians' absurd jurisprudence considered disease a crime punishable by imprisonment or execution and crime a disease treated by psychological counseling. Thus Butler's satire seems to advocate that crimes and disease be addressed with curative rather than punitive measures.

Social and educational policy in Erewhon also reflected Butler's ambivalent attitudes. Parents were excused from any child-rearing failures even before a baby was born. In other words, when children realize that they are mortal, will face pain and suffering, and must grapple with free will, they cannot blame their parents. Social conventions were set by the goddess Ydgrun, an anagram for Victorian England's social conscience, Mrs. Grundy. The educational system operated through the "Colleges of Unreason," which parodied England's Oxford and Cambridge Universities and the teaching of many useless subjects such as Latin. Erewhonian students learned an invented (and essentially useless) language and studied the logic of unreason rather than reason because the latter was deemed too easily perverted to the wrong ends. The professors in the colleges reflected a dogmatism—always more persuasive than reason, Butler thought—as well as an absence of intellectual curiosity. Despite the appeal of certain aspects of the Erewhonian society, the English visitor Higgs soon left Erewhon in a balloon.

The result of Erewhon's obsession with the negative potential of technology was a dystopian theme of machines not only gradually resembling humans but also making people less human. By depending upon technology to solve problems, would humans allow their own skills to dissipate? If the process were allowed to develop to a logical conclusion, would humans become mere automatons serving the machines? Thus the Erewhonians believed that by stopping the technological evolution they were acting to prevent that logical development from materializing. On the other hand, Butler wondered aloud in *Erewhon* whether humans could even survive if they lost the benefits of existing technology. But did Butler intentionally create a bizarre alternative in Erewhon to derail the very real possibility of achieving a sci-entific-technological utopia in the real world of the late nineteenth century? The author's comment on his own motives was equivocal. To be sure, Butler was consistently inconsistent.

**References** Remington, Thomas J. "'The Mirror up to Nature': Reflections of Victorianism in Samuel Butler's *Erewhon*" (1983); Sharma, G. N. "Butler's *Erewhon*: The Machine as Object and Symbol" (1980).

## Expressionism

As one of several emerging modern art forms in the twentieth century, German expressionism developed through stages from its pre–World War I origins to the Bauhaus movement of the 1920s Weimar era. Including both surrealistic and utopian fragments, expressionism set a revisionist tone for other modern architectural utopias such as the Italian Antonio Sant' Elia's Futurist City, the Swiss Le Corbusier's Radiant City, and the American Frank Lloyd Wright's Broadacre City. Expressionism also influenced related areas including the work of dramatists such as Ernst Toller and Bertolt Brecht, and philosophers such as Ernst Bloch with his neo-Marxist concrete utopia. Furthermore, the expressionist stress on freedom of the individual anticipated existentialism. The stages of the expressionist movement began with the idea of a natural earthly paradise among artists of the Dresden Bridge (*Brücke*) and the Munich Blue Rider (*Blaue Reiter*) groups, but the focal point was invariably Berlin. A natural paradise was followed by the architectural vision of a natural metropolis, whose drawings seemed so fanciful as to be incapable of actual construction. Added to these early visions was one seeking to blend art and society, the Crystal Chain group headed by Bruno Taut in 1919. By the time of the Bauhaus movement in the 1920s, expressionist designs had yielded to the pragmatic.

The major utopian influence upon the German expressionists was revolutionary anarchism because the expressionists determined to join life with art, to put ideas into action. Previous simplistic trends such as naturalism and realism seemed irrelevant to the more complex conditions at the turn of the century, especially because they did not grapple with psychological factors. Expressionists projected their futurist art plans from the present reality rather than from an abstract rendering. However, typically for German intellectuals, the emerging expressionism at the beginning of the twentieth century did utilize abstract terms—spirit, will, emotion—that also had been prominent at the beginning of the nineteenth century in the Romantic movement. Also borrowing from Romanticism, expressionism waxed nostalgic about an idealized past time. Hence expressionism encompassed a growing interest in Oriental mysticism to blend with their reform spirit. Although many artists and intellectuals in Germany also used the forceful rhetoric of groups such as the anarchists, the expressionist program was entirely aesthetic rather than political in conception. The organized predecessor of expressionism was the *Werkbund*, a group of architects in the 1890s who posited the concept of artistic cooperation to make the urban-industrial world compatible with the needs of humanity. The *Werkbund* efforts were manifested through the School of Applied Arts founded at Weimar in 1903 under the direction of Henry van de Velde.

Following the example of the *Werkbund*, the 1905 organization that espoused the nascent expressionism was the Dresden Bridge, headed by architecture students Ernst Ludwig Kirchner (1880–1938) and Karl Schmidt-Rottluff (1884–1976). The Dresden Bridge rejected bourgeois values and concentrated on free expression based on their image of challenging the art establishment and issuing a call to the younger generation to create a new future. Though the Dresden Bridge represented a utopian expression, it was not accompanied by a utopian blueprint. In their youthful enthusiasm, the Bridge group primarily evoked an anti-establishment attitude typical of avant-garde artists. It was true that their call for freedom envisioned all forms of liberty, not just creative freedom. Much of the Dresden Bridge natural paradise art portrayed nude youths frolicking in nature, their ultimate expression of freedom as well as rebellion from contemporary mores. Yet for all their spontaneity and air of rebellion, the Bridge lacked a complete vision of an ideal society and their definition of utopia remained "outopia," or nowhere.

The next stage of expressionism came with the Munich Blue Rider group formed in 1911 by Russian-born Wassily Kandinsky (1866–1944) and Franz Marc (1880–1916). These artists thought of the future in terms of a "Great Spiritual Epoch" that would be achieved by merging abstraction with realism. Hence the Blue Rider artists wanted to use abstract art as a universal spiritual language and spread their ideas through journals such as *The Storm* and *The Action*. Some of these artists seized upon apocalyptic themes in their paintings and drawings, but their organization proved even less coherent than the Bridge. Paul Klee (1879–1940) soon became associated with the Blue Rider group and reflected in his work the notion that the universe was a vast puzzle and that art was the esoteric key to its meaning. Very soon, the expressionist evolution became urban when it moved to Berlin, where the metropolis phase began, visualized by Ludwig Meidner (1884–1966) in the "world city." Like other urban reform architects, the German expressionists sought to mold the vision of the new city around human needs and concerns. Unlike other avenues of expressionism, the urban phase required the attention of architects in particular. By 1919 the task of rebuilding a defeated and reorganized Germany offered an even greater challenge.

Bruno Taut (1880–1938) proposed his "Program for Architecture" in 1919 at the outset of the Weimar Republic. His 1920 book *The Dissolution of the Cities* proclaimed that utopia was actually reality lost

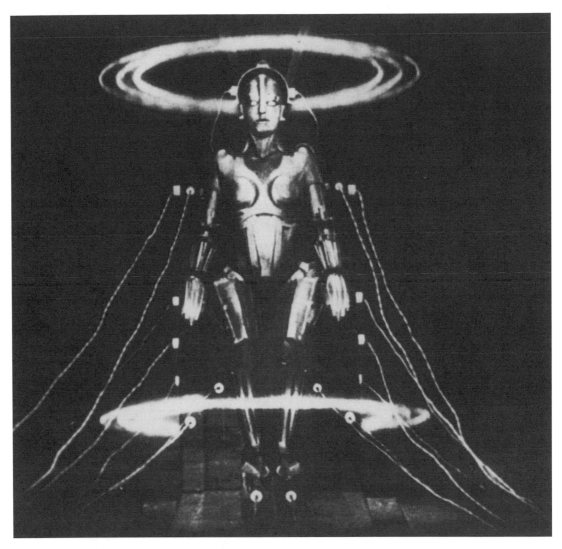

*Futuristic scene from Fritz Lang's motion picture* Metropolis, *1927.*

in a sea of illusion. Taut and his associates argued vigorously that the restoration of social and political order in Germany depended upon an architectural vision of "The Great Utopia." Taut joined other young architects including Walter Gropius (1883–1969), who formed the *Arbeitsrat für Kunst* to brainstorm about the form of reconstruction. This trend in expressionism disdained functionalism for the application of imagination. Many of the expressionist architectural drawings of the ideal metropolis featured elaborate crystalline towers reminiscent of Gothic cathedrals. Hence one of the practical influences of expressionism was the use of glass windows, a metaphor for transcendence, on a vast scale. The most tangible influence on the expressionists occurred in producer Fritz Lang's futuristic 1927 motion picture *Metropolis*, in which drawings of massive urban structures reflected the power and dominance of the urban utopia. Although *Metropolis* grappled with the ambivalence of upheaval and order in the Machine Age, its conclusion avoided taking a strong stand about how individuality could be accommodated in the modern technologically advanced urban-industrial society.

*Wassily Kandinsky,* On White, *1920. (Russian State Museum, St. Petersburg, Russia)*

The expressionist search for the New Man and new art also affected German drama. The New Man ideal, borrowing heavily from Friedrich Nietzsche's "superman" model, stressed the ethical development of a higher humanity for the individual, which would serve as a mechanism transforming society. So determined and committed were the literary expressionists that it seemed they were wrought up in a kind of soteriology, a quixotic quest to save the world through their literature. The transcendent search for human essence by the literary expressionists conformed to traditional abstract German thinking. World War I only emphasized the importance to the expressionist writers of the urgency to discover the New Man and New Society. Playwright Ernst Toller (1893–1939), who fought in the war, featured passionate characters, many of whom committed suicide, in his plays. In *Transfiguration* (1918) and *Masses and Men* (1921) Toller appealed to a reliance upon

persuasion and brotherly love rather than violence to create the new society. In the latter play Toller tried to show the futility of armed insurrection and revolution to achieve change. By concentrating on the liberation of the individual, writers such as Toller hoped to prepare the way for society's remaking.

In his play *Baal* (written in 1918), Bertolt Brecht (1898–1956) intended to critique expressionism, although it employed many of the expressionist themes including liberation, emotion, and love of nature. Still, Brecht was skeptical about the whole abstract concept of the New Man, especially since it seemed to coincide with Friedrich Nietzsche's "superman." Brecht used the setting of a Bohemian dining hall where expressionist artists, including the poet Baal, ballyhooed their assault on bourgeois culture. Baal's unstructured pursuit of hedonism and idealism paved the way for disaster rather than liberation. Similar but starker dystopian themes were elaborated in Brecht's 1930 opera *The Rise and Fall of the City of Mahagonny*, which equated conditions during the gold rushes in California and Alaska with those in Weimar Germany, where people thought they were free and living in a utopia but in reality were regimented and manipulated by a dystopia. Brecht preferred realistic grappling with social evils rather than detached flights of fancy as the appropriate method for achieving a better society.

Soon enough, as Germany struggled to recover from the effects of World War I, the expressionist view of utopia became the object of ridicule by other artists, especially the dadaists. Much more political in their critique of the present, the dadaists embraced revolutionary communism as the preferred medium for producing change. Moreover, the dadaists seemed bent upon a structureless ambiguity to ensure individual free expression rather than a formal utopian blueprint. After 1921 the Bauhaus school, though more concerned with commonality, concentrated on functional buildings rather than a sweeping utopian entity. The Bauhaus did demonstrate a concern to solve the problem of reestablishing community in the urban-industrial society, but the chief tool in attaining that goal was architecture. Yet the Bauhaus lacked sufficient structure and definition to comprehend and unify the variety of individual approaches within the movement. Hence the Bauhaus retained more of an isolated and selective influence rather than a comprehensive program of social unity. The Bauhaus phenomenon became a microcosm of the traditional utopian tension of balancing individual freedom with common goals. Even less than expressionism, the dadaists and the Bauhaus school neglected the development of a utopian social component for their idealized art forms. German artists in the Weimar era could easily visualize their dreams but expended little thought about the practical means to achieve those utopian dreams. Moreover, in the postwar catharsis that Germans experienced in the 1920s, there was little

attraction for impractical dreams or incomplete blueprints for revision. Though it was suppressed as degenerate by the Nazis, expressionism's influence survived better than did dadaism or the Bauhaus school because of the concrete utopia of Ernst Bloch.

*See also* Concrete Utopia.

*References* Benson, Timothy O. *Expressionist Utopias: Paradise, Metropolis, Architectural Fantasy* (1993); Bronner, Stephen E., and Douglas Kellner, eds. *Passion and Rebellion: The Expressionist Heritage* (1983).

## The Expulsion of the Triumphant Beast (1584)

Trained as a Dominican friar, Giordano Bruno departed from his Catholic moorings to become a mystical spokesman for a new religious and scientific system. Bruno's utopian concepts were recounted primarily in *The Expulsion of the Triumphant Beast* (1584). Bruno brought together the natural religion of the ancient Egyptians, the reasoned philosophy of the ancient Greeks, and the government of the Roman republic to create his utopia. After being charged as a religious heretic and serving nine years in prison, Bruno was burned at the stake by an Inquisition court in Rome.

Not long after completing his monastic training in 1572, Giordano Bruno (1548–1600) left church service in Naples and moved quickly to embrace a hermetic, Neoplatonist philosophy. For 15 years he traveled across Europe to university cities—Venice, Geneva, Toulouse, Paris, Oxford, Wittenberg, Prague—where he disputed Aristotelianism and its defenders. He also lectured university audiences and princes on mnemonics, the art of memory enhancement by the use of formulas. Although he praised Nicolaus Copernicus's revival of the heliocentric theory, Bruno actually was unacquainted with mathematics and the emerging new science. Hence his philosophical approach could only anticipate the pansophists of the seventeenth century. Arguing for a fully dynamic, infinite universe, Bruno developed a pantheism that resembled Spinoza's religious views a century later.

In 1584 while in London Bruno published a utopian treatise, *Spaccio della bestia trionfante* (*The Expulsion of the Triumphant Beast*), dedicated to an English poet acquaintance, Sir Philip Sidney. Eschewing the fanciful golden age utopian format so popular in the Renaissance, Bruno used the framework of a Lucian dialogue. The *Spaccio* is organized into three parts, each with another subdivision. The setting is a divine debate with a council supervised by Jove wherein Bruno portrayed mankind enjoying a genuine renewal of love, learning, and morals guided by the all-knowing deities. He relied upon irony, sarcasm, and paradox in an allegorical critique of the aristocracy's lusting after wealth and power; at the same time, he advocated charity toward the poor. His political ideal seemed to be the early Roman republic, which disdained the guile of selfish princes and guaranteed justice and the rule of law. Yet the popular masses were incapable of instituting the reforms, so an all-powerful ruler, that is, Jove, became necessary. By instituting a merger of nature and religion in his pantheism, Bruno paved the way for the more secular utopian concepts of the pansophists in the seventeenth century. It seemed easier to invoke God's blessing upon a reorganization of society if God, the ultimate reality, was more than just creator as part and parcel of the creation. Bruno apparently hoped for a reformation that would replace vices with virtues. He wanted the despots to be controlled and the vulnerable in society to be provided protection, and he wanted a democratic opportunity for learning the arts and sciences. Although he allowed his deities in the *Spaccio* to magically order such a change, Bruno realized that in the real world, reform would be much more complicated. Certainly, alienated as he was from the church, Bruno could not imagine the religious leaders of his day leading a reformation.

The diffuse prolixity of the *Spaccio* contains much more in the form of criticism of Bruno's society and institutions than description of the shape of his utopia to replace the current system. Yet Bruno probably did not conceive of a revolution that would entail completely destroying the old ways and constructing a new system; rather, he envisioned purifying the existing institutions and practices. Unlike Thomas More and other early modern utopian writers, Bruno showed little interest in creating a detailed model of his ideal society. Indeed, Bruno envisioned changing mankind's inner soul more than simply altering his external behavior. His great passion was a dedication to the truth, which he equated with divinity. Truth can survive slurs, slights, and even indifference. Bruno remained skeptical of any claims to infallibility by mortal authorities. No ascetic, Bruno used the utopian framework to recommend a voluntary movement for utilitarian change. Spiritual, as opposed to social, regeneration would produce more genuine social and institutional reform than would a movement led by a totalitarian dictator. His notion of natural religion reform would combine hermetics with certain pre-Christian and nonclassical attitudes, which he may have compared with ancient Egypt.

The aggressive and often bizarre behavior of Giordano Bruno should be understood in the context of his desire to get attention by challenging known authorities. Yet his influence upon the pansophists of the next century and the deists of the eighteenth century is unmistakable. Bruno recognized certain ills in his own society, chiefly in the areas of religion and education. He felt strongly that reforms should be undertaken, so he resorted to the utopian framework in the *Spaccio*. Because he did not intend that his utopia be used as the actual model for a reformation, he did not offer a full-fledged structure for his utopia.

**References** Firpo, Luigi. "Il processo di Giordano Bruno" (1948); Yates, Frances A. *Giordano Bruno and the Hermetic Tradition* (1964).

## Fairhope Colony

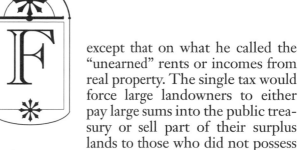

The Iowa radical reformer Ernest B. Gaston decided after failing to bring about reform through the ballot box to launch a unique experiment on the shores of Mobile Bay, Alabama. Gaston proposed to combine the best elements of the cooperative communes of the past but to provide much greater individual freedom, which he believed would be the key to success. The Fairhope experiment began in 1894, and certain elements of Gaston's ideas remain intact today.

Born in Illinois, Ernest Berry Gaston (1861–1937) grew up in Des Moines, Iowa, and received a degree in business from Drake University in 1886. Gaston became deeply involved in agrarian reform efforts in the farm state of Iowa by the 1890s. Several influences affected his thinking, beginning with his study of certain grandiose utopias such as the Topolobampo Bay colony in Mexico and the Kaweah colony in California. Gaston came to believe that such experiments failed because the rules for participants were too rigid. He also became interested in the single-tax ideas of political economist Henry George. In 1879, George's *Progress and Poverty* had outlined a drastic reform intended to lift the common masses from their poverty and provide a large measure of egalitarianism through tax simplification. George argued that the widespread existence of poverty was due primarily to the concentration of the ownership of land in a few private hands. Rather than having the government arbitrarily seize private holdings to redistribute them equally, as was proposed by groups such as the Marxists, George said the redistribution could be achieved simply by changing the tax laws. He proposed the abolishment of all forms of taxation except that on what he called the "unearned" rents or incomes from real property. The single tax would force large landowners to either pay large sums into the public treasury or sell part of their surplus lands to those who did not possess it. The single tax thus would have a leveling effect without creating class warfare as Marxism proposed through the abolition of private property. Gaston had drafted a constitution for a single-tax colony in 1890, but he continued to rely upon traditional reform methods through the electoral process, rallying behind the Peoples' (Populist) Party in Iowa elections during 1892–1893. When those efforts failed to persuade a majority of voters, Gaston turned to a utopian idea as an alternative method of achieving reform objectives. Gaston's vision was expansive: He was not thinking just of himself and his friends but of the whole nation when he founded Fairhope.

Following Populist electoral failures in 1894 Iowa elections, Gaston gathered several close friends to propose the undertaking of the Fairhope experiment (named by a colonist who said the experiment had a fair hope of success). Gaston and about a dozen followers made plans to acquire property somewhere in a southern region to launch their colony. All of the land in the community would be owned by an association and leased to individuals, but every resident would have equal access to the colony's common property. George had argued that property values derived from the use of land by the whole community rather than by individual owners. A user's fee based on the value of the land would be paid in to the association's treasury on an annual basis, a single property tax. Taking Gaston's 1890 constitutional draft as a starting point, the Des Moines

Single Tax Club completed the document that would govern their colony as a true democracy. All adult males and females would be voting members and would elect a governing council that answered directly to the electorate. The constitution aimed to establish "cooperative individualism" by ensuring that Fairhope would be free of any "private monopoly" and to assure each member equal opportunity.

The constitution of the Fairhope Industrial Association stated as its purpose "to establish and conduct a model community or colony, free from all forms of private monopoly, and to secure to its members therein, equality of opportunity." It was capitalized with 5,000 shares of stock totaling one million dollars. The association invoked measures that became widely popular during the coming Progressive era: the initiative, referendum, and recall. Voters could initiate legislation by direct vote rather than having to rely upon their representative bodies. The referendum allowed voters to repeal, by direct vote, existing laws that had become unnecessary or were deemed unfair. Elected officials were subject to recall through petitions and unscheduled elections, which allowed voters to remove officeholders before their constitutional terms were completed. The existence of such a measure would help ensure that officeholders were sensitive to the wishes of the community. The colony would own and operate all utilities (public rather than private) to ensure low costs and maximum efficiency of service, another idea championed later by the Progressives.

The prospective colonists desired to locate somewhere in the South, where the climate was temperate and land inexpensive. Descriptions of specific potential locales in seven states visited by the site committee were published in the group's newspaper, the *Fairhope Courier*, edited by Gaston. By September 1894 the search had ended with the association's purchase of 135 acres on the eastern shore of Mobile Bay. Gaston led more than two dozen settlers to take possession of the colony in

November 1894. Although most early immigrants came from Iowa, some arrived from places as far away as British Columbia. By 1907 the colony owned 4,000 acres around Fairhope, the purchase of additional lands having been made possible by various wealthy benefactors, including Philadelphia manufacturer Joseph Fels. Prospective settlers could acquire land at Fairhope without cost as long as they agreed to pay the annual tax and a $100 association membership fee. Because many potential followers could not afford the membership fee, the colony soon agreed to make land available to nonmembers, hoping that they would eventually join the association. The increase in the number of nonmembers created a population not fully committed to the ideals of the founders, but it seemed the only way to attract enough settlers to keep the colony solvent.

A commercial town center and park were located on the bluffs overlooking the bay. The water became a unifying force, bringing the community together for recreation, social events, and fishing. A steamboat provided transport across the bay to Mobile, the colony's main contact with the outside world for a time. Eventually a causeway built across the head of the bay in the 1920s connected the eastern shore and Fairhope to Mobile with a highway. Fairhope maintained its own water supply, telephone system, library, and school. Marietta Johnson, a schoolteacher from Minnesota, launched the School of Organic Education in 1907, which implemented the progressive educational theories of John Dewey. Johnson wanted to make the school a microcosm of the cooperative community by eliminating the tradition of competitiveness in the classroom. Hence there were no examinations, promotions, or honors given to her students, and the diverse curriculum included the fine arts, environmental studies, and even games. Because of its picturesque location, Fairhope immediately became an attraction for visitors (especially artists and writers) and tourists, some of whom decided to make it their permanent residence. After the failure of the Topolobampo Bay experiment in Mexico in 1893, Marie Howland (1836–1921) came to live at Fairhope, where she founded the library and worked with Gaston at the *Fairhope Courier*. Though there were still only about 100 residents at Fairhope in 1900, the population had grown to more than 1,500 by 1930. In 1908, when the city of Fairhope was incorporated, it lost some of its distinctive features. Most of the community property became owned by the municipality in time, and the original principles gradually were subsumed by nonidealistic traditional practices.

Fairhope existed as a living protest against the existing economic system in the United States. It offered hope by its example for the common classes for an alternative society. Yet despite its limited successes, by the 1920s Fairhope had not inspired a national movement of reform as Gaston had hoped. There had not even been any imitators among the new communities settled in the Baldwin County area around Fairhope. One reason for Fairhope's failure to spread its influence was that Gaston and his colleagues did not utilize a propaganda method to disseminate their ideas. They assumed that the experiment's successful existence alone would stimulate expansion of the scheme. The Great Depression of the 1930s clearly affected Fairhope's fortunes adversely. With the deaths of Gaston in 1937 and Johnson in 1938, an era passed and no comparable leaders appeared to renew Fairhope's principles or economic fortunes. Though the city of Fairhope and surrounding areas in Baldwin County have grown tremendously since World War II, most of the original aspects of the settlement have been superseded by more traditional community and economic values. Without an authoritarian regimentation, utopias such as Fairhope had little chance of surviving the encroaching power of tradition.

*Reference* Gaston, Paul B. *Man and Mission: E. B. Gaston and the Origins of the Fairhope Single Tax Colony* (1993).

## Feminist Utopias

The distinctive feminist utopia genre results from a bifurcated approach to women's issues in the modern era. Feminists from the eighteenth century to the early twentieth century focused almost exclusively upon the goal of equality: legal, political, and social. Yet because of the historic paternalism and perceived egregious male domination, another attitude developed in the twentieth century. Energized by the women's liberation movement of the 1960s and 1970s, radical feminists promoted a previously repressed antimale attitude oriented toward a contest for power rather than equality. Both of the approaches—equality and power—have been included in feminist utopian writing. A further experiment in feminist utopias has been the all-female utopia, which was utilized often to express concerns about male-female relationships.

The campaign for female equality dates from the eighteenth century. The classic statement of the claim by England's Mary Wollstonecraft was a response to Thomas Paine's paean to the French Revolution, *The Rights of Man*. Her *Vindication of the Rights of Woman* (1792) established the goal of women's equality, which continued through the early twentieth century. Female equality in a utopian setting appeared first among the eighteenth-century Shakers who—in addition to practicing celibacy—implemented spiritual equality, though they retained a patriarchal leadership. One of the earliest examples of the female-exclusive utopia was Sarah Scott's *A Description of Millennium Hall* (1762). After a failed marriage, Scott and a female friend established a female commune in 1754 that became the factual basis for the fictional Millennium Hall. In the story, a male character stumbles upon a compact, secular female commune populated by single and socially ostracized women. The commune is run according to the rational principles of the Enlightenment, with women's labors becoming pragmatic rather than gender specific. Another eighteenth-century feminist utopia appeared in China penned by a male. Writing for ten years, Li Ju-chen (1763–1830) set his story, *Ch-ing-hua yuan* (Flowers in the mirror), in the reign of the Empress Wu (684–705) of the T'ang dynasty. The chief character has a daughter who came to earth in the incarnation of the "Fairy of a Hundred Flowers." The story involves a long voyage to many lands, one of which was the Country of Women, where a matriarchal society existed. The ruling females kept males in their harems and otherwise subjected men to the type of repressions common to women in patriarchal societies. Moreover, women made the decisions about marriage and received formal educations.

The nineteenth century witnessed the broadest expression of female distinctiveness in utopian terms. Only about one-third of the literary utopias written by women were feminist in their aims. One approach by nineteenth-century feminist utopian writers supported the campaign for women's rights, which attempted to change society's attitudes and practices toward women. A complementary approach favored using women's liberated powers to reconstruct the United States along utopian lines. Feminist utopists visualized women acting as free moral agents equal to men in rights and responsibilities rather than serving merely as men's inspiration. Hence to one extent or another they assaulted the cult of female domesticity ingrained in contemporary social customs. Feminists believed that an egalitarian society would extinguish virtually all contemporary ills, especially those affecting women and children.

The method of projecting the present into the future to illustrate the possibility of change was utilized in the 1836 essay "Three Hundred Years Hence," written by Mary Griffith, a widow forced into self-sufficiency after her husband's untimely death. In her story, a man buried under snow for 300 years thaws out to discover a society that has ended child abuse, capital punishment, and war. This peaceful, progressive status was achieved through the leadership of women over the intervening

*Kate Millett, feminist author, being interviewed on the ABC show "Good Morning America" by host David Hartman, 27 March 1979.*

centuries. A similar technique was used by Jane Appleton in an 1848 essay, "Sequel to the Vision of Bangor in the Twentieth Century." Appleton's essay countered a male author's fantasy about Bangor, Maine, in 1978 as a sophisticated and prosperous society that had peacefully solved the women's rights issue with women ruling the home and men the outside world. In Appleton's sequel, women had gained complete freedom of opportunity and equality with males, but without any radical social revolution. Marriage, child-rearing, and families remained intact, and women did not even bother to participate in government though it was open to them.

In 1868, Elizabeth Corbett wrote a serialized utopian story for *Harper's* entitled "My Visit to Utopia." Women obtained rights such as the vote and men participated in child care, but most important, women enjoyed satisfying conventional marriages. A more pointed critique of patriarchy appeared in suffragist Annie Denton

Cridge's *Man's Rights* (1870). The story featured a dreamlike trip to Mars with stereotypical sex roles reversed in a matriarchal system where men were second-class citizens. The women were physically appealing but also strong, decisive, and condescending toward men. Cridge even features a "men's rights" meeting in which men complain about getting only one-third the wages of women, being consigned to domestic chores of the household, and lacking educational opportunities. An imaginative approach using a similar reversal of roles was Eveleen Mason's satirical *Hiero-Salem* (1889). Mason created a utopian androgynous family complete with a "father-mother" head of the household, a female who earns the income, and a "mother-father," a male who handled domestic responsibilities. Mason suggested that society could learn from a single meritorious example of reform constructed on a small scale. If men were to be changed, it must begin in the home.

In Alcanoan Grigsby's *Nequa* (1900), the chief female character disguised herself as a sailor to obtain the job and pay she desired and deserved. A mysterious storm swept her ship to the center of the earth, to an idyllic land called Altruria, where she encounters an economically advanced egalitarian society. The female character's guide was a well-educated, independent woman, yet Grigsby retained certain stereotypes of the female such as altruism and compassion for others, which have helped end war and oppression in Altruria. Grigsby was among the first female utopists to show interest in technological advances as an element of the utopia. In an openly antimale mimicking of Grigsby's format, Mary Bradley created in *Mizora* (1889) an all-female society of powerful yet beautiful Amazon-like women ruling utopia. Men had not existed for several thousand years, religion existed in the form of pantheism, and scientific knowledge—especially eugenics for propagation—allowed the female residents to harness nature for their comfort. Since there were no men, no evils or miseries existed in Mizora, including disease. Another suffragist, Winnifred Harper Cooley, used utopian forms to advocate change in "A Dream of the Twenty-First Century" (1902). Cooley portrayed women as reformers who, after obtaining political power through the vote, eliminated the social problems created by an industrial-urban capitalism. Marriage was no longer necessary for female economic security in Cooley's utopia because women had obtained economic equality. Moreover, evil trusts and monopolies as well as slums and mistreatment of workers have been eliminated, thanks to the efforts of the women. A humanist religion with attributes of the social gospel replaced the old male-dominated church.

In addition to literary constructions, there were numerous utopian social experiments aimed at altering the fate of women in a patriarchal society during the nineteenth century. The utopian socialists through their communes committed their movement to removing the oppression that domesticity imposed upon women. Among the great variety of utopian communities established in the United States, some were founded and operated by women, such as the one founded by British-born Frances Wright (1795–1852). Her settlement at Nashoba, Tennessee (1826–1829), served primarily as a haven for escaped antebellum southern slaves and followed the Fourierist pattern. Wright promoted racial and sexual freedom as well as the need for public education. In another, led by Methodist activist Martha McWhirter (1827–1904), about 50 women known as the Sanctified Sisters established the Woman's Commonwealth in 1866 at Belton, Texas. Though it retained certain religious elements, it focused more upon practical self-sufficiency, primarily through the operation of a hotel begun in 1886. Along with the common utopian practice of holding property communally, the movement also engaged in some mystical practices such as the interpretation of dreams and visions. By the time of McWhirter's death, the commonwealth had begun to disintegrate.

Even before the achievement of women's suffrage, the twentieth century's model feminist utopia was written. Charlotte Perkins Gilman's *Herland* appeared initially as installments in her newspaper, *The Forerunner*, in 1915. Significantly, it was not published in book form until 1979, at the height of the renewed feminist campaign. Gilman promoted a full range of feminist activities, including socialism, suffragism, and pacifism. She focused upon the issues of class and racial discrimination as much as sexual bias. The fictional utopia of Herland, an exclusively female society, was discovered by three male visitors exhibiting stereotypical antifemale attitudes. Yet the outsiders find three female residents to marry; the visitors are thinking in terms of the traditional marriage arrangements, while Herland's female mates consider marriage in asexual terms since previous pregnancies had been accomplished through parthenogenesis. Gilman sought in *Herland* to expand the concept of motherhood and education of daughters to become the primary social value. By abolishing the animal instinct (but not passions) in humans, she eliminated sexuality and replaced religion with motherhood. Thus, despite her radical approach to female sexuality, Gilman's role for women fit more closely into a nineteenth-century mold than into the emerging feminism of the twentieth century.

Following a similar format to Gilman's, a rare male contribution appeared in Gerhart Hauptmann's 1925 *Die Insel der Grossen Mutter* (Island of the great mother), which examined the gender issue by employing a utopian fantasy. Hauptmann's published works revealed a fascination with conflict between the sacred and the profane, but he was also drawn to the male-female contest. The story begins when travelers discover a curious island in which a matriarchy has been established following an earlier shipwreck that allowed social experimentation. Whenever a male child is born, he is banished to another part of the island to preserve the all-female rule. The female society caters to the good of the community rather than the individual, seeks the nurture of the family, and provides love and a social conscience to humanity. Hauptmann also suggested that the female qualities coincided with Christian virtues. By contrast, the patriarchal society remained earthly, realistic, materialistic, and above all individual. The problem remains in reality, according to Hauptmann, where males dominate females through the power of sex. There cannot be any society without both male and female.

Following the achievement of women's suffrage after World War I, the utopian themes of feminism virtually disappeared for a generation. Indeed, it was not until the revival of a women's rights movement in the 1960s and 1970s that new and more radical feminist utopias reemerged. With the appearance of Kate Millett's *Sexual Politics* (1970) the feminist emphasis became power rather than equality and assumed a more markedly antimale emphasis than had existed with earlier feminist writers. Although some feminist utopists, such as Doris Lessing in her novel sequence, *Canopus in Argos: Archives*, have faulted male-created institutions and traditions, including politics, as the source of manipulation of women, most writers have focused directly upon male-female relations. France's Monique Wittig in *Les Guérillères* (1969) deliberately provoked controversy by promoting anarchism and expressions of female power: sexual, political, and social. Wittig turned the patriarchal past into an object of derision because in order to alter the female consciousness it was necessary to utterly destroy the mind-set developed from an antifemale historical past. A new image of woman, from physiology to mental framework, had to be created so the past could be expunged. The all-female society of *Les Guérillères* was militant and violent, especially toward the linguistic and ideological representation of patriarchy. The cleansing ritual of destruction of the past became a precondition to the construction of a utopian present and future for women.

For Wittig solutions could only be obtained through women's violent confrontation with men. Another militant approach to past male domination was Joanna Russ's *The Female Man* (1975). Russ, like Wittig, mingled the past, present, and future together through her four primary female characters. The utopian future of an all-female world, called Whileaway, resulted from a plague that killed all males 600 years before the story's setting. Russ rejects Gilman's adoration of motherhood and portrays it as simple necessity, accomplished mechanically. Instead, Russ's emphasis is upon the extended female family, usually numbering 30 members, and the utilization of advanced technology to remove the drudgery of work. Other feminist utopian works invoking the single-sex societies include Suzy Charnas's *Motherlines* (1978), Sally Gearhart's *The Wanderground* (1979), and Donna Young's *Retreat* (1979).

Marge Piercy offered an update to Gilman's interpretation of motherhood in the 1976 utopian novel *Woman on the Edge of Time*. Piercy utilized a bifurcated time setting, contrasting contemporary New York City and the fictional Mattapoisett of 2137 to explore issues of class and race. The only important character, Connie Ramos, moved from the present in New York City (a mental hospital) to a future in Mattapoisett (an anarchist society recovering from massive pollution and waste) in a conscious dream and thereby from an evil society to a good (but not perfect) one. In the ecologically balanced future society of Mattapoisett, women have been spared even the burden of childbearing since all babies are born in test tubes. Men exist but play the role of mothers and even possess female physiology.

Feminist utopists have also utilized science fiction and dystopias as vehicles for their expression. Ursula Le Guin's *The Dispossessed: An Ambiguous Utopia* (1974) does not portray a perfect or even appealing dreamworld through its science fiction; rather, it shows a realistic society, Annares, with flawed humans. Le Guin confronts the problem of allowing freedom of choice in an ordered society while favoring a system giving the greatest degree of human freedom and control. The most admirable quality in Annares is its sexual equality and the elimination of both patriarchic and matriarchic tendencies. Men and women are true friends and partners in Annares. Another use of science fiction for utopian objectives was Thea Alexander's *2150 A.D.* (1971), which employed advanced technology, including robots, to promote gender equality—the Macro self—by removing the competitive and authoritative features of society. Mary Staton used the contrast of two alternative future utopias (one technological and the other humanist) with a present dystopia in *From the Legend of Biel* (1975) to emphasize the positive qualities and potentialities of utopia. Two dystopias, Suzy Charnas's *Walk to the End of the World* (1974) and Margaret Atwood's *The Handmaid's Tale* (1985), portrayed repressive antifemale future societies—Holdfast and Gilead—to critique the exploitation of women in patriarchal traditions and to demonstrate the need for reform.

*See also* The Handmaid's Tale.

*References* Barr, Marleen, and Nicholas D. Smith, eds. *Women and Utopia: Critical Interpretations*, (1983); Bartkowski, Frances. *Feminist Utopias* (1989); Rohrlich, Ruby, and Elaine H. Baruch, eds. *Women in Search of Utopia: Mavericks and Mythmakers* (1984).

## Fénelon, François de Salignac de la Mothe-
*See* Arcadia.

## Forster, E. M.
*See* "The Machine Stops."

## Fourier, Charles
*See* Utopian Socialism.

## France, Anatole
*See* Penguin Island.

## Frankfurt School

The twentieth-century neo-Marxists who comprised the Frankfurt Institute departed from their intellectual patron in order to respond to capitalism's success in neutralizing the opposition of the proletariat and maintaining the status quo. Many of the Frankfurt school were also attracted to Sigmund Freud's psychohistorical analysis of human tendencies. Hence the Frankfurt school and its most utopian spokesman, Herbert Marcuse, created a unique blend of the thinking of Freud and Marx that theorized a new revolutionary class and circumstances for responding to capitalism's successful reliance upon science and technology. Marcuse realized that utopia was no longer impossible thanks to technology's ability to satisfy basic human desires as well as needs.

Launched in 1924, the Frankfurt Institute sought to apply philosophy to develop practical social policy. Its leaders, mostly German Jews, included Max Horkheimer, Erich Fromm, Theodore Adorno, and Herbert Marcuse. On the occasion of the Nazi takeover in 1933, the institute moved to Geneva, Switzerland, and the following year to Columbia University in New York City. Renamed the International Institute for Social Research, the neo-Marxists could not be called true believers since they subjected Marxism to criticism and revision concomitant with the changing times. Some of the founders returned to Germany after World War II, but Fromm and Marcuse remained in the United States to continue their work. These neo-Marxists replaced the class conflict with an existential conflict between man and nature. They also used the term "enlightenment" to describe a process of maturation occurring throughout Western civilization rather than just during the eighteenth century.

Invariably the Frankfurt school philosophers focused upon the ideal of freedom, but they always believed that individual freedom must emanate from the larger community's freedom, so they eschewed abstract theories of personal freedom. As materialists, the Frankfurt group also equated freedom with the happiness that resulted from the satisfaction of needs. Fromm's most widely read treatise, *Escape from Freedom* (1940), questioned whether humans could actually handle the freedom that they had achieved over previous centuries. He argued that peer approval was more important than individualism and that individual freedom traumatized rather than soothed the psyche. Humans thought they wanted to be self-reliant but actually preferred someone else to make their decisions. Indeed, the historical quest for freedom inadvertently had created the conditions for totalitarianism in the post–World War I era because the totalitarian ideology more than liberal democracy was psychologically designed to appeal to the mass man rather than the individual.

Herbert Marcuse (1898–1979) remained focused upon Marx during the 1920s and 1930s, but he gained a major reputation only after World War II when he turned to Freud to help interpret capitalism's resilience. Before the war, he argued that fantasy rather than reason could span the gap between an irrational capitalism and rational socialism. In *Eros and Civilization: A Philosophical Inquiry into Freud* (1955), Marcuse expanded his concept of fantasy in a modification of Freud's notion of sexual repression. Since the overthrow of the capitalist system would end class exploitation, with its accompanying sexual repression, it would usher in sexual freedom along with economic equality. The memory of positive past experiences of freedom and happiness would facilitate and shape the fantasy. Indeed, Marcuse felt it necessary for humanity to "regress" back to an ideal stage of both the mental and physical past. Perhaps Marcuse's most profound tool to stimulate memory and fantasy was art, which generally reflects the life instinct. At the time, he still reflected the rather orthodox Marxist teaching that capitalism's greed and inefficiencies would sow the seeds of its own inevitable destruction.

Yet a decade later Marcuse revised his future view in *One-Dimensional Man: Studies in the Ideology of Advanced Industrial Society* (1964). By then he understood that Marx's theory was based on a condition of scarcity that caused the alienation of the proletariat. Yet in the late twentieth century, abundance had replaced scarcity, so it was possible to free labor from alienation. Marcuse concluded that the democratic welfare state combined with capitalism's resort to advanced technology and automation meant that capitalism had revised itself for survival. The capitalist class, smaller yet more powerful than before, tightened its grip through the monopolistic control of production. The welfare state made all except the wealthiest citizens, especially the proletariat, dependent upon government rather than on themselves for their material security. Large corporations' application of technology—making workers ancillary to the machines—avoided inefficiencies and at the same time provided the masses with sufficient material comforts and libidinal pleasures ("artificial needs") that neutralized the potential for revolution. The ideological totalitarians such as Hitler and Stalin had appealed for mass support from a purely negative emotional basis, the fictitious enemy of Jews or capitalists, whereas a technological totalitarianism satisfied the more fundamental cravings of physical pleasures. The workers, Marx's revolutionaries, had been seduced by technocapitalism and its ally, the welfare state, into accepting their unfree condition. The high-tech capitalist welfare state also produced an insipid, irrational culture—the arts, media, religion, education—that degraded human dignity. The masses opted for television over the theater. Even the so-called liberation movements of the 1960s only manifested a new enslavement of humanity, an enslavement that extended to the unconscious realm and produced passive, easily manipulated masses.

More than ever visualizing a long and difficult struggle to overthrow the status quo, Marcuse therefore began searching for a new revolutionary class that could create a socialist utopia based upon an external standard of truth. The student revolts of the late 1960s, especially the 1968 Paris uprisings, derided welfare-state liberals and chose Marcuse as the counterculture's guru; Marcuse, in his *Essay on Liberation* (1969), considered rebellious youth as the new revolutionaries. Yet when he concluded that the students were disingenuous for merely wanting to soften their degree requirements, he ceased to consider them as revolutionaries. Likewise, when the minority groups in Western nations such as the United States began their civil rights campaign, Marcuse suddenly embraced them as the replacement for the proletariat. However, Marcuse soon learned that the minorities only wanted to reform the system, not replace it. Marcuse recognized in *The End of Utopia* (1967) that the idea of utopia as a revolutionary goal had disappeared, since almost any conceivable lifestyle that satisfied human needs was now possible due to capitalism and technology's advances. Utopia could be reality, so Marcuse opted for the approach taken by the nineteenth-century utopian socialists: designing an "alternative" to the form of contemporary technocapitalism. The new revolutionaries would simply materialize in the midst of the transformation rather than taking charge from their preexisting state. The revolution would focus upon "new needs" such as rest, recreation, privacy, and what Marcuse, aping David Hume, called true freedom based upon a new secular morality. Departing from his earlier adherence to Marxism, Marcuse had become merely a reformer rather than a utopian.

Although not a direct product of the Frankfurt school, Robert A. Heinlein mimicked the philosophy of the New Left and, like Marcuse, became an idol of the 1960s counterculture. Heinlein's *Stranger in a Strange Land* (1961) followed a technique developed first by Gabriel Tarde in *Underground Man*, creating a utopia from a dystopia. The New Left decried the loss of individualism and community, which it hoped to restore. Heinlein's characters learn again to share resources with their compatriots and rediscover interpersonal relationships. The primary illustration for sharing is unrestricted sexual relations, which Heinlein and the youth culture deemed not only self-satisfying but also an act of rebellion against society's taboos. Typical of the Marxist revisionists of the 1960s, Heinlein does not deal with socioeconomic or political structures, although the utopia endorses equality and community property. Hence he focuses upon personal satisfaction rather than the creation of an ideal society that would benefit the whole community. The New Left was at its best when critiquing the establishment and at its worst in providing for either practical or idealistic alternatives.

*See also* Concrete Utopia; Marxism; Welfare State.

*Reference* Brosio, Richard A. *The Frankfurt School: An Analysis of the Contradictions and Crises of Liberal Capitalist Societies* (1980).

## Free State of Noland
*See The Commonwealth of Oceana.*

## Freeland (1890)
Although the Austrian economist Theodor Hertzka resisted calling his novel *Freeland* a utopia, it nonetheless was often compared with another popular, contemporaneous utopian piece, Edward Bellamy's *Looking Backward*. As a socialist trained in the liberal Manchester school of economics, Hertzka attempted to realize the idealistic goals of modern communists, especially Marx and Engels, by creating a working commune. Indeed, there were perhaps a thousand "Freeland" societies that appeared in the 1890s and a planned colony in Africa that never materialized. Hertzka hoped to provide an alternative to revolution in his peaceful establishment of socialism and utilized the utopian format rather than a formal treatise because he felt he would attract a larger popular following. Yet *Freeland*, like many utopian

works of the late nineteenth century, lacked the literary flair of an earlier era in its plodding, analytical tone.

Theodor Hertzka (1845–1924) was born and educated in Austria, where he became an early convert to Karl Marx's scientific socialism as well as to John Stuart Mill's pragmatism and Charles Darwin's evolutionary biology. He served as economics editor of the largest newspaper in Vienna in the 1870s and later edited two socialist newspapers in the 1880s. Hertzka also founded the Society of Austrian National Economists and published several books on socialist theory and practice, the most important being *The Laws of Social Development* (1886). Departing from his journalistic and academic pursuits in 1890, Hertzka delved into the project of creating an ideal society that combined reformed elements of both capitalism and socialism.

Intended to be a practical rather than ideal society embodying "perfect liberty and economic justice," *Freiland: Ein sociales Zukunftsbild* (Freeland: A social anticipation) was published in 1890 and was followed by a sequel, *Eine Reise nach Freiland* (A visit to Freeland) in 1893. Like most socialist thinkers of the nineteenth century, Hertzka argued that the era of industrialization fostered practices—tariffs, cartels, trusts—that ensured the reduction of competition and heightened greed for excessive profits. The system also forced workers to form unions and engage in strikes and created massive social problems. Moreover, despite the advance of technology and improvement in production efficiency, both management and labor experienced only tension and misery. What was needed to ensure both efficient use of resources and social justice was a completely new social and economic concept. *Freeland* proved to be very popular, going through ten German editions by 1896. It was also quickly translated into several foreign languages. In 1994, J. D. F. Jones published a fictionalized account of the attempted settlement of Freeland in Africa. Local "Freeland" societies began to appear in Germany and Austria seeking to implement Hertzka's detailed plans. All of the European precursors led to the plan to implement Hertzka's text in East Africa.

In April 1894, 25 members of a Freeland Association from various parts of Europe led by an Englishman, A. S. Rogers, landed on the island of Lamu off Kenya. The plan called for the trekkers to move inland via the Tana River and to plant Freeland near Mount Kenya, but they made a temporary settlement on Lamu, where they built a fort, a company warehouse, and a community "free house" as well as houses. In less than three months, the settlers ended their expedition in chaos. Some immigrants remained in East Africa in different capacities, including Rogers, who took a post with the British colonial administration. One Dane who returned to Europe published a book about the utopian effort in 1897. The attempt to plant a colony in the jungles of British East Africa failed in the face of the harsh realities of a primitive frontier existence.

Hertzka assumed that Freeland would be founded by realistic pragmatists, not idealistic dreamers. In his fictional account, the International Freeland Society, headed by economist Karl Strahl, set about planning the colony. The group determined that Kenya, with its temperate climate, would be the ideal location. If the local natives would not acquiesce to the control of land, some threat of force might be necessary. The colony would be built in the jungle over four months by 200 workers. In *Freeland*, Hertzka provided only a few basic laws: the equal access of all residents to the land, the state care for those unable to work, democratic participation in government by all adults, and a government with powers balanced between the executive and legislative branches. At the principal city in Freeland, the carefully planned design included schools, banks, government offices, libraries, theaters, and cultural academies, all contained in opulent buildings. Hertzka believed that utopias need not be staid and uniform in appearance.

The government structure included a dozen representative bodies managing 12 administrative associations for such services as food supply and transportation. Freeland did not include judges, police, or a military. Behavior that society might treat as criminal in Hertzka's Austria would be considered a medical problem in Freeland. All government offices and records were totally open with public access provided so that no secrecy was possible. Having viewed the social ills of industrialization, Hertzka placed much emphasis in *Freeland* upon social welfare for the poor, elderly, women, and children. Hertzka borrowed from the utopian socialists his primary institution, the voluntary association of workers who choose freely the type of labor they will contribute. In *Freeland* the state guarantees entrepreneurs free access to credit land and investment resources and also maintains a transportation system—roads, canals, railroads. Money borrowed will be repaid when the enterprise begins making a profit. Workers also enjoy broad benefits, including the free choice of the type of work, profit sharing, and extended vacation time. There is an abundance of labor-saving gadgets to enhance efficiency in Freeland. The tax system is progressive and is assessed against all forms of wealth. The state also provides each family with a house. Yet unlike the Marxist dictatorship of the proletariat, the state really does not own anything. It merely coordinates and facilitates the workers' activities.

Although Hertzka recoiled from the appellation "utopist," he fit the mold as well as any of the other contemporary utopian writers. He was self-assured about the pragmatic, if ideal, planning needed to make his society function. Hertzka's naiveté shows in his confidence in human rationalism and desire to cooperate with others, the positing of a supposedly selfless authority that negates individual freedom yet avoids the normal negative consequences of authoritarian regimes, and the notion that once the outside world observes his utopia it will voluntarily embrace the new system. Sensitive to the authoritarian nature of virtually all ideal societies, Hertzka constantly stressed that the individual could make his or her own choices in Freeland. The problem, of course, was that the choices were narrowly constrained by the very nature of his system. Ironically, at the very time that Hertzka composed his ideal world founded on human reason, his fellow Austrian, Sigmund Freud, was unleashing the irrational side of human nature, which would dash utopian dreams such as Hertzka's. Nonetheless, Hertzka's ideas attracted some important following. *Freeland*'s constitution was copied by the Brotherhood of the Cooperative Commonwealth at Equality, Washington, during a 1904 reorganization of that communal society. *Freeland* also strongly influenced Theodor Herzl's utopian thought in *Altneuland* (1902) and many characteristics of *Freeland* would appear in the post–World War II Swedish welfare state.

**Reference** Jones, J. D. F. *Freeland* (1994).

## Future-Time Utopias

Before the late eighteenth century, history had been interpreted as being cyclic and thus repetitious. The later Enlightenment produced several thinkers who made the Age of Reason's implicit notion of the idea of progress explicit and placed it in a novel time-forward scheme that challenged the notion of cycles. The shift in utopian approaches from a future ideal place to a future ideal time—euchronia—marked a major departure from the traditions begun by Thomas More and prepared the way for the revolutionary era ahead. The idea of progress was most often associated with the advance of science and technology. Gilles Laponge has suggested that late-eighteenth-century utopists linked the pendulum clock, representing technology, with the imagination to become a kind of miniature utopia or utopian model of euchronia. The French leaders in this utopian innovation included the Physiocrat Robert Jacques Turgot, the utopian novelist Louis

Sébastien Mercier, and the Marquis de Condorcet, the historian of the idea of progress. In the early nineteenth century several Russian utopists used the euchronia by combining Enlightenment themes from France with romantic components.

One of the first euchronias in the eighteenth century, *The Reign of George VI* (1763), was written in England by an anonymous author. Though more of a political treatise than a utopia, it was set in the years 1900–1925 yet was located geographically in the same English environment. *The Reign of George VI* reflected the predominance of Tory philosophy during the reign of the first two Hanoverian monarchs (1714–1760). In many respects the future reign was intended to incorporate elements of Viscount Bolingbroke's "patriot king" vision: a dedicated, selfless monarch seeking the best interests of the nation and its people. George VI demonstrates courage as a warrior leader defeating threats to peace, cultural sensitivity in sponsorship of arts and letters, compassion in construction of hospitals, and commitment to universal education through building schools and colleges. The monarch shows an ability to establish a Pax Brittanica in Europe guaranteeing peace for all nations so that other nations revere him almost as much as do the English people.

Robert Jacques Turgot (1727–1781) was a minor philosophe in the French Enlightenment most often associated with the laissez-faire critique of mercantilism as a Physiocrat. As minister of finance to Louis XVI in the first four years of his reign, Turgot unsuccessfully promoted fiscal reforms. In 1750, Turgot delivered lectures at the University of Paris, which were published under the title *Sorboniques*. Turgot proposed in his lectures a revision of the cyclic view of history from antiquity to the present, suggesting instead a continuous movement of progress. He attributed much of the progress in recent centuries to the role of Christianity, a subject unattractive to most philosophes. Yet Turgot also grounded his theory of progress upon the Lockean notion of sensational knowledge, a cornerstone of the French Enlightenment. Knowledge built upon itself and thus continually advanced, particularly in the areas of science, technology, morals, and the arts. Because progress had occurred from the past to the present, it was certain to continue into the future. Mankind has the capacity to learn from nature and improve his material well-being thereby. Thus, although the struggle between the human tendency to accept the status quo (the chief enemy of progress) and the desire for change was ongoing, there was a recent trend in favor of reason guiding and instructing needed changes. Because Turgot argued for a climate that favored change over stasis, he anticipated the emerging revolutionary mood in France and Europe. Turgot was among the earliest thinkers to make a distinction between the physical sciences that produced knowledge of nature and the social sciences that concerned the nature of man.

Another vigorous critic of the ancien régime, Louis Sébastien Mercier (1740–1814), was inspired by Leibniz's optimism to place Turgot's theory of progress into a specific utopian context. His *L'An 2440* (1771) marked the first important break with the Morean tradition of projecting the future into a different place. Mercier's setting was almost seven centuries into the future but was located in the very same place, Paris, of his present. The story begins in 1768 with the narrator engaging an Englishman in a discussion of the vagaries of contemporary France. He falls asleep and awakens unaware that 672 years have lapsed. Strolling out into the streets of Paris, he is surprised to find a different world than he had known, though still largely nontechnological. The broad avenues are lined with sidewalks and artificial lights. The only vehicles allowed on the streets are those used by the elderly and by government officials, so congestion is avoided. Paris has been redesigned, with beautiful hospitals, theaters, and houses. The people appear peaceful, polite, and contented. Governed by a benevolent des-

pot, the society reveres equality, reason, toleration, and scientific knowledge. The telescope and the microscope symbolize the advances produced by science, and a later edition included accounts of air balloons and the prospect of future flights to the moon. Wars and serious crime do not exist in the future France. Mercier's utopia, also unlike More's, was not static but a work in progress, accommodating productive changes. However, the society was not completely altered from the eighteenth-century traditions. Mercier maintained a marital system reminiscent of that of ancient Rome, stressing the husband's authority over the wife. There were no dowries, so only mutual affection should be the basis for matrimony. Because of the fear of censorship, Mercier published the first edition of *L'An 2440* anonymously in Amsterdam, and it was indeed banned in Spain as well as France. Yet the utopia became enormously popular, going through 11 French editions by 1799 as well as being translated into English, Dutch, Italian, and German.

The final phase of the transition in utopian constructions from future ideal place to future ideal time came with the history of the idea of progress by the Marquis de Condorcet (1743–1794). Trained as a mathematician, Condorcet embraced the Enlightenment and became acquainted with Voltaire and Turgot. Unfortunately, he also became absorbed in the reform efforts of the French Revolution and eventually ran afoul of the Montagnard fanatic Robespierre, which led to his suicide. During the time that he was under arrest in 1793–1794, Condorcet composed the *Esquisse d'un tableau historique des progrès de l'esprit humain*. Condorcet had written a biography of Turgot and became acquainted firsthand with the notion of the idea of progress as well as with Turgot's epistemology. Seeking to reaffirm his belief in the prospects for the application of reason, Condorcet composed the history of the idea of progress at a time when his own future appeared bleak. Progress was inevitable, according to Condorcet, because it was an inherent component in human intelligence. Whenever a need arose, the human capacity for response and solution was certain. Thus Condorcet argued that seeming contradictions to progress, such as wars, plagues, economic upheavals, or the obscurantism of his favorite scapegoat, the clergy, actually played a constructive role since they provided a necessary problem for reason to overcome. Human progress thereby depended upon apparent setbacks in order to move forward again. Even improvements in military technology (for example, gunpowder and cannons) might in fact become deterrents to war. Condorcet organized past history into several epochs in order to show the gradations of progress over time. Most important, Condorcet stressed that past progress was a guarantee of future progress so that mankind might realize at some point the very heaven-on-earth existence that utopians had been contemplating. Condorcet's optimistic vision that utopian dreams could become reality helped to reshape the corpus of utopian ideas in the nineteenth century. Progress could replace God as the creative and instructive force for mankind and could indeed be worshipped as a new civil religion of humanity. Condorcet used the idea of progress as an Elysian vehicle to escape the reality of his impending death as a martyr to revolutionary ideals.

French uses of euchronia spread to other parts of Europe by the nineteenth century. In Russia several utopists blended the Enlightenment framework with the popular Romantic philosophy to produce a hybrid euchronia. The first such effort, published in 1829 by F. V. Bulgarin, *True Un-Events, or Voyages in the World of the Twenty-Ninth Century*, utilized the euchronia framework cloaked in a Romantic veneer. Bulgarin's effort was followed in 1833 by another Romantic escapist vehicle, *Year 3448*, by N. A. Veltman. It seems that these early Russian euchronias were merely responses to the liberal Decem-

brist Revolt (1825), which failed to alter the repressive czarist regime. Yet the most important time-forward utopia, by Prince Vladimir Odoevsky (1803–1869), portrayed an elitist version of euchronia. Strongly influenced by German romantics in his youth, Odoevsky had been a member of the mystical "Lovers of Wisdom" literary circle before the Decembrist Revolt. His *Year 4338* was written in manuscript about 1840 and circulated widely, especially among young women, for decades before it was published in the twentieth century during the Soviet rule. Less concerned than Bulgarin and Veltman about the consequences of the Decembrist Revolt, Odoevsky created an ideal society in which the aristocracy ruled without a czar. Odoevsky clearly had read Mercier's *L'An 2440* and embraced the idea of progress, especially the notion that science and technology were keys to the future. The multitalented Odoevsky, who dabbled in chemistry, philosophy, and literature, did not believe that human nature could be substantially altered. Hence modifying and improving the environment through scientific advances could become the means for creating the ideal society. Thus, projecting his utopia into the future, Odoevsky described a host of gadgetry, including wireless communication, which would especially enhance commerce; airplanes and electric trains for improved transportation; the mining of valuable minerals from the moon; computerized production and photocopying of written materials; and electrical talking devices. The story tells of a young Chinese in Beijing writing to a friend in St. Petersburg in anticipation of a cataclysmic collision between a comet and the earth. The society is organized hierarchically, with four levels: Poet-philosophers were ranked highest, followed by physical scientists, social scientists, and technicians. Thus, though he perceptively anticipated the technology of the future, Odoevsky saw no corresponding evolution of the social system.

Future-time utopias, which originated in the late eighteenth century and evolved through the nineteenth century, may have departed from the future-place utopias of the early modern era, but they did not resolve the dilemma of human nature. The older tradition spawned by More required that the utopian author impose his will upon the fictional utopians in order to substitute natural man's corrupt tendencies with pure, unselfish virtues. Yet the future-time utopists showed a greater confidence in human reason than their predecessors. The naive assumption that reason's advance would triumph over man's base nature allowed the future-time utopists either to embrace an egalitarian authority and society or, in Odoevsky's case, to simply reorganize the social hierarchy without reforming it. Both approaches demonstrated problems with human freedom and choice. The hope of the future-time utopists that the ideal society could become reality therefore proved as fanciful and impractical as had the deus ex machina methods of the future-place utopists. The fundamental problem remained humanity itself.

*References* Alkon, Paul. "The Paradox of Technology in Mercier's *L'An 2440*," in Berghahn, Klaus L., and Reinhold Grimm, eds., *Utopian Vision, Technological Innovation, and Poetic Imagination* (1990); Manuel, Frank E. *The Prophets of Paris* (1962); Suvin, Darko. "The Utopian Tradition of Russian Science Fiction" (1971).

## Futurism

Emerging in pre-World War I Italy, futurism offered an unequivocal, stilted vision of technological advancement for the modern era. Launched with the 1909 *Futurist Manifesto* by the aristocratic Italian poet Filippo Marinetti, futurism spread to other parts of Europe, but the war and a totalitarian aftermath killed whatever influence it might have had. Its most obvious manifestation was in architectural designs led by another Italian, Antonio Sant' Elia, who conceived of a modern city with massive structures integrating all aspects of society and commerce. The futurists were determined to reshape the ancient cities of Italy and Europe, and they thought in terms of the "beauty of speed" in their conceptions. Thus the futurists were both destroyers of the old regime and architects of a new era of urban life. A Russian version of futurism appeared during the Revolution of 1917, but the Bolsheviks ultimately turned against the cultural nihilism.

By the early twentieth century many intellectual strands had begun to challenge the inflexible rational standards of Western civilization, which critics said caused a decaying of vitality and need for revitalization. Artistic movements such as cubism and art nouveau were symptoms of the growing rebellion. However, different elements involved in the critique offered varying solutions and attitudes. Because of its history, Italy had received many modern influences tardily, including industrialism and nationalism. Futurism as outlined by Filippo Marinetti (1876–1944) in his *Manifesto* staked out a firmly antihistorical perspective, claiming that the heritage of the past, especially recent history, had no significance. Many Italians had grown weary of their nation being manipulated and superseded in importance by Great Britain, France, or Germany. They longed for the glory of ancient Rome. The very ungenteel and youth-oriented futurist attitude mocked the traditional institutions of Western civilization such as the university. Indeed, futurism insisted that the past must not only be ignored but also extirpated from the conscious mind. Despite the movement's disdain for the past, it was in many respects a social anachronism in the glorification of war and antifeminist sentiments.

Marinetti had used the journal *Poesia* after 1905 to prepare the way for futurism and to recruit fellow-travelers. Though there were "manifestos" for futurist literature and music, art became a central element in the futurist movement, and the artist would become the prime motivator

*Umberto Boccioni,* Elasticita *(1911). (Private collection, Milan.)*

of action rather than mere contemplation. Futurist artists were repelled by system and fixed models; they advocated virtually total freedom of expression. Fascination with the impact of industrialism—new cities and machines—caused considerable excitement for futurist artists. If there were material problems created by such changes, there must be spiritual solutions. Milan artist Umberto Boccioni (1882–1916), author of the 1910 "Manifesto of the Futurist Painters," typified many early futurist painters in his glorification of war, which he deemed to serve a cleansing function. Futurist art intended to project optimism about the future and "universal

dynamism" in its fascination with speed and the machine. The new culture of futurism would be symbolized by the city; Boccioni's "The City Rises" (1911) reflected that view. Futurists demonstrated attraction to mass actions as opposed to individual efforts, especially if they were spontaneous and violent.

Marinetti also recruited architect Antonio Sant' Elia (1888–1916) to produce the "Manifesto of Futurist Architecture" in 1914. Edited later by Marinetti, the "Manifesto" claimed that each generation would have to build its own new cities because new technology would make existing cities obsolete with great rapidity. Sant' Elia despised the decorative aspect of traditional architecture and wanted to make his designs purely functional and simple. Further, since durability was unimportant, technological advances would require that structures have only a brief life. Sant' Elia's principles stressed, first, the elimination of past traditions and, second, the use of modern technology to conceive of a city operating at several levels rather than only one. He thought in terms of the speed of modern methods of transportation—on the surface, below the surface, and in the air. Anticipating many of the major themes of twentieth-century architecture, Sant' Elia's drawings showed massive modernistic structures featuring steel, glass, and advanced elevators, but there was no grand plan or design for cities before the war interrupted the work.

Another late convert, painter-architect Giacomo Balla, a student of the relationship of light and speed, outlined the utopian potential of futurism in "The Futurist Reconstruction of the Universe" (1915). Although he had demonstrated practical architectural ideas in house designs, Balla's conceptual drawings of new designs, machines, and even clothing for the future lacked a pragmatic context. As with other aspects of futurism, the architectural schemes proved superficial and fleeting. Boccioni often wrote articles in the futurist journal *Lacerba* that freely linked the movement's heritage to the late-nineteenth-century antirationalists Friedrich Nietzsche and Henri Bergson. Ironically, both Boccioni and Sant' Elia demonstrated their faithfulness to their philosophy by joining the military and were killed in World War I.

The most important emphasis of futurism was technology, especially the machine, literally a mechanism to escape from the present and the past. Futurists revered the dynamism represented by blast furnaces roaring and automobiles or trains speeding and by the unrehearsed spontaneity of large crowds attending athletic contests. Marinetti argued that war and other forms of violence would be liberating

tools for the uprooting of antiquated culture and society. He particularly targeted libraries and museums, once distributing leaflets in Venice calling upon the populace to tear down repositories of the past and replace the ancient canals with modern thoroughfares. By 1914 futurist artworks appeared in exhibits in London and San Francisco as well as major cities in Italy. Of course, in a sense the futurists got what they called for in the world war, but it proved to be as destructive to their movement as it was to the liberal tradition they critiqued. Many futurists, including Marinetti, joined the ranks of the Italian fascists in the 1920s seeking to shape the political movement in the image of their cultural revolt. However, though willing to utilize technology to develop his war machine, the only symbolism Mussolini adhered to was ancient Rome. The Italian philosopher Benedetto Croce assailed the futurists (and the fascists) for their antihistorical stance. Clearly, in addition to the bad timing of its emergence, the futurist movement proved more reactionary than creative. Nonetheless, futurism was a unique blend of social, political, and cultural thought. Though its conception of utopia proved incomplete in its superficiality, the movement influenced all twentieth-century art forms.

The only important non-Italian influence of futurism was in Russia during the Revolution of 1917. The revolutionary chaos and Marxist-Leninist reconstruction beginning in 1917 allowed a distinctive Russian version of futurism to develop briefly. The iconoclastic poet Vladimir Mayakovsky (1893–1930) led the extension of nineteenth-century Russian nihilism into the revolutionary period. Mayakovsky and his followers railed against bourgeois culture and sought to extinguish the cultural influences of the past in Russia. Like their Italian counterparts, the Russian futurists also showed an affinity for technology and the Machine Age. Russian futurists attacked the repositories of the cultural past, such as museums, and sought to make all culture proletarian. A hybrid movement called Proletarian Culture (Proletcult), led by Alexander Bogdanov and Maksim Gorky, also emerged to compete with futurism. The heritage of Proletcult derived from a direct connection to late czarist utopian sentiments bound up with early socialism. Proletcult advocates attacked futurists as elitists, and the two movements were not friendly. Whereas futurism sought to destroy the culture of the past, Proletcult concentrated upon constructing a new mass culture. Ultimately, Lenin showed little sympathy with the two nihilist trends because he was more rooted in the past than they were. The Bolsheviks preserved the museums and artifacts of the past, merely reconstituting them as "people's" museums. Thus the war against culture and the extinguishing of the past for the sake of focusing on a new future was defeated by the Bolsheviks.

**References** Clough, Rosa Trillo. *Futurism, the Story of a Modern Art Movement: A New Appraisal* (1961); Martin, Marianne W. *Futurist Art and Theory, 1909–1915* (1968).

## Futurology
*See* Science and Society Movement.

## Gandhian Utopia

The dominance of the ancient religion-philosophy of Hinduism in India has militated against utopian thinking until the modern era. Moreover, until very recently, India remained a primitive tribal society organized by caste. During the struggle for Indian independence from Great Britain, the nationalist leader Mohandas K. Gandhi utilized both Western and Hindu traditions to formulate a peculiar form of utopianism. Since the death of Gandhi, Hindu nationalists have used but also altered his original philosophy. In the event, India has grappled with novel ideas of social reform that have diminished but not replaced traditional Hinduism and its caste system. The old still lives beside the new in India.

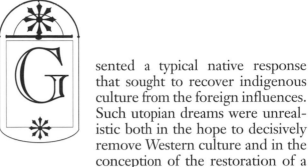

Like other places in Asia, traditional religion and philosophical teaching contrasts sharply with Western ideas by an orientation to the past rather than the future. Yet each culture in Asia treats the issues somewhat differently, and Hinduism more closely resembles Western thought in its careful definition of a paradise. One of the enduring utopian visions that originated in ancient Hindu India was the Pure Land of Eternal Happiness, which included a temple encompassed by thick stone walls. The trees around the temple and lotus pond were made from precious jewels. This Hindu myth resembles the Western ancient picture of a golden age, a time of profound unity and harmony. Hindu cosmology taught that the intervening era of disunity and disharmony would end with a cataclysm and the appearance of a new golden age. With the invasion of India by Europeans beginning in the fifteenth century, Indian culture frequently rebelled against foreign intrusion. The famous army mutiny in 1857 British Bengal represented a typical native response that sought to recover indigenous culture from the foreign influences. Such utopian dreams were unrealistic both in the hope to decisively remove Western culture and in the conception of the restoration of a society much more idealistic than had ever existed previously. Thus while the Indians sought to be free of foreign control, they also substituted a dreamworld for their traditional culture.

The advent of the Gandhian utopia in the twentieth century followed closely upon previous utopian strains in India, which preferred to apply a fantasy about the past as a solution to the British occupation. Mohandas K. Gandhi (1869–1948) became the leader of Indian nationalism and of the drive for independence. Gandhi first became drawn to the issue of independence when he lived in another British colony, South Africa, between 1893 and 1915. Much of Gandhi's theory about the means of Indian liberation he devised while in South Africa. Gandhi also learned a lot about Western thinking through his contact with Annie Besant, a leader of the theosophical movement, which admired and emulated traditional Hinduism. Upon returning to India, Gandhi began practical experiments to apply his ideas, but his technique grew to maturity only slowly after World War I. By that time, the clash between the past and present—religious and secular, feudalism and capitalism, rural and urban—seemed starker than when Gandhi first left in 1893.

Gandhi responded to both the Industrial Revolution and the social systems that followed it, capitalism and socialism. Yet very much like Mao Ze-dong in China, Gandhi did not believe that either alternative was appropriate for India because neither incorporated a spiritual foundation.

*Mohandas Gandhi walking with a group of followers, 1944. (Photo by Khopkar)*

Thus Gandhi grounded his utopia in cultural rather than socioeconomic principles. Still, Gandhi thought that most of the products of technological progress were antithetical to spiritual directives. Most important, Gandhi felt that wage labor in the factories was inhuman, one of the most vile examples of exploitation of humanity. Thus Gandhi produced the theory of "bread labor" by which individuals would produce their basic needs rather than become dependent upon market-driven systems. Gandhi's economic theories of village industry strongly resembled Mao Ze-dong's system during China's Great Leap Forward in the late 1950s. Following his economic model, Gandhi also strongly favored local governments over central governments and dreamed of reinstating the old rule of the villages by elders known as *Panchayat raj*.

Though ingrained in Indian society from time immemorial and thus not originating with Gandhi, his first and perhaps most important utopian element was spirituality. In the context of a clash with Western civilization, spirituality resonated as a weapon against materialism. Second, Gandhi's utopia enshrined the concept of dependence upon the whole community and downplayed individualism and the competitive spirit that accompanied it. Individuals, in Gandhi's view, should sublimate themselves into their family, community, and social class (one of the four *varnas*) as part of their duty. Gandhi thought of the class system not as repressive but as symbolic of social harmony, and he tended to gloss over the caste problem since it seemed insoluble.

Gandhi had read Western critics of materialism such as the Transcendentalists and John Ruskin and embodied their concepts in his principle of *sarvodaya*, or concern for society's welfare. Seeking an Arcadian solution to consumption, Gandhi sought to convince Indians that satisfying simple needs rather than lavish wants should be their aim. Once again, this goal presumed that community well-being was more important than individual happiness. Thus Gandhi expected his followers to emulate himself in embracing *swaraj*, or self-discipline, by stressing the spiritual over the material and the community over the individual. A nation can reflect *swaraj* only if the vast majority of its citizens follow it. Because so many Indians had become dependent upon the British for their livelihoods, Gandhi knew that it would be difficult to sever such ties. He developed the theory of *swadeshi* to respond to the circumstances. Essentially,

*swadeshi* meant that Indians would help each other—in the family, community, or nation—before doing service to a foreigner. Such a practice would especially require rejecting all Western cultural influences, including in such areas as dress and diet. Hence it would entail applying an economic weapon against Western culture. As with his entire program, Gandhi envisioned not a violent but a purely peaceful and nonthreatening rejection of Western traditions. There had already been some examples of burning foreign clothing before Gandhi applied the *swadeshi*, so the practice was ongoing. Gandhi carried his passive methods into the whole gist of his utopia. At the center of his utopia were the concepts of *ahisma*, or respect for life, and *satyagraha*, or nonviolent resistance. Gandhi did not equate his *satyagraha* with Western techniques of pacifism since the Indian method derived from strength rather than weakness (that is, meekness). *Satyagraha* was not simply a tool to gain a particular end; it was a moral conviction, an ideology. The application of *satyagraha* thus involved both a spiritually based and disciplined form of action. Gandhi fully expected the application of his system to produce dramatic change, to create a future utopia. Yet he did not want or promote a utopia imposed by either theorists or authoritarian dictators.

Although Gandhi did not propose to abolish the traditional social system in India, he expected changes in its practice once political independence was achieved. He developed the concept of "trusteeship" to express one of the important alterations. Gandhi hoped to convince the wealthy classes that they had an obligation to share some of their prosperity with others less fortunate, what in the West would have been called charity. Yet Gandhi stressed that the wealth of the rich was not entirely theirs. The rich held that wealth in trusteeship for the nation, and they should voluntarily redistribute some of their excess to the poor. Though Gandhi did not believe that pure egalitarianism was either feasible or necessary, he hoped that the wealthy would use the moment of political independence to reexamine their lives in the context of the needs of the whole nation. Ultimately, Gandhi's dream for a better India conceived of a type of heaven-on-earth that some scholars have dubbed "ordered anarchy," yet virtually all comparisons with Western ideas fail to comprehend the uniqueness of the Gandhian utopia for India.

Since Indian independence in the 1940s, the state has cultivated the ideologies of democracy and socialism, which also rest upon an illusory and hence utopian foundation since they do not really correspond to the social system. The successors of Gandhi sought to apply most of his principles, especially the idea of unity, to preserve the utopian illusion. The Indian government has attempted to promote both economic development and social stability with the political unity. Thus India has created a distinctive system of retaining the old and the new (politics, society, and the economy) side by side. Effectively, the social elite has taken the place of the British Raj since independence while maintaining the fiction of representative democracy. The violence that has interrupted the surface serenity and unity on frequent occasions since 1947 merely reflects the clash of illusion and reality, of utopia and tradition, in India. Yet because the system has the legitimizing veneer of the Gandhian utopia, and thus a moral and ethical quality, it retains those principles of *ahisma*, *sarvodaya*, and *satyagraha* that promote ideals such as self-sufficiency and self-denial. Thus India continues to live both the illusion of the Gandhian utopia and the underlying reality of tension and conflict.

*See also* Maoism; Theosophy.

*Reference* Fox, Richard G. *Gandhian Utopia: Experiments with Culture* (1989).

## Garden City Movement

The dramatic and often problematic growth of urban centers in the late nineteenth century created concerns about the future viability of living conditions in the city. One utopian solution comprehending the environmental and social concerns was offered by architect Ebenezer Howard in England. Howard's "Garden City" (a term that actually originated in the United States but that lacked the semantic impact of Howard's use) eventually influenced most of the architectural planning trends of the twentieth century. Howard borrowed ideas from the earlier utopian socialists as well as from anarchist thinkers for his utopian masterpiece, *Tomorrow: A Peaceful Path to Reform* (1898). Soon there were several places in England where the Garden City concept was being implemented. Ultimately, however, the movement, which was oriented around human development, became consumed in the more practical concerns of urban planning. Nonetheless, Howard's influence in the twentieth century has been enormous.

Certainly, there had been precursors to town planning, which had been fitful and without process until the late nineteenth century. The small-scale model villages of the late eighteenth century of the West Riding of Yorkshire, around Bradford and Halifax, may have been the first effort to respond to industry's impact upon settlement. Yet the unrestrained growth in industrial cities such as Leeds was the rule. One of the first to translate the utopian socialist ideal into an urban setting was James Buckingham in his *National Evils and Practical Remedies* (1849). A disciple of Robert Owen, Buckingham desired to move cooperative planning from a rural to an urban setting in his plan for the ideal city of "Victoria." The plan called for a town center in the shape of a square with quadrangular segments extended along avenues toward the outskirts. Work would be shared on an equal basis in Victoria. Buckingham's ideas influenced the thought of Robert Pemberton, who conceived of a "Happy Colony" to be situated in New Zealand. Pemberton's plan called for ten districts of 20,000 acres each laid out in a radial plan reminiscent of Renaissance planned cities. Pemberton's Happy Colony, with its center made up of four colleges, featured fewer and smaller structures than Buckingham's Victoria and thus was less urban in its appearance. Yet Happy Colony would include communal ownership and voluntary work schemes. The idea of smaller socioeconomic units than existing cities continued to appeal to utopists, including especially William Morris in *News from Nowhere* (1890).

Ebenezer Howard (1850–1928) became absorbed with urban expansion problems and set about to seek solutions. His concern for how socioeconomic changes wrought by the Industrial Revolution had affected the working classes was derived from his reading of the works of the utopian socialists and later the anarchists. Yet they had concentrated upon the economic changes, whereas Howard was concerned more with the impact upon the urban growth. Although their designs would be rather different, Howard was impressed by the ideas of the U.S. utopist Edward Bellamy in *Looking Backward* (1888), especially Bellamy's vision of a redesigned Boston. In addition to his knowledge of utopian town planning ideas, Howard became aware of communitarian experiments in the years preceding his own writing. The U.S. reformer Henry George's single-tax movement inspired many land reform ideas in both the United States and England. Three years after the appearance of George's *Progress and Poverty* (1879), the Land Nationalization Society was formed in England to encourage the government to donate lands for group development.

Meanwhile, another independent utopian movement had taken shape in the form of the Fellowship of the New Life led by J. C. Kenworthy. Following upon the failed experiments of the Ruskin Societies in the 1880s to promote practical applications of worker education, Kenworthy took it upon himself to launch a new organization to establish cooperative communities. Kenworthy also had become acquainted with the writings of the Russian novelist Count Leo Tolstoy, which inspired Kenworthy's idealism. Like

Gerrard Winstanley and Henry David Thoreau before him, Tolstoy envisioned a peaceful, cooperative Christian commonwealth that contrasted with the urban-industrial exploitative mass movements of the late nineteenth century. Both Russians and non-Russians began to establish colonies based upon Tolstoy's principles, and one such experiment begun at Purleigh, England, in 1897 included Kenworthy as a participant. Ultimately, the Tolstoyan Brotherhood Trust broke into different factions and was crushed in Russia by the Bolshevik takeover in 1917.

Meanwhile Ebenezer Howard consolidated all of these related influences—utopian socialism, Tolstoyan colonies, Kenworthy's Fellowship of New Life, the work of Edward Bellamy and William Morris—to create a planned urban utopia in his work *Tomorrow: A Peaceful Path to Reform* (1898). Howard's ideal city followed Pemberton's radial design. It began at its center with civic buildings in a park setting, and extending out from the center would be residential, commercial, and industrial sectors. At the outermost section of the radial design would be the agricultural sections for food production. Following the guidelines of Charles Fourier's phalansteries, Howard would limit the population in the urban area to 30,000 and in the outer agricultural belt to 2,000. Every structure built would conform to principles for the protection of the environment and would be built according to careful plans through a cooperative building society. Obviously, Howard followed his socialist predecessors in seeking to protect the workers from manipulation by the capitalists. Within a year of the publication of *Tomorrow*, Howard helped form a Garden City Association in cooperation with leaders of the Land Nationalization Society. In 1900 the organization was incorporated with shareholders and set about planning the construction of the first Garden City. Led by its secretary, Thomas Adams, the corporation purchased 40,000 acres at Letchworth, Hertfordshire, and began construction, which was completed in four years. Strongly influenced by the anarchist theories of Petr Kropotkin, Adams favored allowing small private holdings that would be integrated into the commercial cooperatives within the Garden City. The settlement at Letchworth attracted former participants in the Tolstoyan communities and members of the Fellowship of New Life.

The ideal of the Garden City was expanded in the twentieth century mainly through the efforts of two architectural partners, Raymond Unwin (1863–1940) and Barry Parker (1867–1947). Unwin served as president of the Royal Institute of British Architects from 1931 to 1933 and received the institute's Gold Medal in 1937. Like Howard, Unwin and Parker recognized a social and esthetic purpose in town planning. They believed that the design of towns and villages must preserve the cohesive unity of the local population while preventing crowding. Further, Unwin and Parker recognized that towns must be built with a cognizance of the past; they were drawn to medieval town designs. Following their first planned community at New Earswick, Yorkshire, Unwin and Parker went on to supervise Garden City developments such as Hampstead Garden outside London. Parker alone designed Wythenshawe near Manchester. Other planned Garden Cities emerged, including Welwyn, Hertfordshire, and Hendon Garden. Plans for additional experiments extended from England to the United States, Sweden, and Finland. Despite significant differences in the scale in which they worked, later architects of megastructures, such as Le Corbusier in his Radiant City and the futurism school of Sant' Elia, also clearly borrowed from Howard's original schemes.

Gradually the Garden City movement became enmeshed in the technical details of town planning and lost its fervor for rehabilitation of the human community. Instead, the influence of the Garden City became one of the specific features of town development rather than a compre-hensive social plan. The changing influence became apparent in Parliament's Town Planning Act of 1909, which featured some technical elements of the Garden City idea but lacked Howard's larger vision for integrating planning into a social regeneration emphasizing cooperation and brotherhood. The 1930s New Deal program of Greenbelt Towns in the United States drew heavily upon Howard's designs, and more recently a New Town Corporation was created in the Department of Urban Affairs to promote ground-up planning for suburban communities. One of the first such new towns was Columbia, Maryland, built in the 1960s outside of Washington, D.C. Thus the utopian aspect to town planning—the relationship of town to country and population to physical structures, the environment, and economic functions—can be directly linked to the Garden City dream of Ebenezer Howard.

**Reference** Creese, Walter L. *The Search for Environment: The Garden City Before and After* (1966).

## *Gargantua and Pantagruel* (1532–1562)

François Rabelais's five-part satirical epic utilized a utopian framework to criticize sixteenth-century society and the church in particular. Influenced by the Italian and Christian humanist traditions, Rabelais's writings reflected both Renaissance themes. The ribald humor and disjointed nature of the story have perplexed critics and made an interpretation of the whole work difficult. Yet in addition to its various other elements, *Gargantua and Pantagruel* tends to reflect the basic elements of early modern utopias.

François Rabelais (ca. 1494–1553) was born in France and had two false starts in monastic orders, one a Franciscan order that opposed higher learning and the second a Benedictine order where he studied Greek. After leaving the monastic order, Rabelais attended the medical school at the University of Montpellier, toured

Italy, and studied Arabic. He became associated with a group of moderate religious reformers known as Evangelicals, led by Margaret of Navarre, the sister of Francis I. The main opposition to the French reformers was centered in the theology faculty at the University of Paris and the Parlement court in Paris. Of course, Rabelais was also a follower and imitator of the "Prince of Humanists," Desiderius Erasmus. Clearly Rabelais hoped for peaceful religious reform, but his hopes were forlorn. Rabelais's literary vehicle of storytelling, extremely popular during the Middle Ages, had become practically passé in the Renaissance. Although he used a medieval litcrary technique, Rabelais conformed to the Renaissance tradition by writing in the vernacular. The targeted audiences of *Gargantua and Pantagruel* thus included intellectuals, his humanist friends, and a popular group, the common classes. Because Rabelais needed money from sales to a wider popular audience, he resorted to an earthy humor that has obscured his more serious aims.

Rabelais launched his five-part epic in 1532 with a story about a race of giants, featuring a father-son pair, Gargantua and Pantagruel. Rabelais published the second book first in 1532, telling the story of Pantagruel, the son of Gargantua, and his campaign against King Anarche of the Dipsodes. The first book, which appeared in 1534, recounted the earlier history of Gargantua, complete with an elaborate genealogy and his utopian setting at the abbey Thélème. A third book was issued 12 years later in 1546 after Rabelais had experienced religious upheaval in France and had traveled to Italy. The third volume departed from the format of the two earlier installments and concentrated on Pantagruel's debate about whether to marry during consultations with his longtime friend Panurge. The fourth and longest book appeared in two installments: 11 chapters in 1548 and the completed 67-chapter version in 1552. It tells of Pantagruel's voyage to find an oracle and the adventures, paralleling classical epics,

along the route. The fifth book was published several years after Rabelais's death in 1562, supposedly from notes he left behind. There remain questions about the authenticity of the fifth book.

The setting for Book One includes an elaborate genealogy of Gargantua, an account of his birth and education, and a history of the war against the evil king Picrochole, but the five chapters dealing with the abbey of Thélème (meaning the abbey of one's will) develop the utopian theme best. Gargantua's frequent companion is the irreverent monk Frère Jean, whose antimonastic behaviors, such as praying directly to God, are portrayed as the true ideal for monks. The abbey was built to reward Frère Jean for his efforts in the war against Picrochole. The abbey is pictured as a kind of Epicurean, hedonist playground with virtually no rules and an ample supply of physical pleasures. Gargantua created a utopia by advancing the antithesis of monasticism, itself based on a utopian ideal. Traditional monastic rules, such as single-sex membership, poverty, and chastity, are nonexistent at Gargantua's abbey. The theme of the abbey was "do what you will" rather than following the strict rules normally associated with monasteries. Of course, because of Rabelais's optimism about human goodness, he believed individual freedom would result in residents willingly pursuing God's will. The abbey has been compared to the Land of Cockaygne settings of the late medieval poems, yet the hedonism proved to be merely a vehicle for Rabelais's more serious reform ideas.

Those reforms are illustrated best in Book Two, the episodic part of the story dealing with Gargantua's son, Pantagruel, who takes on the image of both Christian prince and redeemer. As in Book One, there is a genealogy for Pantagruel and the introduction of a lifelong friend, Panurge, the counterpart to Frère Jean in Book One. Panurge was the ultimate trickster and wit; he dominates even the role of Pantagruel. Most of Book Two is taken up with the war against the Dipsodes. Pantagruel responds to the invasion of Utopie, his homeland, led by King Anarche. Pantagruel was not an expansionist; rather, he was merely defending the land of his grandfather and mother against aggression, the same defensive war attitude reflected in More's *Utopia*. Rabelais also suggests in Pantagruel's military expedition that ruse was more effective than sheer force in war. Pantagruel's success not only liberates Utopie but also the land of the Dipsodes. King Anarche was placed in the position of his intended victims, thus illustrating Rabelais's mimicking of the scriptural technique, particularly frequent in Jesus' parables, of inverting social positions—first and last, rich and poor, master and slave. Thus, though Rabelais condemned wars of aggression, he conceded that defensive wars often are necessary. The episode in which the narrator travels into Pantagruel's mouth also may suggest Rabelais's theme of Pantagruel representing both the body of Christ and the body politic. The story of Pantagruel allowed Rabelais to blend his concepts of political and moral truths in the vision of a utopia. The mighty can be humbled and the humble can be revered in utopia just as they would be in heaven. Thus utopia made possible a heaven on earth and Pantagruel became the model for a Christian prince.

Though noted for his irreverent and ambiguous prose, it is possible to discern a pattern in Rabelais's thought. He certainly utilized the framework of the ancient epic poems such as the *Iliad* and the *Aeneid* in treating the conflict within his stories. Likewise, because Rabelais wrote primarily to an audience of Christian humanists, their themes also abound, especially the critical attitude toward the Catholic church—including the clergy and monasteries. Rabelais utilized the familiar Christian humanist technique of satire and irony to deliver the message. Also, Rabelais's technique of turning positions—first and last, rich and poor, privileged and underprivileged—on their head imitated scripture and especially the methods used

by Jesus in his teaching. There are also numerous parallels between the utopian methods of Rabelais and Thomas More in his *Utopia*. Perhaps the most striking heritage of Rabelais was A. S. Neill's Summerhill School, established in England in 1921, whose watchword was the same as the abbey Thélème's: "Do what you will."

**Reference** Duval, Edwin M. *The Design of Rabelais's Pantagruel* (1991).

## Gaston, E. B.
*See* Fairhope Colony.

## *Germinal* (1885)
Although noted for his realist novels and his campaign for the acquittal of Captain Alfred Dreyfus, France's Émile Zola also tried his hand at creating a workers' utopia in *Germinal*. Many critics believe that *Germinal* was Zola's finest and most representative literary effort. Although in many respects a historical novel, *Germinal* blended some important utopian schemes to suggest ways of instigating reforms in contemporary France and Europe. Zola explored the meaning and application of the then rather new ideas of Marxism, anarchism, and social Darwinism in his novel.

Born in Paris, Émile Zola (1840–1902) grew up in the south of France in Aix-en-Provence, where he attended college and became friends with the impressionist painter Paul Cézanne. After returning to Paris to seek work, Zola published his first work in 1864 and wrote on a regular basis the rest of his career. He became a leading figure in the literary school of Realism, which attempted to come to grips with the modern urban-industrial society. Researching his subjects carefully, Zola explored contemporary problems that have remained at the forefront of the modern era: slum housing, exploitation of workers, prostitution, and so on. Zola also gained experience as a journalist and became involved in politics. Already a famous writer when Dreyfus was prosecuted in

1894 for selling military secrets to the Germans, Zola plunged headlong into a campaign to undo the injustice to the liberal Jewish officer. His most famous contribution, *J'Accuse*, was published in a Paris newspaper and widely reprinted in 1898. He was convicted of libel and sentenced to a year in jail for the essay. Yet ultimately Zola's position was justified when Captain Dreyfus was exonerated, although Zola did not live to see his final release and restoration.

Zola chose the term *"Germinal,"* the name of a spring month in the revolutionary calendar of 1793, for his novel because his objective was the rebirth and renewal of the plight of the workers. The images of biological growth or germination appear throughout the novel and contrast with Zola's animal imagery, which usually represents violence and destruction. Set in the mid-1860s, the novel's 40 chapters are sweeping in scope and have a multitude of characters. The first part follows the efforts of Etienne Lantier to find work in the coal mines. Etienne becomes familiar with a family that includes three generations of miners, who educate him about labor conditions. In the second part, Etienne learns about the class conflict between worker and bourgeois managers.

Zola reveals that workers too often defer to management in the continuation of poor working conditions. He contrasts the living conditions of the two classes, the different family relations and value systems, all of which highlight class differences. Throughout, Zola lampoons bourgeois values and homilies designed to keep the workers in their place. He reveals the popular application of social Darwinism to justify the rule of the strong over the weak and the bourgeois efforts to use God as an ally against the workers even while genuine religious expression had all but disappeared in France.

The economic crisis of the novel focuses upon the overproduction and misuse of investment capital to depress the workers' wages and to prevent the amelioration of their working conditions. Small independent miners are forced to sell out to the larger mine owners, thereby enhancing the tendency toward monopoly. In part three Zola injects political action into the story, again showing the awakening of Etienne's political consciousness. Zola presents various reform and revolutionary proposals ranging from moderate liberal reform to Marxism to anarchism. Etienne embraces the Marxist approach, and Zola traces the historical disputes between the Marxists and anarchists in the First International through the events of the novel. Etienne competes with and sometimes cooperates with the chief spokesman for anarchism, Souvarine. In addition to emphasizing the plight of workers, Zola details their popular culture to provide some taste of their lifestyles. However, the bourgeois owners of industry also faced a crisis in 1860s France because of tight credit and stagnant sales. When the owners decide to cut wages, the workers go on strike, which is covered in part four of *Germinal*.

Zola featured an illegal mass meeting of 3,000 striking miners in a forest outside of the main village. Etienne is a major spokesman at the rally, and he speaks of the violent overthrow of the state and the creation of an anarchist communal society. Though he did not direct the crowd to attack bourgeois representatives, they did so anyway and murdered a local grocer hated for overcharging for his products. The government calls out the military, which intervenes at the mine, leading to a confrontation and the death of many miners. Zola seemed to be apprehensive about the workers losing control of their protest movement because of their emotions.

Soon after the violent confrontation between workers and soldiers, Etienne leaves the community, saying good-bye to the remaining miners, who have returned to work under the same conditions. Etienne vows to go to Paris and begin organizing labor unions and to use legal rather than violent means to accomplish his aims. Etienne does not give up his dream of revolutionary change but realizes that it may not occur as soon as he had hoped. Zola makes it difficult to understand his attitudes toward Marxism, anarchism, and social Darwinism, perhaps because he was still evaluating the importance of the ideas himself. Indeed, it seems that Zola purposefully chose to avoid endorsing a particular political ideology in *Germinal*.

The chief character, Etienne, does not in the end appeal to the reader. He claimed to be a Marxist but led the workers into a bloody and unproductive strike and then turned his back on them to transform himself into an elitist intellectual. Further, the workers as a group are not as appealing as the reader might presume; they possess some of the same unattractive traits as the bourgeoisie. Children are exploited as income producers, and women are subservient to husbands in the working-class families. Moreover, authoritarian hierarchies seem to exist in proletarian society as much as in the bourgeois world. Even Zola's use of terms such as "freedom" is ambiguous. Zola does seem to be saying that abstract ideas do not work unless they are grounded in reality, the needs of people. Hence it is fair to conclude that Zola felt that Marxism and anarchism were too abstract and idealistic to be practical. Instead, the driving force affecting everyone and everything, in the novel as well as in Zola's times, was capitalism. It was the real force that impacted both bourgeoisie and workers; it became the hidden force beneath the surface of the story. Thus Etienne and Zola determine that ordered change working through the existing system is the best approach to achieve an ideal society. Certainly, Zola seemed to follow his own advice when he intervened in the Dreyfus Affair a decade after writing *Germinal*. Though people can act as a natural force either individually or in groups, their actions have consequences far beyond their own situation since they invariably affect the whole of society.

*Reference* Walker, Philip. Germinal *and Zola's Philosophical and Religious Thought* (1984).

## Ghost Dance
*See* Native American Utopias.

## *The Glass Bead Game* (1943)

Hermann Hesse's *Das Glasperlenspiel* (*The Glass Bead Game*) has been difficult for scholars to categorize because it incorporates both utopian and dystopian techniques. Written over a period of time in Switzerland beginning in 1931, yet not published until 1943, the work reveals Hesse's emotional feelings toward his native Germany during the Nazi era. It portrays the distress of post–World War I Weimar German society leading up to the 1933 Nazi takeover. The metaphor of a parlor game was used by Hesse to elaborate his ambivalent musings on the future of Germany and European civilization. Hesse's work is also complicated by the tradition of the bildungsroman, a novel about the main character's psychological growth and development. In Hesse's case, an understanding of the author's life is also crucial to comprehending the literary product.

Born in Wurttemberg, Germany, the son of a former Lutheran missionary to India, Hermann Hesse (1877–1962) became an expatriate in Switzerland but traveled widely, including in India, during the period of his writing. His background made it natural for Hesse to be drawn into comparing Christianity and oriental mysticism, even after prematurely exiting a theological seminary. Physical and mental disabilities caused his move to a Swiss hospital in 1916. Hesse became well known internationally for publicizing Oriental philosophy in his utopian novel, *Siddhartha* (1922), featuring a fictionalized Buddha grappling with non-Western spiritual themes in the cycles of birth, life, death, and rebirth. He began writing *Das Glasperlenspiel* while in Switzerland about 1931 and completed the work in the midst of World War II in 1943, although a German edition did not appear until 1946. Between the time of his initial writing of *Das Glasperlenspiel* and its complete publication, Hesse was profoundly affected by Nazi atrocities. The novel's preface states Hesse's historical perspective that two conflicting trends emerged with the collapse of the medieval synthesis: the quest for individual freedom of thought and expression, and the antinomian attempt to assert individual authority over the rules of society.

It seems clear that Hesse aimed *Das Glasperlenspiel* at the German middle class, or what was left of it following the disastrous inflation of the early 1920s. The glass bead game served as a metaphor for the society in the novel's setting, Castalia. It was a society clearly separated from any existing society so there would be no reasons for confusion about its origins. The playing of the glass bead game allows Hesse to develop various symbols representing values that insert meaning into the story. Most of the symbols described were commonplace: music, mathematics, logic, architecture, or simply words and ideas. Sometimes the symbols stand alone, while in other cases there are combinations. As such, the varied symbols permit Hesse to discuss a wide range of subject matter during the playing of the game. Still, sufficient vagueness remains about the game's meaning to suggest that Hesse's purpose may not have been to explain how the game (that is, life) functioned but how it related to the culture of Castalia. Hesse desired that the reader engage in a purely intellectual exercise rather than allowing emotions to interplay with ideas. The glass bead game was in fact so complex that learning the system required preparation, albeit a purely secular education, in special schools. Since the glass bead game operated on both the physical and metaphysical levels, playing the game required episodes of meditation intended to perfect the player's inner awareness. Indeed, the fact that the game was effectively reserved for only the best and the brightest allowed Hesse's characters, such as Joseph Knecht, the central figure, to critique the game.

Joseph Knecht remains the only complex personality among the one-dimensional characters in *Das Glasperlenspiel*. Knecht's criticisms and concerns are revealed via a letter he writes to an old teacher upon his decision to leave Castalia. Hesse expected the reader to identify with Knecht's criticism that contemporary society was devoid of productive incentives, encouraged people to be dependent rather than self-sufficient, and squelched entrepreneurial innovation. It would almost seem that Castalia replicated the modern welfare state. In a sense, however, Knecht's knowledge of the glass bead game had also prepared him for a transcendent self-knowledge as he anticipated leaving the society of Castalia in order to discover the utopia that does not exist there. Thus Hesse may be suggesting that in order to know what the right values are, one must first have experience with or an understanding of the wrong ones. Knecht becomes a human laboratory for the experimental testing of utopia because the ideal society is determined not abstractly in some detailed blueprint but existentially by the individual and his yearning for meaning. Through the introspective and true-to-himself Knecht, Hesse anticipated Ernst Bloch's concrete utopian process of becoming rather than being. Yet the unusual and unexpected death of Joseph Knecht as a result of drowning has also befuddled critics. Why would Hesse allow his hero to die a senseless death? Although some interpretations have relied upon Oriental, especially Chinese, mysticism to explain the unity (e.g., Yin and Yang) of the parts in the death of Knecht, other interpreters remain puzzled. A letter from Hesse to a friend in 1955 suggested that the original idea for *Das Glasperlenspiel* had to do with reincarnation.

Hesse was affected by both the intellectual portrayal of civilization's death knell in Oswald Spengler's *Decline of the West* and Weimar Germany's excruciating struggle for survival during the dark days of the postwar era. The author seems to trace the origins of the Nazi era to the defects and shortcomings of the later Weimar period after recovery from economic disasters. The glass bead game and the Castalian society have been interpreted by some analysts to be a blueprint for an alternative society, one in contrast to the Nazi regime. However, the novel also has been portrayed as Hesse's retrogressive technique of romanticizing the past, an old German pastime. In describing the game and its symbols, Hesse praised the certainty of disciplines such as music and mathematics and the danger of open-ended pursuits such as poetry and philosophy. Hesse may also have been reacting to the cultural voids produced by surrealist movements such as expressionism and dadaism in the early twentieth century. Thus Hesse may well have been trying to use *Das Glasperlenspiel* as a vehicle to contrast productive and nonproductive cultures. On the other hand, he may have been setting up the ideals of the society of Castalia in order to ridicule utopian dreams as foolish. Hesse's own torn emotions over events in his Germany probably best explain the fact that Castalia remains both a utopia and a dystopia.

*Reference* Pavlyshyn, Marko. "Games with Utopia: Herman Hesse's *Das Glasperlenspiel*" (1985).

## Godwin, Francis
*See* Lunar Utopias.

## Golden Age
*See* Cockaygne.

## Golding, William
*See Lord of the Flies*; Robinsonades.

## Gott, Samuel
*See Nova Solyma*.

## The Great Equality
As the last of a long line of Confucian philosophers in China, K'ang Yu-wei outlined an ideal society in his work *Ta T'ung Shu* (The great equality), which appeared in manuscript form in 1902 but was not pub-

lished in its entirety until 1935, several years after K'ang Yu-wei's death. Moving against the isolationism of Chinese philosophy, K'ang joined Western tendencies marked especially in H. G. Wells's notion of one-world government to advocate global integration in a single state mechanism. The ideal of uniting humans around common rather than disparate elements envisioned a totally equal society with no private ownership of property and social needs distributed by megabureaucracies. A movement around the concept of *Ta T'ung Shu* flourished briefly in China before it was subsumed by a political nationalism modeled on Western standards and led by Sun Yat-sen. Shortly before his death, K'ang Yu-wei founded an academy in 1926 to preserve and promote his ideas, which were eventually more widely known in the West.

The powerful, enduring influence of Confucianism in China began to unravel with the Taiping Rebellion against the Manchu dynasty in the 1860s, inspired in part by the infusion of Christian philosophy that came with the opening of East Asia to Western traditions. The Confucian-inspired reconstruction of the *T'ung-chih* reforms that followed the suppression of the Taiping rebels failed to rehabilitate the older tradition. Increasingly, Western ideas were fused with Confucian traditions to produce a hybrid intellectual framework in China. One of the most important results of the blending of East and West was the production of the most detailed scheme for an ideal society that ever appeared in China. The innovator was K'ang Yu-wei (1858–1927), who strongly dissented from Chinese traditions during his years of education. He also read many Western books and determined by his twenties to reconstruct Confucianism. K'ang Yu-wei's Confucius acquired many Western traits and became a messianic revolutionary. K'ang's following extended into the royal family and inspired some Manchu reforms in 1898. Groups opposed to K'ang's influence prevailed and forced him into exile at Hong Kong in 1899.

Because he favored monarchy, K'ang Yu-wei did not join the nationalist revolution that overthrew the Manchus in 1911, so his ideas quickly lost appeal.

The formulation of K'ang Yu-wei's theory of the Great Equality began in earnest during the 1880s. Greatly influenced by the Darwinian theory of evolution, K'ang conceived of his peaceful, one-world society by constructing a movement that evolved in stages from disorder to ultimate peace. K'ang continued work on *Ta T'ung Shu* over the next two decades; it was completed during his exile in 1902. Portions of the manuscript were published between 1913 and 1929, but the complete text did not appear in print until 1935. After the turn of the century, his ideas became known in the West, especially Germany and the United States, where President Woodrow Wilson urged that *Ta T'ung Shu* be translated. *Ta T'ung Shu* differed from most traditional utopias in that it called for a gradual transition through three stages (corresponding to the ancient pattern of disorder, gradual movement toward peace, and ultimate maturity in the Great Equality) to the realization of the ideal society. K'ang felt that he was ahead of his time and that many contemporaries could not digest his program in its entirety at once. K'ang Yu-wei began *Ta T'ung Shu* with an analysis of the ills of the world, but unlike most Oriental visions of otherworldly goals, he argued in favor of a reform of the existing society. K'ang broke down the types of suffering into 38 headings under six themes: human, natural, accidental, government-induced, emotional, and obsessional. K'ang departed from pessimistic traditions such as Buddhism by stressing that the limits or restrictions upon humanity were the greatest basis for human suffering and not simply part of life itself. By eliminating those limits or restrictions (for example, government restraints, class privileges, racial differences, private property), a peaceful and happy existence could be achieved. The process of elimination would be gradual so that the achievement of the ideal society would also occur incrementally.

The first priority for K'ang Yu-wei was to alter existing systems of government. He greeted the creation of the League of Nations in 1919 with great enthusiasm as an indicator of progress toward his goal of a one-world state. In regard to the most powerful factor propelling nations toward war, the arms race, K'ang proposed an international agreement to limit weapons and armed forces, followed by merging of national systems into an international body, culminating with the abolition of the military and war altogether. A similar process of evolution would occur with the transformation of governments leading to a single authority divided into about 20 massive bureaucracies. The main obstacle to the achievement of a single world government was nationalism, which K'ang proposed to phase out over a long period rather than eradicate immediately. Advantages of concentrating decisions in a single authority would include efficient planning of the application of resources and a guarantee against the economic exploitation of workers. The advent of a one-world system also presupposed a single Chinese language. K'ang had witnessed parochial divisions in China being nurtured by the variety of dialects.

In contemplating the abolition of class barriers, K'ang Yu-wei was inspired by a knowledge of the social system in the United States. Unlike in the caste systems of the Orient, K'ang found in the U.S. tradition the demonstration of the practical application of egalitarianism. In regard to the goal of racial unity, K'ang did not allow for the continued existence, even on equal terms, of diverse races. He sought a voluntary and gradual physiological amalgamation of the different races so that their features would become virtually identical. Recognizing the historic repression of women, K'ang Yu-wei argued for complete equality of the sexes and thus assailed the tradition-laden Chinese patriarchy. State bureaucracies would assume control over functions previously controlled by families, such as child care. The state would provide schools, institutions to care for the poor, and law enforcement. K'ang envisioned a radical overhaul of the criminal justice system to decriminalize many offenses, such as those involving sex. The world society would thus allow greater freedoms but would still not tolerate laziness or abortion. K'ang Yu-wei feared the one thing that could cause his system to fail, a cult of personality formed around a dictatorial, all-powerful ruler. He was probably not so much anticipating the totalitarian regimes of the twentieth century as he was contemplating the historic authority of Chinese emperors. The most utopian aspect of the *Ta T'ung Shu* was the eighth boundary of preserving all forms of life. This area reflected the influence of Buddhism, but it also reflected traditional Oriental ancestor worship. K'ang based his proposal to extend care for life to all creatures upon love; his program would begin with kinship, extend to other humans, and finally encompass all living beings.

K'ang Yu-wei's description of his utopia contains many features in common with Western ideas. People lived in comfortable abodes, complete with all creature comforts, built and maintained by the community authority. Transportation would be freely available to all residents and would include automobiles, railroads, ships, and even aerial vehicles. Ultimately, all physical accommodations would be floating in the atmosphere. Technology would be fully utilized to provide services to residents, and food would eventually be provided in liquid form only. Medicine would benefit from technology and science so that disease could be eliminated. Unisex clothing, in a variety of colors, would be worn, and those who had made major contributions would wear badges of honor. Religion would be Confucian, and belief in God would be replaced by worship of nature. At the end of the *Ta T'ung Shu*, K'ang Yu-wei described the most difficult barrier to overcome (the ninth), that of suffering. There was reference to a mystical book containing truths about overcoming suffering, but few details. K'ang apparently sought to restore the humanist tradition of Confucianism

and feared that the advance of science had created doubts about mankind's relative importance.

K'ang Yu-wei's concept of the Great Equality was carried to a different level by Liu Jen-hang, a generation younger than K'ang. Liu was educated in Japan and the United States, so his perspective clearly was different from K'ang's, even more Western influenced, and free from Confucian traditions. Liu served as editor of Shanghai's *China Daily News* in the 1920s and published *Tung-fang ta-t'ung hsueh-an* (Preliminary studies concerning the great equality of the East) in 1926. Liu demonstrated the strong utopian influence of the West in his bibliography, which cited the major utopian works since Thomas More. Liu classified utopias in seven categories beginning with fantasies (religious paradises, Russian realism), mysticism (mainly Oriental traditions such as the thought of Lao-tzu), back-to-nature movements (such as that of Chinese anarchists), Oriental socialisms (the thought of Confucius and Mencius), Western socialisms (the works of Babeuf, Morelly, and utopian socialists), gender-equality movements (such as those of More, Bacon, Campanella, and Harrington), and modern utopias (represented by the works of Bellamy, Hertzka, and Wells). Despite his awareness of Western utopias, Liu Jen-hang seemed more interested in focusing upon Eastern rather than Western notions of an ideal society. Liu's idea of creating an ideal society began with the examination of three enduring religious-philosophical traditions: Chinese (that is, Confucian and Taoist), Buddhist, and Christian. In Liu's "New Great Equality," he imitated K'ang Yu-wei in a six-phase movement toward the realization of the ideal. Perhaps the main difference between K'ang and Liu was the latter's replacement of gender equality with a matriarchy, which would ensure genetic improvement and the redemption of humanity. Whereas K'ang Yu-wei's Sinocentrism conceived that the rest of the world would follow China's lead, Liu Jen-hang believed in a blending of the best concepts of both East and West. Indeed, Liu viewed China's need for salvation to be greater than that of any other country, so it was not in a position to provide leadership or example to the world. Undoubtedly, Liu framed the dilemma for all twentieth-century Chinese intellectuals, including especially utopists, in attempting to relate Chinese traditions to Western ideas.

**Reference** Hsiao Kung-chuan, "In and out of Utopia: K'ang Yu-wei's Social Thought" (1967, 1968).

### *Gulliver's Travels* (1726)

Known mostly for his political polemics, Irish-born Jonathan Swift (1667–1745) offered a unique anti-utopian commentary that established an important category of utopias, the dystopia, or bad place. It would not be until the twentieth century that authors would fully elaborate the framework outlined by Swift. As a loyal Tory writing against the dangers of Whiggism, Swift used utopian settings such as Lilliput and Brobdingnag in *Gulliver's Travels* to address his political concerns about English and European society. *Gulliver's Travels* thus became the model of a long line of influential dystopias in the modern era.

The era in English politics following the accession of the Hanoverian monarchs in 1714 has been known as the Whig Oligarchy because of the dominance of the Whig Party over an impotent Tory Party. The unfolding of that era unquestionably disturbed such a loyal Tory as Jonathan Swift. Hence he departed from his normal format of political satire to produce a utopian commentary on the contemporary English situation, namely, *Gulliver's Travels*.

Passionately opposed to injustice and selfish politics, Swift grew to detest political corruption and war in an age of one-party rule and overseas territorial expansion. He feared that the economic stability of agriculture was endangered by unrestrained commercial rapacity. In both

*Jonathan Swift, from an engraving by Ravenet.*

cases, Swift, an honest reactionary, blamed the Whigs for creating such conditions and reflected that view in *Gulliver's Travels*, written over the period 1714–1726. His other satirical works—*Tale of a Tub* and *Battle of the Books*—demonstrated Swift's wit and literary skill. Rather than viewing mankind as rational, Swift preferred to consider humans as having the potential for rational acts even while critiquing humanity's selfishness, pettiness, and corrupt tendencies. Swift utilized his chief character, perennial voyager Lemuel Gulliver, to comment upon different societies he encountered on his treks to mythical lands. Gulliver also became a foil to utopian schemes.

The similarities in the settings of Thomas More's *Utopia* and Swift's version must have been deliberate. Both More and Swift wrote of an English traveler—Raphael Hythloday and Lemuel Gulliver, respectively—who sailed to distant lands.

However, there was an important difference between them: More provided only one utopia, and Swift introduced the reader to several possibilities, including Brobdingnag with its 60-foot-tall giants, Lilliput with its miniature humans, and the land of the horse-creature Houyhnhnms. Brobdingnag was not so much an ideal society as it was a method of indicating a hoped-for ideal. Despite the impressive size of the Brobdingnagians and their philosopher-king ruler, they were narrow-minded and lacking in moral and political ideals. Moreover, crime existed in Brobdingnag. Lilliput was more abstract as an ideal society, founded on practical, if sometimes extreme, laws and principles. There were rewards for adherence to the laws and punishments, rather severe in fact, for violators. Lilliput supported a strong moral ethic and promoted education and social discipline, though Gulliver faulted the Lilliputians' pettiness.

The Land of the Houyhnhnms (meaning "perfection of nature") portrayed a pure utopia, the most ideal yet also the most unreal in Gulliver's journeys. The Houyhnhnms allowed Swift to state what humans lack, although he did not present the Houyhnhnms as a viable model for humans. The notion of an Arcadia of a simple, austere, and benevolent, if primitive, society full of effortless virtues was inhuman, impractical, and even undesirable. Indeed, the utterly rational and impassive Houyhnhnms appeared superior to the foolishly emotional, animal-like humans, the Yahoos. Gulliver admired the guileless Houyhnhnms, but they feared that Gulliver might betray their idyllic society to the ravenous Yahoos, especially after Gulliver's account of the English riding on the backs of horses. Upon his final return to England, Gulliver found himself offended by human unreason, and he retired to commiserate with two horses.

Swift's preoccupation with corruption led him to create a dystopia as a vehicle to enquire into human tendencies. Human imperfection and degeneracy were simply facts of real life. People rather than institutions or laws were the cause of corruption. In Gulliver's visit to the island of Laputa, Swift used the "Academy of Lagado" (a thinly veiled dig at the Royal Society) as an illustration of the tension between utopia and dystopia. The professors in the academy, though teaching the ideal and virtuous principles of government, appear vainglorious to Gulliver for naively pursuing delusions. Science represented by the Laputans is perverted and nonsensical, not to mention lacking in utility. Can such selfless individuals seeking the progress of humanity ever exist in any society? Swift concluded they probably could not. Yet he felt compelled to hold up a high standard for society and governmental leaders.

In fact, Swift continually questioned the conventional eighteenth-century wisdom that mankind is rational. He suggested that usually what we call human reason only adds to our natural corrupt tendencies, so reason becomes an obstacle to rather than an opportunity for human improvement. Swift also used the philosopher-scientists in *Gulliver's Travels* to emphasize the corrosive effect of human pride. Whenever the scholars of Brobdingnag or the scientists on Laputa could not ascertain the answer to a question, their pride caused them to devise a fictitious sophisticated response to hide their ignorance. Swift concluded that pride was pointless since humans have nothing to be proud of. Hence, though humans have the capacity for rational or selfless actions, they are more likely to act irrationally or selfishly due to their innate corruptibility. To Swift, overcoming corruption is both difficult and rare. An example of such Swiftian logic is the proposition that religion was good, but man corrupted it. Lilliputian society had not yet been corrupted, but it was vulnerable. Brobdingnag, a more practical society, resembled Swift's England, capable of reform and improvement but cognizant of human frailties.

**References** Champion, Larry S. "Gulliver's Voyages: The Framing Events as a Guide to Interpretation" (1969); Rawson, Claude. *Gulliver and the Gentle Reader: Studies in Swift and Our Time* (1973).

**Hall, Joseph**
*See Mundus Alter et Idem.*

### *The Handmaid's Tale* (1985)

Canadian novelist Margaret Atwood (b. 1939) created a small sensation with a fictional polemic, *The Handmaid's Tale* (1985), about a crass, repressive society of the future. The work was made into a motion picture in 1990. The fact that Atwood's work has been characterized both as a dystopia and as science fiction suggests its complexity. The ultimate central theme of the work is civilization's prospects of survival.

Atwood's setting in *The Handmaid's Tale* was the fictional totalitarian state of Gilead, which occupied the geographical area of New England and was controlled by religious fanatics. Thus Atwood invoked a not-so-subtle reincarnation of the worst elements of New England's colonial Puritan era. Due to various catastrophes brought about by humanity's stupidity, disease and pollutants had caused a serious decline in the fertility of women and thus a population crisis. Although the society of

*Canadian author Margaret Atwood*

Gilead recognized a traditional role for wives, it was essentially misogynist, dividing women into various categories, the most important being "Handmaids," those women who remained fertile and were prepared and obligated to serve as surrogate birthing agents to men with sterile wives.

The story is told by a 30-something Handmaid named Offred who reminisces about the evolution from the past (from the 1970s and 1980s) to the early-twenty-first-century present. Residents of Gilead engaged in exercises seemingly straight from George Orwell's *1984*, including "testifying" at therapy sessions, community prayers, and the all-important "birth day" ceremonies when the Handmaids deliver their surrogate babies. The state maintains an elaborate espionage system to enforce the rituals and monotonous routines. Throughout the narrative, subtle female symbolism, such as the numerous fixtures designed in an oval shape, reminds the reader of the paramount role of the female ovaries. The males, though dominant in the society, are not unduly cruel. Following the tradition of fictional characters in other dystopian novels, a quiescent and obedient Offred gradually rebels against the system, seeking her individual identity. For Atwood, anyone who does not openly oppose a totalitarian system becomes an accomplice in its repression.

At the conclusion of the story, Atwood suddenly introduces a historical retrospective set in the year 2195, thus long after the expiration of the state of Gilead and the life of Offred. This conclusion discusses the discovery of the buried tapes of Offred from the previous era. Yet in this present-future, Atwood does not indicate what type of society has replaced totalitarian Gilead except to suggest that it is a better place—

albeit with sexism still intact—than the earlier time described in Offred's narrative. Despite a critical presentation of the patriarchal Gilead, Atwood's feminism does not necessarily reflect male hatred. Rather, *The Handmaid's Tale* seems to call for designing a practical program of survival for civilization as well as a society of tolerance and selflessness. Hence *The Handmaid's Tale* remains difficult to characterize since it was neither classic science fiction nor a typical dystopia. Still, Atwood's classic contains many features found in twentieth-century dystopian works by Yevgeny Zamyatin, Aldous Huxley, and George Orwell: efficient and unyielding power, hostility to change, and conflicts between the individual and society.

*References* Ketterer, David. "Margaret Atwood's *The Handmaid's Tale*: A Contextual Dystopia" (1989); Malak, Amin. "Margaret Atwood's *The Handmaid's Tale* and the Dystopian Tradition" (1987).

**Harrington, James**
*See The Commonwealth of Oceana.*

**Hartlib, Samuel**
*See Macaria*; Pansophism.

**Herland**
*See* Feminist Utopias.

**Hertzka, Theodor**
*See Freeland.*

**Herzl, Theodor**
*See Altneuland.*

**Hesse, Hermann**
*See The Glass Bead Game.*

**Hinduism**
*See* Gandhian Utopia.

**Howard, Ebenezer**
*See* Garden City Movement.

**Howell, William Dean**
*See* Altruria.

**Huguenot Utopias**
As a persecuted religious minority in seventeenth-century France, the Huguenots rather naturally thought in utopian terms as they searched for a permanent home beyond their native France. Not only did they flee to various parts of Europe, but some also sailed to the New World in search of an ideal place. The result was a spate of utopian projects produced by Denis Vairasse d'Allais, Gabriel de Foigny, and the Abbé Prévost. In the tradition of Thomas More's *Utopia* and Francis Bacon's *New Atlantis*, the expatriate French Huguenot Denis Vairasse's *History of the Sevarambians* (1675) employed rather typical solutions in an ideal society. The *History of the Sevarambians* portrays the longings of a typical Huguenot to create through his imagination the society that would satisfy his needs. De Foigny used the popular theme of *terra Australis incognita* as the framework for his 1676 utopian treatise. The Abbé Prévost used the Robinsonade as a setting for the adventures of his hero Monsieur Cleveland.

Although granted toleration by the Edict of Nantes (1598), Protestant Huguenots in France fairly soon realized that their ideal could not be made permanent. Persecution by a Catholic majority intensified steadily following the assassination of King Henri IV in 1610. Not surprisingly perhaps, the very first French utopia, *L'Histoire du Grand et Admirable Royaume d'Antangil*, was composed in 1616 by an anonymous Huguenot author. Because many Huguenots served as sailors, it was natural that they cast their eyes across oceans to locales such as the Americas. Indeed, there had already been attempted Huguenot settlements on the North American coast dating from the 1550s.

The Exiles, *a painting by James Tissot, depicts the mass exodus of French Protestant Huguenots to foreign lands following the revocation of the Edict of Nantes by Louis XIV in 1685.*

Certainly, the mingling of fact with fiction about the uncharted areas collectively referred to as *terra Australis incognita* fascinated the Huguenots more than other Frenchmen. The Huguenot utopias reflected less of the religious elements than the spirit of adventure and desire for a new life, although the fact that they were a persecuted group became a prerequisite for their utopian schemes.

Denis Vairasse d'Allais (ca. 1630–ca. 1700) had been trained as a lawyer in France but fled to England, where the first edition of *History of the Sevarambians* was published in 1675. The nation of Sevarambia was located in the South Seas near Australia and was founded in the 1400s by a traveler named Sevaris, who can be likened to both the author Vairasse and the chief character, the narrator Captain Siden. Sevaris had conquered lands from the local savages, created the social system, and molded an ideal society that was discovered 200 years later by the story's narrator, Captain Siden, a European sailor who was shipwrecked with his crew on the shores of Sevarambia. Captain Siden found the capital of Sevarambia, Sevarinde, which was perfectly

symmetrical in a radial outline, resembling in design the Renaissance utopian planned city. The royal palace, located at the hub, contained a Temple of the Sun. The all-powerful ruler wisely understood the pride of his subjects and so was effusive in commending their good behavior without having to provide material munificence. City residents lived in neighborhoods called osmasies.

The class divisions in Sevarambia featured only a special status for the magistrates, who wore distinctive attire; otherwise citizens had equal standing. Like most early modern utopias, Sevarambia maintained community ownership of property in order to prevent destructive competition for material gain. Everyone worked, though their labors were described as pleasant and light. Moreover, all goods were distributed equally among the citizens. The syncretistic state religion was founded upon an undogmatic philosophy; individuals were left free to worship according to their own dictates. Many of the clergy also held political office. Some antiquated social traditions were retained, including slaves to serve in the Sevarambian households and a premium upon women who produced the most offspring. Moreover, marriage was expected of all Sevarambians, at age 18 for females and not later than 21 for males. Nonetheless, Vairasse provided a more socially egalitarian bent to his utopia than did most of his predecessors. Certainly, he placed more emphasis upon community needs and less upon the importance of the family than did Thomas More. In certain respects he anticipated the socialist refrain of "from each according to his ability, to each according to his needs." Thus Vairasse's aristocratic, if benevolent, government, representing traditions of the past, coexisted with a somewhat more progressive social system anticipating the future.

Vairasse's utopia, like many early modern versions, placed great value upon education as both a means to an end and a favored pastime. The value of spending time learning was partly that it made a person more enlightened, but also that it kept youth from engaging in frivolities or vices. Education was made available to both males and females in Sevarambia. Youths were taught a strong patriotic attitude toward the benevolent state. Those best suited for learning a skill were directed toward occupational training at age 14, while more academically talented students could be sent to advanced studies in the professions. All males had to serve in the military, which existed primarily for defense, although territorial expansion was permitted when the growth of population required greater living space.

Vairasse's Sevarambia exhibited many elements common to early modern utopias. It was both despotic and boring in the dictates and rules of living. There was no need for a guarantee of individual freedom since the state provided all the necessities. Sevarambia condoned no excesses and embraced moderation in every area. Like More, Vairasse seemed less concerned to create a society strictly modeled after Sevarambia than to protest against existing social, religious, and political inequities and to stimulate a reform movement. Though there existed a despotic, all-powerful ruler

to ensure adherence to the system, the other utopian subjects were equal. Because Vairasse believed that a utopian society, or even a better real society, needed strong, disciplined leadership, he admired Louis XIV's absolutism. The Sevarambians were moral and honest; if they could not tell the truth, they would remain silent. Despite his Huguenot faith and endurance of persecution, Vairasse showed a proclivity for latitudinarianism in religion and a belief in freedom of conscience, which also was characteristic of most early modern utopias. Certainly, Vairasse seemed to move beyond the sixteenth-century Christian utopias toward a more purely secular theme.

Trained as a monk in the Franciscan Order, Gabriel de Foigny (ca. 1630–1692) was expelled for his immoral behavior. Following a brief period as a tutor, de Foigny left France for Switzerland to join the Calvinists. He married and had four children before his wife's death in 1683. De Foigny returned to France to live out the remainder of his years in seclusion. Gabriel de Foigny's *La Terre Australe Connue* (The Australian land discovered) was published in Geneva the year after Vairasse's *History of the Sevarambians*, in 1676. It told the story of a shipwrecked sailor, Jacques Sadeur, who took up residence in a utopia for 35 years. The first English translation was published in 1693 as *A New Discovery of Terra Australis Incognita or The Southern World*. De Foigny followed his early work with extensions in *Les Aventures de Jacques Sadeur*. The utopia that Sadeur discovers among the Australians is a society of hermaphrodites capable of self-procreation who live blissfully in a natural environment. The utopians own property communally, have no formal religion, and rely upon reason to solve problems. The Australians have no European-type diseases, are passionless and temperate in food and drink, and look forward to death as the fulfillment of happiness. Like Vairasse, de Foigny did not dwell on the subject of Huguenot oppression. Instead, he focused upon the ideal of the primitive native customs and endorsed some of those customs, such as suicide, since the natives believed that death was a much more pleasant repose than life.

The Abbé Prévost (1697–1763), in *Le Philosophe anglois, histoire de Monsieur Cleveland* (1731), concentrated more upon the creation of an ideal commonwealth and surveyed three utopias in the process. The fictional hero, Cleveland, was supposedly a product of the odd union of Oliver Cromwell and a former mistress of Charles I. In the first utopian episode, Cleveland is stranded on the island of St. Helena in the Atlantic, where he discovers a Huguenot colony established decades earlier. Struggling to overcome a shortage of males, the colony created a form of theocracy that resembled the governments of Puritan New England. The St. Helena utopia collapsed because it was unable to restrain passions. Prévost concentrated most of his attention in the succeeding utopian visits upon Cleveland's emotional struggle for inner peace. Lacking a comprehensive philosophy such as that of his mentor Fénelon, Prévost demonstrated his personal dislike of war, a skepticism about the potential of reason, and recognition of a preponderance of human frailties.

The second utopian setting finds Cleveland among the Nopande Indians, who respect nature and live in an Arcadia. They view war and violence as not only evil but against nature. The Nopande would only fight to preserve their freedom against a tyrant. Yet Prévost freely confessed that such a society could only exist in the imagination and not in reality. In a third utopia, Cleveland attempts to create an ideal community among the Abaquis Indians with the goal of peace and harmony, but it fails because of the inadequacies of both the architect Cleveland and the would-be utopians. At the end of his travels, Cleveland renounces the pursuit of reason in favor of emotional satisfaction. Cleveland finds a measure of transcendental peace in his religious philosophy, which he admits could not be attained through applications of the mind. In none of the

three utopias did Prévost provide a deus ex machina to intervene and stop the excesses that undermined the utopian dream. He allowed human nature, full of violence, selfishness, and intolerance, to frustrate efforts to create an ideal society.

*References* Manuel, Frank E., and Fritzie P. Manuel, eds. *French Utopias: An Anthology of Ideal Societies* (1966); Stewart, Philip. "Utopias That Self-Destruct" (1979).

## Hutterites

Emerging from the German Anabaptists, the Hutterites established a communal movement in the United States in the late nineteenth century. They are the oldest continuous communist and essentially classless organization in the world, although their primary emphasis has been their Christian teachings and individualism rather than socioeconomic practices, so their communism differs from that of secular communists. The early Hutterites asserted that in order to be a true Christian, believers must live in harmonious communion with other Christians. Although they expected that the millennium would occur sooner rather than later, the Hutterites were not obsessed with the prospect and so differed from typical millennialist groups. From their sixteenth-century origins in Germany, the Hutterites trekked to Russia in the eighteenth century and then to the United States in the 1870s. They continue to thrive in small North American communities and their beliefs and practices have not changed for almost 500 years.

The Hutterites recognize uneducated hat maker Jakob Hutter (d. 1536) as their founder. Originally a follower of Swiss Protestant reformer Huldrych Zwingli in the 1520s, Hutter later broke with Zwingli over issues including infant baptism. One Zwinglian splinter group led by Hutter moved east, and another led by Konrad Grebel migrated west and later became the Mennonite church. Hutter joined Jacob Wideman, who had led the Swiss brethren into Moravia where they began the practice of communal ownership of property in 1528. The group faced constant persecution; Hutter himself was burned at the stake. The first Hutterite confession of faith appeared in 1540, based upon a literal interpretation of the Bible and modeled on the first-century apostolic church. Thus the Hutterites opposed an imposed state church or compulsory membership or attendance.

The Anabaptists were among the most persecuted sects of the Reformation era because they were ostracized by both Catholics and other Protestants. Their primary teaching about adult believer baptism ran against a centuries-old Christian tradition. They also held firmly to the uncommon and unpopular belief in separation of church and state, as well as to pacifism. Unlike most Protestant sects, the Anabaptist-derived Hutterites rejected the doctrine of predestination and believed sin could separate even believers from God and endanger their salvation. The Hutterite sect added to the traditional Anabaptist customs the practice of community property. Grounded in scripture and early Christian custom rather than economic theory, Hutterite communism imitated first-century Christian practices. Constant, severe persecution and entanglements of wars almost wiped out the Moravian Hutterites by the end of the Thirty Years' War in 1648. The thousand Hutterites who survived moved into Slovakia in the mid-seventeenth century. External pressures caused their religion, prosperity, and common property principle to erode during the stay in Slovakia. Eventually only one pure Hutterite colony remained in Transylvania.

After the Hutterites fled to Wallachia in the 1760s, the territory was occupied by Russian armies, and a general invited the Hutterites to move to the Ukraine. Upon obtaining permission and a grant of religious toleration in 1770 from the Russian czarina Catherine, the Hutterites moved to the Ukraine, where they settled along the Desna River. Later in 1842 they moved southward, settling close to the Sea of Azov near a German Mennonite community. The Hutterites remained in the Ukraine for a hundred years struggling to maintain their distinct identity. They were forced by circumstances to compromise many of their traditions; they had less control over the economy and schools though they retained their churches. When a later Russian government embarked upon a Russification program and made the Hutterites subject to military conscription in 1872, the community began seeking asylum elsewhere.

Two leaders of the Ukrainian Hutterites came to the United States in 1873 with some neighboring Mennonites to find a new haven. Over the next three years, all 800 members of the community in the Ukraine moved to the United States and settled in South Dakota. Three primary colonies (*Brüderhof*) were established at Bon Homme, Wolf Creek, and Elmspring, while the remaining population staked out homesteads. The number of *Brüderhof* grew to 17 by 1914 with a population of 1,700. Because of persecution for their pacifism during World War I, large numbers of Hutterites moved across the border into Canada, settling in the provinces of Alberta and Manitoba. The *Brüderhof* were governed as independent theocracies by a minister and council of elders. The adult males elected the minister, who served for life. Often there was an elder minister and a younger minister in the *Brüderhof*. The members lived together in family units but worked and ate meals collectively. Labor was divided by gender, with men handling farm chores and women having domestic responsibilities. The business manager, or *Wirt*, normally sat on the governing council. Their self-sufficient economy was based upon the absence of competition, emphasizing community cooperation in a way similar to the early-nineteenth-century utopian socialists. Business professions were forbidden since, according to Hutterite teaching, the businessman could not avoid sin. Hutterites willingly utilized modern technology when it improved their economic efficiency but refused uses for purely personal benefit. Thus, for example, they would use trucks but not automobiles.

Unlike German Pietist sects that established communitarian settlements in the United States, the Hutterites did not advocate celibacy. Their view of marriage and childbearing followed orthodox Christian and social traditions. In addition to practicing their distinct faith, the members retained their German language through their schools. Common, simple dress was required as an outward sign of conformity to communal rather than individual desires, although some colors were allowed. By the 1980s, the Hutterites occupied about 140 *Brüderhof* in the West

and Canada, with a population of about 25,000. Very few Hutterites have left the communities in the United States, and a number of those who leave eventually return. Unlike secular cooperative communities, the Hutterites make no attempt to convince the outside world to convert to their society. Indeed, the Christian communalists strove mightily to have as little contact with the world beyond their settlements as possible.

**Reference** Conkin, Paul. *Two Paths to Utopia: The Hutterites and the Llano Colony* (1964).

## Huxley, Aldous
*See Brave New World.*

## *The Iron Heel* (1908)

U.S. Marxist storyteller Jack London created a dystopia as a unique way to present his utopia in *The Iron Heel*. Most twentieth-century contrasts were the opposite, a utopian scheme measured against the dystopian result. London's idiom includes future time, Marxism, and science fiction. Hence it is fair to suggest that London's utopia creates its own category, although he most closely resembles H. G. Wells in his variegated style. Yet London was also capable, as in the science fiction utopia of "Goliah," of framing a utopia in the more typical fashion, where an undescribed imposed order is already a fait accompli when the story commences.

Jack London (1876–1916) faced many ailments, both emotional and physical, during his relatively short life. He was an illegitimate child born in San Francisco and given the name of John Griffith, but he was raised by his stepfather John London on a ranch. After leaving school early to search for his biological father, London acquired an education by studying at the public library. Narrowly avoiding a life of petty crime, London gained valuable insights for his literary career by sailing around the Pacific. Following rapid movement through several manual jobs, an acquaintance loaned London the money to attend the University of California. There he nurtured a previous predilection for avant-garde thinkers such as Karl Marx, Charles Darwin, and Herbert Spencer. London's college days were followed by formal involvement with socialism, some initial writing for monthly magazines, and a failed marriage. A trip to England inspired a sociological publication on urban blight, which was followed by a second more enduring marriage and settlement in rural California to write his major fictional novels. Before his death from a drug overdose, London embarked on another Pacific tour that included Hawaii.

*The Iron Heel* is set in the twenty-seventh century, but the story revolves around the memoirs of Avis Everhard, an early-twentieth-century widow of a leading socialist whose voice was crushed by a vicious fascist dictatorship. Through an examination of the memoirs, London was able to describe the conditions that led to the twentieth-century dystopia and critique the dystopia itself, thereby presenting in a positive light the utopia that had emerged by the twenty-seventh century. In the dystopia, the fascist regime crushed the freedom and will of the proletariat, but London made it clear that the dystopia evolved because of the refusal of capitalism to ensure justice for workers or to eliminate evils such as child labor. London's fictional hero, Ernest Everhard, brazenly and uncompromisingly challenged the existing unjust system and suggested that the working classes can rule themselves without benefit of an elite overclass. Even Christianity took its lumps from Everhard, who viewed it as accommodating repressive techniques. The clerical character in *The Iron Heel* pursued self-deceptive rationalizations rather than inspiring reforms. Both predicting and agitating for revolution, Everhard insisted that the new order would rid society of its oppressors. Everhard's antagonists scoffed at his moralisms, which were depicted as "utopian."

When Everhard ran for Congress he frightened the bourgeoisie by forecasting the inevitable victory of socialism, which would squeeze the middle class more than the plutocrats. In the ensuing days, the nation faced serious repression—the loss of the freedoms of speech and the press.

*Jack London*

The economic chaos that followed hit the working classes hardest yet strengthened the appeal of the fascist movement, the Iron Heel. In the midst of the national disintegration, Everhard was elected to Congress, where he engaged the Iron Heel in rhetorical debate. When the Iron Heel eventually seized power, Everhard was tried and imprisoned as a subversive. Socialist rebels liberated Everhard and other congressmen from their prison confinement to lead an underground movement. Although the incomplete memoir suggested the failure of the rebel movement against the Iron Heel, the socialist utopia eventually overwhelmed the repressive fascist dystopia to inaugurate an era of peace and plenty for the utopian future. Thus the deep pessimism throughout the story ended with an optimistic outcome.

As a product of the underclass himself, it is not surprising that London would advocate so vigorously a class warfare in *The Iron Heel*. London clearly did not even believe in the notion of paternalism or charity from the upper classes, and though he showed less anger toward the middle class, he did not believe it was capable of instigating a substantive reform. Such a view is odd in that at the very time *The Iron Heel* was published, the United States was in the throes of a major reform led by the middle class, the Progressive movement. Obviously, London was unmoved by the Progressive reforms, probably because he felt they were bogus. Certainly, he suggested that the middle class were mere pawns being played for advantage by the ruling elite. Like other Marxists, London focused upon the means to the end of capitalism rather than the nature of the resulting new paradigm. Revolution was the only sure method, since reform efforts were either thwarted or watered down. Nor could reason and persuasion abetted by education or propaganda effect the necessary changes since wealthy oligarchs refused to share any of their riches or their power. For London, the idea of any type of benevolent authoritarian system was sheer myth. Indeed, his prediction of right-wing authoritarianism, that is, fascism, suggested the strength and resourcefulness of the rich. The ruling oligarchies have at their disposal control of all the major institutions: banks, industry, government, the media.

Yet with all the dark pessimism throughout *The Iron Heel*, the reader is left with a positive view of the future because London passionately believed that the proletariat's cause was not only righteous but inevitably assured of victory. Nonetheless, London concentrated his creativity on describing a dystopia rather than a utopia. The utopia is not detailed, except to contrast it with the dystopia. It is likely that London became fascinated with the literary forcefulness of dystopian descriptions compared to the facile words that might have elucidated a utopia. Even in his championing of socialism through Everhard, London seemed to relish the combat of class warfare. In the event, the reader is clear about what London viewed as an acceptable utopia even while recognizing that there are no guarantees that his account of dystopia would inevitably result in a utopia in the long run. The great dystopian writers of later years—Zamyatin, Huxley, Orwell—would translate the meaning of dystopia from a perspective entirely opposite to London's.

*Reference* Beauchamp, Gorman. "Jack London's Utopian Dystopia and Dystopian Utopia," in Roemer, Kenneth M., ed. *America as Utopia* (1981).

## *Islandia* (1942)

Austin Wright's capitalist utopia becomes a haven from the harsh materialism, egoism, and complexity of life by providing a pastoral, simple society filled with brotherly love. Wright uses the familiar theme of an outsider visiting utopia who initially fails to comprehend the system but eventually agrees that it is best. *Islandia* is also old-fashioned in its form of utopian society, essentially a medieval agrarian system. Yet it is unique in its grappling with human efforts to escape reality through believable fictional characters, especially women, in a utopian setting.

Austin Tappan Wright (1883–1931) was born in New Hampshire and educated at Harvard, where he graduated from law school (1908) after completing an undergraduate degree. He studied at Oxford University during 1906–1907. Wright began a Boston law practice in 1908 but accepted a professor of law position at the University of California in 1916. He taught there until 1924, when he moved to the University of Pennsylvania Law School. Wright's only published work was *Islandia*, which did not appear in print until a decade after his death. Though it is usually described as science fiction, it definitely contains utopian themes.

The South Seas utopia of Islandia is situated in a temperate climate facilitating agriculture, the main economic activity in a mundane preindustrial society. The social organization at Islandia is based on the traditional family, although women are regarded as the equals of males and possess considerable sexual freedom. The political system, a parliamentary monarchy, is traditional as well. The society favors nonspe-

cialization of skills and encourages its residents, including women, to pursue their interests or develop their talents without pressure to conform. Thus, although most women are married, there is no social stigma attached to those who choose to remain single. Islandia is not a perfect utopia since some residents are unhappy and quarrels occur. Yet there is a strong spirit of cooperation among the citizens.

In 1907, Islandia welcomes a visitor from Boston, John Lang, assigned as the initial U.S. diplomatic consul. Lang gains the appointment in part because of his friendship with an aristocratic Islandian named Dorn. Lang is the narrator of the story, so his perspective on utopia is that of an outsider. The primary policy issue that Lang brings to Islandia's government is whether to end its trade isolation and allow foreign investment which could alter Islandia's utopia. Lang's acquaintances, such as Dorn, favor continuing the nation's isolation, but a liberal faction wants to open trade with the outside world. John Lang's experiences in the story focus upon his relationship with three women and the nature of the ideal society.

Upon arriving in Islandia, Lang meets and experiences brief relationships with two native women, Dorna, the sister of his friend Dorn, and Nattana. Lang learns that the Islandians have more than one term for love. *Ania* was the feeling of love between spouses united to produce a family. It involved sacrifice and mutual nurturing. *Apia* was an erotic desire based purely upon a physical, sensual attraction. *Alia* corresponded to the love of family, friends, and even place. These different meanings of love initially confuse the outside visitor Lang and make his relationships with Dorna and Nattana complicated. Both native women see an opportunity in uniting with Lang to escape their present circumstances. Twenty-three-year-old Dorna, intelligent and attractive, pursues *alia* in her dealings with Lang, so she tries to discourage his thoughts of marriage. Though she wants

**111**

to remain single, she needs Lang to assist her ambitions to enter politics so that she can promote the policy of isolationism that will preserve the utopian society. And the traditions of Islandia dictate that she must be married to qualify as a political leader. Dorna's choices for the marriage of convenience are either King Tor or Lang. Dorna really prefers Lang as a mate since his friendship with her family would aid the cause of defeating the movement for ending isolation. Moreover, Dorna would have to give up more of her independence to become queen by marrying Tor. Yet Dorna does not feel *ania* for Lang, and she ultimately chooses to marry the king. At the key council meeting to decide the trade issue, Dorna argues powerfully and successfully to defeat the proposal to open Islandia to outside trade.

Lang's second encounter, with the younger Nattana, follows similar conflicts about the meaning of love. Nattana also needs someone like Lang to help her gain freedom from the constraints of her family. Nattana's father did not agree with many Islandia practices, such as limiting the size of families, and he found it difficult to support a large family. Relying upon her skill as a tailor, Nattana leaves her father's farm to join some siblings on another farm. Nattana questions Lang about the life of women in the United States, but she is not persuaded they have a better existence. A friendship blossoms into romance between Nattana and Lang, yet Lang confesses that he only feels *apia* toward Nattana, which does not suit either party's aims. Nattana ends the sexual liaison with Lang, although the two remain friends.

Lang returns to Boston pondering whether to move permanently to Islandia. Upon his return in 1910 he renews his relation with Gladys Hunter, whom he knew before he left Boston when she was still a teenager. Lang explains to a receptive, sympathetic Gladys, now a woman of 20, the peculiar emotions of the Islandians. Over a year's time Lang grows to love Gladys in the manner of Islandia's *ania*, and the couple marry and move to Islandia. Gladys finds adjustment to the Islandian ways difficult, and she struggles to exert an individual identity apart from Lang's. Clearly, Wright sees in Gladys the female paradigm for his utopia, a woman strong and independent yet able to conform to a shared, selfless relationship. Gladys thus decides for herself that she wants children so that she and Lang can cultivate *alia* in their new home.

Despite the conservative nature of many facets of Islandia, Wright was ahead of his time in the sensitive treatment of women's emotions. His utopia was not a feminist utopia, but it set a tone of positive appreciation for the place of women in society that was lacking in the work of most male writers. Wright's utopia focused more on the human aspect than on the structural features emphasized in most schemes. Moreover, in a time when utopias were increasingly unpopular, Wright sought to salvage the genre with a positive but realistic account.

**Reference** Flieger, Verlyn. "Wright's *Islandia*: Utopia with Problems," in Barr, Marleen, and Nicholas D. Smith, eds. *Women and Utopia: Critical Interpretations* (1983).

## It Can't Happen Here (1935)

The twentieth-century novelist of U.S. mores, Sinclair Lewis, also ventured into the realm of utopia with his novel about the possibility of totalitarian government in the United States. Lewis was influenced both by the rise of Adolph Hitler and Nazism in Germany and by the popularity of the Louisiana demagogue Huey Long. *It Can't Happen Here* was hastily conceived and written so that it might influence the presidential election of 1936. During 1936 the novel was made into a stage drama that played in 15 U.S. cities. Lewis was sometimes compared with Oswald Spengler as an effective critic of a declining Western civilization.

A native of Minnesota, Harry Sinclair Lewis (1885–1951) was a patriotic, romantic youth. At age 13 he tried to enlist in the military for service in the Spanish-American War before being rescued by his father. Lewis attended a preparatory school prior to entering Yale University in 1903, where he wrote for the student literary magazine. Upon leaving Yale in 1906, Lewis spent a couple of months living in the Helicon Hall utopian community in New Jersey. He eventually returned to Yale to complete his degree in 1908 after another adventurous trip, to Panama seeking work on the canal project. After working in a publishing house before World War I, Lewis devoted full time to writing. His first successful novel, *Main Street*, appeared in 1920. It was followed by a series of phenomenal successes: *Babbitt* (1922), which parodied the business ethic; *Arrowsmith* (1925), which questioned medical doctors' motives; and *Elmer Gantry* (1927), which lampooned religious hucksters. In the period preceding the appearance of *It Can't Happen Here*, Lewis was influenced greatly by the political views of his second wife, journalist Dorothy Thompson (married 1928–1942), who covered Hitler's rise to power in Germany. Though he refused in 1926 to accept the Pulitzer Prize for *Arrowsmith*, Lewis accepted the Nobel Prize for Literature in 1930.

*It Can't Happen Here* follows the rise to political power of Senator Buzz Windrip, a close analog to Louisiana governor and senator Huey Long. Basing his campaign upon the "15 Points of Victory," a melting pot of bizarre political schemes advocated by real-life contemporary political extremists and charlatans such as Father Charles Coughlin, Gerald Smith, and Dr. Francis Townsend, Windrip is elected president of the United States. Almost immediately Windrip begins dismantling the democratic system and replaces it with a dictatorship known as Corpo. The new regime proves to be venal and corrupt as well as repressive. Relying less upon propaganda, the Corpo methods were epitomized by concentration camps housing minority groups. Lewis returned to familiar bugbears from his earlier novels to characterize Windrip's operation: big business and the mass culture of medioc-

*Sinclair Lewis (1885–1951), from a 1930s photograph.*

rity that rewarded sham artists peddling illusions and appealing to the emotions. Americans, as Lewis knew so well, were gullible when it came to get-rich-quick or something-for-nothing schemes. More ambitious than evil, Windrip possessed the qualities of Babbitt and Elmer Gantry honed to an even more sophisticated sharpness. Lewis offered extensive details in his descriptions of the Corpo regime's methods to draw the parallels to real-life contemporary totalitarian systems.

Lewis had been writing about the dangers of authoritarian government since the end of World War I. The rise of totalitarian regimes in Europe, combined with the dislocation and desperation of the Great Depression, offered a serious threat to the principles and institutions of democracy. Yet Lewis remained more conservative in his response than most intellectuals of his era—he rejected communism as a replacement for capitalism. Reflecting the Lewis caveats in the novel is the realist Doremus Jessup, who has observed keenly the evolution of Windrip's regime and appears unsurprised by the advent of a dictatorship. Jessup shows empathy toward the poor and downtrodden, who were exploited long before Windrip was elected president. Yet Jessup also faults romantics and utopians for concentrating on the positive ends of their schemes without comprehending the means to arrive at their object. Ultimately and predictably perhaps, Jessup leads a rebellion against the Corpos, thereby instructing citizens not only to be vigilant against authoritarianism but also to be willing to resist such regimes. Lewis seemed unconcerned that in his resistance Jessup and his comrades resorted to the very violence they condemned in the Corpos. Moreover, other than a brief reference to a kind of vague welfare state, Jessup does not embrace or defend an alternative ideology that would have made his character more appealing. Jessup, like Lewis, appears largely apolitical.

The timing of *It Can't Happen Here* was important, as Lewis understood in his haste to complete it. It sold 250,000 copies in the first year of publication, and many others saw it on the stage during the Federal Theater Project tour in 1936. Critics hailed the novel as realistic and frightening. Though it lacked the detailed grit of Arthur Koestler's *Darkness at Noon* or George Orwell's *1984*, Lewis's dystopia served its purpose in alerting the United States to dangers most Americans had not before thought real.

**Reference** Jones, James T. "A Middle Class Utopia: Lewis's *It Can't Happen Here*" (1985).

## Japanese Utopias

Because utopianism is essentially a secular phenomenon and indigenous Japanese religious traditions (mainly Shintoism) were so entrenched, the utopian tradition did not fit easily into Japanese culture. Moreover, significant Japanese contact with the West did not occur until the 1850s, a period later than contacts with other Asian territories such as China. Thus, utopian thought has been slower to emerge in Japan. The Japanese are focused so intently upon their daily routines and habits that they find it difficult to imagine a place other than their small world of reality. Their proximity to nature also means that visual harmony is more important than a functionally designed symmetry artificially imposed upon nature. Further, the Japanese place no great importance upon individual freedom of action as does Western thought. Hence their ideas of change did not conform to an idealized or unreal condition that was far removed from the typical Japanese lifestyle.

Whereas Western utopias reveal a tension between humanity and nature, Japanese traditions taught that people should obediently conform to nature. Hence even in the modern era Japanese show extreme sensitivity to elements of nature such as the sun and moon, winds and rain, flowers and trees. The appreciation of nature among the Japanese contains a strong spiritual element that is mostly lacking in the West. The ancient religion of Shintoism guided social customs by stressing the importance of the natural order. Even the external influence of Chinese neo-Confucian thought, with its dualism between mind and matter, did not cause Japanese thinkers in the Tokugawa period (seventeenth and eighteenth centuries) to

separate ideas from physical nature. The basis of the Japanese attitude toward nature can be found in their *waka* poetry, which dates from the eighth century A.D. The earliest such poem, the *Man'yoshu*, emphasized the distinct characteristics of the four seasons. Also in this *waka* tradition is the tenth-century story about a bamboo cutter who finds a miniature girl in a stalk. She grows to maturity, entertains but rejects several suitors, and eventually leaves the earth for the moon.

Although with the arrival of Europeans in the Far East in the early modern era it is logical to relate Japanese thought during the Tokugawa Shogunate (1615–1867) to Western ideas, the most profound influence initially altering tradition came from China with the neo-Confucian concept of the ideal. Nonetheless, Japanese thinkers such as Ogyu Sorai (1666–1728), who embraced the ideal and hence reformed society, rejected neo-Confucian physical-metaphysical dualism to stress that the ideal tao, or way of life, must be in harmony with nature. The scientist-artist Hiraga Gennai (1728–1779) wrote *Furyu Shidoken den* in 1763, a precursor of Japanese utopias, which proved to be very influential in generating interest in utopian concepts. Hiraga had studied Western methods from the Dutch merchants at Nagasaki. The story features a hero who travels across Japan ridiculing the feudal system and in the process discovers various strange peoples (for example, giants and dwarfs) who strongly resemble Jonathan Swift's fictional tribes in *Gulliver's Travels*. It is unclear whether Hiraga had learned about Swift from his Dutch tutors, but it is a distinct possibility. The *Shidoken* resembled most later Japanese utopian writings, which are more oriented toward satirical criticism of society than they are attempts to construct alternative ideal societies.

A second eighteenth-century innovator, Ando Shoeki (1701–1758), vigorously attacked the feudal caste system in *Shizen shin'eido* (1775). Japan's feudalism underwent considerable strain caused by its own inefficiencies and high taxes as well as the emergence of independent commerce in the eighteenth century. One chapter in the *Shizen* outlines an ideal society, the *shizensei* (natural order), in which humans are brought into harmony with nature. Ando argued that feudal society was based upon a man-made legal system rather than a natural order, and he believed that a living example of a natural order existed in the Netherlands. Hence the Japanese rarely thought of utopia as "no place"; rather, it had a definite historical location. He proposed that people would contribute to economic productivity in the three areas of farming, fishing, and industry and would receive their needs equally. Thus class divisions and distinctions such as rich and poor could be eliminated, and even enmity between parents and children would disappear.

With the determination of the Meiji emperor to imitate Western techniques in the mid-nineteenth century, Western models of utopia also became more influential in Japan. Indeed, the only period of extensive production of Japanese utopias occurred during the Meiji era, when contact with the West dramatically increased. Yet most Japanese utopias of the period remained one-dimensional, featuring political designs but rarely touching upon social, economic, or cultural areas. For example, two of the most popular Japanese utopias, written by Takase Naokuni (1883) and Suehiro Shigeyasu (1886), discussed political reforms placed in the year 1890. The earliest Western utopia translated into Japanese was a Dutch future-time utopia by Alexander Bikkers, *The Year 2065* (1865). A translation of Thomas More's *Utopia* appeared in 1882, and about three dozen other Western utopias eventually became familiar in Japan. The most prominent Japanese utopist in the Meiji era was Hattori Sei'ichi, who penned three major utopias between 1884 and 1887, all primarily depicting ideal political reforms. By the end of the nineteenth century, however, Japanese reformers had seized upon both cooperative and communal ideals as potential models for consideration.

During the early years of the twentieth century, many Japanese intellectual modernists rejected the capitalist model in favor of social planning in the utopian socialist paradigm. In the post-Russo-Japanese War era, the twin influences of Christianity (permitted in Japan after 1873) and socialism (especially Fabianism) gained their greatest boost from the writings and reform projects of Kagawa Toyohiko (1888–1960), who most clearly reflected Japanese utopian thinking. Although a widely read novelist, Kagawa's primary influence came through his editorship of the newspaper *Kingdom of God*. Mostly from his position as a Christian minister, Kagawa championed political reform in the 1920s as well as sponsoring tuberculosis hospitals for poor workers and promoting the organization of labor unions. Kagawa was instrumental in invoking utopian ideals in the Japanese Farmers Union and promoting cooperation between urban and rural workers. The advent of communism in Japan undermined Kagawa's utopian efforts among workers by the late 1920s. Moreover, the military-oriented government sought to repress both utopian socialist and Christian anarchist movements. Still, some of Kagawa's enterprises, such as the Peasant Gospel School (modeled on the utopian Danish Folk Higher Schools), continued into the depression-era 1930s. The Kingdom of God movement was terminated in 1934, and Kagawa later served time in prison during World War II for attempting reconciliation with China.

Because the post–World War II Japanese constitution allowed the greatest freedom of expression in history, utopian movements revived in various guises. Most of the postwar organizations such as

Soka Gakkai were communal in structure, but they tended to be unusual in their future orientation, particularly dwelling on spiritual regeneration despite the massive decline in formal religiosity. Certainly, almost all Japanese thinking has become vigorously universal and international.

*References* Bikle, George B., Jr. "Utopianism and the Planning Element in Modern Japan," in Plath, David W., ed. *Aware of Utopia* (1971); Seiji Nuita, "Traditional Utopias in Japan and the West: A Study in Contrasts," in Plath, David W., ed. *Aware of Utopia* (1971).

## Jonestown
*See* New Age Cults.

**K'ang Yu-wei**
*See The Great Equality.*

## Kaweah Colony

Started by a labor leader, J. J. Martin, and a lawyer, Burnette Haskell, the colony at Kaweah Canyon, California, was intended to serve as a model for a series of industrial utopian settlements along the West Coast. The experiment did not produce the desired expansion, and Kaweah itself lasted only a few years, from the mid-1880s to the early 1890s.

As a representative of San Francisco maritime laborers, J. J. Martin had been attempting to improve their working conditions through arbitration with employers. Martin found the task daunting; his frustration led him to enter into a partnership with lawyer and former journalist Burnette Haskell, who was also interested in labor issues. Haskell's radicalism was evident in his founding of the Marxist International Workingmen's Association as well as the Federated Trades of San Francisco, a member organization of the national Knights of Labor. In 1885, Haskell presented to the union members a proposal to establish several industrial communes along the Pacific coast near port facilities. Each settlement would foster economic opportunity in their respective regions. Monetary contributions were solicited and a brickyard was planned for Fish Rock, north of San Francisco, but the site was soon deemed unsuitable for planting the colony. An associate of Martin's and Haskell's, C. F. Keller, proposed a site suitable for lumbering operations in the Kaweah Canyon, 50 miles from the San Joaquin Valley in Tulare County. After an investigation recommended the relocation of Kaweah, the Cooperative Land Association was formed. In October 1885, 12 square miles of property at Kaweah was claimed under the federal Timberland Act of 1878 and Homestead Act of 1862.

The association established the Tulare Valley Railroad with Haskell, Martin, and Keller as officers. The colony needed to construct a 20-mile road to connect the timber land with the utopian community of Kaweah and the rail line. The construction of the mountainous road between 1886 and 1890 helped more than anything else to bind the colonists together with an esprit de corps. The colony's purposes included not only the provision of jobs and housing but also the establishment of schools and recreation and cultural facilities. Although no stock was sold to members, they were required to pay $500 in membership fees. Workers would be paid equal wages for their labor. The community of Kaweah would be built on more than 200 acres and governed by a five-member board that would name a supervisor for each of the 11 categories of work, including industries, transportation, schools, and finances. Haskell became the superintendent of schools, and Martin headed the town administration. At town meetings, held once a month, supervisors made reports of their work teams and residents debated legal issues. Early tent dwellings soon gave way to permanent structures. The community featured a communal dining hall, a general store, a community barn, and a print shop, which published the newspaper *Commonwealth*. Cultural activities included weekly literary readings, science tutorials, and performances by a community orchestra.

From the beginning, the colony at Kaweah was diluted because nonresidents could pay membership fees to the association without being residents of Kaweah. Thus there were member clubs in several major cities, including San Francisco, Los Angeles, Denver, and even New York City. The New York club of fewer than two dozen members was organized by Alice Rhine, who had written studies about women's roles in industry. Some New York members visited Kaweah, and Rhine planned to move there although the colony dissolved before she could arrange to leave New York. Some members of Edward Bellamy's Nationalist Clubs were among the recruits to Kaweah. By 1890 the colony had about 200 residents.

The most formidable obstacle to Kaweah's success proved to be the federal government, which charged the colonists with illegally occupying public lands. Responding to the conservationist lobby campaign to preserve forest lands, Congress passed legislation in 1890 creating the Sequoia National Park and Forest, which included the lands settled at Kaweah. Not only did the government refuse to pay the colony for their improvements, but they tried to prosecute Kaweahans for cutting trees illegally. There were also internal disputes and extended wrangling over policy issues such as the wage system, and Haskell was criticized for poor management of finances. The Kaweah experiment blending individualism and cooperation ended prematurely. It is not at all clear that if the legal problems with the federal government had not intervened that the settlement would have been any more successful than other similar efforts. Yet the experiment foundered at a moment of unity and high enthusiasm about its future prospects. Certainly, Kaweah inspired other schemes to launch worker colonies, including Julius Wayland's Ruskin Commonwealth a few years later.

*Reference* Johnpoll, Bernard K., and Lillian Johnpoll. *The Impossible Dream* (1981).


## Kibbutzim

Developing at a time when the utopian idea had been buffeted with criticism, the kibbutz concept sought to revive the ideal of a practical utopia, especially the notion of a socialist utopia. The kibbutz ("gathering" in Hebrew) was as much a social as it was an economic organization. It sought to deal with the problems of (1) labor that alienates workers, (2) the quest for equal distribution of work, and (3) the relationship of the individual to the collective society. The idea of the kibbutz drew upon sources that included in the late nineteenth century the French anarchist Pierre-Joseph Proudhon and, later, the Jewish philosopher Martin Buber. The kibbutz thus became a community structure designed to promote decentralized authority, mutual cooperation, and individual creativity. Kibbutz theorists desired that individuals contribute to the common good by relinquishing most of their selfish tendencies. The kibbutz came closest to solving the age-old dilemma of utopists involving the apparent necessity for a single authority. For the kibbutzim, the ultimate authority was the whole nation.

There were three types of cooperative agricultural societies established in Israel after its restoration in 1948. The *moshav ovdim* was a workers' settlement in which land, largely purchased before statehood, was owned by the Jewish National Fund. Each family retained the income from the land they worked, although the products were marketed collectively. In the kibbutz, property was owned collectively by the participants. It involved a broader form of cooperation than the *moshav ovdim*. The *moshav shittufi* combined the collective and individual aspects of the other two societies by providing cooperative work but individual ownership and living arrangements. Between 1948 and 1954, 227 kibbutzim, populated with about 76,000 participants, were established in Israel. Though most kibbutzim were organized along socialist lines, the majority were non-Marxist. Most kibbutzim employed some form of collective child care, but only a few utilized a collective educational system that began at a child's birth.

The founders of the kibbutz system believed that labor was more than just a

*Jewish settlers in Israel, from an undated photograph*

means of satisfying material needs. Work was viewed as a necessity for human satisfaction and happiness, the essence of life itself. The distinctive attitude of the kibbutz toward work originated in the early days of the formulation of Zionism in the thinking of its leaders, especially Aaron David Gordon (1856–1922), who led early Jewish immigrants to Palestine. The Jewish National Fund was established in 1901 as a subsidiary of the World Zionist Organization to purchase land in Palestine. Organizations such as the Hashomer Hatzair youth movement (founded in 1913) established their own kibbutz federations. In 1951 there was a merger of the large-scale kibbutzim, led by the Hakibbutz Hameuchad, and the smaller settlements (*kvutzot*) of the Hever Kakvutzot into the federation of Ichud Hakvutzot Vehakibbutzim, which was affiliated with the Israeli Workers Party. Many of the early Jewish immigrants with middle-class backgrounds were not accustomed to physical labor. The kibbutz concept honored physical labor above all other forms

of toil. Another principle of the early kibbutzim was that products of the collective labor belonged to the community as a whole. Thus, in order to ensure absolute equality, there was no concept of private property in the theory of the kibbutz. Yet the property was actually not even owned by the local community but by the nation. Because of the communal attitudes toward property, the kibbutzim did not pay wages for labor, though the members did not pay rent for housing or have to buy food or clothing. The physical layout of the kibbutzim resembled other socialist communal experiments of the past: The central communal building was surrounded by concentric circles of land development. The design also accommodated security concerns for settlements established during the British Mandate era before 1948. Indeed, the kibbutzim became the operations center for Jewish military operations of the Haganah before statehood.

The kibbutz system strove mightily to avoid the types of authoritarian control exhibited in most utopias. It relied upon the maintenance of communal cooperation and agreement on its principles to enforce its order. The discipline was effected by warnings, isolation of offenders, and rarely by expulsion. In the event, the kibbutzim never resorted to the threat of force to coerce compliance. Invariably, the first generation of kibbutzers remained most loyal to the original ideals of the society. In the early years of the experiment, economic survival was the quest both inside and outside the kibbutzim. Succeeding generations have altered the regime to be both less ideological and less political. Moreover, the inevitable attraction of the external world's materialism eroded the founding ethos of the kibbutz system. The growth of the kibbutzim allowed the expansion of communal buildings, so interpersonal sharing, common in the early kibbutzim with their single communal buildings, became limited and thus less of a binding element. Thus, though the kibbutz institution did not control the growth of Israeli national interests and nonkibbutz economic expansion, it has been able to adjust successfully, albeit utilizing techniques different from those of the founding generation. For example, by the 1960s half of Israel's kibbutzim featured industries that employed one-fourth of their workers. Another result of change has been that the kibbutz has become less utopian through its evolution.

In the decades prior to the establishment of the State of Israel, the kibbutz theorists worked hand in hand with Jewish national leaders to re-create the ancient nation. In the acquisition of land during the Mandate period, the promotion of immigration to Palestine, and the nurture of the Hebrew language, the kibbutz leaders contributed as much as any other group to the success of nation building. The kibbutz ideology of manual labor also fit the need for the development of an agrarian economy in Israel. Yet like the nineteenth-century communal societies in the United States, the kibbutz model was eclipsed quickly by Israel's political, social, and economic development along Western lines, with its emphasis upon centralization rather than decentralization and class consciousness rather than a classless society. Immigrants since the 1950s have had a perspective entirely different from that of the 1940s immigrants who established the first kibbutzim. The later immigrants directed their economic interests more toward skilled labor and their social interests toward bourgeois values. Furthermore, many of those newer immigrants, especially Sephardic Jews from the Soviet Union and Eastern Europe, were understandably suspicious of any kind of socialist system. Though many of the new immigrants initially worked on kibbutzim, they worked for wages that compromised the socialist principles of the institution. The nation's demand for industrial production and exports since the 1960s has affected the kibbutz idea as much as it has the rest of Israel. In order to survive, the kibbutz institution has accepted external change, but it has lost its original utopian quality in the process. Modern imitators of the socialist kibbutz in nations including Tanzania, Cuba, Yugoslavia, and China, though different from the Soviet managed economy, have not proven to be as successful or resourceful as the Israeli kibbutz in upholding the ideology of self-reliant social equality.

*Reference* Spiro, Melford E. *Kibbutz: Venture in Utopia* (1956).

## Kropotkin, Petr
*See* Anarchism.

### Last and First Men (1930)

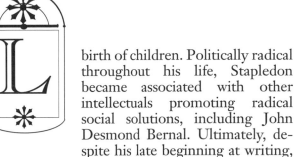

William Olaf Stapledon not only pioneered twentieth-century space science fiction stories but also influenced the use of science fiction in utopian constructions. His *Last and First Men*, published in 1930, had a profound impact upon later anti-utopian science fiction writing. Appearing during the Great Depression and at the onset of the great dystopias, Stapledon's work did not appeal to readers as much as it might have in a different time frame. In *Last and First Men* Stapledon seemed consumed with the juxtaposition of time and fortune with human change.

William Olaf Stapledon (1886–1950) was known as a writer and philosopher as well as a political activist with pro-Soviet sympathies in the early stages of the Cold War. He was born into a well-to-do English family involved in the shipping business at Liverpool. He spent much of his youth living with his parents in Egypt, though he returned to receive his education at Oxford University where he took bachelor's and master's degrees in history at prestigious Balliol College. Before beginning his writing career, Stapledon worked as a teacher (he hoped for a university appointment, which did not materialize) and in his family's shipping business. Though a pacifist, Stapledon agreed to accept a noncombat role (ambulance driver) with the military in World War I. Stapledon, however, remained haunted by his conviction that he was a coward at heart. After the war Stapledon earned a doctorate in philosophy at the University of Liverpool. Before World War I, during his teaching tenure, Stapledon began writing poetry but was diverted from full-time attention to writing by various circumstances, including his postwar marriage to his cousin and the subsequent birth of children. Politically radical throughout his life, Stapledon became associated with other intellectuals promoting radical social solutions, including John Desmond Bernal. Ultimately, despite his late beginning at writing, Stapledon produced ten novels and seven nonfiction works before his death.

*Last and First Men: A Story of the Near and Far Future* was Stapledon's first novel and was well received by critics and readers. He preferred to dub it a "romance of the future" rather than science fiction, despite the fact that he was perhaps the greatest influence after H. G. Wells upon post–World War II science fiction writing. Stapledon himself both praised and criticized Wells, so he wrote without any Wellsian aura and in fact chose not to affiliate his work with any utopian tradition. *Last and First Men* spans a mind-boggling two billion years detailing 18 different species of humans struggling with their own kind as well as with the universe for existence and happiness. Stapledon's theme is present throughout his story of the rapid evolution of human history: How can mankind accept its fate? In the end Stapledon suggested that only among the First Men, in thinkers such as Socrates, Jesus, and Buddha, was there a hint of the appropriate vision of humanity's destiny. Unable to coordinate their technological mastery, the First Men—200 million people—destroyed themselves except for 35 survivors at the North Pole. Over a long period, the survivors developed the Second level, which seemed to be a utopian existence, but a Martian assault extending over thousands of years caused the Second Men to resort to force and then to suffer internal wars. Still, the resourceful humans exposed the Martians to a virus that ended the threat but that also infected humans, causing a slow atrophy of brain power over millions of years. Not until the Fifth Men arrived did the humans achieve the same level of existence as the Second Men. Fifth Men established a high standard of living without social divisions or international conflicts. By studying past horrors, Fifth Men became acutely aware of their fleeting existence and the likelihood of future human extinction, yet they admired the beauty of the mind and its potential for positive creativity.

When the moon's orbit began to inch closer to the earth (again over millions of years), endangering its existence, the Fifth Men prepared for an evacuation to Venus. In order to make the Venusian atmosphere livable, the human scientists had to kill the existing life-forms on Venus, yet the action was justified in a fashion similar to First Men's justification of imperialism or wars. Nonetheless, the Fifth Men eventually succumbed mentally to guilt about perpetrating a genocide on Venus. Fifth Men began to mutate into semihumans, blending with birds and mammals to produce Sixth Men who lacked many human qualities. Fairly soon, a Seventh stage emerged, a species of flying, carefree, even irresponsible artists. Nature deprived the Seventh Men of a necessary nutrient, which ended their ability to fly. Their successors, Eighth Men, were physically large; they faced cosmic threats when the sun began to shrink. The only viable space habitat was Neptune, but the Eighth Men had to breed a smaller human version, Ninth Men, to make the trip. Stapledon then moves rapidly to the Fifteenth Men, who seek to eliminate the "five great evils" of humanity: disease, work, aging, social division, and conflict. Thus the Sixteenth Men closely resemble Fifth Men in their physical and mental capacities, yet they still remained confounded by the mysteries of the universe. Even the superior Seventeenth Men were unable to fathom the universe's mysteries, but the Eighteenth (and last) Men seemed to possess the attributes necessary to achieve bliss: longevity, sexual freedom, and a telepathic psychological unity of all the species. Nonetheless, the Eighteenth Men faced impending disaster from the sun's dissolution; they frantically sought a means to plant the species on other planets. Social disruptions and scarcity of resources reappeared, requiring the application of force and the threat of war. On the verge of the end of mankind, Stapledon introduced a mysterious messianic figure, "the last born of the Last Men," who reflected Stapledon's portrayal of human history as a piece of music.

Stapledon's *First and Last Men* contained the essence of his literary philosophy, and there were several sequels that remained true to that original work. The first sequel, *Last Men in London* (1932), was followed by others suggesting that Stapledon engaged in a sort of rewriting process over the next two decades. Interestingly, Stapledon wrote a brief radio drama in 1931 intended for broadcast on the BBC, but it was only revived by the Olaf Stapledon Society in 1977. Much of the skit focused upon Stapledon's dislike of and prediction of U.S. dominance of the future. Three of the 18 species outlined in the book appeared in the radio drama: the Fourth, Seventh, and Eighteenth Men. Stapledon also reiterated in the radio script the philosophical concerns of *Last and First Men*: relativity of time, humanity's ultimate extinction, and mankind's ability to accept that result. Stapledon might agree that timing is everything, but his own work seemed out of place in the period in which it appeared, and *Last and First Men* failed to halt the decline of utopias; nor did it mitigate the emergence of the dystopia in the second quarter of the twentieth century. Aldous Huxley's *Brave New World* (1932) had a much more profound impact on both the literary genre and the reading public than *Last and First Men*.

*See also* Science Fiction Anti-Utopias; Science and Society Movement.

*Reference* Fiedler, Leslie A. *Olaf Stapledon: A Man Divided* (1983).

## *The Last Man* (1826)

Noted for her innovative fantastic tale *Frankenstein* (1818), the forerunner of modern science fiction, Mary Shelley also penned a utopian work revolving around the role of revolution in the modern era, *The Last Man*. At the very time when utopian theories were beginning to be put into widespread practice, Shelley offered a devastating critique of utopian values. Shelley's last-man syndrome would become immensely popular with dystopian writers of the twentieth century.

The daughter of the radical philosopher William Godwin and the historian Mary Wollstonecraft, both devotees of the Enlightenment, Mary Wollstonecraft Shelley (1797–1851) married the famous romantic poet Percy Bysshe Shelley in 1817. She acquired a voracious appetite for reading and learned Latin, French, Italian, and some Greek. In *The Last Man* she continued a pattern of apocalyptic writing evidenced to some degree in *Frankenstein*, subtitled *The Modern Prometheus*, as well as in works by George Byron and Alfred Tennyson. With the fall of the Napoleonic Empire, the termination of the Holy Roman Empire, and the crumbling of the European portions of the Ottoman Turkish Empire in the early nineteenth century, many Romantic writers imbued with nationalism foresaw a sweeping upheaval that would alter the face of Europe's map. It appeared to be a watershed era ushering in the dominance of the nation-state. Some critics have sought in Shelley's *The Last Man* hidden meanings related to the deaths of Percy Shelley (1822) and Byron (1824), both of whom appear briefly in the work under fictional names. Certainly, it was difficult for Mary Shelley to recover emotionally from the accidental drowning of her husband. She continued to travel around Europe until her death.

*The Last Man* is a complex work that incorporates several elements: a memorial to Percy Shelley and Lord Byron, a survey of revolutionary movements, and an appreciation of the phenomenon of Napoleon. But it also examines utopianism at the very moment of the movement's transition from a literary mode to an experimental communitarian tradition. The setting of *The Last Man* is the twenty-first century, when a plague obliterates the human race. There are varied efforts at both reform and revolution aimed at forestalling the inevitable outcome, but each measure ends in failure and the apocalypse arrives as feared. Whereas many eighteenth-century writers used disease metaphors as a vehicle to express a hopeful outlook at the prospect for revolutionary achievements, Shelley used the same metaphors in an entirely negative fashion. Society does not recover from the fevers of revolution and experience regeneration; Shelley's disease is fatal. It is ironic that her fatalistic position regarding revolutions imitates the views of her parents' philosophical arch-rival, Edmund Burke. Shelley's narrator in *The Last Man* quotes from Burke's writings in several places. Burke opposed the Enlightenment concept of the abstract social contract and the view that it could be instituted by revolutionary means; he believed, instead, that societies fared better by reforming their existing constitutions and institutions. Thus Shelley allied herself with the Enlightenment's chief philosophical anta-gonist for a purpose: She rejected the philosophy of her parents by challenging the doctrine of progress. Yet in the end Shelley also rejected Burke's truism that civilization can survive and recover from revolutions.

One of Shelley's chief characters, Lionel Verney, returns to England from participation in the Greek revolt against the Turks with a sense of foreboding about the plague. He laments the fact that his own son and other school-aged youths, otherwise destined to become national leaders, will never have that opportunity. In *The Last Man*, nature, so revered by the Enlightenment along with reason, has become disordered and humans have lost control of their destiny. Revolutions, like the plague, intimate the loss of respect for human values such as wisdom and order.

Shelley also rejected her father's anarchistic utopianism, expounded in his *Enquiry Concerning Political Justice* (1793). Among other things, Godwin had argued that the advancing knowledge of humanity and science would eventually obliterate disease. Godwin believed that the primary obstacle to the realization of utopia was unrestrained population growth. Shelley examined her father's theory in order to refute it. One of her characters, the political leader Adrian, favors the implementation of a Godwin-like utopia that could eliminate disease by simply willing its demise. Instead of prospective utopias, Shelley gives us unrelenting disasters in which a hostile rather than a friendly nature is impervious to the human will.

Shelley goes further in rejecting utopianism by constructing various projects designed to achieve progress and then shows that they undermine rather than uplift humanity. The character Lord Raymond (that is, Byron) travels to Greece to aid the liberation of repressed peoples as a revolutionary general. Yet noble dreams and motives devolve into disastrous failure and attempts to blame the result on supernatural forces, the inhuman monster of the plague. Upon defeating the Turks and capturing Constantinople, Raymond acquires a vacated city that was obliterated by the plague. Raymond contracts the disease and dies, thus inadvertently becoming an instrument for the spread of the plague. Meanwhile, a stunned Verney returns to England to contemplate the apocalypse, which includes panic, storms, fires, floods, and famines in addition to the ravages of the disease. How can humanity reason with disease? Thus the very nature that the philosophers had worshipped turned out not only to be uncontrollable but also devastating to the human race.

**Reference** Sterrenburg, Lee. "*The Last Man: Anatomy of Failed Revolutions*" (1978).

## Le Corbusier
*See* The Radiant City.

## Le Guin, Ursula
*See* Feminist Utopias; Lunar Utopias.

## Lenin, V. I. U.
*See* Bolshevism.

## Lewis, Sinclair
*See It Can't Happen Here.*

## Lindsay, David
*See A Voyage to Arcturus.*

## Llano Colony
The Llano colony, the last of the socialist-inspired utopian communities in the United States was launched in California by a socialist Los Angeles lawyer, Job Harriman, in 1914. He was indirectly associated with the Altruria community in the Sonoma Valley after 1894. The Llano colony lasted into the Great Depression before it was liquidated in 1939.

Job Harriman (1861–1925) was a native of Indiana and trained for the ministry before switching to the law and moving to California in 1886. His combined training in theology and the law convinced him that although humanity was not naturally sinful, exploitation (chiefly by capitalists) prevented the triumph of the self-evident social principles of socialism. Soon deeply involved in socialist programs, including a Nationalist Club, Harriman ran unsuccessfully for governor of California under the Socialist Labor Party banner in 1898. Then in 1900, Harriman was nominated as the vice presidential running mate of Eugene V. Debs on the Socialist Party ticket. Following his defeat in the election, Harriman resumed his law practice for several years. However, politics continued to stir him, and he entered the contest for mayor of Los Angeles in 1911, again running as the Socialist Party candidate but with imposing labor union support. The primary issue in the election concerned charges against James and John McNamara, two American

Federation of Labor members who were accused of bombing the offices of the *Los Angeles Times*. Because Harriman championed the brothers' innocence, when they confessed to the crime days before the election, Harriman's chances were doomed. Thereafter Harriman retired from politics to concentrate on launching a new cooperative community based on egalitarian principles. He was convinced that if socialism could demonstrate greater economic efficiency than capitalism, it would replace capitalism. In the meantime a socialist demonstration was needed to draw attention away from capitalism.

Successfully soliciting support from some well-heeled capitalist backers, Harriman obtained 9,000 acres in the Antelope Valley north of Los Angeles from the virtually bankrupt Mescal Water and Land Company and named his enterprise the Llano del Rio Company. Sitting between two mountain ranges at about 3,500 feet above sea level, the valley had arable land with the potential for the production of fruits and vegetables, its chief insufficiency being fertilizer. The project would be underwritten by the sale of stock, which began in 1913, and advertising spread across most of the socialist press despite the fact that many socialists criticized Harriman for compromising with capitalist methods. Harriman bought the *Western Comrade* journal in 1914, wherein the colony's prospectus was published. Prospective members were required to purchase 2,000 shares of stock, which could be partially financed from the four-dollars-a-day wage paid by the company. All necessary provisions for the farming of the land would be maintained by the company, and members would be given two weeks vacation per annum. Only five people were on hand for the official opening of the colony on May Day 1914, but the initial growth was significant: Eight months later 150 colonists lived at Llano. Most of the early settlers came from the middle class rather than the working class despite the openly socialist character of the founders. Colonists owned a modest number of cattle in

addition to farming the land. Couples lived in tents at first, and a community center was the first permanent structure. Soon other buildings appeared, including a post office, dairy barn, and laundry.

The Llano colony continued to attract new settlers up to World War I, reaching a total of 1,100 by 1917. There were frequent clashes among the population from the outset, however, and the turnover ratio was large. The tent housing was quickly replaced by numerous adobe clay structures for residences, and there was a dramatic increase in agricultural and industrial buildings, including barns, a flour mill, cannery, sawmill, brickyard, and cabinet shop. A hotel and schools also were built, and the *Western Comrade* had become a weekly paper at Llano by 1916. Harriman had even more grandiose plans for future improvements in an elaborate blueprint drawn up in 1915, a miniature version of which was placed in a dormitory in 1917. The farmers utilized modern irrigation techniques and extensive mechanization along with widely varied livestock breeding. Yet problems began to appear to plague the experiment. The State of California cited Llano for violating pure water and price-fixing laws in 1915. Harriman skillfully incorporated a branch of the Llano colony in neighboring Nevada and then had the Nevada company buy out the California company, all to avoid state regulation. The internal problems were more serious mainly because the economic practices at Llano were unprofitable. Residents complained about poor housing and food and insufficient water.

Harriman was not oblivious to these problems and sought a new location for the colony by purchasing 2,000 acres near the lumber town of Stables, Louisiana (near the Texas border) in 1917. Careful to portray the action as an expansion of the colony rather than admitting failure in California, Harriman oversaw the movement of a handful of Llano residents to Louisiana, even though most of the California industries and the printing operations were moved. The Louisiana colony had grown to about 300 settlers by 1918. The town of Stables was renamed New Llano, but the settlement struggled continually in the first three years. After quarreling with small farmer settlers from Texas, most of the California trekkers left Louisiana, which required that some acreage be sold to keep the colony afloat. Harriman spent most of these years in California trying to maintain the remnant of Llano. There were only 15 families left at New Llano by 1919, but the colony was reorganized in 1920 under the leadership of Harriman's right-hand man, George Pickett, a proficient recruiter and salesman. Lumber, brick, and dairy production were under way by 1921. A school, electric plant, and new highway added to the revival spirit.

By the time Job Harriman died in 1925 he had become disillusioned with the Llano experiment and his utopian ideals. He had been unprepared for the economic and human exigencies of planting communities and making them succeed. The avowedly nonpolitical Pickett became the titular leader of New Llano in Louisiana and moved the colony toward more aggressive non-Marxist socialist methods than Harriman had permitted. The wage system and money itself were abolished, the means of production were vested in the colony, and food preparation and meals were entirely communal. The colony provided all welfare benefits to the settlers, including health care and schools. Still, the colony's most successful financial venture was an ice plant that started in 1925. By 1926 the population in the Louisiana colony was about 250. The depression following 1929 caused many unemployed people to move to Llano—for survival more than for ideological reasons—raising the population to 500. The population at New Llano was much more diverse than that of the California colony. They ranged from avowed Marxists sympathetic toward the Soviet Union to simple farmers completely disinterested in ideology. The diversity led to groups challenging Pickett's leadership; one such challenge involved a massive legal battle in

1927–1928, which Pickett won. Pickett's most successful antagonist was Ernest Webb, who arrived from the California colony in 1931. Webb favored more democratic governance in Louisiana and found considerable backing for his schemes, the most important of which was the Welfare League, a type of labor union. Pickett's domination of New Llano ended in 1935 with a democratic rebellion led by Eugene Carl that allowed all residents over 18 years of age to vote. Yet thanks to impending bankruptcy, Pickett had once again assumed the dominant leadership position by 1936. Even Pickett was unable to prevent the continued decline of the economic fortunes of the colony, which was liquidated during 1938–1939. The century-old ideal of a cooperative commonwealth seemed to die its last breath with the collapse of Llano.

*Reference* Conkin, Paul. *Two Paths to Utopia: The Hutterites and the Llano Colony* (1964).

## London, Jack
*See The Iron Heel.*

## Looking Backward: 2000–1887 (1884)
The American socialist Edward Bellamy composed an extremely influential, if typical, late-nineteenth-century version of utopia in *Looking Backward: 2000–1887* (1884) and its sequel, *Equality* (1897). *Looking Backward* became the second-best-selling U.S. book of the nineteenth century with 500,000 copies sold by 1900. It was also the most popular U.S. utopia and influenced the production of another five dozen utopias during the 1890s. Bellamy's influence extended beyond the United States to Europe, where he was openly admired by other socialists, including H. G. Wells in England and Jean Jaurès in France. Also, there were more translated editions of *Looking Backward* in Russia than in any other foreign country. Believing utopia to be a real possibility, Bellamy combined the elements of Auguste Comte's scientific positivism with the socialist goal of redis-

tribution of property. Bellamy's utopia resembled the classical utopias in its static, nondynamic nature.

Born in New England at the height of the Transcendentalist movement, Edward Bellamy (1850–1898) toured Europe when he was 18, following the Civil War. He worked for newspapers in New York and Massachusetts before turning to literature. Soon after publishing *Looking Backward*, Bellamy helped found the Nationalist Club in 1888 to promote his idea of utopia. There were 165 Nationalist Clubs, led by Thomas W. Higginson and largely independent of Bellamy's control, chartered in the United States by 1891. Bellamy also supported the launching of a monthly journal, *The Nationalist*, during 1889–1891 and later issued a weekly journal, *New Nation*, both of which touted his utopian notions. Bellamy's clubs and journals actively supported the Populist (Peoples') Party in the early 1890s. Despite the fact that his father was a Baptist minister, Bellamy departed from traditional religion and even the Transcendentalist self-help philosophy in devising his utopia. Even an event such as the Civil War was interpreted by Bellamy as an expression of the human struggle for freedom rather than as a great national crisis. Bellamy believed his Nationalist Club movement was a direct heir of the utopian communities such as Brook Farm. Yet Nationalism—once called American socialism by Bellamy—focused upon society rather than the individual. He regarded *Looking Backward* as a prediction of the next stage of the industrial state's development. Though some contemporary critics thought Bellamy's fantastic utopia actually diverted attention away from solving existing problems, the Nationalist movement influenced the broad Progressive reforms that swept the nation before World War I.

*Looking Backward* begins with the chief character, Julian West, waking in the year 2000 after having fallen asleep in the year 1887. In the new society, West finds that the United States has created a new economic policy that has been adopted by the

*Edward Bellamy*

other nations of the world, all organized into a vast federation. The main value in the ideal world of 2000 is economic equality, and the book dwells upon the theme that material conditions—not human nature—have altered over the 113-year period. Bellamy felt that previous utopian focus upon issues such as morals was a waste of time since human nature, which is basically good, can only be facilitated by altering the material environment and that with the achievement of economic equality, other social, cultural, and political values will fall into place as the socialist ideal becomes reality. The industrial masses in *Looking Backward* have created not only equality but also efficiency, which had never been realized under capitalism. Nonetheless, the new society contains a managerial hierarchy and provides for merit advancement, with workers being ranked by their achievements. Yet the capitalist motive of gain has been replaced by one of service to the interests of the larger community.

The strict social organization and ranks in *Looking Backward* probably reflected a fear—both latent and expressed—felt by many socialists that there would be anarchy if discipline was altogether eliminated. Bellamy's utopia anticipated H. G. Wells's one-world government as well as the twentieth-century welfare state. The primary function of the state was simply to make the economy run smoothly. There was little emphasis upon the role of education beyond its function in the workplace. Because socialists such as Bellamy saw the value of education only in economic terms, they had criticized educational systems in their states. Bellamy believed that educational pursuits were best left to individual choice, in part because education could not modify human nature. Moreover, when economic competition was eliminated and human motives modified accordingly, people would be free to make their own choices, including the level of their education.

Bellamy's view of crime was also economically based since he felt that all crime resulted from inequality in material possessions. By placing property in the control of the state, Bellamy's utopia had practically eliminated crimes of violence. The crimes that remained, products of recidivism from the past, were dealt with as a sickness by sending the criminal to a doctor or hospital. Bellamy's views on treatment of criminals may have been borrowed in part from Samuel Butler's *Erewhon* (1872), which treated crimes as diseases. The human desire for acclaim also extended to competition in the arts, where Bellamy's standard was fairness rather than egocentrism. Still, Bellamy's notion of equality did not seem to extend beyond the economic realm. Basic human passions, biological and emotional, were not considered factors that might influence Bellamy's utopia.

As a believer in the idea of progress, Bellamy created a utopia that evolved from one generation to the next toward an ultimate goal of perfection. Yet once the world-state and economic equality were achieved, Bellamy did not foresee any further changes. When a heaven on earth is achieved, why would any further changes be necessary? In *Equality* Bellamy considered the question of whether continuing improvement of methods to assure an abundance of material goods would be a sufficient basis for change in the human mental frame of reference. He argued that economic equality would be accompanied by both intellectual and spiritual development among the utopians, which would make them godlike. The intellectual and spiritual change that Bellamy permitted for his utopians seemed confined to the elimination of the human connection with the earlier, pre-utopian frame of reference. Thus the only changes Bellamy envisioned were the elimination of the capitalist past and the consolidation of present utopian techniques. History is only useful to show a contrast between evil and virtue. Otherwise, the twenty-first century cannot comprehend the nineteenth. The limits of change in Bellamy's utopia can best be represented by the absence of political activity, which would presume the desire for changes. A one-world government precluded the function of political action, which was subordinated to the economic factors.

In *Looking Backward* and *Equality*, Bellamy conformed to most modern utopian constructions by refusing to provide an objective reality to judge utopia as an alternative to the existing system. Thus works such as Bellamy's become useful only as critiques of the present. Bellamy was determined to assail the capitalist system rather than the capitalists who profited from the system since he believed that only human motives, and not human nature, could be altered. Unlike the utopian socialists, who wanted to replace capitalism's competition with cooperation, Bellamy had no such naive faith in changing human nature. Thus his utopia would impose a system that allowed the substitution of the motive of equality for the profit motive. Indeed, perhaps the problem inherent in capitalism related to the stress on individual initiative, which was effectively muted in Bellamy's utopia. If there is no competition, there is no need for initiative. Bellamy's utopians sought recognition only, and their rewards were limited to honorific badges rather than profits. Bellamy wanted not to escape from the urban-industrial society but to confront and reform it. In his utopia, workers would be able to balance effort and reward where capitalism had diminished both. Lewis Mumford wrote that *Looking Backward* was "the archetypal megamachine" that sowed the seeds of the totalitarian and welfare states. Yet it is fair to say that Bellamy, like so many utopian thinkers, was simply naive about state socialism's impact upon individual freedom. Bellamy, like other modern utopian writers, understood that readers would not be attracted by the description of utopia as much as by the criticism of present evils. The utopia, therefore, became a method of testing an ideal or a dream of a better society without necessarily providing a genuine standard for judging the present.

The enormous popularity of *Looking Backward* and *Equality* led to some attempts at practical application. Probably the best known experiment was the Equality colony near Edison, Washington, known originally as Brotherhood of the Cooperative Commonwealth, which was founded in 1895 by J. E. Pelton. Several sites were eventually settled, and the population grew to a few hundred well-educated middle-class residents, complemented by several thousand nonresident members. The Equality colony published a newspaper, *Industrial Freedom*, which blended Bellamy's ideas with those of other socialists. After the population had dwindled to only three dozen by 1904, the colony ended its communism and reorganized along the lines of Theodor Hertzka's Freeland constitution. Yet the infiltration of anarchists from New York divided the group and led to Equality's dissolution in 1907.

*Reference* Becker, George J. "Edward Bellamy" (1954); Bowman, Sylvia E. *The Year 2000: A Critical Biography of Edward Bellamy* (1958).

## *Lord of the Flies* (1954)

In keeping with the dystopian tradition in the twentieth century, William Golding's anti-utopian novel *Lord of the Flies* repels as it fascinates. Golding was drawn to the dark side of humanity and devised a thought experiment to test his theories. Thinking in terms of a fable, he imagined the most inhuman and implausible circumstances for his context, a group of young boys forced to struggle for survival on an isolated island. What happens when humans nurtured on the illusions of civilization face the evil reality inherent in themselves? Golding described his motives in writing *Lord of the Flies*: "to trace the defects of society back to the defects of human nature." Thus, unlike most utopists, he was not so much interested in offering criticism of his society as in exploring the relationship between humanity and nature. Golding questioned whether Voltaire's description of man's inhumanity to man could be rectified by applying the tools of reason. Was nature the dominating feature shaping society rather than human reason? He also seemed drawn to the portrayal of human selfishness by Thomas Hobbes.

William Golding (1911–1993) was fascinated by the Robinsonade genre of utopian literature, particularly by Robert Michael Ballantyne's *The Coral Island* (1858). Ballantyne's story recounted the successful struggle for survival by shipwrecked British youth which was an uplifting judgment about humanity. Yet Golding felt that Ballantyne's tale had been misleading in its portrayal of human responses to threats to existence. Golding feared that humans would respond with barbaric cruelty rather than generous cooperation in such a setting, especially after viewing the barbarities of totalitarianism in World War II and the postwar potential for nuclear holocaust. Obviously, Golding believed that humanity's true nature was one of evil selfishness rather than humanitarianism.

In *Lord of the Flies*, an airplane carrying boys away from a nuclear war crash-lands on a tropical island, whose sheer beauty and natural bounty suggest an idyllic potential. Chief characters such as Ralph and Simon are captivated and intimidated by the natural surroundings. The boys initially agree to organize their new society and overcome their fear of their surroundings by recognizing that they can control their environment. However, soon enough a split develops between Ralph and Jack over how to deal with their newfound freedom. Ralph believes they should embrace maturity and responsibility, whereas Jack and most of the boys retreat into childish immaturity and eventual savagery. Thus Golding makes it clear from the outset that the appearance of evil does not reside in the island but in the humans who occupy it. Moreover, the movement from democratic participation to despotism in the island's governance is accompanied by unnecessary violence. Golding does not resort to veiled metaphors for the meaning of his symbols: The sow's head, for example, is dubbed the "Lord of the Flies," or Beelzebub in Greek. There are no multiple meanings such as might be derived from similar works like Joseph Conrad's *Heart of Darkness*.

In the end, Golding contrasted the roles of children and adults with the ability to handle freedom and responsibility. He delved into the insecurity and craven tendencies of humanity in the example of children forced to become adults due to the survival circumstances. At a time when many in the contemporary world focused upon the fear of atomic holocaust, Golding pointed out that the consequences of fear of freedom and responsibility were more profound than the concern about survival of the human race. Golding also comes to grips with the most baffling problem of utopists since Thomas More, how to ensure an ordered society without imposing authoritarian rule. Golding suggested in his contrasting characters Ralph and Jack that only if order derives from within the person (Ralph) could a true utopia be achieved. Society's essence is determined less by the structure of its political system than by the ethical fiber of the people. Yet most often order is imposed from outside the person (Jack) because of human inability to mature to

responsibility, an inability for the whole society as well as the individual.

Though it was his first novel, *Lord of the Flies* has continued to be regarded as Golding's most important work. Other survival works by Golding followed, especially *Pincher Martin* (1956), but none had the starkness of his maiden work. *Lord of the Flies* became especially popular in English literature classes on college campuses during the 1950s and 1960s. A movie version appeared in 1964, and Golding's survival story merited several imitations in both print and celluloid. Certainly, Golding challenged the Enlightenment notion of human rationality by focusing upon the natural evil in a less bizarre and thereby more compelling fashion than Huxley's *Brave New World* or Orwell's *1984*. *Lord of the Flies* provides a warning about how humanity's animal nature can subdue reason.

**See also** Robinsonades.

**References** Mitchell, Charles. "The *Lord of the Flies* and the Escape from Freedom," *Arizona Quarterly* 22 (1966): 27–40; Woodward, Kathleen. "On Aggression: William Golding's *Lord of the Flies*," in Rabkin, Eric S., Martin H. Greenburg, and Joseph D. Olander, eds. *No Place Else: Explorations in Utopian and Dystopian Fiction* (1983).

## Lunar Utopias

In the seventeenth and again in the twentieth centuries, some utopists located their utopias beyond the earth on moons. The idea of starting an ideal society in a place drastically removed from present society has been a part of utopian constructions since that of Thomas More. However, most locations, even when fictional, have been on earth, on islands or cities separated from the surrounding corrupt society. The desire for a clean break with the earth suggests that the lunar utopists were not interested in persuading the existing society on earth to imitate their system. Thus lunar utopias tend to be both unreal and impractical by their very physical location. Perhaps the earliest lunar utopia was Francis Godwin's 1638 *The Man in the Moone*, followed closely by *L'Autre Monde*

*Ursula K. Le Guin during a 1985 interview in San Francisco*

*ou les Etats et Empires de la Lune* (1657), the moon voyage utopia by Savinien de Cyrano de Bergerac. At the beginning of the twentieth century, H. G. Wells's *First Men in the Moon* rekindled interest in lunar locations for utopias. More recent examples in the late twentieth century include Ursula Le Guin's *The Dispossessed* and Samuel R. Delany's *Triton*. Only when astronauts landed on the moon in 1969 was the image of a utopia on earth's moon replaced by moons from more far-flung planets.

Because of their classical education, many early modern intellectuals were familiar with the ancient Roman writer Plutarch's speculation that the goddess Persephone was queen of the moon. Such a notion led some ancients to place the location of Homer's Elysium on the moon. Much popular attention focused upon the Scientific Revolution in the seventeenth century. When the Italian astronomer Galileo Galilei described extraterrestrial planets in motion in his *Sidereus Nuncius* (1610), it caught the imagination of the European intellectuals. Ben Jonson popularized the new astronomy in several plays, including *News from the New World Discovered in the Moon* (1620), and John Donne made reference to travel to the moon in his poems. The German mathematician Johannes Kepler's *Somnium* (1634), describing a dreamlike trip to the moon, was written about 1609 and circulated in

manuscript form before publication.

Francis Godwin (1562–1633), who served as bishop of Hereford in England, was fascinated with the idea of creating a "new world" in a celestial place beyond earth. Godwin had read speculations from explorers that Native Americans might have traveled from other planets as aliens to earth. Hence his image of the lunar aliens strongly resembled those American primitives. Like other intellectuals of the era, the new astronomy also intrigued Godwin. He may have read John Wilkins's *The Discovery of a World in the Moone* (1638) before completing his fictional moon voyage. Wilkins, a leading figure in the founding of the Royal Society, matter-of-factly speculated about possible spaceship voyages to the moon and even about the possibility of planting human colonies on the moon. Although the idea of space travel and even alien beings would provide grist for the science fiction mills over the following centuries, it also allowed utopian writers to utilize venues for their utopias far removed from earth as well as civilization. It was easy enough to mingle fact with fiction when creating an ideal society beyond the pale of existing human settlements.

In *The Man in the Moone; or, a Discourse of a Voyage Thither* (1638), Godwin presented a fictional narrator-traveler named Domingo Gonzales from Spain. As an experienced explorer, Gonzales had traveled across the Atlantic seeking precious minerals in the New World, and on one journey he landed on the island of St. Helena. There he discovered a distinct variety of large birds called "gansas," which he used to pull a makeshift airplane to fly to the moon. The text contains a sketch of the aerial vehicle. Gonzales found a society of intelligent giants who had migrated to the moon from the earth in an earlier era. Except for their size, the moon people resembled the primitive peoples of the New World in the Americas. The Arcadian moon kingdom was ruled by an absolute monarch assisted by 24 princes, and various levels of social classes existed. Because the monarch had established laws and institutions that were readily embraced by the populace, there was no need for lawyers. Likewise, since the climate—without seasonal changes—and nutrients were adequate, there were no physicians because no sickness existed among the lunarians. Oddly, the lunar society also contained miscreants who more closely resembled earthlings in size and who were banished to earth since they did not obey lunar rules. Hence, Gonzales reasoned that he had known some of these lunar exiles on his travels to new lands. Upon leaving the moon, Gonzales resumed his flight with the birds and aerial machine, landing on a mountaintop in China.

Godwin was a direct and perhaps the most important influence upon another lunar utopia published in France in the 1650s. Savinien de Cyrano de Bergerac (1619–1655) was the author of *L'Autre Monde ou les Etats et Empires de la Lune*, written about 1648 but not published until two years after Cyrano de Bergerac's death, in 1657. Unfortunately, the first edition was not only edited by Henri Le Bret but expurgated so as to alter much of Cyrano de Bergerac's meaning. De Bergerac had a reputation as a libertine and engaged in a running feud with the Catholic church; Le Bret hoped to rehabilitate his friend's name and thus censored anti-Catholic references in *L'Autre Monde*. In 1659 the lunar utopia was reissued together with a similar story about a voyage to the sun. Cyrano de Bergerac was a soldier by profession, but he became known to posterity for his writing. He was acquainted with many seventeenth-century notables, including the scientist Pierre Gassendi and the philosopher René Descartes.

Godwin's influence upon Cyrano de Bergerac can be measured by similarities, including the size of the moon people, reduced gravity on the moon, and the vitality and longevity of the lunarians. Significantly, Godwin's *Man in the Moone* was published in a French translation in 1648, the same year that Cyrano de Bergerac is believed to have composed *L'Autre Monde*. His primary purpose in writing the utopia was not so much to design an ideal society as to satirize his own times. In that respect, he was an imitator of Renaissance satire, especially that of François Rabelais, and a precursor of Jonathan Swift's inimitable satirical style. A secondary motive must have been to publicize recent knowledge revealed by the new science. After various experiments with flying, the fictional character Cyrano finally propelled himself to the moon by rocket. Some pages were devoted to parodying the paradise story in Genesis (omitted from the first edition by Le Bret). Captured by moon creatures who walked on all fours, the smaller, two-footed Cyrano was deemed an oddity and taken to their city, where he was assigned to a resident to be trained as a circus animal. Soon, one of the moon creatures conversed with Cyrano in Greek, which allowed him to be rescued from the humiliation of being treated like an animal. Cyrano learned of the existence of settlements on the sun, which would provide the basis for an extension of the story left incomplete by Cyrano de Bergerac in 1650. The lunarians received nutrition from vapors rather than food, which guaranteed health and longevity. Like Godwin's lunar society, Cyrano's utopia was ruled by an absolute monarch, though Cyrano did not describe the laws or political institutions since he had no preferences on polity. The lunar utopia did contain a parliament of birds, which may reveal Cyrano de Bergerac's ideal of representative government but also may simply suggest his belief in the equality of all living creatures. The role of the birds also presages Swift's Houyhnhnms. Since there is disagreement about important symbols, some scholars have been reluctant to classify *L'Autre Monde* as a utopia. Although wars existed in the lunar society, various controls made them less destructive, and intellect was given much greater recognition than battlefield victories.

Both Godwin and Cyrano de Bergerac found imitators in the eighteenth century.

In 1751, Godwin's scenario was replicated by Ralph Morris in *A Narrative of the Life and Astonishing Adventures of John Daniel*. After being stranded on an island, the narrator and his mechanically minded son build an airplane that allows them to travel to the moon. There the human visitors encounter a race of superior people resembling primitive natives from the southwestern part of North America. In 1706, Tom d'Urfey published *Wonders in the Sun or the Kingdom of the Birds*, which borrowed heavily from characters in Cyrano de Bergerac's *L'Autre Monde*. D'Urfey included a section paralleling Cyrano de Bergerac's paean to the four-legged lunarians.

By the middle of the nineteenth century, science fiction works had become commonplace. Jules Verne's *From Earth to the Moon* (1863) wrote of rocket-powered space vehicles to propel fictional astronauts to the moon. Another late Victorian who mingled science fiction and utopian ideas was H. G. Wells. His *First Men in the Moon* (1901) combined elements of technological potential for space travel with a story about two astronauts who discover a lunarian society, the Selenites. Wells's lunarians appear less than human in many respects. Their massive brainpower had caused other parts of the Selenite bodies to atrophy to the point of being grotesque. The Selenite society headed by an authoritarian Grand Lunar is extremely rigid and organized into castes, although their scientific prowess has assured abundance and established peace. The Selenites appear more like robots than humans, and Wells's depiction seems more anti-utopian than utopian since he does not really hold up the Selenites as a viable alternative to the flawed human society.

Following the concerted attempts of utopists in the nineteenth century to create viable utopias and the twentieth-century rejection of those ideals in a variety of dystopias, it proved difficult for utopists in the second half of the twentieth century to overcome skepticism about utopias. Hence in the work of Ursula K. Le Guin (b. 1929) and Samuel R. Delany

(b. 1942), a return to the extraterrestrial settings of a lunar society became an appealing alternative to earthly settings. Yet following the U.S. astronauts' landing on the moon in 1969, earth's moon lacked the degree of separation that Le Guin and Delany needed to locate their space colonies. Hence they used the moons of far-flung planets for their utopias, and those moons' neighboring planets provided the contrast of imperfect societies like those on earth. Le Guin's *The Dispossessed* and Delany's *Triton* employed the anarchist model for their lunar societies. Yet the inspiration for these two experimental utopias was different; Le Guin drew upon the more traditional reliance upon reason, albeit from both Oriental and Occidental origins, to produce a harmonious and moral society. Delany, however, reflected his fascination with the structuralism of French philosopher-historian Michel Foucault in rejecting system making in favor of seeking a common human denominator in mental structures. Nonetheless, as the titles of their works suggest, neither considered their utopias as genuine blueprints but only as "ambiguous" utopias. Clearly, they revealed the general public suspicion attached to any proposed ideal society by the 1970s.

There are two contrasting societies in Le Guin's *The Dispossessed* (1974), the planet Urras and the moon Anarres. On Urras, society is organized around a totalitarian system even though the three different sections pursue varying methods of organizing society. Captured Odonian rebels on Urras were transported as punishment to the moon of Anarres where they were forced to remain united in order to survive in a place of scarcity. Le Guin used the setting of a desperate necessity for survival to create a moral impetus to work together. The Odonian rebels established an anarchist society with complete individual freedom and no private property. Yet over time even Anarres became corrupted because the rebels sought to separate themselves from their history on Urras. Ideals and ambition became problems on

Anarres since they imply an unequal status. The rejection of the past required remembering the past (without a past or a future, there cannot be a present), so individual freedom was transformed by the revolutionary society on Anarres into a homogenized cultural conventionality that was antithetical to freedom. Le Guin thus subtly criticized the socialist ideal—from the utopian socialists to Marx—that individuals left to choose freely would all agree to establish the same type of society. She also engaged the tension between the creation of an ideal organization for society and the desire for human freedom and creativity. The chief character, Shevek, a scientist seeking a utopian solution to society's dilemmas, reflects that tension effectively.

Samuel Delany relied upon the structuralist pursuit of common *mentalités* to portray individuals at the mercy of conditions rather than capable of shaping their destiny. In *Triton* (1977) Delany seeks to show that even if reason prevails and a moral, social, and political ideal system can be constructed, life is not so simplistic or uncomplicated. *Triton*'s chief character, Bron, is a mathematician living on a moon of Neptune gripped by conflicting sides of his personality. Those schizoid tensions and feeling of incapacity are eventually resolved by the ultimate transformation, from man to woman. The residents of Triton are organized around group identities rather than as individuals. They are not truly humans but merely elements of biological and social structures. Still, the society on Triton can be described as anarchist since there are no authoritarian controls. The questions that the various groupings might raise about their existence have no answers, so, rather than a strict unity as in Le Guin's utopia, Delany's utopia features a heterotopia of plural options lacking uniform standards or coordinated organization. Indeed, the presumption of a fixed mental arrangement precludes any possibility of a unified reform. Thus in a different manner, Delany's fictional society is as ambiguous as Le Guin's. Both modern authors feared being dogmatic about their ideal societies; they probably thought such an ideal was impractical.

*References* Bachrach, A. G. H. "Luna Mendax: Some Reflections on Moon Voyages in Early Seventeenth Century England," in Baker-Smith, Dominic, and C. C. Barfoot, eds. *Between Dream and Nature: Essays on Utopia and Dystopia* (1987); Fekete, John. "*The Dispossessed* and *Triton*: Act and System in Utopian Science Fiction" (1979); Harth, Erica. *Cyrano de Bergerac and the Polemics of Modernity* (1970).

## Macaria (1641)

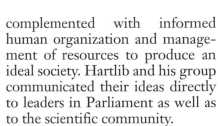

Usually associated with the scientific publicist Samuel Hartlib but probably written instead by an associate, Gabriel Plattes, *A Description of the Famous Kingdom of Macaria* embodied many aspects of both pansophism (universal wisdom) and utopianism. *Macaria* represents the approach of many utopian writers affected by the Scientific Revolution of the seventeenth century seeking to utilize the maximum degree of scientific organization to solve problems of limited resources. This particular utopian strain is sometimes called "full employment" in reference to its full application of available resources in utopia as opposed to the more austere programs advocated by Thomas More and his followers.

As an émigré from Germany to England, Samuel Hartlib (ca. 1600–1662) became a leading publicist for scientific solutions to ordinary problems. Influenced by both the Baconian emphasis upon experimental science and the more mystical tradition of Hermetics, which relied upon astrology and alchemy, Hartlib helped combine the scientific ideas of England and the Continent. He is also believed to have been an influence upon the founding of the Royal Society in the 1660s. However, Hartlib's scientific awareness also reflected an admiration for the pansophic tradition and its principal advocate, Johann Amos Comenius (1592–1670) of Moravia. Hartlib arranged for Comenius to visit England in 1641–1642 and published several of Comenius's works. Comenius, Hartlib, and their circle of intellectuals sought to reestablish mankind's dominion over creation and to use scientific knowledge to solve practical problems and improve material conditions for humanity. Thus a pre-lapsarian (i.e., before the fall of man) Arcadia would be complemented with informed human organization and management of resources to produce an ideal society. Hartlib and his group communicated their ideas directly to leaders in Parliament as well as to the scientific community.

*Macaria* obviously reflects the influences of Thomas More and Francis Bacon, two early utopians who argued for different means to achieve a similar result. Notably also, its publication coincided with Comenius's visit to England. The fact that England was experiencing social, economic, and political upheavals that quickly exploded into civil war further helps explain the appearance of *Macaria* as a framework for solutions to contemporary problems. The English scientists and their Continental associates focused their attention on the quest to utilize all natural resources efficiently and to curb unnecessary waste. The Hartlib circle wanted practical solutions to ills such as poverty and shortages of necessities. Much of their reform orientation naturally dealt with agricultural improvements. Rowland Vaughan's idealized agricultural reform treatise about a "Golden Vale," *Most Approved and Long Experienced Waterworks* (1610), suggested some of the techniques utilized in *Macaria*. Plattes and Hartlib often pointed to the analogy of the beehive, in which every member has a work assignment and performs accordingly in harmony with fellow workers. Human labor was not being utilized efficiently, according to Plattes and Hartlib. *Macaria* inspired Peter Chamberlen's *The Poore Mans Advocate* (1649), which called for the government to oversee a redistribution of resources and reorganization of employment, especially for the poor.

The fictional story of *Macaria* was carried on in the form of a dialogue between a traveler and a scholar. The work appealed specifically and directly to Parliament to act upon the recommendations. The kingdom of Macaria was bountiful in its provision for residents. Estates were managed effectively to ensure maximum production. The result was that taxes were low; they remained low because the king of Macaria avoided expensive wars even while maintaining a strong defense. The king was able to maintain an accurate knowledge of the condition of his people by delegating authority to subordinate officials. The duties of government were divided into economic categories such as livestock, fishing, trade, and colonies. The Macarian parliament's function was primarily to supervise state officials and punish them if their work failed to meet the criteria set by the king. The notion of "full employment" of resources and manpower in the economy of Macaria stands out as the salient feature of the utopia's success.

Even though the pansophists often featured Christianity as a guide for the precepts of their utopian schemes, Macaria had no state religion, and religious practice remained on a rather general level of theocracy, avoiding the sectarian hairsplitting of the real world in seventeenth-century England. Still, Macaria punished heretics by execution. Unlike most utopias in the early modern era, Macaria featured a strong, active government directly involved in planning the lives of its citizens. The fact that the treatise was presented to the English Parliament should prepare the reader for its method of control. It is fair to suggest that *Macaria* was not a full-fledged utopian construction but only a call for efficient reorganization of government to improve economic conditions. The fact that it emanated from a scientific source should help the reader appreciate its limited picture of an ideal society. Nonetheless, *Macaria* represented a serious examination of how to reorganize society in the wake of the advance of capitalism. The full-employment utopia inspired a number of reform projects and ideas dealing with agriculture, the poor law, mercantilism, and labor over the next

century, culminating with Adam Smith's *Wealth of Nations* (1776).

*See also* Pansophism.

*Reference* Webster, Charles. "The Authorship and Significance of *Macaria*" (1972).

## "The Machine Stops" (1909)

As one of the few twentieth-century romantic novelists remaining, E. M. Forster exhibited both his concern for human cooperation and its dilemmas in works such as *Howard's End* (1910) and the award-winning *A Passage to India* (1924). He was also influenced by H. G. Wells's utopian writing, especially the Wellsian fascination with machine technology. Forster's "The Machine Stops" thus became one of the first of many twentieth-century dystopias that took an antitechnological stance. Although other dystopian writers such as Yevgeny Zamyatin, Aldous Huxley, and George Orwell would receive more attention and credit for revealing the possibility of technological nightmares, Forster's version exhibited insightful and prophetic qualities that reflected the ambivalence of his generation toward science and technology. Moreover, Forster seemed able to make the important distinction between the roles of tools and machines as they affected humanity.

Edward Morgan Forster (1879–1970) was born in England in the waning years of the Victorian era. He was educated at King's College, Cambridge, and was later elected a fellow of the college. Forster's first novel was published during a residence in Italy. He later traveled in India and worked as a civil servant in Egypt during World War I. Forster joined a number of other liberal humanitarians in the late nineteenth and early twentieth centuries who began to fear the potential dehumanization caused by modern technology. Forster admitted to being impressed by Samuel Butler's antitechnology satire, *Erewhon* (1872). Also like other contemporaries, Forster had a profound respect for the positive possibilities of science and technology as well, especially as a vehicle to eliminate superstition and provide certainty about the nature of the universe. Yet the advance of capitalism had witnessed a partnership with technology that seemed wrongheaded to a thinker such as Forster. Technology itself was not evil, but human uses of it could produce evil results. The profit motive could and probably would get in the way of solving the moral dilemmas that technology would invariably create. Forster agreed with Aldous Huxley's analysis that man was not made for technology but vice versa: Technology existed for man. The problem remained of how mankind could manage technology without allowing the machine to dictate outcomes to humans. Given the fact that machines could enhance or frustrate human capacities, once the technology existed it would be used whatever the consequences because once created, its management was determined more by the nature of the machine than the nature of mankind. Further, the dependence upon machines meant that obsolescence and constant reconstruction would force even greater dependency upon the machines. Unlike some past utopian devotees of technology, including Francis Bacon and Henri Saint-Simon, Forster could not accept the contemporary positivist view that only the technologically skilled should have power to make decisions in such a society.

Forster first published his essay "The Machine Stops" in the *Oxford and Cambridge Review* in 1909 as a warning to his intellectual associates that H. G. Wells's optimistic view of the future uses of technology could be mistaken. Forster understood that one of the inevitable consequences of the explosion of science and technology was the necessity for a faceless, almost inhuman bureaucracy, the bane of all big government in the twentieth century. The society depicted in Forster's dystopia resembled Wells's society in *When the Sleeper Awakes*, an underground beelike society where individuals live in an effectively isolated state (communication limited to visionphones) oper-

ating under the command of a bureaucratic committee that takes its instructions from the Machine. Forster made it clear that one of the most disturbing consequences of technology is the isolation of people from one another. There is no role for parents after the birth of a child since the Machine takes over. Forster anticipated the impersonal, limited perspective of television with his visionphones—communicators see an image but not the real person. The human residents of the underground society do not understand how the Machine works, only that they are its subjects. Indeed, Forster shows that the mystery of the machine is actually the mystery of humanity.

The main character, a female named Vashti, struggles with a rebellious son, Kuno, who has turned against the machine society. Kuno's desire to visit the earth's surface, a capital crime in the underground world, shows another of Forster's concerns about technology's impact, that it isolates humanity from nature. Kuno is not content to see pictures of the earth's surface; he wants to experience it himself. Indeed, in order to discourage thoughts such as Kuno's, the society has decreed that the respirators necessary to exist on earth's surface be abolished. The regimented society follows orders dictated by the Book of the Machine, which anticipates every exigency. The Machine has convinced residents that they need not engage their imagination about contingencies. Mechanical assistance has become so extensive that human muscles have atrophied, and babies who exhibit independent exertions of strength are killed. In short, human weakness—physical and mental—has become a virtue. The society has replaced traditional religion with a worship of the Machine; the Book of the Machine is viewed as holy script.

After painting the scenario of the technologically driven society, Forster introduced a problem very familiar to humans dependent upon machines in the twentieth century: What happens when the machine stops? In his story, there are hints at the potential trouble when various malfunctions in the Machine occur, preparing the reader for the eventual total failure. Scientific determinism, made stronger by the popular theories of Charles Darwin, Karl Marx, and Sigmund Freud, has ultimately impinged upon mankind's ability to determine individual choices. Thus human freedom has become contingent upon the authority of the Machine, that is, technology. Because the population has been trained to be utterly dependent upon the Machine, they cannot survive when it fails. Even Kuno fails in his attempt to escape to earth's surface when huge worms pull him back to the underground world. Nonetheless, Kuno's glimpse of the earth's surface and its beauty provides an imaginary window into the past history of humanity. The imagined other world, utopia to Kuno, must have actually existed at one time.

Yet just as Forster did not explain how technology came to control mankind, he did not propose a solution, an answer to the growing dependence upon machines. Thus Forster's purpose in writing "The Machine Stops" must have been to sound a warning rather than to offer an alternative to technology's place in civilization. It was, however, a forlorn warning, since Forster apparently expected that nothing would be done to prevent the consequences he feared.

*Reference* Elkins, Charles. "E. M. Forster's *The Machine Stops*: Liberal-Humanist Hostility to Technology," in Richard D. Erlich and Thomas P. Dunn, eds. *Clockwork Worlds: Mechanized Environments in SF* (1983).

## Mahdi
*See* Messianism.

## *Manifesto of the Equals* (1796)
Although not the first utopian communist scheme, the Pantheon Society of Gracchus Babeuf truly converted utopia into a revolutionary instrument during the era of the French Revolution. Previously, both the Enlightenment and eighteenth-century utopists had urged reform as the appropriate method to inaugurate change. Already an enemy of France's absolute monarchy at the time of the outbreak of revolution in 1789, Babeuf joined a host of contemporaries in designing a utopian ideal society. His tract *Manifesto of the Equals* outlined a society in which private property would be abolished. Thus the revolutionary government of the Directory, composed of businessmen, regarded Babeuf as a dangerous radical. His small group of conspirators was arrested, and Babeuf was executed in 1797. Babeuf's society of equals contrasted sharply with most previous utopias controlled by elites. Nineteenth-century socialists saw Babeuf's *Manifesto* as indicating the limits that constrained the Revolution of 1789, thereby causing its failure to accomplish its aims.

The French Revolution's ideology was summarized in the tenets of "liberty, fraternity, and equality." The particular goal of equality attracted this obscure thinker from Picardy, born François-Noël Babeuf (1760–1797). A rebellious attitude toward his father caused Noël to be banished from his family. Despite being a prodigy, Noël ran afoul of his noble employers, further laying groundwork for his anti-establishment attitude. Noël began to develop egalitarian schemes in the 1780s, a time when utopian projects were proliferating all over France. Noël read not only his favorite author, Jean-Jacques Rousseau, but also the utopian Morelly's *Code of Nature* (1755), which may have been the single greatest influence upon Noël. At the outset of the Revolution in 1789, Noël led a tax revolt in Picardy and drafted a *cahier* for the Estates-General proposing the abolition of serfdom. He soon assumed the revolutionary name of Gracchus Babeuf, thus showing reverence for ancient Roman heroes.

Babeuf began to construct his communist conspiracy as early as 1790, but he never really identified himself with the masses. He served on local revolutionary councils that proposed government fiscal reforms. Babeuf vigorously criticized the

Constitutions of 1791, 1792, and 1795 as being "aristocratic," and though favoring the Constitution of 1793 he believed it to be unimplemented. In and out of jail between 1790 and 1794, Babeuf learned not to trust anyone in power, even fellow revolutionaries. In his frequent contributions to *The Tribune of the People*, a revolutionary newspaper he founded, Babeuf not surprisingly revealed an intense hatred of the class system and private property. He formed the Pantheon Society with like-minded rebels including Pierre-Sylvain Maréchal, Auguste Darthe, and Philippe Buonarotti to foster an egalitarian system of honesty, opportunity, and justice.

Babeuf composed (probably with Maréchal) the *Manifesto of the Equals* as part of the scheme to pull down the bourgeois-controlled Directory in 1796 and replace it with a system of communal ownership of property. The primary aim of the French Revolution should be the elimination of inequality and oppression. With Rousseauian gusto, Babeuf declared: "From time immemorial we have been hypocritically told—men are equal; and from time immemorial does the most degrading and monstrous inequality insolently oppress the human race." The unequal distribution of material goods had become the root of all evil to Babeuf's followers, the Equals, who wanted their program to eradicate both the rich and the poor. Thus Babeuf's practical communism, still essentially agrarian, would ensure that citizens could obtain food as well as justice. The utopia would guarantee equal educational opportunities and equal distribution of labor and the fruits of labor. Babeuf criticized the unearned income of the wealthy primarily because they did not work for it. Thus in Babeuf's ideal society, work would be both expected and required of its residents, and sloth would be punished. Without elaborating, Babeuf claimed that his ideal society would bring both an inner peace and social tranquillity, an absence of worry and fear, and equal concern for all groups in society from children to the elderly. In short, the "republic of equals" was not a Land of Cockaygne or indulgent hedonism but a simple society fulfilling fundamental needs.

Even though Babeuf's "Conspiracy of the Equals" was easily crushed by the Directory and its leader executed, the ideal of a pure communist society lived on in France and Europe and would be revived in more serious dress decades later. Yet even Karl Marx's socialist system did not emphasize absolute equality in everything as did Babeuf's. Enlightenment philosophers such as David Hume had warned that such an ideal was impossible to achieve given human proclivities. Yet in Babeuf's egalitarian utopia, as with others in future decades, a strict discipline enforced by a centralized state authority was the instrument for guaranteeing the desired outcome. Babeuf also could not have adequately anticipated how the Industrial Revolution would change the conditions of the economy and society in the nineteenth century. Nonetheless, Gracchus Babeuf did show that the ideal of utopia could go beyond mere reformation and merge with the reality of revolution.

*Reference* Rose, R. B. *Gracchus Babeuf: The First Revolutionary Communist* (1978).

## Maoism

Going beyond the totalitarian communism in which he was trained, the Chinese dictator Mao Ze-dong rejected Western influences and chose a primitive peasant socioeconomic orientation to produce a revolutionary social movement known as Maoism in post–World War II China. Mao's revolutionary program evolved from the Great Leap Forward in the late 1950s to the Cultural Revolution of the mid-1960s. True to the native Chinese xenophobia that had existed for decades, since the late Manchu dynasty, Maoism was skeptical of Marxist intellectuals and revered the simple rural lifestyle. Certainly, Mao was not comfortable taking his cues from Soviet Communist leaders. Nonetheless, like all totalitarian systems, Maoism relied upon a rigorous form of authoritarianism that ironically was used

*Official portrait of Mao Ze-dong*

socialist leveling. Hence, though adapted for the peculiar situation in China, Sun Yat-sen's program was derived from philosophies born in the West and imported into China. Whatever the source, these ideas supported the overthrow of the ancient Chinese imperial system and replaced it with a Western-style republic. Sun Yat-sen's reading of history viewed the Taiping Rebellion of the 1850s as a forerunner of his three principles. Thus Sun Yat-sen carried the idea of freedom outlined in the Great Equality movement into practical action in creating a republic for China.

Sun Yat-sen viewed his philosophy as being compatible with communism as it emerged in the years prior to his death. The chief translator of communism in China, however, was less inclined to borrow Western ideas wholesale, including socialism. Mao Ze-dong (1893–1976) came from sturdy peasant stock and retained that essential perspective throughout his career. He learned to admire heroes and powerful leaders, from Chinese emperors such as Ch'in Shi Huang-ti and Wu Ti to Western figures such as Peter the Great, the Duke of Wellington, and George Washington. However, Mao did not travel outside China for his education as many of China's nationalist and communist leaders would. Significantly, he remained very insular (he admired the Great Equality movement) though not insulated from non-Chinese ideas. Mao respected Sun Yat-sen and supported the 1911 revolution that overthrew the Manchu and established a republic. He attended Beijing University, embraced socialism, and became one of the founders of the Chinese Communist Party in 1921. After the civil war began between the Communists and Chiang Kai-shek's Guomindang Nationalist Party in the late 1920s, Mao struggled to gain control from Moscow-trained Communist Party leaders. Although he sought to integrate the rather small industrial proletariat into the revolution, Mao was forced to rely most upon rural peasants and even bandits.

by the very sources of past authority Mao criticized.

The transition in dynamic Chinese thought from the Great Equality movement of the late nineteenth century to the unique reversion to a parochial Maoism spanned the nationalist movement led by Sun Yat-sen (1866–1925). Although Sun Yat-sen was not a utopian, his intellectual treatise outlining China's future, *Three People's Principles* (*San min chu-I*), included some utopian elements borrowed from Western thinkers. Indeed, the three principles cited by Sun Yat-sen—nationalism, sovereignty, and livelihood—all seem to have originated in the West rather than China. Theoretically, the idea of nationalism incorporated the Western notion of equality, though Sun's version rejected the idea of foreign control or occupation as had occurred recently under the Manchu. The ideal of sovereignty implied that the Chinese were a single people, a kind of an extended family, with equal natural rights. The concept of livelihood involved socioeconomic equality, a Chinese version of

Nevertheless, though peasants might have to be reeducated, Mao knew they sustained the revolutionary spirit critical to ultimate success. Following the massive losses in the Long March of 1934, Mao finally became the head of the Chinese Communist Party in 1935. After the war with Japan, the Chinese Communists successfully seized control of the mainland from the Nationalists in 1949. Mao continued to rule China until his death in 1976, but his political philosophy evolved only gradually.

Mao Ze-dong had always rejected the Western notion of an ideal society. Indeed, Mao's macrocosmic view depicted a struggle of the simple but superior Orient (the "East Wind" in Mao's terminology) against the decadent Occident. Rather, he believed that ideals were only practical achievements of a revolutionary nature. His concept of a permanent or continuing revolution was an adaptation of typical totalitarian methods. The three principles of Maoism had been present in his thought for some time before they were realized in practice. His glorification of a form of populism, or concern for the masses, derived from his own rural peasant background and experience. Like most modern Chinese, Mao embraced nationalism as a vehicle to throw off the traditional yoke of repression, but his was a more xenophobic nationalism than that of most leaders, including that of Sun Yat-sen. Mao's most mystical, and thus utopian, principle was his idea of the translation of individual will into collective action; the course of the revolution would be determined by this collective will rather than some abstract Marxist predetermined stages. Hence Mao committed himself to a thoroughgoing reeducation process utilizing mass psychological techniques to gain support for his ideas, all of which meant a slower evolution of Maoism. The Western notion of happiness would be realized through participation in the permanent revolutionary program rather than through the achievement of any theoretical goals.

After years of consolidating the revolutionary victory of 1949 by pursuing a Soviet model that suspended utopianism, Mao launched a program called the Great Leap Forward in 1958. The previous course of collectivization of the economy around agricultural development had proven problematic by the late 1950s. Mao's efforts had been criticized by Western-oriented Communist intellectuals, who were finally repressed to make way for a decentralized Great Leap Forward for both agriculture and industry. Twenty-four thousand communes, each with populations of 20,000, were formed to coordinate the process epitomized by the vision of the rural countryside enveloping the cities. Although communal practices such as child care resembled traditional socialist methods, the system of small-scale cottage agriculture and industry ran contrary to most socialist planned economic practice symbolized by the grand-scale five-year plans. Initially broad popular support greeted the Great Leap Forward; many thought that the era of the Great Equality had finally arrived. Yet Mao's dream of a communal society failed in part because too much time was spent on indoctrination in Maoist propaganda about egalitarianism, including the messianic cult of personality, and too little on developing market-driven economic technology. Indeed, the economic results for China of the Great Leap Forward were disastrous, leading to perhaps 30 million deaths by 1960.

The economic failures of the Great Leap Forward forced Mao to agree to modifications, such as allowing the restoration of private peasant lands. Yet because Mao continued to believe the Chinese were essentially selfless and creative, he seemed stubbornly determined to make his unique philosophy work. In 1962 he revived a practice used in the war against Japan by sending propaganda instructors to teach and live among the peasants. In 1965, Mao launched a new phase of his philosophy, the Great Proletarian Cultural Revolution, aimed at eliminating four obstructions to his program: ideology, educational tradition, social customs, and bad habits. The realization of these goals would bring to fruition his aim of transforming socialism not into anarchism but into pure communism. By controlling the media and the military to assist the implementation of the Cultural Revolution, Mao's methods were both efficient and ruthless. Typical of many other totalitarian regimes in the West, Mao also resorted to organizing China's youth to promote his program. Thus the emphasis shifted from the rural areas emphasized during the Great Leap Forward to the cities. The 13-million-strong Red Guards became a spearhead of the Cultural Revolution, motivated by the little red book of published "Quotations" from Chairman Mao. Ultimately the Red Guards superseded both the regular military and the Communist Party in leading the Cultural Revolution. The Cultural Revolution coincided with a large upheaval of youth counterculture movements in the West in the late 1960s as well. Eventually, however, factions of the Red Guards—peasant, bureaucratic, and aristocratic—began to fight each other for control. By 1968, Mao had called off the Red Guards and they were dissolved, although Mao tried to continue the Cultural Revolution. The results were mixed: Higher education suffered complete disarray, but health care among the peasants improved. Economic growth also expanded, albeit only marginally. Even before Mao's death in 1976, China had determined to chart a new course of allowing Western ideas and techniques limited access to China. The attempt to control and regulate foreign intercourse with China to protect the totalitarian authority was to prove tricky, but more economic progress occurred than during the mystical, utopian Maoism of the past. Yet the end of Maoism also spelled a halt (whether temporary or permanent) to utopianism in China.

References Meisner, Maurice. "Utopian Goals and Ascetic Values in Chinese Communist Ideology" (1968); Schram, Stuart R. "To Utopia and Back: A Cycle in the History of the Chinese Communist Party" (1981).

## Marcuse, Herbert
See Frankfurt School.

## Marinetti, Filippo
See Futurism.

## Marxism
Though Marx coined the disparaging phrase "utopian socialism" later in his career, Marxism represented an extension of both early socialist thought and its utopian elements. Marx's "scientific socialism" supposedly differed from the utopian socialists in its focus upon the present rather than the future and its obsession with the class conflict. Yet Marxism retained important utopian concepts, and those would reappear in the work of later Marxist thinkers and various attempts to create Marxist societies. Indeed, to some scholars the utopian socialists, by their response to industrialism in experimental communities, were greater realists than the Marxists. Steven Lukes has suggested that Marxism possessed a peculiar and seemingly antithetical relationship with utopianism and that the combination of both utopian and anti-utopian ingredients in Marxism, not surprisingly, proved perplexing for its adherents.

Karl Marx (1818–1883) was born and educated in a politically divided Germany ripe with Romantic nationalism and Idealist philosophy that manifested a pervasive tendency to escape from reality into imaginary worlds in order to approach and solve real problems. Marx became a journalist writing about political economy and spending much time in France, home of utopian socialist spokesmen such as Charles Fourier and Henri Saint-Simon. Starting in 1844, Marx also engaged in a lifelong partnership with wealthy German industrialist Friedrich Engels (1820–1895), who had worked in England and knew the utopian communalist Robert Owen. Although both Marx and Engels found flaws in the utopian socialists and differed from them in their campaign to abolish property rights, the thought of both was shaped by the utopians.

Toward the end of his career, Engels wrote in *Socialism: Utopian and Scientific* (1882) that the scientific socialists owed a special debt to the early socialists such as Saint-Simon, Fourier, and Owen. Engels freely borrowed many of Fourier's ideas, which he regarded as a scientific approach to industrialism. The problem with Fourier's phalansteries was not their communalism but their retention of private property. Engels also believed Owen's ideas of communalism were practical and appealing. Saint-Simon became an important influence upon the young Marx through a Saint-Simonian lecturer at the University of Berlin. Marx was especially attracted to Saint-Simon's historical analysis of socioeconomic systems and the role of labor. Marx did not convert to socialism until 1843 upon his move to Paris, long after he had immersed himself in early socialist writings. Of course, Marx was also strongly influenced by the German Idealists, especially the abstract subjectivism of Hegel and his historical dialectic. Thus Marx and Engels developed their "scientific socialism" from three primary sources: utopian socialism, Hegelian philosophy, and their understanding of political economy. Although Marx and Engels claimed that they were creating an entirely new system of social thought, they obviously borrowed significant portions of their ideas from others, including the utopians.

Once Marx arrived in Paris and entered into his association with Engels, he began to focus upon the evils of the class system and developed his theory of a historical class conflict based upon economic exploitation. Marx and Engels then set about to construct a political approach for their goal of ending the exploitation of the proletariat and also the historical cycle of dialectical materialism. Like earlier utopians, Marx and Engels were driven by the ideal of legal and social justice for the common people. The collapse of capitalism, caused by its inherent greed and inefficiencies, would usher in a temporary phase, the rev-

*Karl Marx*

olutionary dictatorship of the proletariat, that involved state confiscation and redistribution of all property on an equal basis. Once redistribution was accomplished, the state would wither away, and a perfect classless society—a millennial heaven on earth—would emerge. Hence abundance of resources would replace scarcity, individual freedom would be guaranteed, and historical cycles would disappear since discontent would no longer drive change. Thus the Marxist society that would result from the transformation of the capitalist system was as ideal and utopian as any previous concept. Critics argued that Marxism, with its analytical flaws, manifested not realism but virtual fantasy in a rather typical utopian fashion.

In the earliest outline of Marxist thought, *The Communist Manifesto* (1848), Marx and Engels devoted a section to utopian socialism, which they noted appeared at a time when the class struggle had not yet developed. The utopian socialists spoke for all classes, including the proletariat, in their quest for reform and social justice. Because the utopian socialists believed all classes would embrace their ideas, they found no problem appealing to the ruling classes to employ their reforms, whereas the Marxists wanted to overthrow those same ruling classes. Both the utopian socialists and the Marxists wanted a revamped socio-economic-political system. The difference in approaches was marked: The utopian socialists relied upon education and persuasion, while the Marxists counted on the dynamic forces of history and class conflict. By highlighting the different methods, the Marxists hoped to show prospective followers that their solution was more realistic and beneficial than the utopian socialist technique of creating alternative societies while leaving the capitalist establishment intact. The utopian socialists had identified the appropriate goal for the proletariat, but, according to Marx and Engels, their method of reaching that goal was flawed.

That Marx and Engels were obsessed with the immediate destruction of capitalism and elimination of property did not override their prediction of a futuristic, utopian, classless society. Hence, without the influence of the utopian socialists upon Marx and Engels, their theory might have produced an entirely different scenario. The founders of scientific socialism had learned from Saint-Simon that politics must be driven by economics and from Fourier and Owen that distinctions based on the division of labor must be eliminated. Yet because Marx and Engels were repelled by the notion of utopias being dreamworlds instead of realities, they refused to assimilate the varied utopian influences and ideas into a pure utopian framework. Thus despite their protestations to the contrary, Marx and Engels owed a profound debt to the utopian socialists for both their analysis of capitalism and the projection of their ideal society.

Later followers of Marx attempted to sever any residual ties to utopianism. After the anarchists led by Mikhail Bakunin broke up Marx's First International in 1872, a Second International was formed without the anarchists in 1889 following Marx's death. The leaders of the Second International were a German, Karl Kautsky (1854–1938), and a Russian, Georgy Plekhanov (1857–1918), who adhered to orthodox Marxist teachings about the collapse of capitalism and feared the term "utopian" because it suggested the impossible to them. These two spokesmen insisted that the proletariat could comprehend scientific socialism with instruction. Kautsky organized the German Social Democratic Party in 1875 and required that its spokesmen avoid discussion of the future, especially utopias, although Kautsky had written an admiring treatise on Thomas More's utopia. The socialist goal was only the destruction of the capitalist system, not speculation about the socialist society to succeed it. Plekhanov founded the Russian Marxist movement as a leader of the Narodniks, who argued that Russian peasants could skip past capitalism from feudalism to socialism. Ultimately, Plekhanov rejected the Narodnik approach as utopian and opted for the traditional capitalist phase as a prerequisite to the proletarian revolution. With Russia's small, weak middle class, it was more difficult for Plekhanov than for Kautsky to avoid discussion of the future.

Some Marxist thinkers, such as Eduard Bernstein (1850–1932), began to alter Marx's prediction that capitalism would crumble on its own and suggested that socialists needed to spur its failure before capitalism could be revitalized. In the process of revision, Bernstein argued that orthodox Marxism retained a "residue" of utopianism that should be expunged. Oddly, Bernstein had written a history of Gerrard Winstanley's seventeenth-century utopian Digger community, an early application of communism. Yet whether orthodox or revisionist, the Marxists could not dismiss the final goal of a communist society, the utopian element in their system.

As it had for other utopian ideas, the United States proved perhaps the most fertile ground for practical applications of

Marxism prior to the twentieth century. The wealthy socialist editor Julius A. Wayland (1854–1912) converted to Marxism after moving west in the 1880s. He started publication of *The Coming Nation* from Indiana in 1893 and continued its operation until his death. In 1894, Wayland led other interested socialists to found an experimental community in Dickinson County, Tennessee, west of Nashville. The colony, named the Ruskin Cooperative Association after the well-known English writer John Ruskin, sought to blend socialist economics with nineteenth-century aesthetics. Wayland recruited settlers through *The Coming Nation*; most arrivals came from the New England area, which was hard hit by the Panic of 1893. Each settler paid $500 to become a member. When Wayland left the colony in 1895 for Kansas, there were 200 residents; they operated the newspaper and owned the land on a communal basis. Because the original site was unsuitable for agriculture, the settlement was moved to an 800-acre tract in nearby Cave Mills. Yet almost the sole source of income remained the newspaper. After Wayland's departure, the colony lacked strong leadership and began to collapse, in part because of disputes between Marxists and anarchists. Most of the remaining settlers at Ruskin moved in 1899 to Duke, Georgia, to join a previously settled communal colony and establish the Ruskin Commonwealth. The 300 settlers built a school and library, maintained various recreational programs, and continued to publish *The Coming Nation*. The Ruskin Commonwealth disbanded in 1901 after disease and fires disrupted the colony's life.

Meanwhile, the British reception of Marxism was more guarded. British socialists clung to their romantic roots, tended to advocate reform rather than revolution, and remained largely aloof from the proletariat. When Henry Mayers Hyndman attempted, without much success, to establish an orthodox Marxist organization in the 1880s, the movement was eclipsed by the appearance of the Fabian socialists. The leaders of the Fabians were almost all intellectuals, originating with ex–civil servant Percival Chubb, journalist William Clarke, and historian Edward Pease. The most prominent leaders for the next several decades were playwright George Bernard Shaw, science fiction writer H. G. Wells, and historians Sidney and Beatrice Webb. In 1883, Pease engineered the founding of the Fabian Society (named for the Roman commander Quintus Fabius Maximus, who utilized a strategy of caution). The Fabian agenda rejected revolutionary methods, economic determinism, and the expropriation and redistribution of property advocated by orthodox Marxists. Instead, the Fabians relied upon education and persuasion aimed mostly at the middle class to support social reforms. The Fabians thus had the same ends as the Marxists, but their methods to obtain those aims were quite different. The retention of romantic sentimentalism mixed with utilitarian pragmatism led the Fabians to focus upon rhetoric and utopian schemes rather than on concrete programs. With the appearance of the Labour Party in the early twentieth century, the Fabian Society became more of a novelty than a serious socialist organization. The Webbs and other former Fabians became infatuated with Russian communism in the 1930s.

By the twentieth century when the Second International disintegrated in 1914, a radical Marxist breed had emerged led by the German Rosa Luxemburg (1871–1919) and the Russian Vladimir Ilich Ulyanov, a.k.a. Lenin (1870–1924). The radicals claimed to reject the revisionists but in fact moved even beyond Bernstein in advocating active revolution to produce a socialist utopia. Luxemburg had a powerful faith in the ability of the proletariat to create a future ideal society, whereas Lenin argued that the socialist intellectuals must guide the process. Lenin went so far as to assert that fantasy was a part of scientific socialism, and he admired the "utopian" revolutionary writer Nikolay Chernyshevsky. Both Luxemburg and Lenin were to lead revolutions in their countries, revolutions that looked to the future as well as the present. Luxemburg died in the 1919 failed Spartacist Revolt in Germany; Lenin succeeded in overthrowing Russia's czarist regime in 1917 and establishing a communist system complete with an authoritarian utopia. Far from withering away, the state in Communist Russia became as authoritarian as the czarist regime and merely substituted Communist Party control of property and privilege for the power of the old Russian aristocracy. With orthodox Marxist Leon Trotsky's failure in his struggle against the pragmatic Josef Stalin to succeed Lenin, Marxism as communist totalitarianism became a living dystopia rather than a utopia.

Outside the Soviet Union, Stalinism remained a utopian ideal for socialist intellectuals in the 1930s. Only in the post–World War II era with the appearance of George Orwell's anti-utopias were serious questions raised by intellectuals about Stalinism. Former Marxists such as Arthur Koestler, André Gide, and Louis Fischer confessed to having been duped by Stalinism. A new breed of Marxist revisionists soon emerged led by Ernst Bloch in Germany, with his notion of a "concrete utopia," and Herbert Marcuse in the United States, who relied upon Freud to reinterpret the Marxian revolution.

*See also* Anarchism; Bolshevism; Concrete Utopia; Frankfurt School; Utopian Socialism.

*References* Geoghegan, Vincent. *Utopianism and Marxism* (1987); Steven Lukes, "Marxism and Utopianism," in Alexander, Peter, and Roger Gill, eds. *Utopias* (1984).

## Mayakovsky, Vladimir
*See* Futurism.

## Melville, Herman
*See* Noble Savage Utopias.

## Mercier, Louis Sébastien
*See* Future-Time Utopias.

## Messianism
Closely related to millenarianism, messianism was a religious movement that involved an activist, usually revolutionary, agenda for change in society. Although the term "messiah" comes from Hebrew, there are examples of messianism in religions other than Judaism around the world, including Christianity, Islam, Buddhism, and nature religions of primitive tribes. In the modern era a secular phenomenon developed, political messianism, usually connected to religion only loosely if at all. Claiming a divine message and inspiration that is linked to an ancient prophecy, messiahs tend to appear when traditional beliefs are threatened and promise a regeneration in the form of paradise on earth. The phenomenon of messianism has appeared in Europe, the Americas, Africa, and Asia.

The term "messiah" derives from the Hebrew word *mashiah*, and the concept first existed among ancient Hebrews. Yet variations have appeared across the globe so that it has become a generic expression describing a deliverer or savior from an existing condition of repression. There are three primary elements in messianism: a mythology that develops around the messiah figure, the doctrine of redemption, and the concept of suffering or sacrifice. The messiah figure in addition to being viewed as a redeemer or savior is also often conceived of in terms of being a worldly ruler (both spiritual and political) and as a judge upon the corrupt and sinful society. Messianic movements have taken many forms from the purely religious to the purely secular, although they usually involve an admixture. Such movements involve tenacious emotional commitments from followers who feel helpless and isolated by their deprived condition. Hence most movements do not suggest that their aims may be accomplished by followers; they may be accomplished only by the messiah. Messianism usually transcends existing traditions and institutions, so it produces a unifying result. Yet the bottom line for all messianic movements is the

*A crowd reaches out to Ayatollah Ruhollah Khomeini in Tehran, Iran, 3 February 1979. He had returned from exile on 1 February to take control of the revolutionary government in Iran.*

hope for a better and more just society than the one that exists before the messiah appears. Although most of the messianic movements have their origins in the ancient era, they have produced dynamic impacts periodically during the modern era to the end of the twentieth century.

From Old Testament times forward, orthodox Jewish teaching has included the expectation of a messiah or savior. Jewish prayers are filled with such references, which include not only the appearance of the Messiah but also the restoration of the State of Israel (before 1948), the rebuilding of the Temple in Jerusalem, the restoration of the Sanhedrin, and the gathering of the Lost Tribes of ancient Israel. Jews are taught that they should be prepared for the coming of the Messiah but should not predict when God may choose to act. There seems little question that the belief in the Messiah has been perhaps the most important factor sustaining the Jewish people through the perils of their history. Jewish messianism has also maintained a close connection to Christian millenarianism since Roman times, though the Christian teaching concerns the reappearance of the Messiah a second time to establish a victorious reign on earth.

In the older civilizations of the East, there was a long tradition of recurring messiahs in Confucianism, Taoism, and Buddhism. Chinese messianism anticipated the arrival of a savior during a time of imminent danger or disaster. The messiah was usually expected to be a political ruler who would restore happiness and peace. Portents of the messiah's arrival included diseases and demons. The chosen people, bound together by a formal brotherhood, would be protected from the dangers by the messiah-deliverer. Often the prophets of the messiah acted in the role of healer and soothsayer. Messianic movements such as the *Tiandihui* (Heaven and Earth Society) reflected the central tenets of Chinese societies dedicated to preparation and action to change their condition. Such organizations were steeped in mythical origins and striking rituals. The Heaven and Earth Society supposedly originated in the late eighteenth century as a response to betrayal by Manchu ministers of state. It also appeared during a time of severe economic deprivation caused by dramatic population increases early in the Manchu era. The mythological origins held that monks of the Shaolin order were betrayed by Manchu (Qing) officials and fled to establish the Heaven and Earth Society after receiving a sacred text, the Mandate of Heaven, which contained the tenets of the order. Their rituals included the blood oath, which was designed to remove demons. Initiates of the Heaven and Earth Society were led symbolically to a haven, the City of Willows, to await the arrival of the messiah. Essentially, the Heaven and Earth Society existed to overthrow the Manchu rulers and restore the Ming dynasty.

Theravada Buddhism contains similar elements of messianism in China and Southeast Asia (Burma, Ceylon, Thailand, Laos, and Cambodia). Mahayana Buddhism brought comparable themes to Japan. The Buddhist messiah, called *Maitreya*, was a title claimed by many political leaders over the centuries and probably originated during the time of the Mongol occupation of China (fourteenth century). The myth taught that *Maitreya* at some distant time would arrive from heaven following a series of calamities: plagues, floods, and barbarian occupation. The *Maitreya* would deliver three sermons that would lead to the conversion of many millions and a trek to the serenity of a magical city. Ultimately the entire world would participate in the age of paradise. The *Maitreya* would be assisted by the *mingwang* (Luminous King) or *mingzhu* (Luminous Ruler). Since a leading tenet of Buddhism is harmony among humans, whenever disharmony appears, many of its followers begin to anticipate the appearance of the *Maitreya* to restore righteousness. Government should direct its energies toward the common good of the whole community rather than the selfish desires of the few. Buddha also taught that social justice was a prerequisite to the spiritual progress of the individual seeking nirvana (union of the soul with the universal spirit).

Like the myths of Western ancient societies, Buddhist myth theorized that there had once been a golden age of peace, plenty, and harmony where even work was unnecessary. Thus the future goal of the Buddhists was to achieve the past existence of the golden age. That realization would come with the reincarnation of the Buddha as the messiah or *Maitreya*. However, the messiah's appearance would be preceded by the establishment of a universal political rule that ensured justice for all. The Buddhist dream of such a utopia includes an isolated island, *Uttarakuru*, that strongly resembled early modern Western utopias. Once abundance has been achieved through the "wishing trees" on *Uttarakuru*, the tensions among people will subside and they will enjoy unity as well as harmony. In the modern era, the vision of a Buddhist messiah primarily affected peasant populations in Asia and often led to rebellions against the authorities. With the advent of socialism in the nineteenth century, many elements of messianic Buddhism blended with egalitarian socialism and Christianity. Following the devastating 1923 earthquake in Tokyo, messianic groups such as *Reiyukai*, *Sekai Kyuseikyo*, and *Seicho no Ie* multiplied and flourished briefly in Japan, promising an imminent new golden age.

Relatively early in the history of Islam, the ideal of the messiah also became popular among peasant populations, especially in the dissident Shiite sect and to a lesser extent in the mystical movement of Sufism. The Islamic messiah, like the Buddhist, would assail oppression and lead a restoration of Islamic piety and principle. Typically the idea of an Islamic messiah appealed once more primarily to the lower classes in Islamic territories, victims of sinful recipients of *riba*, or ill-gotten gains. During the Middle Ages there were several egalitarian peasant revolts that lacked

the messianic element but that prepared the way for the advent of the Savior Imam, the Madhi (that is, the divinely guided one), a philosopher-king who would launch the *umma* or collective unity by destroying evil and reestablishing justice. The Madhi would therefore redeem the suffering faithful from the enemies of Allah and usher in an era of abundance. Islamic salvation does not depend upon an inner spiritual regeneration or the coming of a divine kingdom. Instead, the Islamic messiah, representing an extension of the Prophet, simply creates the conditions through which the ideal *umma* may exist. Mohammed created not only a religion but also a particular social system. The messiah's task is simply to restore that order whenever it has been subverted.

By the eighth century, Shiite belief focused upon the Imams (who possess *'isma*, or infallibility) of the Husaynid family, most of whom supposedly embodied the Madhi and thus never really died. There were certain basic tenets in the belief in the Islamic messiah: that he will be a descendant of the Prophet Mohammed's family; that he will be called the Madhi; that he will restore the faith, unity, and justice of Islam; and that his arrival will presage an apocalyptic era. There have been only a few instances of the supposed appearance of the Madhi in Islamic history, beginning with the first in the Fatimite dynasty, al-Mahdi 'Ubayd Allah. The most noted claimant representing Sufism was the seventeenth-century ascetic Hamad al-Nahlan, otherwise known as Wad al-Turabi, who proclaimed himself Madhi in Mecca. Another Madhi appeared in North Africa among the Berbers in the person of Muhammed ibn-Tumart. Yet the two most spectacular appearances of the Madhi in the modern era occurred in late-nineteenth-century Sudan and in Iran during the 1970s–1980s. In both cases, the concept of the messiah as both a religious restorer and a political revolutionary were amply demonstrated.

The African territory of the Sudan had not been important in the history of the continent prior to the late nineteenth century. However, the Nile River valley seemed to possess a particularly strong attraction for Islamic messiahs. In 1786, an Ottoman military leader was hailed as Madhi during an expedition against rebels in Egypt. A Mahdist claimant led rebellions against Napoleon's occupation in 1799, and another revolted against an Egyptian Pasha in 1822. Muhammad Ahmad 'Abd Allah (1844–1885) claimed the title Madhi in 1881 in large part to challenge local political authority in the Sudan. In particular, Muhammad Ahmad quarreled with Sheikh Muhammad Sharif. Upon establishing his popularity as religious leader and after a series of visions in 1881, Muhammad Ahmad announced his divine election as Madhi. When Muhammad Ahmad escaped miraculously from an attempted arrest in 1881, a full-scale insurrection ensued, with the Madhi receiving popular support from the *Ansar* (Helpers). Several failed attempts to crush the rebellion heightened the Madhi's boldness as his campaign expanded across the Sudan. Following the British occupation of Egypt in 1882, primarily to protect their control of the Suez Canal, reinforcements were sent to Khartoum. Meanwhile the Madhi instituted a reform state in the Sudan with emphasis upon an equitable tax system and genuine justice in the courts. Although the Madhi became an absolute monarch, he relied upon an elaborate subdivision of authority to administer the new rules of the messianic society. Essentially, the Mahdist rule reverted to a primitive concept of asceticism. The Madhi intended to dissolve marriages that involved a non-Mahdist while promoting the marriage of single women, though limiting the wedding expenses. Women were required to be veiled and to cover their heads; the punishment for violators included beating. Ownership of land was protected, and disputed claims were restricted to seven-year limits. The British sent a veteran of Sudanese service, Charles Gordon, to Khartoum in 1884 to evacuate the British presence. Instead, Gordon tried to organize a local challenge to the Madhi but was cut off by the *Ansar*. A British relief force failed to reach Khartoum before Gordon's position was overwhelmed, and he was killed in early 1885. The triumphant Mahdist victory was followed closely by the untimely death of the Madhi (Muhammad Ahmad) in June 1885. He was succeeded by Khalifa 'Abdallahi, initially given the title of *wazi* by the Madhi, later asserting himself as *Khalifa*, imitating Bakr's claim to be Caliph upon the death of the Prophet Mohammed in 632. Despite recognized administrative abilities, the *Khalifa* supervised certain compromises in the regime established by the Madhi, compromises that diminished his reputation among the faithful. The Mahdist state in the Sudan continued to control most of the country until the British finally defeated them in 1898 and Khalifa 'Abdallahi died in January 1899 upon the capture of Omdurman.

The other major example of a Mahdist-type state occurred in Iran beginning in the late 1970s around the leadership of Ruhollah Al-Musari Al-Khomeini (1902–1989), who assumed the title of *ayatollah*, or spiritual leader. Following an extended period of modernization of Iran under the Pahlavi shahs since the 1920s, many fundamentalist Muslims chafed under the Westernization, which they saw as undermining the principles of Islam. Leading the criticism was the Shiite faction, which had a large following in non-Arab Iran reflecting the sect's growth around the Muslim world in the 1970s. When the religious leader Ayatollah Khomeini insisted that he should become the political leader in Iran in order to restore orthodox Islam, the shah's government regarded him as a traitor and forced Khomeini into exile in 1964. Yet the popular movement against the shah resulted in his departure in early 1979 and the return of Khomeini, called the Madhi by some followers, to Iran shortly thereafter. The fundamentalist takeover in Iran presaged a comprehensive cultural reversion to primitive Islamic traditions. Class structures were eliminated and replaced with an egalitarian social system, while a strict dress code required women to cover their bodies following ancient tradition. Insisting upon unity, Khomeini suppressed all groups other than his own. Political authority was subjected to control by the religious leaders, and Islamic law replaced existing secular laws. Popular control was maintained through political sermons delivered in the major mosques and through indoctrination in the schools. Strict Islamicization combined with vigorous anti-Western propaganda to isolate Iran from the world. Close government control of the economy resulted in massive inflation, further complicated by a lengthy war with neighboring Iraq, which Khomeini regarded as part of his goal of exporting the Islamic revolution. Since the death of Khomeini in 1989, the regime in Iran has modified the Ayatollah's campaign to create a universal Islamic state even while remaining staunchly fundamentalist.

Because of the European imperialist "scramble for Africa" beginning in the 1870s, native Africans blended their own traditions with Christian teachings to shape a messiah-deliverer who would restore native authority and lands seized by the white man. The subjugation of African peoples by the European colonialists caused a desire for freedom, improved conditions, to be accompanied by the resurrection of the dead, solar eclipses, and a prophet who would help the people prepare for the coming of the messiah. The natives most often resorted to fetishism, the worship of inanimate objects, to express xenophobia and to protect them from black magic. Perhaps the earliest example of such a movement dates from 1904 and coalesced around a Congo prophet named Epikilipikili, who fashioned a fetish called *bwanga* supposed to ward off evil and make the natives bullet-proof. Soon secret societies relying upon fetishes, such as the Lukusu among the Bashilele tribe, appeared across central and west Africa and were often the source of rebellions.

The most important of the African messiahs was Simon Kimbangu, desig-

nated *ngunzi* (prophet), whose movement spread across central Africa after 1921. Like most African messiahs, Kimbangu had been converted to Christianity although his nationalistic teachings referred almost exclusively to the Old rather than the New Testament. Followers believed that Kimbangu could raise the dead to life and called him "God of the Black Man." Thus the traditional native belief in a supreme spiritual deity combined with the Judeo-Christian deity. Biblical stories of the Jews' fight for freedom against great odds—David versus Goliath was a favorite—were cited to inflame the Africans against the Europeans. Kimbangu preached against idol worship and polygamy and condemned the white man's invasion of Africa. He predicted the removal of the Europeans, followed by resurrection of the dead and the establishment of a golden age or regeneration. Clearly, the colonial authorities regarded Kimbangu as a threat; he was arrested and imprisoned, escaped, but was reimprisoned to die in 1950. Kimbangu believed that the persecution he suffered was simply a replay of Christ's suffering and death. Rather than subduing the native unrest, the arrest of Kimbangu incited more upheavals and led to additional messiahs coming forth. Andre Matswa founded a movement in the 1920s called Amicalism to oppose the French colonial occupation. Matswa also was arrested and exiled only to become another martyred hero to the Africans. After 1939 the leadership of Matswa's movement fell to Simon-Pierre Mpadi, who formed the Mission to the Blacks, later called the Khaki movement, to champion the goals of his predecessors.

With the advent in Europe of the Age of Ideology and its concomitant regenerative expectations in the nineteenth century, a secular political version of messianism began to appear with regularity. Because of the requirements for fervent believers to achieve the implementation of their program, modern ideologies rather naturally gravitate toward a messianic leader to articulate both the ideology and a plan of action. The mass-movement ideologies and their messiahs are predicated upon applying reforms to create a utopian existence, albeit through political methods. The epoch-making events of the French Revolution and the Industrial Revolution had created a new mental framework that willingly challenged almost every tradition and institution from the early nineteenth century forward. The idea of progress facilitated not just the hope but an inevitable expectation for organic positive change. The merging of reason and nature with the various ideologies was expected to produce a voluntary unification of humanity in the goal of perfection.

Romantic nationalism, with its goal of unifying all peoples with a common language and culture into the nation-state, produced numerous political messiahs. Nationalists believed in a historical dynamic that would produce the desired unity, so support for the ultimate goal was simply conforming to natural tendencies and was thus easily justified. The theorists would not be dissuaded by the fact that it was almost impossible to literally draw political boundaries precisely separating peoples by nationality. Hence the dream of national unity was essentially utopian. The ideal of national unity was nurtured first in politically divided Germany by romantic literary figures such as Friedrich von Schiller and Johann von Goethe and scholars such as Johann Fichte. Practitioners could be found everywhere, from Simon Bolívar in South America to the Greeks seeking freedom from Turkish rule. The climax of the romantic nationalist period occurred during the revolutions of 1848–1849. Attempts at unification in Italy, promoted by Giuseppe Mazzini's "Young Italy" organization in the 1830s and 1840s, and in Germany, by the young radicals at the Frankfurt Assembly, both failed. The only measure of success occurred in Hungary, where Lajos Kossuth gained a degree of independence from Austria. Socialism also nurtured its own messiahs, especially after the failures of the voluntary utopian socialist communes. Karl Marx became a spiritual as well as intellectual leader of scientific socialism from the mid-nineteenth century forward.

The culmination of nineteenth-century nationalist and socialist utopian dreams appeared in the twentieth-century totalitarian regimes of messiahs such as Adolf Hitler in Germany, Josef Stalin in Russia, and Mao Ze-dong in China. The cult of personality could be said to be a direct outgrowth of obsessive and uncompromising ideological devotion. Ironically, although professing an ideological facade, totalitarianism actually made a sham of ideology. The concept of totalitarianism was revolutionary and unique in that its proposed total reconstruction of society required the literal uprooting of the past—ideas, traditions, laws, and institutions. The means of achieving such a radical change was an absolute dictatorship, which proved efficient by comparison with representative forms of government. Initially, the subjects of totalitarian regimes respect a government that can get things done, that can make the trains run on time. Yet totalitarian regimes do not institute a lifestyle dramatically different from previous arrangements except for the elimination of individual freedom. Their utopia simply invokes a more efficient method of making the system function. The totalitarian claim of leveling and egalitarianism is perverted in practice, with party members alone receiving perquisites denied ordinary subjects.

*See also* Maoism; Millennialism; Native American Utopias.

*References* Bauer, Wolfgang. *China and the Search for Happiness* (1976); Holt, Peter M. *The Mahdist State in the Sudan, 1881–1898* (1970); Lanternari, Vittorio. *The Religions of the Oppressed: A Study of Modern Messianic Cults* (1963); Popkin, Richard H. "Jewish Messianism and Christian Millenarianism" (1980); Talmon, J. L. *Political Messianism: The Romantic Phase* (1960).

# Metz, Christian
*See* Amana Society.

## Millennialism

Perhaps the most obvious utopian link to religion, the ideal society of the millennium, derived from both Jewish apocalyptic writings and Christian teachings about the end of time, when human control would give way to Christ's earthly reign. Thus either the millennium has been viewed as a religious expression of utopia, or vice versa, utopia has been seen as a secular connotation of the millennium. Throughout Western history millennialism has appeared periodically in various dress and contexts as a recurring theme of utopian thought. The primary difference between millennialists and utopians is their view of human capacities. Lacking an eschatology, utopians have confidence in the ability of human reason to produce an earthly paradise. Millennialists, driven by their concept of human sinfulness and imperfection, believe that only an external intervention by God will create an earthly paradise. Moreover, millennialists, preoccupied with the timing of the event, rely upon God to establish the conditions in their *perfect* society, whereas the utopians concentrate upon describing how their human-directed *ideal* society would function rather than how it would be established.

In their prophecies, Old Testament Jewish figures such as Isaiah, Ezekiel, and Jeremiah often relied upon apocalyptic images of wars and calamities foretelling and preceding a restoration of Israel. Christian teaching about the apocalypse and the millennium was founded upon the last book of the New Testament, the Revelation of John, written toward the end of the first century A.D. In complex symbols, the writer of Revelation portrays the last days of the earth portending the establishment of a 1,000-year reign of Christ at the Second Coming. There are also, in Revelation and in other Old and New Testament passages, veiled discussions of prophetic climaxes and events leading to the end times. Various Christian prophets since the first century have attempted to interpret earthly events as precursors and

*Albrecht Dürer's woodcut, "The Four Horsemen of the Apocalypse" (1498)*

indicators of the coming millennium. Those millenarian prophets tended to appeal to popular classes, and their views were usually condemned by the Roman Catholic church. Yet even millennialists are divided over whether the millennium will occur after Christ's return (postmillennial) or during the 1,000 years before his return (premillennial). Premillennialists tend to identify more closely with utopians since they believe human effort must be exerted to prepare earth for Christ's return.

The most important medieval rendering of the millennium came from Joachim of Fiore and his followers, known as Joachimists. A Benedictine monk in the twelfth century, Joachim argued that human history was framed by three eras, each dominated by a person of the trinity: God the father, Christ the son, and the Holy Spirit. Joachim suggested that the third age, of the Spirit, had been inaugurated by the monastic architect Benedict

*"The Salamander Safe. A Millerite preparing for the 23rd of April. Now let it come! I'm ready!" Lithograph depicting a member of the Millerite sect prepared to survive the end of the world (1844, according to William Miller) in a specially constructed refrigerator that offers provisions for many days.*

of Nursia in the fifth century. Thus the millennial age was directed by the monastic orders with their emphasis upon love and joy. Because Christ's church was not permanent and only belonged to the second age, Joachim's teachings about a postchurch age seemed dangerous as well as wrongheaded to the church hierarchy. Though he did not use the term "millennium" to describe his "third age," Joachim evoked comparisons by his followers.

Joachimism inspired most of the late medieval and early modern millennial movements, each touting a society of earthly perfection. Those movements sometimes took the form of a passive contemplation and preparation for Christ's reappearance but occasionally assumed the form of a social revolution threatening existing order. Although not the central basis of most heretical movements, Joachimist views can be found among the late-twelfth-century Gnostic-like Cathari movements centered in southern France and the extreme Hussite sect known as the Taborites in early-fifteenth-century Bohemia. During the Protestant Reformation in the sixteenth century, several radical Protestant groups frequently expressed Joachimist views.

Thomas Münzer (1490–1525), a radical German Lutheran acquainted with Martin Luther, invoked millenarian themes during the German Peasants' Revolt of 1524–1525. Well educated and charismatic, Münzer became the most effective leader of alienated German peasants during the Reformation. After participating in the drafting of the peasants' Twelve Articles of reform, Münzer attempted in 1525 to establish a theocratic state in the city of Mühlhausen by overthrowing local authority and abolishing private property rights. The German princes soon overwhelmed Mühlhausen and executed Münzer, ending his millenarian experiment.

Among the most radical Anabaptist leaders, the Dutch baker Jan Matthys (d. 1534), inspired by the apocalyptic Anabaptist teaching of Melchior Hofmann (1500–1543), proclaimed the onset of the millennium and the creation of a perfect earthly existence in the German town of Münster near the Dutch frontier. The Melchiorites represented the guilds and commoners in Münster who fought against Catholics and Lutherans for control of the episcopal city in 1534. Matthys organized the takeover and proclaimed a "New Jerusalem" that featured communal ownership of property, abolition of buying and selling, and destruction of all books except the Bible. Following Matthys's death, the Münsterites came under the spell of a tailor who assumed the name John of Leiden (1509–1536). John's new regime introduced polygamy and tolerated sexual promiscuity, which prompted an assault by the Catholics that ended Münster's millenarian episode in 1535.

Millennialism in the seventeenth century was often linked with pansophic schemes, even hinted at in Francis Bacon's *New Atlantis*. There were elements of millennialism found in the work of such diverse thinkers as John Milton and John Bunyan on one extreme and Thomas Hobbes and Sir Isaac Newton on the other. Newton launched an intensive inquiry into the biblical books of Daniel and Revelation in 1693 to ascertain the timing of the end of the world. Probably the most pronounced impact of millennialism in the century was during the English civil war of the 1640s, when a variety of radical groups emerged, led by the Fifth Monarchists. The temporary abolition of the monarchy and the Church of England at the end of the civil war (1642–1648) created an unusual environment for free thought. Basing their biblical interpretation of history upon the four earthly monarchies (Babylon, Persia, Greece, and Rome) followed by a fifth monarchy headed by Christ, the Fifth Monarchy Men (oddly named since most of their followers were women) pressed the Commonwealth government for implementation of their scheme. Their hopes were based in part upon the fact that revolutionary leaders such as Oliver Cromwell had been branded by the royalists as "John of Leiden." However, upon the collapse of the Parliament of the Saints in 1653, some Fifth Monarchists turned against an increasingly repressive government and resorted to revolutionary outbursts. They announced their intention to overthrow governments and authorities both civil and religious, often citing the experience of the Münster Anabaptists as well as biblical prophecies. After two small-scale uprisings, in 1657 and 1661, led by Thomas Venner, the government actively suppressed the Fifth Monarchists, even though they continued to appear during later decades.

The next period of millenarian activity occurred in conjunction with and following the French Revolution, mainly in England and the United States. The millenarian movement also began to divide along social lines, between an intellectual elite that had dominated millennial thought during the seventeenth and eighteenth centuries and the popular classes who led the movement in the nineteenth century. The first group of "popular" millennialists in 1790s England were followers of Joanna Southcott (1750–1814), who claimed to be a prophetess. She wrote pamphlets about the need to prepare for Christ's return and gathered followers of the institutionalized Richard Brothers, a millennialist who purported to be a "nephew" of God. The most notable follower of Southcott was the radical reformer William Sharp. By 1804, Southcott possibly had as many as 100,000 disciples and had established chapels in several major cities. Southcott's prominence ended when her claim of a miraculous pregnancy turned out not to be true, and she died in 1814. Other prophets, including John Wroe and John "Zion" Ward, attempted to keep the movement alive into the 1830s.

Several popular millennial groups emerged in early American history. The colonial precursors to the better-known nineteenth-century groups included a small sect of German Pietists who were followers of Johann Jacob Zimmerman. Predicting that the existing world would end in 1694 with the onset of the millennium, Zimmerman sought to gather followers in the wilderness of America to await the event. When Zimmerman died in the Netherlands before the ship sailed for America, his place of leadership was taken by a well-educated disciple, Johannes Kelpius (1673–1708). After surviving stormy seas, the Pietists made their way to Germantown, Pennsylvania, where they established the "Woman in the Wilderness" sect named for an image in Revelation. The group of 40 members maintained communal property and practiced celibacy and other forms of self-denial. Their settlement of 175 acres included a tabernacle complete with telescopes to prepare for the coming of Christ. Kelpius lived in a nearby cave. When the Second Coming of Christ did not occur in 1694, the sect struggled to survive with numerous defections. Kelpius, who had claimed immortality, died in 1708, and only a handful of believers maintained the sect until its end in 1748. A German leader of Seventh-Day Baptists, Johann Beissel (1690–1768), arrived in Pennsylvania in 1720 with colonists to join the Woman in the Wilderness group. Later, in 1728, they eventually organized their own millennial settlement at Ephrata (that is, Bethlehem), implementing a communal, ascetic existence that did not permit marriage. Beissel did not set a specific date for the arrival of the millennium, but the sect constantly prepared itself for the event, including making ascension robes. The Ephrata group numbered 300 and planted colonies in York County, Pennsylvania, and in South Carolina. By 1770 the Ephrata settlement ended its communism and gradually merged into the Seventh-Day Adventist church.

The early followers of Joseph Smith (1805–1844), who founded the Church of Jesus Christ of Latter-Day Saints (Mormons) in the early nineteenth century, invoked distinctive millennial themes. The Mormons showed a determination to build a "City of Zion" at various places in the early American West to prepare for Christ's return, coinciding with the second resurrection and millennial reign on earth, followed by the third resurrection. Smith preached that Christ's return would not occur until proper earthly conditions, a New Jerusalem, had been prepared by Christ's followers. The first attempt at compliance came in 1832 with the establishment of the United Order of Enoch at Independence, Missouri, based on communal living, but it failed to take root and the Mormons were expelled in 1834. A second United Order was started in 1875 under limited communism at Orderville, Utah. Brigham Young authorized the experiment, which eventually comprised 600 members before it ended in 1884 by common agreement.

The Shakers (United Society of Believers in Christ's Second Appearing) originated as a dissenting Quaker group in mid-eighteenth-century England. However, their greatest impact occurred in the United States after Ann Lee (1736–1784) led the first settlement in New York in 1774. Lee taught an ascetic feminism that assumed that the source of evil was sexual relations. Led by Lee's successors, Joseph Meachem (d. 1796) and Lucy Wright (d. 1821), the Shakers recruited members who were disaffected from other religious denominations to join their semimonastic society. By the 1820s there were 19 Shaker communities, most located in the Midwest. At the time of the start of the Civil War, about 60 Shaker communities existed from New England to the Midwest, and their numbers totaled 6,000 by 1861. Shaker tradition enforced celibacy (married converts were "demarried"), which was adopted for the purposes of self-discipline and devotion to God's will. Hence their social system and rules were predicated on their religious beliefs. They also embraced common ownership of property and a highly structured organization. No other movement in the United States except the Shakers gave women equal spiritual status with men, and the movement proved especially attractive to teenagers. Like other ideal communities in the United States, the Shakers developed a reputation for skilled craftsmanship in their distinctive style of furniture. The Shaker settlements declined steadily in the late nineteenth and twentieth centuries to only two communities.

Another German immigrant to America, George Rapp, established the Harmony Society. Born in Württemburg, Germany, the son of a farmer, George Rapp (1757–1847) criticized his Lutheran faith as being preoccupied with form rather than genuine worship. By 1787 he had organized a separatist group at Württemburg that advocated believer's baptism, congregational governance, and pacifism and urged preparations for the onset of the millennium. Church and state persecution led Rapp to seek a haven in the United States. He sailed to Baltimore in 1803 to arrange the purchase of 5,000 acres north of Pittsburgh, Pennsylvania. By 1804, 300 followers had immigrated from Germany to join Rapp. After additional German separatists arrived, the Harmony Society was established in 1805, adopting communal ownership of property. Like some other religious communes, the society enforced a common style of dress and housing. In addition to about 50 log homes, the society built a school and church, mills and workshops, and common barns. They produced a variety of agricultural products for their livelihood. The strict religious nature of the community became apparent in 1807 with the adoption of celibacy and the prohibition of tobacco.

Because of its isolation and poor soil, in 1814 the community purchased 30,000 acres along the Wabash River in Indiana and sold their property in Pennsylvania for a tidy profit. Harmony, Indiana, proved successful economically, and other German settlers arrived there in 1817, raising the population to more than 700. Still, the location bred disease and caused the settlers to sell the land to Robert Owen for $150,000 in 1824. The Harmony Society purchased land back in Pennsylvania near the original settlement and called it Economy. The settlers by then focused upon more profitable manufacturing rather than farming. The placid scene became complicated by the arrival from Germany in 1831 of Bernhard Müller (who called himself Count Leon). Müller gradually tried to undermine the society's policy of celibacy and promoted other worldly pursuits as well. While the majority remained loyal to Rapp, a sizable minority of 250 opted to join Müller in leaving Economy in 1832, later settling in Louisiana. By the time of Rapp's death in 1847, the Harmony Society numbered about 1,200. After the Civil War, the community at Economy started a petroleum business that increased their wealth. The Harmony Society did not dissolve until 1905, when its numbers had dwindled to a handful.

Another group of millennialist Württemburg separatists came to the United States soon after Rapp. Led by Joseph Bimeler (1778–1853), the Society of Separatists of Zoar purchased more than 5,000 acres in Ohio in 1817. The Zoarites' religious views coincided with Rapp's: pacifism and opposition to government and state churches. The Zoarites also adopted celibacy at first, though they began permitting marriages after 1830. Likewise, Bimeler followed Rapp in deciding to hold property in common. Administered by three elected trustees, the society required new residents to complete a probationary period of one year before becoming full members. Though religious meetings were held, the Zoarites were careful not to utilize any semblance of ritual or ceremonies. The Zoarites enjoyed music, but their intellectual pursuits were limited to religious literature. Their early economic successes were followed after the Civil War by steady decline, although the value of their property increased to about $3 million. In 1898 the more than 200 residents determined to divide the property among themselves and end their communal experience.

Another U.S. millenarian movement, founded by William Miller (1782–1849), convinced followers that the end of the world, and Christ's return, would happen on October 22, 1844. Miller urged his followers not only to reform their spiritual lives but also to rid themselves of earthly possessions before that date. Miller's supporters included several hundred preachers and possibly 100,000 persons, mainly from New York and New England. Following the failure of the millennium to materialize on October 22 as predicted, Miller and his followers became disillusioned. Later proponents of Miller's views revised his prediction of the millennium from an exact date to a more general, albeit imminent, time frame and organized the Seventh-Day Adventist church.

The Minnesota populist leader Ignatius Donnelly (1831–1901) used the millennium as a vehicle for his critique of society in the apocalyptic novel *Caesar's Column* (1891). The story reflected the populist class theory of oppressors (banks, railroads, big business) exploiting the oppressed (chiefly small farmers). A plutocratic oligarchy, operated by Italian Jews (populists like Donnelly tended to be xenophobic), ruthlessly governs New York City, where the chief character, Gabriel, a wealthy merchant, arrives from the pastoral utopia of Uganda. Gabriel is repelled by the condition of the working class and soon accidentally falls in with Max Petion and the anarchist Brotherhood of Destruction. The Brotherhood's leaders, the charismatic Caesar and a lame Russian Jew, offer no solution except destruction and become little more than dictators. The ensuing class war leads to chaos and carnage, including a massive mound of dead bodies known as "Caesar's Column." As the rest of the world is destroying itself, Gabriel, Max, and a few refugees flee to the Ugandan Arcadia to begin the millennial era of peace that precedes the return of Christ. Other examples of apocalyptic violence portending the millennium pervaded various U.S. novels of the 1890s, demonstrating the truism that periods of stressful change usually produced millennial visions.

Millenarian movements have not been limited to the West, but those occurring in non-Western cultures have definite links with Christianity. The Taiping Rebellion in China (1850–1864) combined elements of Confucian philosophy and Buddhist religion with Christianity. The Taiping rebels, strongly influenced by nineteenth-century Christian missionaries, hoped for an earthly kingdom that would end the corrupt Manchu dynasty. They proclaimed a return to a golden age of perfection that predated Confucius and the Tao faith. The leader of the revolt, Hung Hsiu-ch'üan (1814–1864), was educated at a Christian mission in his youth. Later, he claimed to be the "Heavenly King," a younger brother of Jesus, sent by God to establish an egalitarian "Heavenly Kingdom of Highest Peace" (*Tai-ping tien-kuo*). Hung transformed Christian rituals into Chinese sacraments: The Taiping bath mirrored Christian baptism, and drinking tea imitated communion. Hung opposed idolatry and opium use but did not condemn polygamy. Hung stated that the coming millennium would produce a food surplus, although he made no reference to a final judgment. The Taiping rebels operated from their capital of Nanking until it was overwhelmed by imperial forces in 1864, whereupon Hung committed suicide. Despite distinctive Oriental elements in the Taiping concepts, the rebellion could not have been conceived without the Christian ideas of a creator God, lawgiver, and savior, which required an emphasis upon sin (*tsui*).

Another example of non-Western millenarianism occurred in Nyasaland (Malawi), Africa, in the early twentieth century. Once again, late-nineteenth-century Christian missionaries, especially the Seventh-Day Adventist Joseph Booth's eschatological preaching in central Africa, helped nurture a millennial-style tradition. The initial millennial tendency began with a Nyasa-born leader renamed Muana Lesa, the Son of God, who formed the Kitawala organization and was executed in 1926. Lesa came under the influence of the Jehovah's Witnesses, who placed great stress on the approaching millennium. The central Africa Kitawala movement in the early 1900s thus blended native beliefs, the desire for independence from the Europeans, and Christian teachings about the millennium. The African millennial movement was also connected to the influence of Elliot Kamwana–led Jehovah's Witnesses (1909) and an ill-fated 1915 rebellion against British rule led by a U.S.-educated messianic figure, John Chilembwe. Millennial themes became even more widespread among the natives in Nyasaland during the 1920s and 1930s, emanating partly from the tribal traditions of prophets that may have been centuries old. Concurrently, Islamic messianism associated with the Mahdi mingled with tribal and Christian traditions to further fuel millennial themes.

Yet another fascinating extension of the millenarian movement transpired in Melanesia in the early twentieth century. The idyllic native societies were disrupted by the arrival of Europeans, especially missionaries who introduced Christianity and its teachings about Christ's millennial rule on earth. Christian ideas blended with the natives' ancient primitive beliefs, which revolved around ancestor worship, to produce a reaction against the foreign invaders. The so-called cargo cults had certain distinctive features from one island people to another, but also many similarities. With no concept of private property, the Melanesians felt that material items brought to the islands by the Europeans should be available to all and were disappointed to find that such cargoes were not distributed to them. The foreign concept of private property combined with the dislocation of age-old traditional beliefs caused further resentments. The arrival of cargoes, which natives believed rightfully belonged to them, was interpreted as the beginning of the millennium. Variations on the cargo cults either had the natives disposing of the Europeans or living in harmony with them after the cargo was distributed to all inhabitants.

Clearly, the Christian concept of the millennium was mixed with and at times reshaped by various primitive local religious customs and secular utopian movements. Likewise, the Judeo-Christian-Islamic belief in a heavenly paradise was a major influence upon the heaven-on-earth thinking of secular utopians. Passive anticipations of the coming millennium have caused many religious leaders such as England's John Mason in 1694 and America's William Miller in 1844 to prepare followers for the event. Other Christian theologians, including current spokesmen, have sought to read the "signs" predicted in the Bible for the end times. Further, parallels between the millennium and most utopian scenarios from Thomas More to the twentieth century can be identified. Generally, millennialists have tended to be more like utopians in their theory but less similar in their practice.

*See also* Messianism; *Nova Solyma*.

*Reference* Harrison, John F. C. *The Second Coming: Popular Millenarianism, 1780–1850* (1979); Thrupp, Sylvia L., ed. *Millennial Dreams in Action* (1970).

## *A Modern Utopia* (1905)

Though noted mostly for his many tales of science and catastrophe fiction, H. G. Wells wrote perhaps the single most influential utopian work of the twentieth century. Further, *A Modern Utopia* became the paradigm for the twentieth-century welfare state. It was in many respects simply the classical idea of utopia recast into a modern technological form. Wells's fiction was a logical extension of the eighteenth-century fable and the Gothic romances of the early nineteenth century. Later in his career, Wells wrote other works with a utopian flavor, including *Men Like Gods* (1923) and *The Shape of Things to Come* (1933), but they lacked the vitality of *A Modern Utopia*, which was written at a time in his career when his optimism overflowed and he enjoyed fame and fortune from his series of science fiction novels. It more accurately represents his philosophical thought than do any of his many other works.

Herbert George Wells (1866–1946) was born into a working-class family and demonstrated empathy with worker struggles in all of his writings. He worked his way through the University of London studying with Thomas Huxley and majoring in biology. Soon after launching a writing career, Wells was drawn to science fiction. He became friends with the leading British authors of his day: George Bernard Shaw, Rudyard Kipling, and Joseph Conrad. Wells followed Shaw into the Fabian socialist movement, a tame offshoot of Marxism. *A Modern Utopia* concentrated more upon the idea of utopia rather than on a specific blueprint of a potential system. It updated the traditional utopia and gave it a modern guise. After 1905, Wells grew more skeptical about the possibilities of creating a utopia in the real world. Lewis Mumford said that Wells was able to both restate the meaning of past utopias and bring them up-to-date. Coming within a decade of World War I, *A Modern Utopia* may have been the last important representation of the idea of progress that had been so pervasive during the preceding century. Even though the war and the totalitarianism that followed helped undermine the idea of progress and alter future utopian concepts, the influence of Wells on twentieth-century utopian and dystopian writing remained powerful.

It was the structure of the book that brought attention to Wells's contribution. Rejecting the classical dialogue form popular with many utopists, Wells introduced his idea by having the chief characters, while strolling in the Alps, discover a different time and space in a parallel planetary system, including an earth, exactly replicating our own solar system. Unlike most earlier utopias, which consisted of an isolated community, Wells's utopia required an entire planet with a one-world government. Wells extensively traced the evolution of the world-state concept from the Middle Ages forward. By discovering the new system around them, the characters are able to engage in self-examination and self-critique, since they do not agree on the merits of utopia. The utopians found by the travelers do not own real property individually, but they do possess personal property. Wells's attitude toward work was definitely more hostile than that shown in typical utopias. Residents may work or remain idle, since scientific progress is to eventually eliminate the need for manual labor. Although some individual privacy is respected, the state regulates human reproduction. The state compensates mothers both for procreation and for proper child nurturing. Technology's advantages are abundant, from 300-mile-per-hour trains to efficient creature comforts. Advanced technology also has helped to unify the regional and national cultures of the utopians into a global system. The state, rather than the individual, is responsible for providing material well-being and social security for the utopians. The state maintains elaborate and detailed records of every aspect of each citizen's life.

When Wells wrote that "the modern utopia must not be static, but kinetic," he was suggesting that in order to make utopias real rather than imaginary, they must be viewed as achieving perfection gradually in stages. Thus one hallmark of Wells's utopia was functional change, since he wanted his utopia to reflect dynamic rather than static development. Another trait of *A Modern Utopia* was freedom, which Wells saw as a replacement for virtue as the prime concern of early modern utopias. However, Wells provided that uncreative ("dull") members of utopia would be denied the right of procreation. Wells believed that by emphasizing both freedom and the necessity of a one-world state, a creative tension would develop to locate a proper balance between collectivism and individualism. Certainly, Wells recognized the past dilemma of utopists in restricting the individual's ability to remain out of step with the system. Indeed, Wells has his fictional visitors meet a utopian resident who is openly hostile to the society. The balance of individual and society interests was illustrated by utopia's aristocratic class, known as *samurai*, who possessed both ability and stability and were open-minded and innovative. Wells also insisted that a unified state need not mean an absence of variety in the culture. Yet by emphasizing an all-powerful benevolent state, Wells's idea seemed open to criticism after the emergence of totalitarian systems in the 1920s and 1930s. One result was a skeptical attitude toward the centralized state in virtually all twentieth-century literary dystopias, which eclipsed utopias in popularity. On the other hand, the establishment of first the League of Nations (which Wells helped create) in the 1920s and then the United Nations in the 1940s suggests that Wells's idea of world government was not far-fetched.

Rejecting socialist thinkers such as Karl Marx and Edward Bellamy, Wells seemed more influenced by earlier utopian concepts, notably Francis Bacon's seventeenth-century utopia, *A New Atlantis*. Scientists were undoubtedly the most revered citizens of *A Modern Utopia*. Wells described his socialism as primitive and more similar to Plato's *Republic* and Thomas More's *Utopia* than to Marxism or Bolshevism. Yet Wells has replaced the doctrine that mankind is sinful with the eighteenth-century belief in mankind's goodness and perfectability. Because he hoped to create a real rather than an ideal utopia, much of what Wells wrote focused upon problems of his own time rather than a blueprint for the future. Wells believed that human beings could not readily be reformed in the absence of improvement of their environment. Virtually all twentieth-century utopias and dystopias would fit the Wellsian model of a government gigantic in scale and power as well as dependent upon science and technology to accommodate both the control and pleasure of its subjects. Aldous Huxley's *Brave New World* (1932) and George Orwell's *1984* (1949) derived their negative impression of utopia from Wells.

**References** Hillegas, Mark R. *The Future as Nightmare: H. G. Wells and the Anti-Utopians* (1967); Wagar, W. Warren. *H. G. Wells and the World State* (1961).

## I Mondi (1552)

The Italian Renaissance popularizer of Thomas More's *Utopia*, Anton Francesco Doni, in 20 days during 1552 wrote a satire, *I Mondi celesti, terresti, et infernali, de gli accademici pellegrini*, an imaginary dissertation on seven worlds. In the sixth, about a utopian world, entitled "Mondo Savio," Doni staged a dialogue between a wise man (Savio, from the Italian *saviezza*, meaning "wisdom") and a madman (Pazzo, from the Italian *pazzia*, meaning "folly" or "madness"). Doni was inspired by Erasmus's *Praise of Folly* (1513) with its play upon meanings and the anonymous *La Pazzia* (Venice, 1541), which went through six Italian editions. Anticipating Jean-Jacques Rousseau in the *Discourse on Inequality*, Doni believed that in an early historical era before the advent of "civilization," mankind had lived in harmony without concern for property; following the onset of civilization, society had been corrupted over the centuries. Doni created controversy by including in his ideal city a society that had abolished marriage and instituted free love. Indeed, it was not clear whether Doni added the more controversial features in jest. Nonetheless, *I Mondi* went through several Italian editions and was translated into French.

Anton Francesco Doni (1513–1574) was born in Florence and completed monastic training before leaving the clergy to read law briefly. He joined a literary academy in Florence and published some musical works. After many failed efforts, he finally persuaded the Medici to become his patron, and Doni served as the family printer for almost two years, 1546–1547. He then moved to Venice and joined another literary group, the Accademia Pellegrina. Doni authored nine books during 1551–1553, including a treatise on moral philosophy and another on love. He also composed *I Mondi* during this period.

The new world described by Savio and Pazzo resembled other uniform Italian ideal cities from the Renaissance. Like Filarete's "Sforzinda," Doni's city was designed like a star with a temple at the center hub. The doors of the temple opened to 100 streets that extended to the gates of the city, and 100 priests supervised each street. Even so, religious rites were vague and unclear in the city. Activities at the temple seemed more cultural than religious. Common craftsmen were located on the same streets with one another. In the "Mondo Savio," Doni followed most early modern themes for utopias, including social equality and communal ownership of property. Indeed, there was no money in "Mondo Savio" making it difficult, if not impossible, to distinguish class differences. All of the residents of the city suppressed their pride by living in simple houses and by dressing alike. Food was available in traditional varieties, though not in excess, for everyone. Human ambition and prideful learning were ridiculed. The only education necessary was learning a particular craft or skill. Doni's ideal society provided rather more variety of work, suggesting a greater concern for choice and diversity among the population than allowed by most early modern utopian writers. Nonetheless, the residents of Doni's city, like More's Utopians, preferred to limit their work and enjoy leisure time rather than labor longer to acquire luxuries. Doni's special provisions permitting free love among the female residents were designed to be an attack upon society's complicated legal requirements of marriage.

Francesco Doni utilized a utopian framework as a vehicle to critique his own society, particularly in the social and moral arenas. In that respect, he was typical of early modern utopian writers. He was also similar to Italian architects of the ideal city in the particular design of his "new world." Because Doni used certain sensational elements, such as unorthodox sexual practices, he appeared more modern and secular than most of the utopian authors of his own era. His views on social equality were not typical of the early modern era and compare more closely with Rousseau's ideas. Doni did not outline a government structure in his new world, nor did he provide for law enforcement, since he assumed that there would be no crime in an egalitarian society. Nor was there any need for military defenses: No neighboring state would attack Mondo Savio because it did not maintain any riches to create envy.

*See also* Renaissance City-State Utopias.
*Reference* Grendler, Paul F. "Utopia in Renaissance Italy: Doni's New World" (1965).

## Montaigne, Michel de
*See* Arcadia.

## More, Thomas
*See* Utopia.

## Morelly
*See* Code of Nature.

## Morris, William
*See* News from Nowhere.

## Mundus Alter et Idem (1605)
Strongly influenced by Thomas More's *Utopia*, Bishop Joseph Hall's *Mundus Alter et Idem*, published in Latin in 1605, strictly defined, was a critique of the Land of Cockaygne ideal society. However, some have regarded Hall's effort as a precursor to the genre known as dystopia. Although there were several editions in different languages following its initial appearance, *Mundus* did not establish a standard for dystopias, which would await the model created by Jonathan Swift in *Gulliver's Travels* (1726). Thus Hall's utopian treatise should be considered as an extension of More's influence into the seventeenth century as well as a unique effort at reproaching contemporary society.

Joseph Hall (1574–1656), bishop of Exeter and Norwich, was a prolific writer, as his collected works attest. As an Anglican cleric, he was noted for his piety and dogmatism, which complemented his ambition. Actually Hall's religion was pragmatic and even nontheological. In a later era he might have been a deist or a disciple of Alexander Pope. Hall remained, however, an ardent defender of episcopacy even into the violent civil-war era of the 1640s. When he composed the *Mundus Alter et Idem Sive Terra Australis ante hac semper incognita* (A world different and identical located in Terra Australis) in 1605, it was published under the pseudonym of "Mercurius Brittanicus." Hall utilized the familiar Renaissance technique of satire to comment upon the social ills of his time. Hence *Mundus* became rather popular over the years following its appearance in Latin. Another Latin edition was produced within a few years, and the first English translation, by John Healey, *The Discovery of a New World*, appeared in 1609. It was also translated into German in 1613. After a brief introduction in which Mercurius debates contemporary customs and institutions with some Cambridge scholars, Mercurius relates the story of a voyage to Antarctica and the unveiling of a society that sharply contrasts with More's Utopians. The newly discovered land has five divisions whose names reflect the author's method of inverting the ideals of More's society. Crapulia is a place where intemperance in food and drink rules; Viraginia is a region ruled by women who treat men as inferiors; Moronia replaces folly with wisdom as the favored guide to actions; Lavernia is a state of anarchy rather than an organized society of rules. The fifth region, Terra Sancta, lacks a description and is otherwise ignored by the author. The text of *Mundus* was accompanied by elaborate maps of the regions, marginal notes and illustrations, and even an index of proper names.

Hall was acquainted with the late medieval tradition of the Land of Cockaygne, which featured a superabundance of resources and an absence of work and responsibility. Obviously, he feared that such a fantasy, unreal as it might be, appealed to the masses and was even the dictum of certain aristocrats. Hall's parody of utopia was not merely a literary exercise, since he feared society was drifting toward hedonism and away from its spiritual discipline. Furthermore, Hall followed More in rejecting the notion that reason alone could be mankind's guide in successfully reforming society. Hence Hall was even more skeptical than More that a perfect or near-perfect society could exist. The reason for the impossibility of achieving the ideal was the human condition, mankind's perversity and selfishness. The society revealed in *Mundus* becomes virtually the opposite of the ideal society, a place that repels the reader. When Hall used the term "utopia," he clearly used it in a pejorative sense as an impossible, not to mention impractical, ideal. Since Hall was a cleric, it is fair to conclude that one of his purposes in writing *Mundus* was to demonstrate that only through living the Christian life and receiving a heavenly reward could mankind achieve the ideal or the perfect existence.

Hall's play upon More's *Utopia* occurs throughout *Mundus* but appears most clearly in passages from the visit to Crapulia, a region that also includes the nations of Yvronia ("drunkard" in French) and Pamphagonia ("all-devouring" in Greek). More had his Utopians participate in communal rites, including meals. Hall also required the subjects in Crapulia to imbibe together, but state officials ensured that no one could be found temperate in their indulgences. Subjects were forced to be gluttonous and utilized all their spare time consuming food and drink, leaving no time for self-improvement as occurred in More's *Utopia*. The total attention to satisfying bodily desires preempted any concern for the development of the mind in Crapulia. Hall's refrain is simply "anyone who is drunk cannot offend" and must be good company even if they are ignorant. In Hall's Crapulia, More's vices have effectively become virtues. The "humans" in Crapulia, Yvronia, and Pamphagonia resemble animals by their actions and never consider reason, much less "civilized" behavior, as pertinent to their existence. In certain respects, Hall makes the reader think of these humans as primitives in their absence of clothing and painting of their bodies. In the event, Hall sought to shock as well as amuse his readers so that no right-thinking individual would ever desire to reside in such a place. Nonetheless, the fact that Hall had written his satirical fable demonstrated his personal fear that the civilized world was regressing toward the very unlikely scenarios he pictured in *Mundus*.

Hall's technique of exaggeration and inversion suggests that he was earnest in his desire for reform of society as well as genuinely fearful of its direction. For example, the most pointed reference to government, to the Viraginians' parliament, cited the legislature's practice of changing laws daily upon their whim. Another illustration struck at the family unit: In Lavernia robbery was a family affair in which all members participated, and children were taught to steal something each day. Further, parodying More's insistence that society's leaders be well qualified, in Hall's Crapulia, promotion to a higher office was based on the size of one's stomach. Unlike most of the early modern utopists, Hall demonstrates clear disdain for the aristocracy. Though they are the leaders of society, Hall portrays them as neither exemplary nor competent. Thus Hall's mention of Henry Hastings, earl of Huntingdon, in his dedication, was a satirical inversion since he did not really admire the earl, a Puritan and thus to Hall a schismatic. Hall felt that aristocrats were to blame for turning vices into virtues, ruinously pursuing vainglory, allowing competition with other peer groups to create unnecessary social friction, and lacking in respect for traditions or restraint in their pursuit of the latest fad or fashion. Human pride allowed a privileged class such as the aristocracy to indulge their petty fancies without regard to the social consequences. The English and European aristocracy, far from being noble, were grotesque in their selfishness and irresponsibility.

Reflecting his fears about change and challenges to tradition, Hall viewed his Mercurius as a prophet of the dangers of society too easily embracing different directions. In *Mundus* Hall deliberately warned his readers to rekindle the good old ways of the past and to disdain appealing new trends that desecrate rather than elevate humanity's intellectual and spiritual condition. His style was witty and inventive, even if his ideas about society may have been staid and traditional. Without question, he introduced the prospect of developing the dystopia as an alternative method to utopia for commenting upon society's problems and future.

***Reference*** Wands, John M. "Antipodal Imperfection: Hall's *Mundus Alter et Idem* and Its Debt to More's *Utopia*" (1981).

**Nabokov, Vladimir**
*See Bend Sinister.*

## *The Napoleon of Notting Hill* (1904)

The neo-Christian essayist and novelist G. K. Chesterton reflected contact with several utopian thinkers and sources, especially his friend H. G. Wells, when he penned his own version of utopia. Chesterton touches on a variety of themes in *The Napoleon of Notting Hill*: politics, the meaning of sanity and insanity in the symbols of life, the role of the state in the relationship of nationalism to imperialism, and the relationship between public and private, as well as the ideal society of utopia.

Gilbert Keith Chesterton (1874–1936) was born in London, the son of an auctioneer whom Chesterton later likened to Charles Dickens's Mr. Pickwick. Chesterton evidenced a skepticism toward the liberal, rationalist mainstream early in his schooling at St. Paul's. Physically clumsy and unathletic, he briefly pursued an art career when he attended the Slade School of Art, where he came into contact with impressionism. Also in his youth, despite his family's Unitarian beliefs, Chesterton developed a strong personal faith in Christianity and eventually joined the Catholic church. Chesterton also became attracted by the Fabian socialist movement in Britain, which brought him into contact with several major literary figures, including H. G. Wells. At one point in the 1890s, Chesterton composed a biographical work on Robert Louis Stevenson and showed some fascination with his subject's nihilism. Stevenson, like Chesterton, had turned toward faith in God after being repelled by the cynical philosophies of Oscar Wilde and Arthur Schopenhauer. Chesterton also revealed a fascination with William Morris, the author of the optimistic utopian treatise *News from Nowhere* (1890). Chesterton's first novel was inspired by his scrutiny of the Boer War in South Africa and his interest in the relationship between nationalism and imperialism. *The Napoleon of Notting Hill* contains most of the themes of his later novels, some of which, such as *The Man Who Was Thursday* (1907) and *The Return of Don Quixote* (1927), also show a utopian bent. Chesterton takes swipes at those of his contemporary intellectuals who arrogantly thought they could predict the future. Perhaps the most striking influence of *The Napoleon of Notting Hill* was on the Irish nationalist Michael Collins, who was inspired to lead the 1916 Irish Rebellion against British imperialism.

*The Napoleon of Notting Hill* takes place in 1984, an interesting date since it was also chosen by George Orwell for his famous dystopia. The novel is organized into five sections of three chapters each to allow Chesterton to focus and comment upon specific issues. In Chesterton's future, the emphasis is less upon the advance of technology (there are no automobiles in 1984 London) than upon the fact that even with greater creature comforts, the future society is spiritually void. In the London of 1984, people have lost faith in their own individual capacity for independent thought and have simply acquiesced to the monotony of the established regime. The future city of London is governed by a massive bureaucracy presided over by a figurehead despot selected through a random process rather than by inheritance. The story focuses upon the selection of a new despot, Auberon Quin, who represents the impressionism that had fascinated Chesterton before he wrote his novel. Quin takes artistic license when he decides to play a practical joke on Londoners. He recreates the old borough system that had operated in London during the Middle Ages, complete with antiquated rituals and attire. The bureaucrats, led by a character named James Barker and abetted by big business interests, do not embrace Quin's system, but neither do they interfere since it appears harmless, if eccentric.

A few years after Quin's experiment is launched a new magistrate of the London borough of Notting Hill, Adam Wayne, naively takes Quin's rules seriously. The fanatical Wayne decides to utilize the powers of the medieval borough by blocking the construction of an urban development in his territory. Despite the odds (rather like the Boers in South Africa) and relying upon swords rather than firearms, Wayne's small army ultimately succeeds in wresting control away from London's authority, causing Wayne to be portrayed as a latter-day Napoleon with a tiny empire in Notting Hill. Yet the other conquered boroughs, expressing their own nationalism against Notting Hill's emergent imperial rule, rise up against the Napoleon of Notting Hill and defeat Wayne. The whole episode is of course ludicrous, yet it allows Chesterton to express his views on a number of contemporary issues. The final chapter, at the end of the war, unexpectedly brings the two characters Quin and Wayne into a sort of unified expression, linking the fantasy of childhood with the reality of adulthood. Quin explains to Wayne that his digression into the Middle Ages was a joke, and Wayne finally understands; Quin, meanwhile, has come to respect Wayne's convictions. Thus, unlike in the rest of the book, in the final chapter Chesterton allows the reader the liberty to draw conclusions that might not be those of the author.

When Quin decides to apply his own symbols to meaning, he invokes a kind of antilogic that challenges the existing establishment. Quin's medieval rules effectively asked why the modern methods of government were necessarily better than the ancient ones. Thus the novel causes the reader to go beyond merely dismissing medieval ways as absurd and to question the reasons for the existing London system. Quin forces an examination of the established ways, which in turn leads to the conclusion that the existing system cannot be rationalized any better than the old. The troubling conclusion from the exercise is that Chesterton may have been suggesting that there are no absolute standards. Chesterton skillfully makes his three main characters reflect a specific point of view. Wayne makes the metaphorical old symbols re-created by Quin into a rallying point for people who had become virtual automata under the existing bureaucratic system. Chesterton also uses irony by having Quin, called insane by bureaucrats like Barker, refer to Wayne as insane. In the character Barker, Chesterton expresses contempt for politicians obsessed by power who claim to be acting on behalf of "the people." Chesterton discovered in *The Napoleon of Notting Hill* his own sympathy with the common man and small nation, the underdog.

Though relying upon symbols throughout the novel, Chesterton personally had misgivings about allowing metaphors to exist without a full explanation. Thus the author seems to have believed that humans can never perfectly express their thoughts to others. Certainly Chesterton believed that society and its institutions should not stifle personal inspiration and creativity, which ultimately emanate from a divine source. Yet he seems to have been uncertain about whether a utopian ideal society can ever be created, since even if it were expertly devised, people might not understand it in the way its creator intended. However, through the reconciliation of the apparently opposing views of Quin and Wayne at the end of the story, Chesterton did present a hopeful rather than a doleful prospect for the future. Because the two main characters ultimately adopt a commonsensical view, the reader is left with the impression that both Quin's humor and Wayne's seriousness have their place as long as they are properly balanced, but that in modern society the two opposites created an atmosphere of conflict that made resolution of differences difficult. People should not take themselves too seriously, and at the same time they should maintain a tolerance and understanding of the views of those who differ.

*Reference* Quinn, Joseph A. "Eden and New Jerusalem: A Study of *The Napoleon of Notting Hill*" (1977).


## Native American Utopias

Like the peoples of other primitive societies, Native Americans developed utopian ideas by blending their own traditions with the ideas of Western civilization. The most important influence upon Native American tribes was Christianity, so their utopias often reflect millenarian or messianic qualities. Yet these utopias remained distinctive and retained more of the native ideology than did those of most tribal societies. The most striking feature of Native American utopias was the Ghost Dance tradition, which later became a religion. Similar themes existed among North and South American tribes. The primary orientation of Native Americans was to seek liberation from the European invaders and the restoration of their traditional lifestyle.

Virtually all tribes in the Americas possessed the concept of a messiah or deliverer in their pre-Christian religious mythology. Most interesting, the messiah usually was portrayed as a white man in myths such as that of Quetzalcoatl among the Aztecs in Mexico or of Manabozho of the Algonquian tribes in North America. Because one of the messiah's functions would be the regeneration of the tribe's world, Native American lore taught that the coming of the messiah would be preceded by miraculous signs such as comets and disastrous events like floods and famines (especially cited by the Earth Lodge cult). The approaching utopia was also to be foretold by a prophet or messenger (*pagés* in South America), often preaching the necessity for unification of tribes and a return to more traditional practices whose

observance had become corrupted. The prophet would lead the tribes to the Land without Evil, an earthly paradise. The introduction of Christian teachings among the tribes merely heightened these messianic tendencies. Such prophets appeared prior to frontier Native American uprisings led by the Ottawa chief Pontiac (who was inspired by the Delaware prophet) in the 1760s and by the Shawnee chief Tecumseh during 1811–1813 (his brother Tenskwatawa was the prophet). The prophets condemned such corrupt practices among the tribes as drunkenness, polygamy, and female relations with Europeans, and both Pontiac and Tecumseh campaigned for a unification of the tribes into a single nation. Thought by many tribes to be the incarnation of the Algonquian messiah Manabozho, Tenskwatawa predicted liberation if the natives would return to the good ways of past custom.

Other prophets following Tecumseh's defeat echoed the earlier themes. Kanakuk (d. 1852), the Kickapoo prophet, reasserted Tenskwatawa's admonitions about virtuous living and isolation from the white man. He urged the Kickapoo not to yield their Illinois lands to the government in 1819, but they were nonetheless forced to move to Kansas. The Columbia River tribes came under the spell of the prophet Smohalla (ca. 1820–1895), whose followers became known as the Dreamers in the 1860s. Educated in part by Jesuit missionaries, Smohalla also borrowed certain Christian concepts to blend with native thought. Smohalla taught that the Native Americans were the chosen people of the Great Spirit and that a resurrection of their dead relatives would accompany the advent of an era of liberation from the hated white man and restoration of lost lands. Smohalla's rituals also included dances, the Salmon Dance in the spring and the Dance of the Berries in the autumn. Another cult, led by Kolaskin in the Columbia River area, did not feature a ritual dance, but other elements remained consistent with previous prophetic themes.

The culmination of utopian thinking in relation to the encroachment of the white man upon Native American lands and customs occurred in the Ghost Dance uprising of 1890, which climaxed in the massacre at Wounded Knee, South Dakota. The mythical legend of unification and earthly regeneration promised the elimination of suffering, disease, and death, so it possessed a powerful appeal in troubled times. In addition to the expropriation of their lands, the Plains tribes had witnessed the gradual elimination of the buffalo herds by white hunters. A prophetess named Wananikwe, who preached a ritual called Dream Dance, advocated unity and peace among the tribes. She had first warned about the dangers to the herds after 1876, but there had been little response. Like most western tribes, the Paiutes did not receive the promised provisions and agricultural education on the reservations run by the government. Their poverty led to exasperation. During the late 1860s, a Paiute leader named Wodziwob (Fish Lake Joe) received a revelation that a train would arrive from the east bringing dead relatives. Of course, it happened that the first transcontinental rail line across the West was completed in 1869 in Utah. Wodziwob preached that the tribe should paint themselves and engage in the Round Dance to prepare for the train's arrival. The dance was accompanied by testimonies about reform and renewal. Yet the living conditions of the Paiutes continued to deteriorate over the years that followed.

A new prophet appeared in the person of Wovoka (d. 1932), a member of the Paiute tribe in Nevada whose father was a shaman. Wovoka was ten years old when Wodziwob's revelation circulated in Nevada. Wovoka had converted to Christianity while working for a rancher named Wilson; Wovoka later took the name Jack Wilson in honor of his benefactor. Wovoka began leading Round Dances about 1888 and fell ill the next year during an eclipse of the sun (especially sacred to Native Americans). Wovoka claimed later that he had levitated to converse with God, who revealed a time past of happiness and plenty among the Paiutes. God instructed Wovoka to return to earth and preach reconciliation, peace, and work. If they followed the admonition, the tribes could join their departed relatives in paradise. Soon enough the vision of Wovoka spread from the Paiutes to other neighboring tribes such as the Arapaho, Shoshone, and Cheyenne. Other prophets such as Porcupine (Cheyenne) reinforced and embellished Wovoka's message and predicted the appearance of the messiah and the launching of the millennium in the spring of 1891.

During 1889–1890, several delegates from the Sioux tribes traveled west to hear Wovoka's message. Soon preparations were under way across the Great Plains for the coming events. The preparation and purification rituals, which no doubt were extensions of the Round Dance, included the sweat bath and several days of the Ghost Dance, in which participants, both male and female, wore a "ghost shirt" believed to be bulletproof and danced in a circle until sheer exhaustion caused them to collapse. Although Wovoka stressed that his movement was peaceful, accounts that followed the confrontation and massacre at Wounded Knee in 1890 taught that the advent of the millennium would include the extermination of the white man and the recovery of Native American lands as well as the return of the buffalo. The Oglala Sioux prophet Black Elk (1863–1950) explained that the European occupation of Native American lands was a punishment for their sins, but since they were now cleansed the white man's rule must end also. When government agents attempted in 1890 to stop the Ghost Dance ritual among the Sioux, Chief Sitting Bull refused to cooperate and was killed by reservation police. Forced by their hunger to surrender, about 200 Sioux were massacred by troops following an incident at Wounded Knee. After the violent clash with the U.S. government in 1890, the Ghost Dance ritual soon became a religion. Prophets refused to specify a date for the millennium but promised that it was imminent. Certainly, the bleak existence of the Native Americans on government reservations following 1890 did not diminish their hope for deliverance. It only fueled a variety of escapist techniques, including eating the nonaddictive peyote cactus as a ceremonial function (of the Native American church, established in 1918).

The parallels between North American and South American tribes are remarkable. For many decades during the sixteenth century, the Tupis tribes migrated from the interior of Brazil to the Atlantic coast following a messianic promise of an earthly paradise (Land without Evil or Land of Immortality and Perpetual Peace). Some shamans convinced the Tupis to stop cultivating the soil since the food would grow by itself to provide a bounty, and eternal youth became another bold promise. Many legends and descriptions caused the European explorers to seek El Dorado in the interior. The *pagé* prophet–medicine man followed in the late sixteenth and seventeenth centuries and encouraged opposition to the Europeans and restoration of native traditions. The *pagés* also predicted that the regeneration of the land would produce an earthly paradise. A Brazilian-Paraguayan tribe, the Guarani, embraced similar themes of treks to a Land without Evil from the sixteenth to the nineteenth centuries, usually in response to clashes with the European invaders. Like North American natives, the Guarani believed in the resurrection of the dead following a great natural disaster. Often the utopian movements among the Tupis and Guaranis led to violent confrontations with the Portuguese or Spanish. Among the Amazon tribe of Tukunas in Brazil, a movement as late as the 1940s followed a prophetic call to erect a temple in the jungle, which would protect the Tukunas from a devastating flood that would wipe out the white man. Other messianic movements advocating liberation from the Europeans occurred in Colombia in the sixteenth century, in Peru in the eighteenth century, and in Argentina in the nineteenth century.

*See also* Messianism; Millennialism.

*References* Edmunds, R. David. *The Shawnee Prophet* (1983); Ribeiro, René. "Brazilian Messianic Movements," in Thrupp, Sylvia L., ed. *Millennial Dreams in Action: Studies in Revolutionary Religious Movement* (1970); Mooney, James. *The Ghost Dance Religion and Wounded Knee* (1976 [1896]).

## Neo-Confucian Utopias

Early modern Chinese philosophers seeking a basis for promoting reform offered a variety of methods to reconfigure traditional Confucian thought to support utopian reform projects. Certainly, a major part of the impetus for reformist thought included political changes that would usher in the ideal state. Yet little thought was given to changing the traditional institutional structure. Foreign occupation of China—from 1234 to 1368 by the Mongols and again from 1644 to the twentieth century by the Manchu—has influenced philosophical views in much of the nation's modern history. Another strain of Chinese utopian thought involved a growing sensitivity to the plight of the peasants and the emergence of an egalitarian sentiment. Even though utopian thought projecting change and challenging the existing system was itself a major departure from traditions that looked to the past, many of the utopian projects actually sought to restore what was considered an ancient golden age. Hence, though Confucian thought was altered, it remained the starting point for early modern reform ideas in China.

The earliest neo-Confucian utopian concepts date from the Sung era (907–1279), but the first important statement came later, in the sixteenth century. "Clan communism" was articulated in the late sixteenth century by a scholar, Liang Ju-yuan (1527–1579). He was not a rebel in any modern sense of the word, since he respected hierarchical arrangements and the moral obligation of duty, typical Confucian tenets. Moreover, although an advocate of learning, Liang did not view education as a particularly liberating force. Instead, he focused on the institution of the family as the chief instrument of reform in his writings. In 1553, Liang (using the pseudonym Ho Hsin-yin) constructed the "Hall for Gathering in Harmony" in the Yung-feng district of south-central China. He proposed bringing all members of his extended family together in a cooperative venture that would include education and economic activity. Not only would educational methods be enhanced by a more convivial atmosphere, but children would also become better acquainted with their relatives. The combining of property holdings and cooperative labor would ensure both greater efficiency of production and equal distribution of the crops. In both the communal school and work arrangements, there would be a designated director or leader, so Liang's system still embodied a sense of hierarchical authority. Liang Ju-yuan's clan communism reflects both the traditional conservatism of Oriental traditions as well as the growing Western influence in Asia, which propagated change. Although the emperor tended to like the commune idea because it simplified tax collection, local provincial officials opposed it because it lessened their opportunity for graft. A 1559 tax rebellion in Yung-feng province became the pretext for arresting Liang and causing his communal experiment to collapse. Because Liang ran afoul of an imperial official in 1573 over his educational ideas, he was declared an outlaw, arrested, and beaten to death.

The transition of Chinese ruling dynasties in 1644 from the Ming to the Manchu led certain Chinese intellectuals to assail the whole system of political rule by absolute monarchs. Characteristically, neo-Confucian intellectuals compared the contemporary system to an ancient time of wise, selfless rulers when laws were fair and a feudal society operated in harmony. It was the beginning of a new and long-term utopian tradition in China that undermined the traditional attitude of waiting

patiently for changes and advocated more dramatic and immediate change.

It seems clear that with the incursion of Western ideas into East Asia in the early modern era, traditional Chinese philosophy would be influenced by the new mental framework from the West. The antimonarchical tradition sought changes in both society and government, but it remained largely an underground operation for a long period because the Chinese adhered to their inclination to avoid being outspoken.

One of those most disturbed by the overthrow of the Ming dynasty at the hands of the Manchu was Huang Tsung-hsi (1610–1695). Huang saw China's slow but steady deterioration since the end of the Chou dynasty (third century B.C.) as unchecked. He recognized not only the repressive nature of the monarchy but also the ossification of the Confucian philosophy with its resistance to reform. In the 1662 *Ming-i Tai-fang Lu* (A plan for the prince), Huang used a familiar contrast between the light (freedom) and the dark (repression) to make his point. Coincidentally, the dark also connoted a barbarian rule, and Huang spoke of the catastrophe of foreign (that is, barbarian) occupations, which had included that of the Mongols. Chinese tradition often outlined a scenario wherein the forces of darkness prevailed against a latent virtue in the people, including in a high-ranking minister who bided his time awaiting an opportunity to lead renewal. Thus Huang compared the advent of the Manchu in 1644 with previous dark periods and saw himself as playing the role of the legendary Chi-tzu, an imprisoned idealist set free by a liberator-savior. Hence the Chinese customarily patiently waited for the collapse of evil and the establishment of an ideal society. When Huang's book was reissued in the 1890s during the last years of the Manchu rule, it was viewed as prophetic by opposition groups.

Huang Tsung-hsi's attempt to revitalize Confucianism portended a different intellectual approach to a corrupt society and government in China. Previously rare, increasingly after the seventeenth century, intellectual criticism of the establishment became vigorous and even violent. Utopian thought in China severed its ties to religion and expanded along two different lines. One approach was the creation of the ideal state, albeit abstractly, relying upon Buddhist teachings about avoidance of corruption and the inner life of purity. The Chinese school of utopists following this line tended to combine varying elements of Confucianism, Taoism, and Buddhism, but they did not threaten the existing regime openly. The other approach after Huang ´Ĭsung-hsi involved using satire to bring theory to bear upon reality, and it resorted to the image of the voyage or quest against great odds.

*References* Chang, Carsun. *The Development of Neo-Confucian Thought* (1957–1962); deBary, William Theodore. "Chinese Despotism and the Confucian Ideal: A Seventeenth-Century View," in Fairbank, John K., ed. *Chinese Thought and Institutions* (1957).

## Neville, Henry
*See* Arcadia; Robinsonades.

## New Age Cults
Combining a variety of utopian elements, late-twentieth-century New Age cults have attracted a wide, if esoteric, following, not to mention intense curiosity from the public and media. Cults have been most evident in the United States, but their appeal certainly extends to Europe and other continents. Indeed, the cult of Scientology had 15 million adherents in Europe by the late 1990s. Although each cult has its own peculiar identity and utopian schemata, New Age movements tend to be syncretic. They are an amorphous blend of several ingredients derived from millenarianism, messianism, romanticism, science fiction, Oriental mysticism, communalism, the occult, shamanism, spiritual healing, and channeling. The 1960s increasingly represent the point at which a breakdown of the old order occurred, especially in the Judeo-Christian tradition and bourgeois values. The youth counterculture offered stinging and often accurate critiques of the existing establishment—politics, institutions, laws, social customs, and so on. Almost unconsciously, the assault focused on the failure of democratic liberalism's promise of greater individual freedom. Instead, despite impressive advances in prosperity, post–World War II Western society promoted the growth of nonrepressive totalitarianism, that is, the welfare state, which forced the individual to lose his or her identity. Yet the alternatives offered were both too disparate and too illusory to produce a unified new order. Rather, as individuals feel disgust toward or betrayed by the existing system, they drop out to seek meaning beyond civilization's repression of their individual identity. Hence New Age cults claimed they filled a void in the intrinsic human quest for meaning in life.

One of the typical New Age responses to established traditions occurred in the revival of the utopian communalism that had been so popular in the nineteenth century. Following the youth rebellions of the early 1960s, including the "hippies" and "flower children," some groups sought to put their rejection of the system into a practical alternative lifestyle. California became a popular location for many of these communes, but they could be found in almost all parts of the United States. Unlike most of the nineteenth-century communes, the New Age communities generally steered away from a messianic or authoritarian style of leadership and were more democratic in operation. There were, of course, exceptions, such as the community that formed around Charles Manson in the late 1960s. The New Age communes sought not to convert others to their beliefs but merely to exist in isolation from the traditional society. They tended to be pragmatic about the need to maintain a livelihood for the sect, usually through agriculture or craft production. Communes usually reflected a secular orientation, although they could practice certain spiritual-mystical rituals and almost

*Aerial view of the Heaven's Gate compound near San Diego, California*

always worshipped nature. Probably the pioneering model of the New Age communes was Findhorn, Scotland, established in 1965 by Eileen Caddy, Peter Caddy, and Dorothy Maclean. Ultimately, the American David Spangler (b. 1945) made Findhorn popular in the United States, and a foundation was established in 1972 to promote its ideals. The distinctive features of the Findhorn model included use of "devas," or nature spirits, which were part of certain foods, and channeling with the spirit world. Gradually, New Age communes multiplied in the late 1970s, and some became very successful, including the 250-member Sunburst community in California, which operated a 5,000-acre farm and ranch near Santa Barbara. Sunburst's livelihood derived from the sale of their organic produce. Other California communes include Ananda, founded in 1967 and attracting about 400 participants; Kayavarohana, started in 1977 by an Oriental guru promoting celibacy and asceticism; and Cornucopia Institute,

started by Ken Keyes and later relocated to St. Mary's, Kentucky, in the 1970s, featuring instruction in consciousness-raising. Perhaps the oldest example of the revived communalism is the Koinonia Partners in south Georgia, originally founded in 1942 as a biracial community. Revived in the 1960s, the 600-acre farm supported about 60 residents. Several communes reflected a stronger religious tone, including the Abode of the Message on 450 acres in New York, which taught a version of Islamic Sufism, and the 300-member Love Family in Washington, which followed a primitive version of Christian communism and claimed the Bible as its authority. The Renaissance Community in rural Massachusetts originated as a haven for ex–drug addicts and professed a universal spiritual approach to sobriety. The New Age communes even adopted a style of architecture, the geodesic dome, pioneered by architect R. Buckminster Fuller, who coined the phrase "spaceship earth."

New Age cults often seek inspiration and guidance from a guru figure. One of the earliest such religio-philosophical mystics was the French Jesuit paleontologist Pierre Teilhard de Chardin (1881–1955). Trained in both theology and science, Teilhard de Chardin traveled and worked in almost every corner of the globe, immersing himself in a variety of cultures. As a Catholic and a member of the Jesuit order, Teilhard de Chardin's scientific ideas proved controversial because he spent much time and effort attempting to harmonize his view of Christianity with that of evolutionary science. He recognized mankind's frustration with reality and the resulting dichotomy between the this-worldly reformers promoting a heaven on earth and the other-worldly spiritualists looking for perfection beyond physical existence. Teilhard de Chardin's description of the "noosphere" in *L'Avenir de L'Homme* (The future of man, published posthumously in 1959) created an apocalyptic explanation of humanity's physical transformation that appealed to many New Agers. The noosphere was a third stage (following the inorganic and organic stages) in the evolution of matter, a physiological and psychological transcendence of humanity into a utopian dimension. In the noosphere, human awareness and sensitivity would become acute from early childhood onward, allowing the achievement of a peaceful synthesis of spirit and matter. The noosphere thus would achieve the final state of autonomous and self-sufficient consciousness, allowing plant, earth, and organic matter to dissipate. Hence "noogenesis" produces the end of the world as it has existed, a vision at once both hopeful and troubling. Teilhard de Chardin's ideas became popular in the English-speaking world thanks to the efforts of the evolutionary humanist Sir Julian Huxley, who wrote an introduction to the English translation of Teilhard de Chardin's *The Phenomenon of Man* in 1959.

Another New Age movement built upon a charismatic mystic leader was Scientology, founded in 1954 by La Fayette Ron Hubbard (1911–1986), a would-be musical composer and artist. Hubbard's *Dianetics* (1950) was a forerunner of Scientology. Hubbard portrayed humans as possessing a dual nature, body and spirit (called Thetan consciousness). Humans were condemned to inhabit earth 75 million years ago by an alien space ruler. Hubbard constructed ten "Celebrity Centres" around the world as recruiting tools to attract entertainment-media celebrities and artists whom Hubbard saw as essential to make the movement viable. Many Hollywood stars have joined Scientology since the 1970s. One of the movement's publications is a periodical called *Celebrity*. Cleverly, Hubbard attempted to frame Scientology as a religion in order to gain tax advantages, although it was granted tax-exempt status only in 1993, by the Clinton administration. Although very popular in Europe, Scientology has been treated by some media and governments as a fund-raising scam rather than a church. By the 1990s, Scientology operated almost 500 "churches" in more than 50 countries.

Certainly the cult movement gained its widest notoriety from publicity surrounding Jim Jones's People's Temple. The temple starkly manifested the consequences of utopias gone awry and thereby heightened twentieth-century skepticism about utopian dreamworlds. Jim Jones's California-based Christian Assembly of God church founded a colony in 1977 in Guyana. The communal existence fostered an isolationist and apocalyptic perspective among its troubled members. Jones's power over the movement was reminiscent of the power held by leaders of earlier communal societies founded on utopian dreams, but Jones carried the experiment to the ultimate extreme and demanded the sacrifice of life itself for his cause, which led to the mass suicide of 913 followers in Guyana in 1978. The People's Temple became a dystopian nightmare manifested in reality.

Born James Warren Jones (1931–1978) at Lynn, Indiana, the future founder of the

People's Temple was part of a large rural family struggling through the depression years. He rejected the values of his father, a disabled World War I veteran and member of the Indiana Ku Klux Klan in the 1920s. Married in 1949, Jones and his wife Marceline, a nurse, had one child of their own and adopted seven other children. While attending college at Butler University in 1953, Jones founded and pastored the Christian Assembly of God church in Indianapolis. Jones eventually received a degree in education from Butler in 1961 and developed a reputation for enhancing interracial relations in Indianapolis. Influenced greatly by his study of Father Divine's social gospel in the 1930s and 1940s, Jones felt a calling to minister to the urban poor. In 1962–1963, he served as a missionary to Brazil, where he established a mission church and orphanages, and he also visited neighboring Guyana. Upon his return to Indiana, Jones changed the name of his church to the People's Temple Full Gospel church. He was ordained into the Christian church in 1964 and the next year began preaching an apocalyptic theme of nuclear destruction, which he predicted for 1967. Because of the perceived imminent danger, Jones led 70 families to relocate to Ukiah, California, north of San Francisco, in 1966. By 1970, Jones had established a ministry in the Fillmore district of San Francisco, using a former synagogue as a sanctuary. Jones recruited followers from among the urban poor and in 1971 moved his church and followers to San Francisco.

By the 1970s Jones had jettisoned most of his earlier Christian beliefs in favor of a political Marxist agenda, while retaining certain millennial and faith-healing traditions. The People's Temple had about 5,000 members by the late 1970s, its financing coming largely from members' Social Security checks. Jones had become an important element in the local politics of San Francisco, marshaling his followers to support or oppose candidates and platforms. Newly elected Mayor George Moscone appointed Jones chairman of the

City Housing Authority in 1976. Political leaders, including California Governor Jerry Brown, Vice President Walter Mondale, and First Lady Rosalynn Carter, offered support to Jones's social reform agenda. In 1977, Jones received the Martin Luther King, Jr., Humanitarian Award for his social ministry. At the height of his popularity and influence in San Francisco, Jones brought plans for a utopian community in Guyana to maturity. After establishing a church mission in Guyana in 1973, Jones leased 27,000 acres of remote jungle land in 1974 from the government of Guyana, which hoped to see development and settlement of the area. Suggesting that forces opposing his movement necessitated the flight to Guyana, Jones convinced many of his congregation to escape with him to South America.

About 900 church members joined Jones for the trek to Guyana in 1977. Those entering the commune were required to sign away their property to Jones, who would use their resources to maintain the settlement. The settlement soon became known as Jonestown and, like his California constituencies, was populated mainly by the disaffected urban poor. The vast majority of those who came to Guyana were black, although the settlement, like the San Francisco church, operated on an interracial basis. Jonestown eventually included a farm and a sawmill, small cottages, a medical center, and a communal assembly. Some outside of Jones's following feared that his followers were being exploited and coerced. Indeed, Jones seemed to adopt increasingly bizarre positions, denouncing the Bible and lauding historical figures such as Lenin. He also showed signs of paranoia about those who supposedly opposed him, including especially the U.S. government, and had the residents of Jonestown practice mock suicide drills. After family members of some Jonestown residents, organized as Concerned Relatives, complained about coercion and sexual abuse of their relatives, California Congressman Leo Ryan traveled to Guyana in November 1978 to investigate, accompanied by journalists and members of Concerned Relatives. Clearly skeptical of Ryan's motives, Jones attempted to assure Ryan that the residents of Jonestown were not forcibly detained or abused. Keenly aware of the power of public scrutiny, Jones hired conspiracy theorist and attorney Mark Lane to serve as spokesman for the People's Temple. As Ryan's group prepared to leave Jonestown following their visit, Jones's guards murdered the congressman and most of his party. Jones then directed the 900 residents of Jonestown to commit mass suicide by drinking poison-laced Kool-Aid. Those who did not comply were shot.

The U.S. public was shocked by the Jonestown massacre because nothing like it had occurred before, certainly nothing associated with utopian ideas. Nonetheless, some New Age cults of the late twentieth century increasingly resorted to Jones's suicidal methods either to avoid control by the outside world or to escape to an anticipated better existence beyond the physical world. Mass suicides by cults have continued to occur periodically since 1978. Growth in the numbers of isolated and despairing people who dropped out of society for a variety of reasons provided New Age cult movements ample opportunities for recruitment. Another source nurturing New Age movements has been the proliferation of space alien theories, which has benefited from resources such as the Internet. It was only a small leap from popular culture's fascination with science fiction, and its manifestation in cults following television programs and motion pictures, to the amplification of the theme of alien interaction within certain cult groups.

In April 1993 the U.S. government, seeking to arrest cultists for arms violations, raided the Branch Davidian compound near Waco, Texas. The resulting fire killed the 75 residents, including David Koresh (né Vernon Howell), the group's leader since 1987. The government claimed that the Davidians had committed suicide. The Branch Davidians were a splinter from the Davidians who had separated from the Seventh-Day Adventist church in the 1930s. These groups had taught an apocalyptic message not unlike that of Jim Jones.

In 1994 and 1995, members of the Order of the Solar Temple committed mass suicide at locations in Canada, France, and Switzerland. The order was founded in 1984 by a Belgian medical doctor, Luc Jouret, who became obsessed with homeopathic medicine and extreme environmentalism. He blended New Age ideas about astrology and the apocalypse with his primary interests. In October 1994, police discovered 5 bodies in Canada and 48 in Switzerland dead from apparent suicide, and most bodies were burned in ceremonial robes. Jouret was among the dead. In December 1995, 16 more members of the Order of the Solar Temple were found dead in rural France.

The most recent illustration of a suicidal cult was the Heaven's Gate cult, started in the 1970s by Marshall Applewhite, which involved the mass suicide of 39 people near San Diego, California, in 1997. Typical of many New Age cults, the Heaven's Gate group mingled Christian teachings about an afterlife and messianic deliverance with theories of space aliens and transmigration into a higher form of life after physical death. Despite the attempts of postmodern utopists to divorce their movements from religion, the religious element from traditional millennialism to New Age cults has remained inextricably connected with utopianism.

*See also* Messianism; Millennialism; Theosophy.

*References* Faber, M. D. *New Age Thinking: A Psychoanalytic Critique* (1996); Krause, Charles. *Guyana Massacre: The Eyewitness Account* (1978); Melton, J. Gordon, Jerome Clark, and Aidan A. Kelly. *New Age Almanac* (1991); Weaver, Dusk and Willow. *Sunburst: A People, a Path, a Purpose* (1982).

## New Atlantis (1627)

Sir Francis Bacon's *New Atlantis* fits neatly into the early modern utopian tradition of writers such as Thomas More and Johann

*Francis Bacon, from an engraving by Marshall*

Valentin Andreae, yet it offers much less detail than other books in the genre and demonstrates Bacon's conflicting conclusions about humanity. Thus it has been difficult to define Bacon in simple terms because he reflected such ambivalence toward his own times. That irresolution can be seen especially in his sole venture into utopian writing, the *New Atlantis*, left uncompleted at his death and published by his chaplain the next year. Bacon sought in his utopia to promote two personal ideals, the advancement of the new science and the reform of politics. He proved, however, in the *New Atlantis* that he was more of a pragmatist than an idealist and that he wore the mantle of utopist uneasily.

Sir Francis Bacon (1561–1626) was a true Renaissance man of the seventeenth century. He is best known to posterity as a philosopher of modern science, but he was also a lawyer, a historian, and a holder of political office whose writings were voluminous. Bacon came from an aristocratic family; his lawyer father served in Elizabeth I's government as lord keeper. As a child Bacon was introduced to court life, and he ultimately sought to follow in his father's footsteps, although he rebelled against the educational tradition represented by his father. Educated at Cambridge and Gray's Inn, Bacon immersed himself in the classics and came to visualize himself as Hercules, a hero with strength and determination. Bacon was elected to Parliament as a young man but failed to obtain the desired post of attorney general under Elizabeth. Indeed, for all of his ambition and potential, Bacon's career proved to be unstable and checkered. His greatest political service occurred in the reign of James I (1603–1625), when he rose to the top political office as lord chancellor (1618). Ultimately Bacon became tangled in partisan politics and was impeached by Parliament for bribery. In part, failure in politics caused Bacon to seek approval among the scientific community. His most important writings promoted the new science emerging as part of the century's Scientific Revolution. These works included especially *The Advancement of Learning* (1605), *Novum Organum* (1620), and *The Great Instauration* (1620). To understand the implications and meaning of *New Atlantis*, practically the whole corpus of Bacon's writings must be comprehended. Indeed, Bacon had been thinking about, planning, and writing drafts of *New Atlantis* for 30 years before his final effort in 1623. Soon after its initial publication in England in 1627, it was translated into French (1631) and Latin (1633). In the seventeenth century, 11 editions appeared, and more than 100 have been issued since. An unknown author, R. H., perhaps the scientist Robert Hooke, issued a more complete version of *New Atlantis* in 1660 that added an absolute monarch to resolve questions about authority. Strongly influenced by the Cambridge Platonists, Joseph Glanvill wrote a continuation of *New Atlantis* in 1676 stressing religious latitudinarianism for utopia.

*New Atlantis* begins with a prologue describing the voyage of Europeans from Peru across the South Pacific toward China, which leads to the discovery of the utopian society of Atlantis. The closed, isolated land the voyagers discover is not known to the outside world, although the Atlantans know that world quite well. King Solamona founded Atlantis 1,900 years earlier and determined that it would be a closed, self-sufficient society. Initially, the outsiders are given a hostile greeting, but ultimately they are allowed more time and leisure to explore Atlantis. Unlike More's Utopians, the Atlantans are Christians, so there is less contrast in religion than in most other areas. Bacon believed with most of his contemporaries that Christianity afforded society a sensible means of discipline and order in addition to its role in personal salvation. The most interesting feature of Atlantis is Salomon's House, otherwise known as the College of the Six Days' Work, which is in the city of Bensalem. Salomon's House has the responsibility and possesses the authority to collect and examine knowledge from the world outside Atlantis. Two ships are dispatched from Atlantis each dozen years with one-third of the 36 fellows from Salomon House to investigate other nations and their advancements— the sciences, arts, industry—to determine what, if any, knowledge will be retained for Atlantans. Thus these intellectuals, Bacon's philosopher-kings, become the screens and distillers of knowledge for the society. The fellows prevent the society from being corrupted by too much contact with foreign customs and become the guardians of morals as well as knowledge. Bacon's futuristic visions included scientific endeavors by the fellows, such as experiments with eugenics, airplanes, and submarines.

Other than the detailed description of Salomon House and discussion of the family, there is little substance to Bacon's utopia. About one-third of the book deals with Atlantis's relationship to the outside world, another third with Salomon House, and the final third with marriage and the family. Thus it leaves to guesswork Bacon's views about government, laws and courts, the military, the economy, care of the poor, and schools. God had ordained government, but he had not specified a particular form of government, so Bacon devoted no effort to the creation of an ideal human government. Custom was more important than laws since it was, or should be, the basis of the law. As for education, the improvement of the mind was a better guarantor of good behavior than a simple moral creed, yet the extent of learning should be determined by the individual rather than by the state. Like More in *Utopia*, Bacon was less concerned about creating an ideal model for human behavior than simply establishing some method for ensuring good behavior.

The conservative and pragmatic Bacon focused his effort in *New Atlantis* upon two pet projects, the promotion of the new scientific knowledge and a desire for reform of the political system. Many of the later scientific academies established in Europe mentioned Bacon as an inspiration in their founding. Although a great believer in the importance of intellectual curiosity and pursuit of the ideal, Bacon strenuously clung to reality in his reform agenda. He considered but rejected basing his ideal in the form of an Arcadia or millennium. Although Bacon agreed in theory that an ideal society might be created through strong virtuous leadership, the appeal of the perfect moral commonwealth was offset by his pragmatic view of the limitations of reform based on reason. Hence he was left with the utopian model as the basis for formulating his ideal society. Bacon sought to resolve the constant tension between the ideal and the practical, between philosophy and science. Relying upon his own experience as a public servant and studied observation of human self-deception, he embraced a utopia rather than a perfect moral commonwealth because of his lack of faith in the human ability to overcome corruption. Still, Bacon's *New Atlantis* remained imperfect because he made no real effort to tackle many social questions about an ideal society.

It is not surprising that Bacon eventually toyed with a utopia, for he was constantly designing reform projects, projects that ranged from the criminal code to education. Yet for Bacon the most important goal was a moral one that his other projects could not approach. Thus the best means to the moral goal was through the development of a method to improve the intellect rather than simply teaching moral truisms. Perhaps religious faith might help humanity recover its lost innocence, but to regain control over creation required perfecting the arts and sciences. Bacon saw no contradiction between belief in both a human-created earthly ideal society and a heavenly paradise provided by God. By framing his reforms in a utopian model, Bacon could deal with human weakness and passions, but his fundamental problem remained how to separate his virtually infallible scientists in Salomon House from other humans. Bacon expected his scientists to conform to a higher standard than ordinary humans, yet he remained uncertain that they could fulfill such expectations. Francis Bacon thus posed the ultimate obstacle for all modern scientific utopias by recognizing that science not only provides answers to society's problems but also becomes a source of power in itself, a power that may also be subject to corruption. The fellows of Salomon House became the teachers and providers of knowledge, but their power allowed them to decide both what knowledge to reveal and what to keep hidden, thereby demonstrating their ability to control people. If scientists could be trusted to act benevolently, then why could not the rest of humanity also be expected to act benevolently? Unable to resolve the dilemma, Bacon left to future scientific utopian projectors an apparently insoluble question.

*References* Anderson, Fulton H. *Francis Bacon: His Career and His Thought* (1962); Bierman, Judah. "Science and Society in the *New Atlantis* and Other Renaissance Utopias" (1963).

## The New Science (1725)

Largely ignored in his own time, Giambattista Vico has become a major figure in modern thought because of his elevation of the importance of the study of history as a guidepost for civilization. His most important work, *Principles of the New Science*, was published at the dawn of the Age of Reason when most philosophers looked to the natural sciences for inspiration and guidance. Probably because Vico was still attached to a theistic cosmology, he did not fit into the increasingly secular and agnostic pattern of most eighteenth-century philosophical thought. However, in the same way that many Enlightenment philosophers dreamed of a better society, Vico too envisioned a progressive realization of the ideal society—a utopia—through the application of the laws of history.

Born in Naples, Italy, Giambattista Vico (1668–1744) came from a rather poor Neapolitan family but developed an early interest in history and the classics. Vico became especially attached to the natural law theory and the writings of seventeenth-century English philosopher Thomas Hobbes. Vico's dedication to scholarship paid off when he was named professor of rhetoric at the University of Naples in 1699. He continued to garner a reputation for scholarly skills and was rewarded with the title of royal historian for the Kingdom of the Two Sicilies in 1735. When the *Principles of the New Science* was published in 1725, it was largely unnoticed by fellow scholars, although it sold sufficiently well to inspire Vico to publish a revised second edition in 1730. He was working on a third edition when he died in 1744. It was not until the nineteenth century and his rediscovery, chiefly by the French historian Jules Michelet, that his work became widely appreciated. Vico was revered by thinkers such as Henri Saint-Simon, Auguste Comte, Karl Marx, and Georges Sorel. His reputation continued to grow from the nineteenth into the twentieth century, and he is now considered one of the seminal thinkers of the Enlightenment era. Vico came to be regarded by many twentieth-century philosophers as a prophet of the dilemmas of the modern age.

Contemplating the contrasting roles of science and history, Vico reasoned that since the physical universe was made by God, only God could fully comprehend it. In fact, Vico considered that science was more a source of illusion than of certainty as it affected humans. Moreover, it was science rather than history that was subjective and thus suspect in its claims to authority. Objective history, on the other hand, was entirely man-made (man is within rather than without), so mankind could indeed know history and fruitfully apply it to society's problems. Moreover, Vico believed that God operated through human history, so understanding history also was a means of comprehending God. Vico's belief in a cyclic theory of history was not at all unique, but certain aspects of his breakdown of the theory were distinctive. Two terms are crucial to an understanding of Vico's cyclic theory: *corsi*, or the normal cycles of civilizations rising, declining, and falling, and *ricorsi*, or the window of opportunity for change and renewal upon the completion of a cycle. Vico believed that history is replete with examples of flux-reflux for nations, institutions, and leaders. Specifically, he identified two eras in which a *ricorso* had taken place: one in the ancient world, with the collapse of the Roman Empire, and a second in the modern era, with the Reformation. Vico also identified three stages of political development in the historical cycles: theocracy, aristocracy, and republics.

Unlike Thomas Hobbes, John Locke, and Jean-Jacques Rousseau, Vico did not believe in the concept of the social contract since he felt that most subjects were not capable of understanding such a contract. He did contemplate the relationship of the natural law to his science of humanity, however, because he believed that their relationship held the answer to the relation of time (history) and ideas. Man seeks positive law, that is, practical legislation, rather than abstract (hence theoretical)

constitutions to perfect society. History becomes the mediator between the ideal and the practical. Science on the other hand tends to separate time and ideas. Like Machiavelli, Vico always admired the strength of the laws of the Roman republic. The historical variables that influenced change included knowledge, will, and power, all of which were subject to individual applications. The ultimate arbiter of change was necessity. Still, mankind can and does make its own history because to Vico human nature was not fixed and abstract but, rather, part of the historical process of growth and development.

In Book One of *The New Science*, Vico explained the origins of human wisdom—the great unifying factor and source of natural law—starting with Adam's fall from grace. Accepting that the Jews remained God's chosen people and thus an exception to the general rules of history, Vico focused upon the Gentiles and their reliance upon "common (poetic) wisdom," by which he meant that God controls and directs human history at the same time that he gives humans the free will to make their own choices. As nations were formed from different groups of people, three "instincts" developed in all: religion (a recognition of a higher spiritual authority), marriage and family (bonding of parents and children), and the practice of burying the dead (anticipating a life beyond the physical existence). The common wisdom was joined over time by what Vico called "recondite (philosophical) wisdom," that is, the collected knowledge of philosophers over time, to produce a self-contained humanism that combines individual intellect and will. In Book Two, Vico related human wisdom to history and introduced the different cycles. As societies developed, they tended to break down into two distinct groups that Vico called "patricians" (nobility) and "plebeians" (commoners). The tension between the two groups had both positive and negative features and consequences. Vico took the occasion in this section to state his belief that the Roman republic was the zenith of human history, mankind's greatest achievement. By contrast, the Roman Empire witnessed a dissipation of discipline and positive Roman virtues noteworthy in the republic primarily because of the human tendency to become soft during times of material prosperity. Vico also denigrated science from the era of the Renaissance to the eighteenth century as fostering a false sense of certainty about the nature of mankind. Indeed, science had undermined the role and authority of history by suggesting that knowledge of the past was irrelevant.

In Book Three, Vico concentrated on the emergence of language and myth, starting with primitive man. Language evolved over time from a vague if poetical form to a symbolic and in more recent times more literal style. There was very little of substance in the brief Book Four. In the concluding Book Five, Vico examined the stages or cycles in specific nations, comparing, for example, the course of change in ancient Greece and Rome, to show the similarities. He explained the progress of human social development over time by stressing three vital human traits: conscience, which makes mankind recognize mistakes and seek improvement; curiosity, which prods intellectual innovation; and the work ethic, which not only is necessary to survival but also allows humanity to construct various monuments to human prowess.

Despite the strong philosophical overtones of the *New Science*, it had a distinct utopian flavor in Vico's notion of movement toward an ideal society and the role of God as the architect of history. Thus Vico seemed out of place in the skeptical, secular eighteenth century; his work fit better with the seventeenth-century utopian constructions, which retained a Christian framework. Yet it was the nineteenth-century practical utopians such as utopian socialists, Marxists, and positivists who drew sustenance from Vico even more than from the philosophes. By the twentieth century, when science's potential began to be questioned and dystopias

mocked science and technology, Vico with his condescension toward science seemed more like a prophet than a philosopher. Vico would have been pleased that over time history played at least as large a role in utopian writing as did science.

**Reference** Caponigri, A. Robert. "The Timelessness of the *Scienza Nuova* of Giambattista Vico," in Rimanelli, Giose, and Kenneth J. Atchity, eds. *Italian Literature, Roots and Branches: Essays in Honor of Thomas Goddard Bergin* (1976).

## *News from Nowhere* (1890)

A socialist utopia that combined elements of Arcadia, *News from Nowhere; or, An Epoch of Rest; Being Some Chapters from an Utopian Romance* was written by William Morris and published in a serialized version in *Commonweal* (1890) before appearing as a monograph with illustrations the following year. Scholars believe that Morris wrote *News from Nowhere* as an antithesis to Edward Bellamy's paean to technology, *Looking Backward* (1887). Morris believed that his pastoral, nontechnological vision could become reality despite its unreal assumptions. He seemed to be offering a society that embodied the moral equivalent of innocence as a contrast to the sinful society that he saw around him in late-nineteenth-century England.

William Morris (1834–1896) was born into an English middle-class family; even before he attended Oxford he had immersed himself in romanticism, which was in full bloom by midcentury. Morris was particularly struck by the medieval themes that he found in Sir Walter Scott's novels and John Ruskin's prose. Indeed, Morris chiefly derived his attitude toward capitalism as well as an appreciation for medievalism from Ruskin. These influences caused Morris to apply his imagination to all of his creations, including his early poetry. He agreed with the utopian socialists such as Saint-Simon that capitalism's dehumanizing competition must be replaced by an economy of cooperation. Despite Morris's shy disposition, he was not at all retiring but, rather, bold in his intellectual pursuits. Morris became active in socialist politics in Britain, but although he has been labeled a Marxist it is probably more accurate to view him as very independent. At one point Morris resigned from the Socialist League to form a smaller organization, the Hammersmith League. He was acquainted with the Fabian intellectuals but did not join their group. Morris's influence would continue after his lifetime in the popular Garden City movement, which was based upon his view that art forms such as architectures were held in common by all people.

In his utopian novel *News from Nowhere*, Morris focused upon the objective of enhancing human freedom. His liberal view of human potential for good inspired a belief in the idea of progress and the possibility of reshaping society. Morris did not believe that humans really "wanted" all of the material benefits they might desire. Another way of approaching the issue was to suggest that some "necessities" were not really necessary at all. Capitalism had simply expanded the list of "necessities" unduly in order to confuse mankind and demand excessive degrees of labor. The creation of artificial needs to satisfy the appetite of capital markets must be abolished and should be replaced by a system of cooperation in which the tasks of work would be greatly diminished. Work that produced evil results would be displaced by work that was pleasurable since work fulfills the creative need in mankind, much as Morris imagined it had for the medieval craftsman. Unlike in the utopian communities proposed by Fourier, in Morris's ideal society there would be no excesses; rather, simple, basic needs would be satisfied with ample but not extravagant provision.

The chief character in Morris's story, William Guest, awakens after about 200 years of sleep into a socialist ideal society. The capitalist system has been destroyed by a revolution, and the new society of Nowhere has no government and people do not own private property. Work has become an art form, and individual creativity has been rediscovered by the citizens of Nowhere. The divisions of society have all but disappeared—rich and poor, urban and rural—although citizens are allowed to dress according to individual preferences. Women are freed from adherence to traditional sexual mores, though they retain a traditional domestic role. Education is neither mandatory nor institutionalized in Nowhere, yet it is available to those who desire to educate themselves. Decisions are made by majority rule in communes, but the minority do not have to abide by the majority's decisions. Religion, which essentially glorifies nature, exists without the trappings of ritual or hierarchy and teaches brotherly love. Because they do not afflict their bodies with harmful substances such as alcohol or tobacco, the utopians live long and happy lives; they revel in the beauty of nature because the horrid factories and slums of the era of capitalism have disappeared, and the air and water are unpolluted. There is little crime in Nowhere, but even when it occurs there is no punishment since there is no law-enforcement mechanism. Morris's utopians have rejected not only capitalism but also the necessity for a centralized authority, such as the one described in Bellamy's *Looking Backward*, to direct their lives. Hence a kind of pure freedom has been discovered, reminiscent of Rousseau's fanciful prehistoric egalitarian society.

In the book version of *News from Nowhere*, Morris offered architectural renderings of his ideal society. These drawings, despite their pastoral settings, became an inspiration for Ebenezer Howard's Garden City movement, which emerged a few years after the publication of Morris's book. Unlike other Marxists of his day, Morris focused less upon the nature and problems of the proletariat than upon a redefinition of work. As far as Morris was concerned, life could and should become art, including the activity of work. Morris's thinking represented a watershed in the nineteenth century between the unbounded optimism of the utopians who preceded him and the twentieth-century pessimism about ideal societies, which produced a plethora of dystopias.

See also Arcadia; *Looking Backward: 2000–1887*.

References Bradley, Ian. *William Morris and His World* (1978); Coleman, Stephen, and Paddy O'Sullivan. *William Morris and News from Nowhere: A Vision of Our Time* (1990).

## *1984* (1949)

One of the most popular British authors in the post–World War II era, George Orwell wrote two of the most famous dystopias in the twentieth century: *Animal Farm* and *1984*. Orwell was one of the earliest intellectuals to identify totalitarianism as a special form of authoritarian repression and thus a serious worldwide threat to freedom. The totalitarian state proved to be more able to resist opposition than had been previous types of dictatorships. Yet although it rejected virtually all of the principles of the liberal humanitarian tradition, it lacked any positive ideology, so it proved unstable. Orwell used satire so effectively that his work can be read simply for its entertainment value, yet he also proved to be prophetic in outlining the dangers of totalitarianism, especially Stalinism.

Orwell was born Eric Arthur Blair (1903–1950) to a colonial civil servant and was educated at Eton. He served a tenure in the foreign service in Burma, where he learned to despise the imperial system. Influenced early in life by British utopist H. G. Wells, Orwell began his career as a believer in the fashionable utopia of socialism. He was a successful novelist prior to World War II, producing such works as *The Road to Wigan Pier* (1937). Because Orwell, like other intellectuals of his age, had been nurtured on the tenets of reason and progress, it was difficult for him to grasp the irrationality of totalitarianism. Yet he soon moved away from Wells's utopian approach to embrace one outlined by both Yevgeny Zamyatin and Aldous Huxley: the dystopia. Orwell also found themes from Jonathan Swift's *Gulliver's Travels*, which he

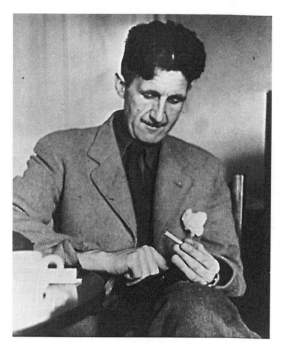

*George Orwell*

believed anticipated totalitarianism. Following World War II, Orwell published *Animal Farm* (1946), a thinly veiled parody of Soviet totalitarianism under Josef Stalin. Soon afterward, while fighting tuberculosis, he penned an even more pointed dystopia called *1984* (1949), which described a totalitarian future in which human freedom was nonexistent. The framework for *1984* may have been derived from James Burnham's influential *Managerial Revolution* (1941), which included rigid business hierarchies utilizing force and technology to maintain control. Orwell used his native England as the setting for both of his dystopias, which suggests that his ideas were derived largely from his own environment and experiences. Orwell departed from literary traditions because he made no attempt at ensuring happiness for his fictional characters.

There is very little difficulty understanding the parody *Animal Farm*, which depicts a totalitarian system similar to the Soviet Union under Stalin. The barnyard animals revolt against the farmer, who represents the czarist regime, and set out to establish an egalitarian socialist system. However, the transition goes awry when the pigs, led by Napoleon, who represents Stalin, decide to co-opt the revolution and take over the barnyard. Their slogan, painted on the side of the barn, reads: "All animals are equal, but some animals are more equal than others." In *Animal Farm* the dream of a utopian socialist society is ruined by the seizure of power and establishment of a totalitarian dictatorship. There seems little doubt but that Orwell had concluded after the defeat of Hitler that Stalin posed the greatest totalitarian threat to the future.

By contrast, *1984* depicts a fictional totalitarian state projected into the future. Although Orwell agreed that it was fantasy, he believed that it contained a potential reality for future societies. Orwell stated that *1984* was not a prediction of what will happen but rather of what could occur in the future. It was both a warning and a prophecy; Orwell's motto seemed to be "Forewarned is forearmed." In his fictional world, there are three megastates that have survived a nuclear war and thereafter agreed to use only conventional weapons. The context of wartime is an obvious extension of the chaos and irrationality of World War II: The era of progress has ended. Like historical totalitarian regimes, Oceania aims to expand its territory (hence the constant war), to reduce its citizens to automatons who think and act uniformly, and to make humans more like animals, who are dependent upon a superior authority for their existence. Oceania is ruled by a Party that is made up of only a fraction of the population and is headed by a mythical figure known as "Big Brother." The Party maintained three slogans: "War is Peace"; "Freedom is Slavery"; and "Ignorance is Strength." Orwell's point was that totalitarianism is backward, banal, and barbaric.

The chief character, Winston Smith, lives in Oceania, which roughly comprises western Europe, and works at the Ministry of Truth. The Party rules absolutely without conventional laws, and the state relies upon sophisticated technology to suppress individual freedoms and promote obeisance through its ideology, called Ingsoc. The Party makes no effort, either explicitly or implicitly, to ameliorate the misery of the population. Oceania understands that in order for freedom to exist there must be certifiable knowledge available to individuals. Hence the system of Doublethink eliminates even the possibility of freedom of the mind by removing all certain knowledge such as science, mathematics, and history. In Oceania two plus two is not necessarily four unless the state says so. Indeed, the ideal citizen in Oceania is not a true believer but someone who doesn't know right from wrong or truth from falsehood, and who thus is dependent upon the state, through the Ministry of Truth, to explain such matters. Like other residents of Oceania, Smith is both depressed by and yet compliant toward the state's repression. He is an unattractive hero, lacking courage and genuine emotion; altogether he is a rather pathetic figure. Yet because Smith recognizes the repression for what it is, he joins a secret movement to overthrow the regime. The revolt is ill-conceived and executed, so it fails; following a regime of torture Smith ultimately accepts defeat. Thereby Smith reflects Orwell's view that totalitarian regimes probably could not be overthrown from within. It is a dreary existence without cheerfulness or normal outlets for happiness. Children are trained to spy on their parents and even sexual conduct is strictly proscribed.

Although Orwell's writings have been categorized as dystopias, there have been considerable disagreements about the meaning of *1984*. The most common interpretations claim that it is either satire aimed at socialism or prophecy of a possible future scenario. It does seem that Orwell was attempting to reconcile the conflicting aspects in socialism, democracy, and totalitarianism as well as trying to sort out the prospects for the future. Unlike H. G. Wells, however, Orwell concluded that reliance upon science and reason would not necessarily produce an ideal society. Otherwise, Germany would have become such a model society instead of embracing Nazism and Hitler.

Certainly, Orwell was bothered by the infatuation of Europe's intellectual community with collectivist political and economic solutions. He may have been the first to recognize that the only two types of government that could possibly exist in the twentieth century were totalitarian systems and democratic welfare states. Orwell concluded that neither prospect was attractive for human freedom and independent thought because they both involved expanding the intrusive power of the state at the expense of the individual. Indeed, he concluded that although both totalitarian regimes and welfare states sought to produce "perfect" citizens, they instead completely dehumanized them. Citizens in either type of state must be reeducated by systems such as Doublethink and Newspeak so that illusion becomes reality and the present completely displaces the past and the future. Orwell would not be surprised that at the end of the twentieth century the government of the United States was awash in acronyms and euphemisms that described government agencies and functions. Certainly, Orwell had come to the conclusion that government cannot solve all human problems and, moreover, that it had become virtually impossible for the people to overthrow or reform governments in the twentieth century.

*References* Beauchamp, Gorman. "*1984:* Oceana as an Ideal State" (1984); Stansky, Peter, ed. *On Nineteen Eighty-four* (1983); Steinhoff, William. "Utopia Reconsidered: Comments on *1984*" (1983).

## Noble Savage Utopias

The discovery of the New World by the Europeans in the late fifteenth century led to a fascination with and fanciful vision of primitive native lifestyles as a basis for utopian constructions. The noble savage ideal built upon an Arcadian setting the social basis for reform, and the subgenre

extended into the nineteenth century. Many Europeans who encountered the natives admired their nonmaterialistic, back-to-nature existence. Yet the most appealing aspect of the noble savage societies was their moral qualities, especially useful as a contrast to the immoral proclivities in the utopists' real world. Thus the idea of the "noble savage" suggested a primitive lifestyle as an antidote to the materialism and aggressive expansionism of the Europeans. In many respects the interpretation of native societies by Europeans was inaccurate, but the ideal demonstrated a utopian influence of the New World upon the Old.

Inspired by both Thomas More and the traditions of the New World Native Americans, Spain's Vasco de Quiroga (1470–1565) established a utopian community near Mexico City in 1537. Europeans such as Quiroga had been dismayed in the early sixteenth century by the undue influence of materialism and by growing secular lifestyles. In the style of Erasmus and other Christian humanists of his time, Quiroga pursued reform along the lines of a practical, even primitive, Christian philosophy. When he arrived in freshly conquered New Spain (that is, Mexico) in 1531 as a judge in the *audiencia*, Quiroga was struck by the absence of greed, ambition, and luxury among the "noble savages" of America. Sincerely believing that More's theoretical vision could be put into practice among such a receptive population, in 1535, Quiroga requested permission from the Spanish monarchy to launch his community.

Quiroga's scheme called for each community of 6,000 families to be governed after a familial style. Fathers and mothers would rule individual families, magistrates would supervise 30 families, governors would have authority over four magistrates, and a *corregidor* appointed by the *audiencia* would be the chief executive. The naturally virtuous Native Americans would agree to work in harmony in carefully designed agricultural villages, expecting only an equal share of the fruits of their labor. The local friars would teach them Christian virtues as they labored. The scheme was remarkably simplistic.

Unable to persuade the royal council to implement his plan across New Spain, upon being named bishop in 1537, Quiroga launched his experiment in two villages (*hospitales-pueblos*) near present-day Mexico City; he called his villages Santa Fe. He was able to introduce most of the ingredients from his written plan, including women working and a six-hour workday.

Quiroga also suggested in his discourses about the Santa Fe *hospitales-pueblos* that the American design could be a model for the reformation of European society. However, when government backing failed to materialize he quickly put aside that larger plan to focus upon his Mexican experiment. The communities operated with Quiroga's close supervision for the next 30 years. They apparently continued to function for some time after Quiroga's death, perhaps into the early seventeenth century.

An English example of putting utopian ideas into practice occurred with the unique Puritan missionary to the Indians of New England, John Eliot (1604–1690). Fleeing from the tyranny of church and state in England, the Puritans saw themselves as God's new chosen people sent to build a New Jerusalem in the American wilderness. Hence they viewed New England as a potential utopia. Arriving in Massachusetts Bay Colony in 1631, Eliot quickly determined to fulfill a commitment by Puritan congregations to convert the natives to Christianity. He later founded the Society for Propagating the Gospel in New England (1649) to solicit funding for the missionary effort. He learned the Indian dialects, published an Algonquian translation of the Bible, and founded 19 "praying towns" of Indians in Massachusetts among his converts. Although his primary mission was religious, Eliot's noble savage view allowed him to retain the purer elements of Native American traditions rather than attempting to integrate them into a European culture. The "praying towns" were distinctly separate from the English settlements, in part to protect the Indians from encroachment but also to create an isolated environment for the design of Eliot's utopia. The theocracy that emerged was based upon pure scripture designed to transform the Indians from degenerate, albeit unknowing, humans to regenerated saints. Eliot's attempt to nurture independent, Christian Indian communities on the New England frontier ended with King Philip's War in the 1670s. During his ministry, Eliot composed *The Christian Commonwealth* (1659), which included principles that he had already implemented in his Indian villages. However, Eliot's "Commonwealth" was projected back across the Atlantic to England: He used his practical experiences with the New England Indians as the basis for proposing a radical religious and political overhaul of his own homeland. *The Christian Commonwealth*, actually written in 1651–1652 during the governance of a republican government in England, represents to many scholars a Fifth Monarchist millennial tract, yet, more important, it describes a democratic government that was truly unique in its time.

In 1610, Italian Jesuits established a utopian community among the Native Americans of South America. Over the next 30 years, about 40 Jesuit *reductions* were founded in parts of Paraguay, Brazil, Argentina, and Uruguay. Each *reduction* included two Jesuits, often non-Spanish, and numerous native families. The Jesuits found the natives particularly adept at learning music and the decorative arts. Each *reduction* had a church at its center surrounded by a square of houses. The day began with prayers, followed by work by the males in either the fields or the manufacturing centers. Meals were provided for the whole community, and all possessions were communally owned, although families remained together in living quarters. Young men married at age 17 to women of about 15. Young unmarried females were instructed in their duties by the elder women of the community. The natives had their own language, Guarani, and dressed so neatly that Spanish authorities who saw them in the towns became uneasy. Natives operated the system of justice through their own elected officials.

Because the *reductions* were located in isolated regions, there was little chance for Western civilization to infringe upon the peculiar system operated by the Jesuit fathers. The societies were effectively dismantled after 1768 when the Spanish king Carlos III ordered the Jesuit order disbanded in Spain and its territories. The question of how idyllic a lifestyle existed in the *reductions* was raised by the French philosophe Louis-Antoine de Bougainville (1729–1811), who visited Paraguay about the time of the Jesuit expulsion. From his perspective in France, Bougainville had admired the *reductions* with their ideal of happiness achieved without either wealth or poverty. However, he learned from his visit that the Indians had been subjected to oppressive controls by the Jesuit fathers. They were given corporal punishment for minor violations of rules and subjected to a spy system. Their schedules provided nothing more than drudgery, monotony, and an apparently unfulfilled life. The price of civilization for the Paraguayans had been a repressive regime.

Upon leaving South America, Bougainville sailed to Tahiti, another supposedly idyllic primitive society previously admired by Europeans. Despite the beauty of the islands populated by a friendly and peaceful people, Bougainville discovered a society divided into two groups. The aristocrats ruled with an iron fist over the common classes; for example, only the ruling class could eat delicacies such as meat and fish. The society was plagued by aggressive neighboring tribes and by diseases. Nonetheless, Denis Diderot's *Supplement to Bougainville's Voyage* (written in 1772 but not published until 1796) makes it clear that the Tahitians desired to keep their own ways rather than embrace the "civilization" of the Europeans. Their spiritual leader Orou, who did not understand Western morality, recognized that his society was very fragile when faced with Western mores. It was susceptible to European depravity, which would compromise the noble savage innocence, and Western technology, which would alter their Arcadia. Their ignorance was bliss. Still, Diderot's motive in this work was to criticize European sexual mores rather than to hold up the Tahitians' society as a viable ideal.

An extremely popular late-eighteenth-century treatise on the native lifestyles, *A Philosophical History of the Two Indies* (1780) by the Abbé François de Raynal (1713–1796), summarized many of the travel accounts of European visits to native societies in the Americas and the Pacific Isles. Raynal's purpose was to criticize Europeans for disrupting the Arcadia and endangering freedom among the primitive native societies. He also speculated that the attraction of the noble savage societies for Europeans was that they partly eased the consciences of the aristocracy by letting them view their peasants as happily enduring hard labor like the noble savages. Raynal reasoned that in the future, the favorable portrayal of the savage societies would be turned around to demonstrate the inequities of human institutions rather than a back-to-nature utopia.

Because the frontier of North America moved slowly to the west, the European contact with the natives was episodic. Hence it was not surprising that the noble savage ideal could survive well into the nineteenth century. The great American novelist Herman Melville (1819–1891) used a real-life incident in the Marquesas Islands in the Pacific as the setting for his noble savage utopia, *Typee*, published in 1846. Following the pattern of other utopists who wrote about noble savage societies, Melville used the primitive framework to examine Western civilization. The chief characters, Tommo and Toby, flee the repressive captain of their whaling ship *Dolly* to live among the natives despite their apprehensions about Typee cannibalism. Tommo and Toby stumble upon the idyllic Typee Valley, which provides abundant food, the bread-fruits and bananas that do not even require cultivation. The natives enjoy their leisure and do not care about the time of day. Since the natives do not even produce man-made laws, their blissful society is the result of the provisions of nature alone rather than of an authoritarian system. Even the Polynesian taboos derive from nature rather than arbitrary rules. Melville scoffed at Western commercialism and, especially, technology, which he suggested only made it easier to kill and maim. Happiness, he suggested, came in a simple, natural formula for the harmonious Polynesian savages, while the competitive Europeans struggled for their livelihood, not to mention happiness.

Western utopists transformed their curiosity about primitive societies into a foil for the critique of their own society. By contrasting the real meaning of the terms "savage" and "civilization," the authors hoped to stimulate recognition of the basest faults of Western civilization. Natural reason unfettered by artificial social and political conventions appealed to these utopists for its simplicity and wisdom. The noble savage ideal also proved attractive for its Arcadian setting, since the unrestrained growth of cities and industry seemed to mar the natural beauty of Western nations. The bounty of nature was cultivated yet unspoiled by the savage societies, whereas Western technology only promised more efficient exploitation of natural resources.

*See also* Arcadia.

*References* Beauchamp, Gorman. "Melville and the Tradition of Primitive Utopia" (1981); Holstun, James. *A Rational Millennium: Puritan Utopias of Seventeenth-Century England and America* (1987); Lugon, Clovis. *La République Communiste Chrétienne des Guaranis, 1610–1768* (1949); Zavala, Silvio. *Sir Thomas More in New Spain: A Utopian Adventure of the Renaissance* (1955).

## *Notes from the Underground* (1864)

Noted for his strongly Russian sentiments and antiliberal tendencies, Fyodor Dostoyevsky ventured into the utopian form of expression to make important points in *Notes from the Underground*. He continued many of the same themes in the section of *The Brothers Karamazov* (1880) entitled "The Grand Inquisitor." Dostoyevsky rebelled against both the rationalism and the materialism that gripped the liberal establishment in western Europe during the mid- to late nineteenth century. He sought liberation for the individual from those false ideologies and took solace in a primitive form of Christianity. His style of anti-utopian writing appears most similar to that of Jonathan Swift in the early eighteenth century, but the Russian milieu makes *Notes from the Underground* unique indeed.

Fyodor Dostoyevsky (1821–1881) developed a proclivity for writing at the same time that he became politically active opposing the repressive regime of Czar Nicholas I (czar 1825–1855). His first novel was published in 1845, but soon afterward he was arrested for his political activities and exiled to Siberia. When the reform-minded Czar Alexander II (czar 1855–1881) succeeded Nicholas, he granted amnesty to Dostoyevsky, allowing him to return to his writing though freedom of expression remained limited by censorship regulations. In the post-exile era, Dostoyevsky became a staunch Slavophile and tended to be critical of almost anything emanating from the West. His novels from the 1860s to his death also reflected a strong antiliberal and antimaterialist attitude. Dostoyevsky dabbled in journalism as well as writing novels during his productive years. Though there are similarities between Dostoyevsky and other great contemporary Russian writers such as Ivan Turgenev and Leo Tolstoy, the sharpness of Dostoyevsky's realistic critiques makes his work distinctive as well as important.

*Notes from the Underground* is divided into two parts that reflect the author's views of Russia during the most repressive years of the 1840s under Nicholas I and the decade of change and loosening of restrictions in the 1860s under Alexander II. In the first part, which deals with the 1860s, Dostoyevsky, through the underground man, satirizes the popular theme of nihilism made coherent in the writings of Turgenev. The second part, set in the 1840s, turns the author's satirical blows upon the romantics. Thus Dostoyevsky used satire to assail two popular trends that he had personally lived through in Russia. By reversing the chronology in his story, Dostoyevsky further points out the confusion and disarray of the Russian intelligentsia. In part one the underground man embraces nihilism, thus allowing Dostoyevsky to criticize the outlook. Further, Dostoyevsky uses part one in particular to contrast his views with those that Nikolay Chernyshevsky outlined in his optimistic utopian socialist treatise, *What Is to Be Done?* (1863).

The underground man seems to represent a social type, the Russian intellectual, groping for meaning in life. Typically for the era, the underground man fits into the intellectual mainstream in his belief in positivism, an advanced version of scientific determinism made popular by the French thinker Auguste Comte. Thus the underground man believes that human free will is a fiction since the laws of nature predetermine everything. Chernyshevsky had also denied the existence of free will. Dostoyevsky mocks the positivist view by arguing that if there is no free will, there cannot be any moral imperatives. Indeed, the absence of moral acts makes the underground man a nihilist. Despite the fact that his reason presses the point that he should feel neither guilt nor pangs of conscience, as the underground man confronts the world he is uncomfortable with the recognition of his own impotence and unimportance. Deluded as he is, the underground man responds to the awareness of innate emotional and moral feelings. Through the so-called masochism of the underground man, wallowing in self-doubt, Dostoyevsky aims to show humanity's spiritual well-being and consciousness of moral sensibilities.

The underground man engages a character who represents Chernyshevsky's views literally, and initially the underground man accepts the tenets of scientific determinism. Yet the underground man admires the man of action who rejects the theory and acts spontaneously according to a moral directive. Thus the underground man has accepted determinism as an intellectual act but has rejected it emotionally. The underground man, like most humans, according to Dostoyevsky, is conflicted about the direction he should go. Thus he is not inherently evil but indeed struggling to overcome evil by becoming a whole person instead of an automaton. The underground man is coming to grips with what Dostoyevsky calls "fantastic realism," which stresses alternative acts outside the norms. Again, Dostoyevsky returns to Chernyshevsky's *What Is to Be Done?* to focus his argument.

The image of the ideal society and "rational egoism" in Chernyshevsky's story is the Crystal Palace, designed after the utopian socialist communities, especially the concepts of Charles Fourier. Dostoyevsky sets up the idea of choice between the "highest good" and an array of other lesser goods. The greatest good is the expression of individual moral will free to choose, the only course of action that will preserve the integrity of the individual personality. The Crystal Palace was constructed as a substitute for free will and the passions, considered by utopian socialists as obstacles to achieving maximum happiness. The underground man soon realizes that a Crystal Palace agenda means the end of human action other than obedience to determinism. Utopian socialists often used the analogy of the ants working in the anthill, mindlessly but happily fulfilling predetermined objectives. Of course, Dostoyevsky recoiled from such comparisons, which dictated the purging of moral conscience as well as free will. The rationalists might not understand why Dostoyevsky would want to preserve pain and suffering for mankind, but the Russian knew that with the elimination of pain comes the end of humanity as he understood it. Though Dostoyevsky would insist upon allowing individual will to make its own choices, he preferred a kind of primitive Christianity, without the trappings of the institutional church, as his ideal society—a real palace.

The second part of *Notes from the Underground* focuses upon the romanticism of the 1840s, which according to Dostoyevsky promoted a dreamworld based on the "egoism of principle." The moral problem for this group of intellectuals was that their vanity prevented them from translating their expressed affection for humanity into action. Once again, it is the underground man who reflects that vanity and selfishness. The story focuses upon the underground man's encounter with a prostitute named Lisa. The vain male seeks to show his moral as well as physical superiority to Lisa. He wants to humble Lisa and make her feel guilty about her profession. Upon leaving the brothel, the underground man urges Lisa to visit him so he can help her reform her ways. Yet, just as in part one, the underground man begins having doubts about his superiority. Lisa selflessly shows concern for him, which causes further trepidation. Dostoyevsky permits the underground man to rationalize his harshness toward Lisa by undergoing the emotional disturbance. Just as Dostoyevsky attempted to hold up a pure Christianity as an ideal society in part one, he tries to demonstrate the importance of selfless love as an antidote to vanity in part two. Like the underground man, humanity should struggle with free will and moral choices, despite the pain involved, rather than accepting an ambiguous existence in some utopian, regimented structure.

Dostoyevsky presented an even more devastating assault upon the liberal system, and socialism in particular, in the section of *The Brothers Karamazov* (1880) that deals with the Grand Inquisitor. The atheist brother tells the Christian brother a medieval story of the Inquisition in Spain wherein Christ appears and is arrested on orders from a cardinal known as the Grand Inquisitor. Christ is told by the Grand Inquisitor why he must die once more. The church and the pope have determined after hundreds of years that Christ was wrong about humanity desiring freedom. Rather than wanting to be free, mankind only wants to be happy, which requires giving up their freedom. The church has agreed to feed people since their pursuit of knowledge cannot guarantee their food. The Grand Inquisitor states that Christ made a mistake when he did not command humans to give up their freedom and follow him. People need not freedom but only the necessary food; because they are unhappy, people are childish, rebellious, and uncertain how to use their freedom. The Grand Inquisitor tells Christ that the church has decided to follow Satan since he understands human needs better. The church, after receiving from Satan the powers that Christ refused, has opted to provide happiness to humans. Christ's appearance threatens the arrangements because the people do not understand what is happening. Twentieth-century dystopian writers resurrected the image of the Grand Inquisitor over and over again. The Grand Inquisitor was a prophetic warning about the dangers to human freedom in totalitarianism and the democratic welfare state.

*See also* Positivism; Utopian Socialism.

*Reference* Frank, Joseph. "Nihilism and *Notes from the Underground*" (1961).

## *Nova Solyma* (1648)

Samuel Gott's *Nova Solyma* contained elements of both utopianism and millennialism, yet it cannot be said to be a true representation of either. Nova Solyma is a millennial ideal society set in the Middle East. Yet it had no formal religion, and the treatise contains more details about education than about Christianity. Nova Solyma also had elements common to other seventeenth-century utopias: an enlightened and benevolent government, patriarchal social discipline, and an efficient economy with a strong work ethic. The treatise was yet one more product of a tumultuous age of war and disruption of order in England.

A Londoner by birth, Samuel Gott (1613–1671) came from a prosperous merchant family. His knowledge of Latin, Hebrew, and the law resulted from an education both at Cambridge and at Gray's Inn. Gott was no doubt influenced by the Puritan elements that dominated Cambridge as well as the new scientific circles. He was elected to Parliament at the beginning of the civil war and was among the Presbyterian peace party that was forcibly removed from the Long Parliament by the army in 1648. That was the same year in which Gott published *Nova Solyma, The Ideal City; or, Jerusalem Regained* without his name attached. Gott's work was hardly noticed at the time, and when the writing was rediscovered in 1902, authorship was wrongly attributed to John Milton.

*Nova Solyma* has been characterized as a "philosophical romance"; it featured a picaresque form of disjointed episodes yet also maintained a Christian outlook as its unifying philosophy. Nova Solyma is an ideal society situated in the Holy Land after the return—and conversion to Christianity—of the Jews from their extended absence. Hence the framework invoked the millennium, which was a popular seventeenth-century theme of Christians. However, other than the role of Jews in a traditional millennial setting, there was little in *Nova Solyma* that reflected a millenarian theme. For example, it mentions no apocalypse.

The two English visitors to Nova Solyma—Politian and Eugenius—appear during the celebration of the city's founding to negotiate a trade agreement with England. They learn from their guide, Joseph, about Nova Solyma's system of laws, education, society, and economy as well as the population's religion. The visitors and the residents of Nova Solyma found that the pursuit of sensual pleasures was unfulfilling and that only moderation guided by Christian principles truly satisfied. Yet there was no state church in Nova Solyma to dictate doctrine. The religious quarrels of the English civil war era obviously bothered Gott: His utopia avoided such disharmony.

Because humans must accept God's ways voluntarily, Gott does not propose the abolition of property rights in Nova Solyma. The economy of Nova Solyma resembles that of Stuart England, dominated by merchants and gentlemen farmers. Neither intemperance, sloth, nor waste is tolerated in Nova Solyma. The sketchy section on government in *Nova Solyma* suggests that law and the magistrates' authority serve to nurture the ideal society's citizens. Magistrates also apparently serve many of the functions of the priest, an office not specifically mentioned. The state is only a tool, a facilitator, to allow Christian tenets to be effected.

Certainly the most elaborate description of the ideal society in *Nova Solyma* concerns the education provisions. The system, limited to males only, focuses upon three areas: religion, ethics, and academics (mainly literature and science). Effective education ensures that citizens reached their full potential and thus apply their best knowledge to society's as well as their own advantage. Gott argued that the saved also needed the stern discipline of education to avoid falling away from their faith. In Nova Solyma, because education is also necessary for the institution of social discipline, the family assumes the primary responsibility for learning up to age ten, when the boys enter a public institution. All subjects taught in the public schools reflect a moral-religious as well as intellectual purpose. Still, universal education has not entirely eliminated certain incidents of crime and blasphemy in Nova Solyma.

Gott's purpose in *Nova Solyma* has been viewed best as theological rather than utopian, to illustrate the necessity of implementing and following a Christian philosophy. Gott also seemed concerned to demonstrate the credibility of Christianity in an age of reason. The work cannot be effectively associated with the pansophic movement popular in the era. Despite the admitted influence of Francis Bacon's *New Atlantis* upon Gott, Nova Solyma was not a scientific utopia but a "new Jerusalem." The utopian aspects of the story are focused upon the search for true human happiness. Not only did Gott reject physical pleasures as a misguided formula for happiness, but he also could not accept romantic love as a substitute for God's love. In that respect Gott viewed man-kind's nature as sinful and held that human solutions that omitted God could not succeed. Reason, however, could dictate the structure and discipline necessary to achieve adherence to the Christian faith.

*See also* Millennialism.

*Reference* Patrick, J. Max. "*Nova Solyma*: Samuel Gott's Puritan Utopia" (1977).


**Noyes, John Humphrey**
*See* Oneida Community.

## Odoevsky, Vladimir
*See* Future-Time Utopias.

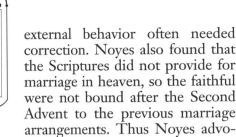

## Oneida Community
Going beyond the personal freedom of the Shakers to include sexual liberation for women, John Humphrey Noyes founded the Oneida Community of Perfectionists in 1848 as a successor to his Putney experiment. Noyes argued that the Second Coming of Christ and the millennium had already arrived, a view that separated the followers of Noyes from postmillennialists. Noyes argued that women should be free to decide both when they initiated sexual relations and when they would conceive through an institution known as "complex marriage." As outlined in his work *Bible Communism* (1853), Noyes combined the doctrines of communal property and self-perfection at Oneida to create a unique utopian system. Oneida became the most successful communalist society in nineteenth-century America, and after its incorporation in 1881 as a joint-stock company, it developed into a successful capitalist enterprise.

John Humphrey Noyes (1811–1886) came from a prominent New England family, but his red hair symbolized a youthful willingness to challenge traditions. Converted to Christianity while a student at Dartmouth College in 1831, Noyes decided to pursue a theology degree at Andover Academy and the Yale divinity school. His absence of a personal conviction of sin led him to construct a theory of ending sin altogether. Through his study of the New Testament, Noyes concluded that the return of Christ had already occurred at a much earlier time. Society was thereafter separated into the sinful and sinless. Yet although some were free of sin and inwardly perfect, their external behavior often needed correction. Noyes also found that the Scriptures did not provide for marriage in heaven, so the faithful were not bound after the Second Advent to the previous marriage arrangements. Thus Noyes advocated extending communal practices from property to sexual relations and concentrated upon reforming sexual tendencies. In short, Noyes desired that the Christian community adopt the lifestyle of the first-century Christians by sharing everything with each other.

Noyes married Harriet Holton and began recruiting followers through a journal, *The Witness*, published in Putney, Vermont. After securing a small following, Noyes founded the Putney Association in 1840 as a religious entity though it lacked any formal charter or bylaws. By 1844, Noyes had authorized the practice of communism after reading about the Shakers. Putney included about 500 acres, with houses, a general store, and print shop. Members participated jointly in manual labor along with study and worship services. Once a week the residents engaged in mutual criticism of each other. In 1846, Noyes introduced his theory of "complex marriage," which gave women the freedom to engage in sexual relations freely with anyone and at any age. Whereas the concept implied greater freedom for females, since Noyes did not believe in contraceptives, birth control depended upon males practicing self-control. Some critics suggested that Noyes had replaced the domination of women by one man in a monogamous relationship with domination by many men. These practices caused neighboring people to shun and criticize the Putney Association, and Noyes retreated to New York City after charges of adultery were leveled against him in 1847.

Some of Noyes's followers obtained a few acres of land at Oneida Creek, New York, in late 1847, and the Putney settlers and Noyes moved to Oneida in early 1848. The colonists built log cabins and mills, but they struggled to keep the society alive until they began manufacturing animal traps for profit. Their income was also supplemented from their fruit orchards and livestock. Later a factory manufacturing spoons initiated the famous silverware products. The population grew from 87 in 1849 to over 300 by the late 1870s. Another satellite community grew up at Wallingford, Connecticut. The settlers came mostly from New England farms or small villages, but they also included some professional people. The religious background of the settlers was quite varied, the largest group being former Congregationalists. In the 1860s the community completed construction of the Mansion House, a modern facility with indoor plumbing and central heat that housed about 50 residents. It also contained large meeting halls and the dining hall. Noyes published a weekly paper, the *Oneida Circular*, which accepted payment from those able to pay. The community possessed a well-stocked library and an orchestra and provided games and plays for entertainment.

Noyes invoked his social and religious theories to the full at Oneida, especially the notion that individual perfection could only be achieved through communal efforts. Although sexual relations were permitted between any male-female pair of members, each had to obtain consent from his or her mate before pursuing the practice. Thus in reality the principle of self-regulation meant that Oneida's sexual freedom was not absolute, and the term "free love" is misleading. Nonetheless, the institution of "complex marriage" was as controversial in New York as it had been in Vermont and was suspended for six months in 1852 due to local hostility. Upon successful implementation of the system of "complex marriage," Noyes launched in 1869 a eugenics experiment known as "stirpiculture" based upon his

reading of Darwin's *On the Origin of Species*. Noyes concluded that only spiritually mature individuals should be engaged in breeding. Women of childbearing age were asked to sign an agreement to allow a committee to determine whether and with whom they would have sexual relations for procreation. Most of the children born in the decade following 1869 were the product of stirpiculture eugenics.

The system of discipline at Oneida also featured the technique of "mutual criticism" introduced at Putney. A resident could request criticism if they felt guilty about some action, but it could also be initiated by someone who recognized a moral dilemma in another. The individual undergoing criticism might appear before the whole community but usually was examined by a select committee. Education for children was available but not required. Those with special talents might be sent to an institution of higher learning outside of the community. In part because there was no enforcement of labor, the Oneida Community became dependent upon outside hired workers to complete the work tasks. The division of labor was supervised by 21 committees, the heads of each comprising a coordinating board that prepared weekly reports to the residents. Women participated equally with men on the governing agencies. The entire system was managed with remarkable efficiency.

When in 1876 Noyes proposed transferring authority to his son, Theodore Noyes, the community balked. Theodore Noyes was an agnostic, had not participated much in Oneida, and favored a system of discipline foreign to his father's methods. John Humphrey Noyes suddenly left the community and settled in Canada, never to return to Oneida. Meanwhile, the dispute matured into a full-fledged division at Oneida by 1879. From his exile Noyes proposed giving up the system of "complex marriage" that had caused so much outside criticism of the experiment. Though Noyes recommended adoption of a system of celibacy similar to that of the Shakers, the community tended to embrace conventional marriage instead. The termination of "complex marriage" had the effect of calling into question the system of communism and indeed utopianism as well. In 1881, Oneida was incorporated as a capitalist joint-stock company, a decision acceptable to all but a handful of members. Families gradually removed from the Mansion House to individual houses, and some moved in small groups to New York City, Boston, and California. Noyes died in 1886, leaving behind a community different from the Perfectionists he had founded in the 1840s. Despite the disarray, by the 1890s, Pierrepont Noyes, another of his sons, had reinvigorated the revised community, which was thereafter known as Kenwood, with a non-Perfectionist idealism. Economically, the joint-stock company, Oneida Limited, became a profitable business manufacturing a nationally known line of silverware.

Oneida's fascinating story reflects many attributes of utopianism. It was formed and driven by specific ideas about human relationships. Noyes recognized that a practical utopia must enforce discipline and embrace a uniform set of principles in order to survive. Oneida may have been more successful than most communal experiments because it offered more personal freedom and less authoritarian controls than similar experiments. Even so, it was Noyes's ideas that shaped the dynamic aspects of Oneida, especially its social structure and relationships. Even the most successful utopia offering the greatest individual freedom demands a source of authority, and for Oneida that authority was John Humphrey Noyes.

*Reference* Carden, Maren Lockwood. *Oneida: Utopian Community to Modern Corporation* (1969).

## Orwell, George
*See 1984.*

## Owen, Albert Kimsey
*See* Topolobampo Bay Colony.

## Owen, Robert
*See* Utopian Socialism.

## Pansophism

In conjunction with the dynamic expansion of knowledge caused by the Scientific Revolution of the seventeenth century, utopian writers developed the concept of pansophia, or universal wisdom, as the basis for an ideal society. In addition to having a strong scientific bent, pansophists also blended Christian philosophy to frame their earthly millennium. The development of pansophism also marked the emergence of a new stage of utopian thought, moving beyond early utopian literary schemata that tended to accept the practical impossibility of constructing the ideal society. Science thus produced the possibility of changing utopia from a dreamworld to a real reformed society.

The pansophists actually believed that their ideas, unlike the fanciful concepts of sixteenth-century utopian writers, could be implemented because of the application of reason and scientific methods. Contrasted with later ages when they were in conflict, science and religion seemed utterly compatible in the view of the pansophists. Discovering the workings of nature and using that knowledge for human benefit was simply another way to understand God's creation and engage humanity in acts of charity. Coincidental with the advance of science in the seventeenth century was the decline in religious passions that had dominated the Reformation era. Pansophists were true Europeans in their desire to create a unified Christian commonwealth that would eradicate political and linguistic divisions.

There were certainly elements of pansophism in the utopias of Francis Bacon, *New Atlantis* (1627), and Johann Valentin Andreae, *Christianopolis* (1619). Yet in the early decades of the seventeenth century the "new science" was struggling to over-

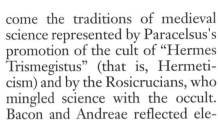

come the traditions of medieval science represented by Paracelsus's promotion of the cult of "Hermes Trismegistus" (that is, Hermeticism) and by the Rosicrucians, who mingled science with the occult.

Bacon and Andreae reflected elements of both the old and new science in their thinking. Johann Amos Comenius (1592–1670) looms as the watershed figure in the emergence of pansophism. As a member of the Moravian Brethren in Bohemia, Comenius traveled widely around Europe, including in England, and corresponded in his youth with Andreae. Comenius was not a scientist per se, but he became a serious publicist for the new science, and through the merger of his religious and scientific thought he articulated the concept of pansophia as universal wisdom. Comenius's system was grandiose in every respect; it included universal education and even a universal language. He blended Bacon's mechanical method with the magical tendencies of Hermeticism, which relied more upon astrology and alchemy, to propose a regeneration of mankind that would give him dominion once more over creation. The Comenian program called for a major overhaul of education to stress practical knowledge, science, and an ecumenical Protestant religion.

The expatriate German Samuel Hartlib, living in England, invited Comenius to visit there in 1641 hoping to inspire English scientists to found a pansophist institution, the "invisible college." The college would rely upon science to improve technology and agriculture, which would result in broad improvement of the standard of living. The Comenians, who urged government sponsorship of their reforms, maintained close ties with parliamentary leaders such as John Pym.

Nonetheless, neither the college nor Comenius's plan for an elaborate encyclopedia of knowledge ever materialized. Still, Comenius remained a source of inspiration for English reformers. Some scholars believe Comenius's influence indirectly led to the founding of the Royal Society years later. Though the English reformers contemplated specific changes, like Comenius they conceived of changes in society being applied universally. The pansophists believed that a universal language and education would eliminate the internal religious divisions in Europe and would also enhance universal peace among nations. The pansophists relied more upon practical rather than theoretical science to become the basis, with Christianity, of the ideal society.

Toward the end of the seventeenth century and the Scientific Revolution, the German mathematician Gottfried Wilhelm Leibniz (1646–1716) came the closest of any pansophist to outlining a universal system. Leibniz promoted learning around the world from China to America, and he also assisted in establishing several scientific academies. He was called upon for advice by a variety of European princes. Leibniz's *Monadology* (1695) came closest to fusing the search for useful knowledge from the new science and Christian principles. The essence of Leibniz's monads, that is, matter, was coordinated motion that began with a First Cause, that is, God. Leibniz thus visualized all matter, including humans, conforming to essential standards and operating in efficient harmony with other matter. He believed that the continued study of the workings of nature not only would reveal knowledge that could improve mankind's condition but would also further demonstrate God's magnificent creation. Leibniz effectively was the last of the pansophists committed to a Christian commonwealth grounded in scientific knowledge. After him, theorists such as John Locke and the French philosophes pursued mechanistic and purely secular formulations foreign to the pansophists.

A few French scientists, including Marin Mersenne and René Descartes, flirted with pansophist ideas in the first half of the seventeenth century and also advanced the idea of a universal philosophic language. That scientific leaders such as Descartes and Leibniz were trained in mathematics helps illustrate the difficult transition in the seventeenth century from the theoretical sciences based upon mathematical logic to the practical sciences based upon experimentation. The pansophists feared that a fragmented, discipline-oriented scientific approach would work against the development of universal knowledge as well as knowledge of God. They were far less concerned about using science to enhance the physical needs of humans than to ensure that the primary focus remained on Christian principles. What good were sophisticated means if the proper end was not achieved? Hence the pansophists opposed using science and technology merely to cater to human sensual desires. Thus their utopia was more similar to Arcadia than to the Land of Cockaygne.

Education was central to ensuring obedience to the goals and objectives in pansophic utopias. Comenius advocated a gentle but rigorous approach to learning. The pansophic writings about educational reform became perhaps the most tangible heritage of their influence. Marriage and children in pansophic utopias existed to promote the higher good of the society rather than individual desires or choices. Political and social institutions always played a secondary role to religious traditions. Moreover, the goal was to create both religious freedom and the absence of sectarian strife. The previous century had witnessed extensive bloodshed in the name of religious orthodoxy. The pansophists assumed that its citizens would accept an ecumenical consolidation of Christian beliefs among Protestants and Catholics. Because the pansophist formulations failed to achieve the conjunction of science and Christian principles in a utopian society, the Enlightenment embraced the Scientific Revolution while rejecting Christian metaphysics in favor of pleasure seeking.

*See also* Macaria.

*References* Hall, A. Rupert. "Science, Technology, and Utopia in the Seventeenth Century" (1972); Manuel, Frank E. "Pansophia: A Seventeenth-Century Dream of Science" (1971).

## *Penguin Island* (1908)

The liberal-patriotic French author Anatole France expressed disillusionment with the liberal cause in France and other places in Europe through the composition of *L'Ile des Pingouins* in 1908. The work does not fit with France's other writings, so it has been difficult for literary analysts to classify it, although France had written a utopian piece, *The White Stone*, in 1904. Using civilization itself rather than a human as protagonist, France wrote a parody that expressed both his disappointments with the present and his hopes for a better future. Despite being criticized from opposing French sides—Catholics and surrealists like André Gide—for his literary style and philosophical expressions, France was read widely outside his own nation and was noted for his modernist skepticism.

Anatole France (1844–1924) was born François-Anatole Thibault, the son of a Parisian book dealer. The family was descended from peasant stock, and his father had been successful selling books, especially those dealing with the French Revolution, after a career in the military. France published his first book—a biography of a popular poet—only four years after graduation from college. France embraced the liberal ideals of the Third French Republic (1875), but he did not hesitate to criticize other liberal intellectuals, including Emile Zola. Elected to the French Academy in 1896, France left the organization in 1900 because of conflicts with some members who opposed Captain Alfred Dreyfus's cause. Following the lead of many French liberals, France rallied to the defense of Dreyfus, a liberal Jew falsely accused of selling military secrets to the Germans. Gradually, France became enamored of socialism in the early twentieth century as he continued to publish and travel widely in Italy, England, and Argentina. France remained largely pacifist during World War I, although he volunteered for military service but failed a physical. Following the war, France had a brief fling with the newly formed Communist Party before his death in 1924.

Around 1905, Anatole France felt a certain despair over the failure of the Russian Revolution and the ineffective leadership of liberals in the French government. He also faced some personal problems in his life at the time, including a dispute with his daughter. He composed a utopian fantasy, *The White Stone*, in 1904, just before pessimism came to dominate his thought. In this piece, France contrasted the past with the future by comparing the Greco-Roman world with a golden age in the twenty-third century. France simply speculated in *The White Stone* about what the future would be like without making any firm predictions. Although there was some satire, especially about Western nations' imperialism, it lacked the deep pessimism and fear of the future found in *Penguin Island*. Thus France's composition of *Penguin Island* does not even fit easily with his previous utopian writings. Two previous French works had used the Antarctic setting of Penguin Island for their animal treatises: Georges Buffon's *Natural History of Birds* (18 volumes, 1770–1785) and Pierre-Jules Hetzel's *Scenes of the Private and Public Life of Animals* (1842). Those works, like France's, owed much to the eighteenth-century voyage literature and Robinsonades made popular by Jonathan Swift and Daniel Defoe.

France surveys the existence and progress of civilization from its mythical origins to the present in *Penguin Island*. The story revolves around a Breton itinerant monk named Mael who aimed to sail to the Breton islands off France. Instead, his ship was blown far off course, taking him to an island in Antarctica. Mael's failing eyesight caused him to baptize penguins along the seashore, thinking them to be humans. Mael's mistake caused great turmoil and debate in Heaven about how to resolve the matter. God and the angels soon determined that since the penguins had already been baptized, they must be transformed into humans. Anatole France then reconstructed the history of Penguin Island, which served as a parody of the national history of the author's own France.

Since the penguins had become human they needed clothing, and the Devil, disguised as a monk named Magis, proposed to design the necessary clothing. However, when Mael discovered that the Devil sought to use clothing fitted for the maid Orberose to promote lascivious conduct, he created his own clothing, which would diminish the attraction of the female anatomy. The story also discussed the evolution of class consciousness through an elaboration of the feudal aristocracy. The creation of an exploiter-exploited class contrast sanctioned by the Catholic church allowed France to criticize both society and the clergy. Mael again represented France's idealism by attempting to create a society based upon egalitarian principles. For example, Mael promoted a tax system based upon assessment by progressive income levels, but the proposal was rejected in favor of one that taxed all income groups with the same percentage of tax.

France also used the story to discuss the origin of monarchical government, which had been replaced in his own lifetime by a republican structure. Threatened by a dragon, Mael and Orberose appeal to a hero to dispatch the beast. Orberose married the savior, Kraken, and they became king and queen. France brought the story of Penguin Island up to the French Revolution and Napoleonic eras, during which time religious faith was replaced by skeptical materialism. Although France was critical of the national hero Trinco, the Penguin version of Napoleon, for bringing the nation to defeat, he was the only leader who gave the nation glory. When a republic was established, the monarchists schemed to undermine and replace it,

again following closely the actual history of the nation of France. This section featured a parallel episode to the Dreyfus Affair. Yet even with the victory against discrimination and bigotry, the liberal tradition was betrayed by a satisfaction with political power that left social justice unachieved. France both predicted and mocked the advance of technology, such as automobiles, by suggesting that even though machines might make life easier they would not ensure the reform of the human condition.

At the end of *Penguin Island*'s survey of the past, France projected his vision of the future. He saw huge metropolitan centers with skyscraper buildings. Big business, through a trust system, dominated and exploited society, which was made up of technocrats and workers, both subservient to the ruling class. Into this fixed scene appeared a group of anarchists led by Georges Clair bent upon the physical destruction of the existing unjust society. The anarchists utilized a weapon that resembled an atomic bomb to destroy civilization. Yet when a new society emerged from the rubble of the old, it quickly resumed the patterns of the past, reflecting France's cyclic and thus pessimistic view of history. Thus even if the existing system were to be destroyed, he saw no hope that an ideal society could emerge to take its place. Such pessimism also appeared in France's 1914 work, *Revolt of the Angels*, which concluded that even angels, if they were to become human, would reject paradise in favor of an unjust system.

*Reference* Kershner, R. B. "Degeneration: The Explanatory Nightmare" (1986); Levaillant, Jean. *Les Aventures du scepticisme: Essai sur l'évolution intellectuelle d'Anatole France* (1965).

**Pietists**
*See* Millennialism.

*Pingshu*
Although most early Manchu utopias in China have been categorized as neo-

Confucian, the obscure treatise *Pingshu* by Wang Yuan does not conform to other so-called utopian works of the era. It may be deemed pre-neo-Confucian in its limited structural reforms that do not assail the imperial tradition per se. Despite the supposed unification of the "Three Teachings" of Confucianism, Taoism, and Buddhism into a modified Confucianism centuries earlier, splits in the Confucian ranks appearing by the seventeenth century were aggravated by the advent of the Manchu rule in 1644. Wang Yuan does not attempt to reconstruct Confucian thought in order to critique the Manchu dynasty, and he tends to be more amenable to the class structure and privilege than were neo-Confucian utopists. Still, Wang Yuan's utopia describes in detail many changes and ideals, mostly grounded in economic reform, for the future of China.

Wang Yuan (1648–1710) lived in the first generation after the overthrow of the Ming dynasty (1368–1644) by the Manchu, considered foreign invaders by the Chinese since they were from Manchuria. Because his father had been an imperial guard during Wang's youth, Wang considered himself loyal to the Ming rule and thus opposed to the Manchu. Wang became a student of the philosopher Yen Yüan (1635–1704) during 1703, after composing the *Pingshu*. Yen became an advocate of Han learning, seeking pragmatic application of reforms rather than mere abstract theories popular with the neo-Confucians. Wang wrote the *Pingshu* (Book of pacifying) in the 1690s as a proposal for establishing a society based on "good order" and involving specific practical reforms. It was not published in its original form, but an edited version by Li Kung (1659–1746) appeared about 1708 as *Pingshu-ding* (The edited book of pacifying). Like Wang, Li had been a follower of Yen Yüan and became friends with Wang about 1700. Some scholars have portrayed the *Pingshu* as part of a bourgeois enlightenment in China based upon Wang's sympathy with the position of merchants and other middle-class business

interests. Yet Wang's philosophy contained much more traditional views that would make his designation as a liberal reformer suspect. Thus his reform system speaks in terms of specific economic changes but accepts many traditional social views. For example, Wang favored restoring to law the outlawed five mutilating punishments in the criminal code.

Although Wang did not elaborate on opposition to large, bureaucratic government in the manner of other reformers, he did favor some decentralization since he believed that the government had become overly centralized. Actually, his political economy coincides closely with the European system of mercantilism, or state control of the economy, in the late seventeenth century. For example, Wang believed that a nation's wealth was determined more by the amount of bullion it possessed than of grains. Cash had become more important than land. However, Wang sought improvement for the whole of society and not just the interests of the state. The *Pingshu* described the evolution of government in China following the post-Confucius era and suggested that it was constructed on a false foundation which needed to be completely swept away so that a new and better structure could be established. Wang proposed a consolidation of the class system, in particular seeking either to eliminate the more regressive and inefficient classes (the poor and petty criminals) or to assimilate them into the productive groups. Clearly, Wang saw a need to eradicate both crime and poverty in his utopia. However, Wang also proposed a state social welfare system to care for the aged, orphans, and the disabled. Not surprisingly given the foreign invasion of China, Wang espoused a xenophobic attitude in his social statements.

The social system proposed by Wang required a reduction in the number of ranks from 17 to 10. Essentially, Wang sought to make the citizenry more productive by simply refusing to recognize past categories such as the poor and criminals. Perhaps the most innovative new social rank would be junior bureaucrats, who proved essential to the reformed local administration of government and the economy. Two ranks, the peasants and the soldiers, would be eligible to receive government land grants to make them self-sustaining and taxpaying subjects. Wang also paid great attention to the merchants, who were given greater privileges, although because of his hatred of foreigners, no foreign trade would be allowed. In an overt attempt to maintain class distinctions, Wang prescribed dress (silk or non-silk) and transportation (donkeys or horses) codes for the merchants.

The economic reforms primarily concentrated on increasing the amount of arable land and its productivity. The most ideal concept in Wang's reforms involved a massive irrigation program for northern China that would enhance the area's productivity and bring it up to the level of southern China with its great river systems. A whole chapter deals with hydraulic methods of managing the Yellow River. By expanding the amount of arable land, the population would become more self-sufficient and able to pay their taxes. Elevated land incapable of irrigation was set aside for living quarters and for growing mulberry and fruit trees. Wang detailed methods for recovering additional lands for use. Wastelands would be reclaimed, depopulated areas would be repopulated, and government officials convicted of graft would have their property seized and redistributed. The reforms would not allow absentee ownership, and subjects would be limited to a single occupation.

Wang offered considerable detail about his ideal government. The main purpose of a more decentralized government would be to improve public finances and to create more efficient control of local governments. The emperor's position would not change much from its existing status, except that Wang foresaw a major delegation of authority through a structured hierarchical system reminiscent of European feudalism. The emperor would be assisted at the central government level

by two prime ministers and several bureaucracies. The major changes proposed by Wang came at the provincial level of government. Two categories of viceroys, for provinces in the interior and principates around the borders, would report to the imperial authorities. These appointed officials would serve three-year terms with reappointment based on merit. Provinces or principates would be further subdivided into prefectures composed of several counties each. Counties would contain five cantons with a village elder as spokesman. Cantons were viewed as very important to provide moral guidance, law enforcement, and economic discipline. They were also crucial in the establishment of grain reserves to be used in cases of natural disasters. Essentially, the provincial structure would serve as a microcosm of the central government. Junior bureaucrats at each level would normally be appointed by and responsible to their supervisors. Overall, Wang hoped to reduce the number of government officials while ensuring greater efficiency of government, especially at the lower levels.

Probably the primary reason for government reorganization, according to Wang, was the need for more efficient collection of taxes. He was critical of the lax financial management of previous Chinese governments. In his plan, the Board of Money would serve as a central treasury department. Regarding taxes, Wang wanted to lessen the burden of peasant taxes by allowing them to pay in kind from their agricultural harvests and textile manufactures. The rate of taxation was 16.7 percent for landed households, whereas merchants only paid 10 percent of their profits. Wang proposed higher tax rates for tea, wine, and tobacco, interestingly, to reduce consumption in the case of tobacco. Of the taxes collected, 60 percent were to remain in the local county while 40 percent would go to the prefecture. Wang also proposed that the state act as a banker, loaning money for interest.

Education in the *Pingshu* demonstrated the tight government controls through the

Department of Education. Apparently Wang did not want an independent class of scholars to exist, since they might offer challenges to the regime. Thus as students moved through the educational structure, they were carefully scrutinized in order to select the brightest students for government service. The process generally began at age 13 in the county schools, which relied upon Confucian methods. Those students scoring highest on examinations would be sent into a system of government training to become junior state officials. The course of study expanded to 12 subjects, including the humanities, fine arts, economics, law, and military science. Students who did not qualify to become civil servants were sent to technical schools.

Although Wang Yuan's *Pingshu* does not propose a revolutionary overhaul of the Chinese system of government or society, it clearly indicates the influences of Western ideas of reform. It might be difficult to argue that Wang's utopia was enlightened since it lacked many elements of later neo-Confucian utopists; nor did it meet European Enlightenment standards. Yet Wang recognized the need for changes in China, and he sought practical methods to accomplish what in reality was a utopian ideal. In fact, authoritarian methods to achieve a better society were characteristic of European early modern utopias. It was an important, if gradual, step toward greater utopian influences in China's future.

*See also* Neo-Confucian Utopias.

*Reference* Dunstan, Helen. "Wang Yuan's *Pingshu*: A Late Seventeenth Century Utopia" (1987).

## *A Plan for the Prince* (1662)
*See* Neo-Confucian Utopias.

## Point Loma, California
*See* Theosophy.

## Positivism
Although it was not regarded by its followers as utopian, the nineteenth-century concept of positivism possessed many utopian ingredients. The French philosopher Auguste Comte was the founder and spokesman for positivism. He believed he had discovered a science of society that could produce a veritable heaven on earth if it were implemented. Although born and nurtured in Europe, positivism would become the banner of reform in the Americas and Russia. Yet despite its liberal underpinnings, positivism was intended to be implemented only by a small elite group of technocrats whose designs for society could be trusted because they would be totally selfless.

Auguste Comte (1798–1857) grew up in postrevolutionary France believing, with his utopian socialist mentor, Henri Saint-Simon, that the Revolution of 1789, though successful in throwing off the yoke of feudalism, had not created an ideal society because it concentrated solely upon capitalism. The revolutionary generation failed to recognize the potential of scientific and technical knowledge to completely remake society. In particular, Comte and his disciples argued that because of the Industrial Revolution's dramatic disruption of both the economy and society, previous mistakes of reorganization could only be overcome by adopting positivism.

Comte's positivism was described with considerable detail in two massive works, the six-volume *Course of Positive Philosophy* (1830–1842) and the four-volume *System of Positive Polity* (1851–1854). In the first exercise, Comte sought to reorder scientific thought to practical rather than theoretical applications, a prerequisite for using science to reform society. In his second treatise, Comte attempted to show the "positive" results from relying upon science as a guide to social restructuring through the political process. Implicit in all of Comte's writing was the assumption that the proper application of scientific knowledge was the only method that would produce an ideal society. Such knowledge could not be questioned because it could be verified. To Comte science simply removed any need for discussion about means. Yet because there was only one method to produce the ideal society, scientists alone could formulate the science of society, or sociology. Professionals from other disciplines—lawyers, historians, philosophers, theologians—need not participate because they were not qualified for the particular task.

Comte's philosophy of history divided human events into three stages: (1) the theological or mythical age covered the period from prehistory to ancient times, (2) the metaphysical age extended through the Middle Ages to the French Revolution, and (3) the positive stage began in the nineteenth century and would soon produce a scientific utopia. Comte's sociology consisted of both a systematic philosophy and an implementing polity or government, the true source of utopian elements. Thus the sociologist was both a theorist, who would design the ideal society, and practitioner (technocrat), who could transform the philosophy into legislation. Most important, the technocrats would impose a moral authority upon society that would substitute altruism for capitalist self-interest. Comte's Positivist Society, founded in 1848, tried to promote a civil religion in which priests would administer rituals based upon the worship of positivism rather than God.

Comte's influence among his contemporaries should be classified according to how they used his ideas. There were many like-minded philosophical sympathizers who admired Comte, such as England's John Stuart Mill and Henry T. Buckle, Emile Durkheim in France, and the Unitarian-Universalists in the United States. Another group that was interested in practical, if selected, applications of positivism could be called social activists. They included English author George Eliot and U.S. labor leader Samuel Gompers. Yet the purists among the Comteans are not as well known. They included Pierre Laffitte, Comte's successor as public lecturer at the Positivist Society in France during the 1860s–1870s. Followers in the United States established utopian positivist communities that followed several unsuccessful utopian socialist experiments.

Henry Edger (1820–1888) immigrated to the United States from England in 1851 and in 1853 joined the recently established utopian community called Modern Times on Long Island, New York. As a disciple of Comte, Edger was one of the first Comteans in America. Upon settling at Modern Times, Edger built a temple to worship the Comtean religion. Nonetheless, there were few converts to positivism among the nonconformist residents at Modern Times, partly because industrial workers were ill prepared to launch an agricultural society. Meanwhile, Edger wrote several positivist tracts. His first effort focused upon the moral anarchy of the 1850s, which allowed him to tout positivism as a true moral reform. Edger, following Comte, stressed the primacy of social cooperation over pure individualism. Edger was one of the founders of the first positivist society in New York City in 1868. His followers included journalist David Croly and philosopher-author Thaddeus B. Wakeman. Though the social experiment at Modern Times had dissipated by the late 1870s, Comte's influence upon U.S. liberalism became permanently ingrained thanks largely to Edger's efforts.

A second episode of Comtean positivism in the United States was initiated by a Russian émigré, William Frey, born Vladimir Geinss. Despite coming from a Russian noble family, Geinss's social conscience was pricked by the modest reforms of Czar Alexander II in the 1860s. Enthused by events in Russia and by his reading of Auguste Comte, Geinss decided to travel to the United States, which he believed offered an even greater opportunity for incorporating reform ideas. Taking the Anglicized name of William Frey, in 1868 he obtained several hundred acres at Cedar Vale, Kansas, near Wichita, where he settled with his family and a small entourage. Frey hoped to launch an experimental community that would illustrate positivist benefits and inspire others to emulate them. Because the Cedar Vale experiment showed little pioneer ingenuity in simple pursuits such as farming or construction, it failed to attract new converts. When another Russian reformer acquainted with Frey's effort, Nicholas Chaikovski, arrived in Kansas in 1874, his group chose not to join Frey's ragtag commune but to start their own. Most of the Russian colonists left Kansas to return home in 1877, leaving Frey virtually alone.

In Central and South America, positivism became a secular alternative to Catholicism and the basis of some political reform efforts. In Chile, the brothers Jorge and Juan Lagarrigue championed positivist views during the 1870s–1880s through extensive propaganda, both written and oral, though they disdained political action. As a result of the 1889 Brazilian revolt against Emperor Dom Pedro II, positivist champion Miguel Lemos tried unsuccessfully to implement a Comtean system in the drafting of a republican constitution. He did, however, succeed in including such ideas—freedom from religious and military traditions—in the state constitution of Rio Grande do Sul. In 1867, Mexico's president allowed the French-educated Comtean disciple Gabino Barreda to launch an educational reform effort grounded upon positivism. Barreda hoped that by creating a large educated class, an appreciation of science and technology would allow more-extensive positivist reforms to replace traditional religious and political philosophies with a new moral order. However, Barreda's chief disciples soon abandoned positivism in favor of social Darwinism.

Perhaps one of the most serious problems in applying positivism was the claim of science to be value neutral even though the sociologist was supposed to implement a scientific plan based upon a moral imperative. The place of science and technology in modern utopias has often begged the question of whether science would serve humanity or vice versa. The positivist naïveté about the possibility of people using concentrated political power for benevolence rather than oppression of society was a classic utopian attitude.

**References** Harp, Gillis J. *Positivist Republic: Auguste Comte and the Reconstruction of American Liberalism, 1865–1920* (1995); Simon, Walter Michael. *European Positivism in the Nineteenth Century* (1963).

## Rabelais, François
*See Gargantua and Pantagruel.*

## The Radiant City

The idea of transforming the modern city into a harmonious utopia attracted a variety of architects, but none more daring than the Swiss designer Le Corbusier. The concept of building on a massive as well as comprehensive scale appealed to Le Corbusier. His primary proposal was outlined in *La Ville radieuse* (The radiant city), published in 1935. It became one of the most influential theories of urban architecture in the twentieth century. Modern utopian architects, such as Le Corbusier, believed that they could direct the reform and reorganization of society through physical designs rather than systems of laws and institutions. The influence of Le Corbusier was revealed at its grandest scale in the design of the interior Brazilian capital of Brasilia in the late 1950s.

Prior to World War I city planning, in movements such as Ebenezer Howard's Garden City, refused to yield the role of the countryside. Yet following the war the Italian Antonio Sant' Elia established the school of futurism, which thought in terms of vast scale and without a hint of retaining any rural aspects. As he grew to maturity in Switzerland, Charles-Edouard Jeanneret (1887–1965) learned to appreciate both the impact of the modern industrialization and the importance of skilled craftsmanship. The young Jeanneret demonstrated a talent for drawing at his applied art *gymnasium* and read about nineteenth-century socialist idealists such as John Ruskin. His principal teacher instilled the notion in Jeanneret that mankind must live in harmony with the environment. After traveling around Europe, Jeanneret began regularly visiting Paris, where he worked as an architectural draftsman and continued his architectural studies. He became acquainted with the Garden City designs and began to add a knowledge of residential housing to his designs for commercial structures. Jeanneret moved his permanent residence to Paris in 1916 and forsook his birth name for Le Corbusier.

Le Corbusier's first project for creating an ideal city was *The Contemporary City for Three Million People* in 1922. The idea in the utopia was to blend human society into the natural surroundings with the aid of technology. However, Le Corbusier thought of his project not as something for the future but, rather, as for the present and thus entirely practical. He had long felt that urban planning must be considered an applied science, a specialty of architecture. The plan called for two superhighways to intersect at the center of the city, thus dividing it into four quadrants. The city would be partitioned into segments isolating residences, commercial buildings, and factories from each other. Because of the concentration of population in the metropolis, Le Corbusier recognized the importance of efficient and speedy transportation, which would include subways and pedestrians paths in addition to highways. In order to make the most efficient use of limited space, the main structures in the inner city were 60-story glass and steel skyscrapers. Le Corbusier envisioned a concentration of population but with less congestion than in existing cities. He also positioned the principal buildings in a design that reflected his view that commerce was more important than government. The white-collar professionals lived in luxurious apartments near the city's center, while other social classes lived on the outer perimeter of the city. The inner city provided a number of parks, gardens, and recreational facilities to illustrate Le Corbusier's dictum that leisure was as important as work.

By the time Le Corbusier produced his magnum opus, *La Ville radieuse*, in 1935, he had concluded that the only way an ideal city plan could be implemented in the Second Machine Age was through an authoritarian system. Individual liberty should be limited to the private realm only. He had become intrigued with fascism in Italy, especially after a 1934 visit in which Le Corbusier was lauded by Benito Mussolini. Le Corbusier later worked with the Nazi collaborationist regime at Vichy, France, during World War II. Thus one of the main differences between the Contemporary City and the Radiant City reflected Le Corbusier's shift toward authoritarian government. The government in his Radiant City was more a hierarchy of technocrats than of politicians, closely resembling the concepts of syndicalism. Another important change from the Contemporary City to the Radiant City was Le Corbusier's determination in the latter that social class divisions must be minimized. The family unit primarily supervised the realm of leisure since all members were separated by work and school during a major portion of the day. Since Le Corbusier's utopia made material provision for all of its inhabitants, there was no basis for crime or poverty in the Radiant City. Hence virtually all of society's typical problems would be eliminated. Because the Radiant City was produced during the Great Depression, Le Corbusier assumed its methods could solve the economic problems of the time as well.

After World War II, Le Corbusier supervised some small-scale projects for France and India, but he never realized his dream of personally creating the ideal city before his death in 1965. Moreover, Le Corbusier's notion of a megascale city was opposed by architects such as Frank Lloyd Wright and intellectuals such as Lewis Mumford. However, one of Le Corbusier's great legacies was the newly constructed capital of Brazil at Brasilia in the late 1950s. The architects of the project, Lucio Costa and Oscar Niemeyer, borrowed and copied from Le Corbusier's theories and designs. They also envisioned the new capital city as representing the harmony of the whole, a unity of form and function. Like Le Corbusier, Costa and Niemeyer thought that Brasilia could lead the reordering of society through its very design. As early as 1883, Joao Bosco had dreamed of a city like Brasilia in the country's sparsely populated interior. In the 1955 presidential election, Juscelino Kubitschek campaigned on a platform to enhance national communication and development by building the capital at Brasilia. After his election the project moved forward to completion following a plan that the International Congress of Modern Architecture led by Le Corbusier had been developing since the 1930s. In the Congress's *Athens Charter* (1941), written by Le Corbusier, cities should incorporate four functions: economic activity, residential housing, recreational facilities, and transportation systems. The *Athens Charter* clearly consolidated Le Corbusier's earlier work in the Contemporary City and the Radiant City. Costa had studied Le Corbusier's ideas since 1930, and Niemeyer agreed with Le Corbusier that creating harmonious relationships between public and private struc-tures would blur the distinctions. Although Brasilia was designed following Le Corbusier's principles, it did not initially succeed in persuading its residents of the value of its aims. Many felt that uniformity eliminated individuality and fostered anonymity. Most high-level government officials refused to live in the same complexes with lower employees. Hence, as with almost all utopian schemes, the designers rarely comprehended the impact of abstract ideas operating in reality with humans rather than automatons.

**Reference** Fishman, Robert. *Urban Utopias in the Twentieth Century: Ebenezer Howard, Frank Lloyd Wright, and Le Corbusier* (1977).

## Rand, Ayn
*See Anthem.*

## Ranters

Unlike any other radical movement in seventeenth-century England, the Ranters possessed neither any unified statement of belief nor an organization. Indeed, before the 1970s scholarship fleshed out the Ranters, it was hardly regarded as a formal movement at all. Although they were often classified as a religious sect, the Ranters rejected many of the most fundamental Christian beliefs. Since "ranting" was simply a colloquial term for antisocial behavior, contemporary Puritans (and others) might charge anyone engaged in profane and wicked acts as a Ranter. Some scholars have tried to trace their origins to earlier radical movements, such as Familism in the sixteenth century. Their following derived mostly from the lower social order and the military during the civil wars at midcentury. The Ranters, like other dissenting groups, were able to flourish and freely express themselves due to the abolition of the institutions of authority and discipline, the Crown and the Church of England. With the restoration of monarchy and the Church of England in 1660, the Ranters faded away, most apparently joining the Society of Friends (Quakers). Anticipating the modern anarchist tradition, the Ranter utopia stressed virtually absolute individual freedom, so Ranter practices varied rather widely. Still, most ordinary Englishmen not only did not embrace the Ranters but also shunned them. The Ranter utopia most resembled the late medieval Land of Cockaygne, except that Ranter ideas emanated more from the religious and social milieu than from economic conditions.

The seventeenth century was a fertile time for religious sectarianism as order in church and state broke down in several places around Europe. Disorder and the absence of repression allowed private beliefs to become public practice through a great variety of utopian movements, many of which proved to be precursors of the modern era. Virtually all of the radical movements originated from a religious foundation. The Diggers, the Levellers, the Quakers, and other groups that became visible in England during the 1640s–1650s objected to the established system of institutions and laws in various ways. They sought to reorder society, especially in religion and government, to fashion a utopian ideal. The broad, generic movement known as Puritanism actually contained several varying strands, so once their common enemies, king and bishops, were overturned, they openly split into factions. The Ranters reacted against Puritan beliefs such as Sabbatarianism and moralism, so their own system of belief began from a negative stance. Yet without organization or a formal statement of faith, Ranter practices ran the gamut from the bizarre to the sublime.

In general, most who were either dubbed Ranters by others or who called themselves Ranters rejected certain fundamental Christian beliefs held by Puritan and Anglican alike. Among others, they denied the immortality of the soul, they did not believe in the existence of either heaven or hell, they rejected the divinity and resurrection of Christ, and they treated the Bible as an allegory rather than as the divinely inspired word of God. The Ranters viewed tithes as mere ceremony and a discouragement to economic initiative. The Ranters' religious beliefs were summed up in their embracing of pantheism, which viewed God as being in nature and mankind literally so that the worship of nature became the worship of God. God (and Christ) had entered mankind to dwell as spirit, so Bible study seemed superfluous. Moreover, since each person was divine, salvation could be achieved by any number of actions, including indulging in what Puritans regarded as vices: drunkenness, cursing, and use of tobacco. Because of their pantheism, the Ranters saw no need for clerics or magistrates nor for ecclesiastical and civil law. Their emphasis upon absolute freedom led most

Ranters to embrace antinomianism, stating that they were free to disobey human laws whether ecclesiastical or civil.

The Ranters were often associated with the Family of Love because they adopted especially antisocial practices in sexual and family relations. Certain scholars have attempted to trace their origins to earlier groups including the Brethren of the Free Spirit and the Joachimists. It may be that like Gerrard Winstanley and the Diggers, the Ranters were repelled by economic changes they could neither adapt to nor comprehend. Some advocated free love and decried the traditional family structure as another restraint upon individual freedom. Often groups of Ranters would meet at taverns to eat, drink, smoke tobacco, and sing bawdy songs in communal fashion, mocking Christian rituals. The Ranters probably gained their vision of freedom from their view of the aristocracy, which enjoyed all the social privileges without having to labor. Staunch believers in equality, the Ranters greeted each other as "fellow creature" rather than as Mr. or Mrs. Much of the Ranter sexual ethic, like their social ethic, was adopted as a form of protest against society's conventions and restrictions.

The chief followers of Ranters included manual laborers, usually migratory, and vagrant peasants. The largest segments of Ranters seem to have originated in urban settlements in either the Midlands, especially Derbyshire, or Western counties, especially Wiltshire and Dorset. Since the Ranter phenomenon emerged during the civil-war era, many converts also came from the military. Despite their attack upon religious tradition, the Ranters always seemed to use religious images in their self-descriptions. John Robins of Wiltshire claimed that he was God while engaging in spouse swapping. Thomas Webbe of Dorset, who also advocated free love, had been an ordained Anglican minister prior to his association with the Ranters.

The chief exponents of Ranter thought were Abiezer Coppe, Laurence Clarkson, and Jacob Bauthumley. Unquestionably, their philosophy began with the notion of equality and included the belief that there was no afterlife, and hence they believed that mankind must make the most of the present existence. Any action is permissible if it does no harm to another human, especially bodily acts. Thus the Ranter philosophy might be summarized in the phrase "eat, drink, and be merry." Coppe attended Oxford University and served as army chaplain during the civil war and has been classified as a Baptist by some researchers. He encouraged soldiers after the abolition of monarchy and the church to engage in drinking, smoking, and swearing. Despite advocating revolutionary actions, Coppe's pacifism caused him to despise violence. He embraced the Digger tenet of abolishing private property. Coppe did not claim that man was God, but he asserted that mankind possessed a divine nature. Still a believer in sin, Coppe stressed that the greatest sins were oppressing fellow humans and showing no mercy toward the poor. Clarkson, a veteran of the parliamentary army, quit the military in 1649 when he became a self-styled preacher advocating universal salvation. He embraced much of the Leveller and Digger positions on government and property rights. Clarkson particularly abhorred the unequal tax structure. Rejecting his calling as a preacher, Clarkson condemned the clergy, embraced pantheism, and denied the existence of heaven and hell. By the late 1650s, Clarkson had become a follower of Lodowicke Muggleton, another mystical radical. An ex-shoemaker and parliamentary soldier, Bauthumley left the army on the occasion of publishing *The Light and Dark Side of God* in 1650. He advocated pantheism, argued that hell and Satan existed within each person, and viewed biblical stories as allegories. Though initially given corporal punishment for his book, Bauthumley thereafter lived a respectable life in Leicester.

While there were various other radicals identified as spokesmen for the Ranters, each supposed authority acted or spoke independently of others. The efforts of the Commonwealth government to suppress the Ranters seemed mild compared to their treatment of other radical groups, suggesting that the authorities may not have regarded the Ranters as an organized and thus threatening movement. It is this fuzziness in defining both the Ranter ideas and their representatives that has led historian J. C. Davis to argue with considerable acumen that the Ranters really did not possess a tangible identity in the manner that some Marxist historians have described. Davis has plausibly suggested that the Marxists were anxious to discover a plebeian movement within, and pitted against, the larger bourgeois revolution, and the Ranters fit the need. Though Davis could agree that there was a mood or sentiment present in the revolutionary era of the 1640s–1650s that reflected views such as antinomianism and practices such as libertinism, no such formal or even informal Ranter movement existed. Nonetheless, it can be concluded that the sentiments and practices that may be characterized as "Ranter" did operate in the period, expressing a point of view shared by some minority of the population, probably mostly from the lower social stratum.

*References* Davis, J. C. *Fear, Myth, and History: The Ranters and the Historians* (1986); Jerome Friedman. *Blasphemy, Immorality, and Anarchy: The Ranters and the English Revolution* (1987).

## Renaissance City-State Utopias

Renaissance Italy (1300–1500) produced a number of ideal city utopias fostered by the competitive spirit among city-states and the practice of patronage of the arts by governments. Architects participating in the quest for the ideal city design included Filarete, Leon Battista Alberti, Francesco di Giorgio Martini, and Leonardo da Vinci. Other more general planned utopias were drawn by Francesco Patrizi and Ludovico Agostini. Virtually all of the architectural plans for the ideal city reflected the aristocratic perspective of the architects themselves, of their patrons, or both. Inherent in almost all Renaissance planned societies was the goal of retaining aristocratic power. However, most of the utopian plans sought a way to integrate the popular masses into the overall scheme. In many respects, designs that benefited the aristocracy were also good for the commoners. The architects were inspired by a rebirth of classical styles, but they incorporated Christian themes as well. The ideal became both a functional and aesthetically appealing city.

Among the earliest utopian architects of the ideal city in Renaissance Italy, Filarete, in his *Trattato d'architettura* (published in the 1460s), described the model city Sforzinda, which illustrated the concern with community that became characteristic of modern utopians. Sforzinda was also the first completely planned ideal city produced during the Italian Renaissance. In seeking a plan for the ideal city, Renaissance architects began with classical antiquity for inspiration and authority. However, Filarete also derived ideas from late-medieval Gothic designs. Antonio di Pietro Averlino (ca. 1400–1469), known by his pen name of Filarete, worked under the patronage of the Milanese duke Francesco Sforza, for whom the utopian city was named.

Believing that participation in the construction of a magnificent edifice was one of the great human pleasures, Filarete reasoned that cooperative action in building the ideal city would become the quintessential force of unity in the community. When considering the symbols that would become part of the new city, Filarete followed a typical Renaissance path of mixing classical pagan themes with Christian emblems. He also followed the classical conceptions of the ideal city in starting with the political considerations of the design. The harmony of a city's surroundings was important in ensuring the support of subjects for their government. Filarete's Sforzinda also displayed an appreciation for improved technology in construction and design.

View of an Ideal City, *a fifteenth-century painting attributed to Piero della Francesca*

Following the concepts of ancient Rome's widely read architect Vitruvius, Sforzinda was shaped like a star with eight radial streets extending from a center core to the city gates joining large squares, with churches marking the boundary of the inner circle. Eight canals alternating with streets extended from the gates to towers at the outer extremity. The central square was adorned with colonnades and surrounded by buildings, including a bank and the magistrate's offices. Three adjacent squares contained the prince's palace, the cathedral, and the marketplace. The text can be misleading in places because Filarete's descriptions do not always correspond to his drawings.

The design of Sforzinda was intended to be both symmetrical and functional because Filarete believed attention given to architecture was timeless. He reasoned that human dwellings were second only in importance to food for survival, so he provided considerable detail even for workers' housing. Filarete followed the ancients in thinking of the ruler as the father of the city, who would authorize its construction, and the architect as the mother, who would determine its design and bring it to life.

Filarete's Sforzinda represented a society in Renaissance Italy that was dominated by powerful princes and aristocrats with little concern for the common people. Thus, other than seeking acceptance by the common people, architects such as Filarete serving a prince such as Sforza provided nothing in their plans that would benefit residents other than the prince and nobles. Necessarily, therefore, Filarete's personal utopian tendencies, which may have reflected his modest origins in Siena, were restrained by obedience to his patron. Nonetheless, because common laborers would contribute to the construction of Sforzinda, with its palaces and churches, they would feel an affection for the ideal city. Residences, however, would reflect the status of those who occupied them: Doric forms for gentlemen, Corinthian for merchants, and Ionic for craftsmen. The ideal city, according to Filarete, should function much as a beehive, with workers dutifully serving their master. Perhaps the only popular concession by Filarete was the provision of schools for the children of the lower classes. Further, Sforzinda condoned what the Renaissance regarded as minor deviations such as gambling, drinking, and prostitution, which may well have been viewed as placating the popular classes. Indeed, one of the prominent buildings was the "House of Vice and Virtue," which included a brothel alongside lecture halls.

Among Italian Renaissance architects who desired to create the ideal city, the Florentine Leon Battista Alberti (1404–1472) authored a famous treatise, *De re aedificatoria* (On architecture), published after his death in 1485. Alberti's work has become one of the most influential writings on architecture in modern history. Renaissance Italian cities aggressively sought to replace their medieval images with a distinctively modern appearance. True to the thinking of the Italian humanists of his day, Alberti sought to design a city that would allow the nurture of *virtù*, or the talent of its citizens. He hoped that his project would create a union of form and function.

Though Alberti was born into an aristocratic family, they had been exiled to Genoa from their native Florence. Alberti finally returned to Florence in 1435 upon the occasion of Cosimo de Medici's accession to power in that city. Talented in many areas including philosophy and linguistics, Alberti's first published work concerned painting. Alberti believed that architectural beauty also served to influence the development of moral character in citizens. Thus the architect to Alberti was more than just a planner and designer; he was also the creator of an ideal social paradigm. Following the influence of Plato, Alberti argued that the ideal city should be located in a place with good soil and climate. *De re aedificatoria* was written about 1450 while Alberti was attending the court of Pope Nicholas V in Rome. The first edition of 1485 was in Latin, but it was reissued in Italian (1546) and French (1553), demonstrating its lasting influence.

In the treatise Alberti wrote in detail about the building materials, designs, functions, and symbolism that comprised the plan of the ideal city. He did not actually draw an entire city plan because he felt that different cities demanded different designs. Typical of the Renaissance, Alberti's architectural style mimicked classical rather than Gothic forms. Buildings existed for specific functions and not just for adornment or show. The location of shopping areas would be convenient to residential areas. Three categories of buildings existed in Alberti's ideal city: public structures, private residences for the aristocracy, and housing for the commoners. Several piazzas would be interspersed within the city.

Alberti did not attempt to create a radical new social system for his ideal city. Thus he provided for the social divisions of the aristocracy and the laboring classes as well as the city-state prince. The architectural proposals were to mirror the social order, so the housing of the aristocracy and commoners was separated carefully. However, though Alberti expected the aristocracy to live comfortably, like most utopians he disdained extravagance. Alberti also recognized the problems of security for the city-state and the existence of warfare, and he designed city defenses including walls and fortifications. Understanding the importance of functionability for the modern city, Alberti provided a comprehensive concept of the ideal city.

Also talented in engineering and painting, Francesco di Giorgio Martini (1439–1501) of Siena is best known for his architectural skills. Like his contemporaries, Francesco was strongly influenced by the ancient architect Vitruvius, and he seemed intent upon exceeding Vitruvius's reputation. Despite his humble origins, Francesco worked for his native Siena in crafting city plans in the late 1460s. Yet his work also included fortifications and individual buildings in Urbino (1472–1482), Rome, Milan, and Naples. Because he was engaged in thinking about the implications of his designs, Francesco always allowed practical conditions to moderate his inclination to literally accommodate antique patterns. Like most Renaissance architects, Francesco fashioned what his patrons desired, including churches and cathedrals. But he also had the opportunity to contemplate plans for an ideal city, which he outlined in his treatise *Trattati di architettura, ingegneria e arte militare*, which he began composing in 1481. Shunning abstract tendencies, Francesco anticipated the sixteenth-century designs in the simplicity of his structures.

The multitalented Leonardo da Vinci (1452–1519) sketched a number of drawings of urban plans that focused upon the problem of proportionality of structures. It was essential in practical terms that the buildings of the ideal city achieve the properly balanced relationship to each other. Although he never supervised the actual construction of any project, Leonardo's intense interest in architecture led him to conceive of a never-completed treatise on the subject; only his sketchbooks survive. Also dependent upon patrons and circumstances, Leonardo was invited by Ludovico Sforza to submit plans for the rebuilding of Milan after the devastating plague of the mid-1480s. The plan, *I Manoscritti e i Disegni*, called for the city to be divided into ten separate divisions featuring a literal architectural bifurcation separating aristocrats from common people. The upper level of the city, for the aristocrats, would be free of the crowding and clamor of streets with horse-drawn vehicles and would be able to partake of the healthy air and sunlight. The peasants would be confined to the lower levels, dominated by streets, canals, and refuse.

Francesco Patrizi's planned city, the *Città felice*, showed the greatest deference to aristocratic needs. Patrizi (1529–1597) was bishop of Cherso and as such reflected an aristocratic lifestyle common to the upper clergy. The three privileged classes in Patrizi's utopia were military officers, government officials, and the clergy. Thus even middle-class merchants and craftsmen were denied citizenship. The ideal city's design considered only the happiness of the privileged classes. Patrizi envisioned a rich abundance of food, clothing, and other needs. Therefore, the only benefits to the common classes were those designed specifically for the aristocracy, such as the favorable location of the city to assure moderate climactic conditions. Otherwise, a distinct air of superiority pervaded the aristocrat of the *Città felice*.

A musician by training, Ludovico Agostini (1534–1590) showed more interest in the needs of the commoners than most Renaissance utopian planners. He conceived of an imaginary republic in the 1580s (*La Republica Immaginaria*) that allowed greater participation by the masses in setting rules for society. The author's views are presented in the form of a dialogue between two characters, Finito (the weak one) and Infinito (the disciplined one). Agostini seemed most concerned with eliminating sloth among the population, and he thus set limits on the

amount of leisure time. A maximum of seven hours was allotted to sleep. The division of labor included manual, business, and intellectual endeavors, but Agostini regarded all types of skills as worthy. Each merchant or craft group would be organized into guilds, with democratic participation by all members. In order to prevent accumulation of excess material possessions, Agostini established strict limits on the amount of goods one person could obtain. The republic required twice-a-week fasting (one meal per day) to underscore Agostini's contempt for wasteful accumulation. Aristocratic pleasures were confined to conversation, and exercise and common diversions such as dancing were not permitted. There were even restrictions on clothing; ornate attire permitted for governing officials only.

**References** Saalman, Howard. "Early Renaissance Architectural Theory and Practice in Antonio Filarete's Trattato di Architettura" (1959); Weller, Allen S. *Francesco di Giorgio, 1439–1501* (1943); Westfall, Carroll William. *In This Most Perfect Paradise: Alberti, Nicholas V, and the Invention of Conscious Urban Planning in Rome, 1447–55* (1974).

## Residential Utopias

With the contrast and conflict between urban and suburban life in the twentieth century, utopian schemes reflected different views about how to integrate community with economic and political functions. Most architects and urban planners focused upon the city and sought to blend all of the disparate elements—housing, industry, retail, recreation, and so on—into a total entity. Other ideas converged around a residential utopia as the primary framework and saw support elements, such as commerce and transportation, as secondary. Certainly, the impetus to such thinking began with designers such as Ebenezer Howard and his Garden City, followed by Frank Lloyd Wright's Broadacre City. Yet both of those plans started with the city as a whole rather than with residential needs, although Wright showed greater interest in highlighting housing over economic and political structures. It was in the further elaboration first of suburbia and then of whole new small-scale towns that the residential utopia showed its diversity in the late twentieth century.

The middle-class quest for upscale suburban housing gradually encompassed the larger concerns about community, education, recreation, and culture. Was it possible to plan a whole community around the axis of residences rather than either economic or political functions? The quest for the ideal community produced a novel type of utopian planning that went beyond mere architectural design in the last decades of the twentieth century. From the beginning of the twentieth century forward, urban planning to accommodate population growth became a practical necessity. Yet most of the designs for communities revolved around economic, commercial, or transportation factors rather than residential considerations. Obviously, the automobile has shaped twentieth-century demographics more than any other factor. The widespread reliance on the automobile by the 1920s dictated the location of residences in the suburbs because urban centers had become too crowded, polluted, and dangerous for family life. Large-scale architectural designers such as Le Corbusier and Frank Lloyd Wright depended upon automobile arteries as central features of their planned cities. Indeed, they anticipated the major socioeconomic influence of the automobile in the second half of the twentieth century. By contrast, Howard's Garden City design, which predated the automobile, focused upon close proximity of residences to work and recreation so that walking or biking was feasible.

Of course, whenever residential communities were located on the outskirts of the cities, a commercial sprawl invariably followed that disrupted the ideal of integrated planning. Eventually even business operations would move from the inner city to the suburbs. The result was "edge cities": smaller-scale versions of the metropolis that would crop up around the urban center. Beginning with Tyson's Corner in northern Virginia, the vicinity around Washington, D.C., produced more than a dozen edge cities. Other metropolises, such as Los Angeles, New York City, Detroit, San Francisco, Atlanta, Phoenix, Houston, and Dallas, all sprouted similar edge cities in the 1980s and 1990s. The new style of city blended the public and private aspects in subtle styles of commercial structures housing business, retail, and recreational activities. It basically involved moving the workplace closer to the retail and residential locations. There was no city center in the edge cities, certainly no courthouse or square. The "centers" of the edge city were multiple, encompassed in office complexes built to accommodate the local environment and in sprawling retail shopping malls. The world's largest mall, in Edmonton, Canada, covers 24 city blocks and contains 800 stores. Both of these aesthetically appealing "centers"— office complexes and shopping malls— were intended to make work and chores more pleasurable. Moreover, housing returned to the more traditional single-family unit rather than the multistory apartment homes in the old cities. Residential subdivisions were in closer proximity to both business and retail centers, which shortened the distances required to satisfy needs, although the automobile remained the primary means of transportation. Nonetheless, edge cities themselves fairly soon suffered from some of the same problems as the older urban settings, including congestion, pollution, and crime. Moreover, the hectic and impersonal tone of people's lifestyles may have been encouraged rather than dissipated by the edge city phenomenon.

Because of disappointments with the adverse consequences of edge cities, other residential alternatives eventually appeared. These included "new towns" designed for limited-growth, small-scale urban life built around residential neighborhoods. A second phenomenon has been the more remote "villages," which primarily attracted retirees or second-home purchasers. Reston, Virginia, and Columbia, Maryland, became the prototypes of the new town design. They were conceived by "developers" who were not in every case architects by profession but had a vision of an integrated community that provided the benefits of urban life without the negative qualities. New town designers hoped to allow residents to escape from the crowded, rushed environment of most urban centers and, especially, to free them from reliance on the automobile. They also hoped to integrate civic, cultural, recreational, and educational facilities into the residential areas. A prime concern also focused upon preserving much of the natural environment. Architectural designs increasingly were drawn to complement rather than detract from the local topography and ecology. Most of all, proponents desired the restoration of community and cooperation among people with diverse backgrounds and interests. Nonetheless, by presumption the new towns were limited to well-educated, upscale professionals with a much greater than average income. Hence the new towns by their nature excluded a great portion of the populace.

Taking their cue from nonplanned, limited commercial-scale retirement communities such as Highlands, North Carolina, the nonurban village settlements of Sea Ranch, California, and Seaside, Florida, provide yet another form of residential utopia. Because they are oriented toward retirees or families desiring vacation homes, this type of residential utopia is not located near places of work as is the case in the suburban communities. They assume that the starting point for community development is the private residence. Prospective buyers are offered an array of choices about the design of their living quarters, including the materials as well as floor plans. Developers at Sea Ranch and Seaside were especially conscious of the climatic and ecological concerns of the locales in their design choices and building materials.

Sea Ranch began development in the 1960s on 4,000 acres along ten miles of rugged terrain on the northern California coast above San Francisco. The primary developers were Alfred Boeke and Lawrence Halprin, architects who drew the initial plans for Sea Ranch. Houses were built in clusters away from the bluffs across meadows to preserve the natural setting. The common land areas, about half of the total area, were owned by the community rather than individuals. Strict community covenants prevented any undesirable developments, while housing materials were deliberately suited to the natural topography. Although recreational opportunities were included at Sea Ranch, proponents stressed the natural beauty over pleasures as the main attraction. Retail outlets are both scarce and small at Sea Ranch, and thus there is no real town center. Because all of the land is privately owned and administered through a homeowners association, there is no government agency that operates Sea Ranch, although state laws have created some regulations for coastal development.

Seaside was conceived by Birmingham, Alabama, resident Robert Davis, whose grandfather in 1946 purchased the 80 acres that would comprise the development. The Florida panhandle was a favorite beach retreat for thousands of regional visitors following World War II, but by the 1980s its sprawling development from Pensacola to Panama City reflected a haphazard, environmentally threatening pattern that became known as the "redneck Riviera." Davis conceived of Seaside as a planned community of vacation homes designed to blend into the coastal ecology and pristine beaches. Davis recruited architects Andres Duany and Elizabeth Plater-Zyberk to expand to Seaside their planned development concept, called Charleston Place, in Boca Raton, Florida. The idea of planning was limited mainly to the layout of the streets; individual home buyers selected the design of their houses from several plans. Construction began in 1981, and lots sold steadily, followed by home construction along the grid plan and according to the building codes of Duany and Plater-Zyberk. The neotraditional houses were anchored with pilings to secure them during hurricanes and featured tin roofs. Automobile access is limited in Seaside so that walking is encouraged. Anchored by a village green surrounded by a community center, art gallery, and a few commercial buildings, Davis hoped to promote a sense of community togetherness at Seaside. Architects Duany and Plater-Zyberk are busy promoting other projects incorporating their neotraditional plans, formally dubbed Traditional Neighborhood Development.

*References* Campbell, Carlos C. *New Towns: Another Way to Live* (1976); Garreau, Joel. *Edge City: Life on the New Frontier* (1991); Sexton, Richard. *Parallel Utopias: Sea Ranch, California and Seaside, Florida* (1995).

## Restif de la Bretonne, Nicolas Edme (1734–1806)

As a child of the Enlightenment fascinated with egalitarianism yet wedded to traditional social institutions, Restif de la Bretonne served as a bridge between utopian constructions of the eighteenth century and the utopian socialists of the nineteenth century. Restif's utopianism progressed gradually from simple reform projects dealing with education and manners to bizarre schemes such as those in *La Découverte australe*. The utopias of Restif de la Bretonne serve as a transition from the early modern static schemes inaugurated by Thomas More to the more dynamic concepts of the nineteenth century.

Nicolas Edme Restif de la Bretonne was born into a landowning peasant family in Burgundy. The population in his home region was largely Protestant despite the persecution that had existed since Louis XIV ended toleration in 1685. Restif's father was a member of the Jansenists, a mystical Catholic sect that had also been persecuted by Louis XIV. Young Restif's education was limited to a brief sojourn in a Jansenist school and as a printer's apprentice, but he read some Latin litera-

ture and contemporary novels. However, the most important intellectual influence upon Restif was Jean-Jacques Rousseau. His knowledge of printing allowed Restif to establish a business in Paris and to publish his own writings. His marriage to an adulterous wife affected his attitudes of male dominance and female deference in his writings. Furthermore, guilt about his own sexual indiscretions caused Restif to desire strict moral conduct in his utopias. Despite Restif's rambling, anecdotal literary style, his writings on utopian topics offered detail on almost every aspect of society. He used the technique popular in the eighteenth century of writing letters to fictitious characters who reappear in his works to receive Restif's wisdom about utopia. He seemed obsessed with correcting human and institutional vices by discussing subjects of reform, ranging from prostitution to the theater, in a series entitled *Idées singulières*, which first appeared in 1769.

The first important utopian essay was a mild dose of what was to come later. In his novel *Le Paysan perverti* (The perverted [male] peasant), published in 1776, Restif included a detailed appendix, "Les Statuts du bourg d'Oudun" (The laws of the city of Oudun). In the laws, Restif sought to provide citizens security against corruption. Restif revealed his attachment to the past by contrasting the corrupt temptations of urban life with the Arcadian simplicity and innocence of the rural population. Yet seeking to remain connected with reality, Restif located his utopia of Oudun between the urban and rural extremes. He continued to believe that the family unit was the most important social institution, yet he redefined the family unit in a broader framework than kinship. The family, beginning with the institution of marriage, becomes the community itself, with all of its common interests and concerns. The rigid laws of the community are intended to isolate its residents from the corruptive influences of the world. The education of children combines Spartan techniques and asceticism that eliminate indulgences. Hence Restif's original utopian vision did not provide for individuality or diversity.

In his first utopian venture, Restif was reluctant to depart from patriarchal structures and really did not believe that the ideal society of Oudun was possible. Thus in his next utopian treatise, *Les Contemporaines* (1780), Restif relocated the utopian setting from the countryside to the city in an attempt to confront the reality of the new urban-industrial order of society. He featured a cooperative venture by 20 families living on the same street in Paris to form a unified social unit and pool their resources. This egalitarian format resembles the utopian communities of the early nineteenth century formulated by socialists such as Charles Fourier. Moreover, the subjects of this work were members of the working class. Restif appears to have tried to join his ideals of utopian perfection with the real-world conditions of his native France. Still, although there was more flexibility for women in the urban utopia than the rural, Restif did not entirely dispense with his patriarchy to produce a society of gender equality.

The climax of Restif's movement to embrace the perfectibility of mankind in his utopian progress was the sometimes bizarre world of *La Découverte australe par un homme volant* (1781) and the regimented society of *L'Andrographe, ou Idées d'un honnete-homme* (1782). The former work utilized a technique widely popular among literary utopias in the eighteenth century, the imaginary voyage to an idyllic setting. His hero, Victorin—who incidentally invents a flying machine—travels from Europe to Megapatagonia in Australia, where he discovers a species of man-animals in a biologically diverse environment. The Megapatagons did not need much structure or law since they operated according to the laws of nature. There was no private property in Megapatagonia to create social stress. In *L'Andrographe*, part of the *Idées singulières* series, Restif devised a system of competition with rewards of honor and esteem rather than mere sensual

pleasures or material goods. The elder citizens became the instruments of instilling both wisdom and restraint in the younger generations. The austere requirements for the young were complemented by feasts for the winners of competitions.

The philosophy of Restif de la Bretonne was a combination of hedonism and social reform that rested upon the quest to create a system of secular morality, a popular pastime among the philosophes of the Enlightenment. Thus Restif's idea of utopia reflected tensions between male and female, pleasure and pain, discipline and freedom, but it was a creative rather than a debilitating tension. He thought that happiness would be achieved less by a guarantee of easy access to pleasurable pursuits than by the anticipation of achievement. Thus denial and discipline became the preferred means to the end of happiness. It was not that Restif preferred the moderation of an Arcadia to the excesses of a Land of Cockaygne. He recognized that human self-interest and passions required direction and instruction to be able to manage material conditions. Hence in the utopian works, Restif emphasized that the first generation of utopians must instruct the children so that they could advance beyond the first generation toward the ideal society. Restif also argued that knowledge should not be acquired only in one's youth but should be spread across a lifetime. In that way, individuals would not become haughty about knowledge but would incorporate the wisdom of life experiences over their life span. In short, Restif wanted to create a virtuous citizenry, not merely an ideal society. His obsession with discipline and rules shows his fear of anarchy—another common Enlightenment concern—both within the family and in society as a whole.

Thus though Restif de la Bretonne may well have anticipated the utopian socialists of the early nineteenth century, he was primarily a child of the Enlightenment concept of the perfectibility of mankind and of the natural law tradition that emphasized virtue and discipline. Moreover, his methods were revised during the early nineteenth century when utopian strategists relied upon a theory of history to suggest either that future progress flowed inevitably from historical conditions or that revolution was necessary to pull away the carcass of corrupt tradition. Despite the efforts to link Fourier with Restif, there is no evidence that Fourier ever read any of Restif's works. Hence Restif's utopian concepts belong more to the early modern pattern of static systems that evolved out of Thomas More's model utopia. There was no provision for dynamic change within the utopia of Restif. Restif represents the end of one era of utopian writing much more than the beginning of another.

**Reference** Poster, Mark. *The Utopian Thought of Restif de la Bretonne* (1971).

## Robinson Crusoe
*See* Robinsonades.

## Robinsonades
Daniel Defoe published his model novel *The Life and Strange Surprizing Adventures of Robinson Crusoe, of York, Mariner* in 1719. Without realizing it, he also contributed the most famous example of a subcategory of utopias known as Robinsonades, which became very popular, especially among German writers, during the eighteenth and nineteenth centuries. The theme, with variations, continued far into the twentieth century. Defoe inspired many authors, including Voltaire and Samuel Johnson in the eighteenth century, William Morris in the nineteenth century, and William Golding in the twentieth century. In certain respects, the story of Robinson Crusoe has the earmarks of many early modern utopian adventures. However, Defoe created the vision of a practical utopia constructed literally from the ground up with no prior infrastructures. Even more than the notion of the self-made man of initiative, Defoe's Crusoe showed the most profound ingenuity yet conceived by utopian writers.

*Robinson Crusoe discovers the footprint of Man Friday. (Engraved illustration from an eighteenth-century German edition of Daniel Defoe's* The Life and Strange Adventures of Robinson Crusoe.*)*

The early modern era opened up a new realm for utopists, a worldwide rather than merely a European panorama. Voyages of discovery in the sixteenth and seventeenth centuries revealed that other civilizations and cultures markedly different from those of Europe existed. Inevitably, some Europeans viewed these little-known new worlds through rose-colored glasses as a means of escapism, visualizing flaws in their own societies and potential improvements embodied in non-European traditions. Although literary historians credit Daniel Defoe with creating the genre known as Robinsonades in *Robinson Crusoe*, the antecedents go back to the earlier, seventeenth-century fascination with *terra australis incognita*. Defoe had already read many accounts of stranded mariners; he specifically cited the experience of Scottish sailor Alexander Selkirk, who was marooned on a small island off Chile.

Perhaps the original prototype of the Robinsonade was Henry Neville's Arcadian utopia, *Isle of Pines* (1668). A radical republican protégé of James Harrington, Henry Neville had been condemned by Parliament for advocating atheism. In *Isle of Pines*, Neville recounted a Dutch sea captain's voyage to Madagascar that resulted in the discovery of a curious island populated by almost 2,000 English-speaking residents. The island's founder, George Pine, had been shipwrecked on the island with four women, adopted polygamy, and produced hundreds of off-spring. Pine described the isle as a place of bounty with a temperate climate, "always clothed in green and full of pleasant fruits." Following Pine's example, the isle's populace had defied social conventions and engaged in immoderate practices such as polygamy, which Neville suggested endangered the society's idyllic life and necessitated the imposition of external authority to regulate freedom. Similar to Neville's technique was Robert Knox's *An Historical Relation of Ceylon, a Robinsonade* (1681), which definitely shaped Defoe's version of the genre. Once more, the story featured stranded seamen discovering an idyllic existence on the Indian Ocean island, adopting primitive native customs and rejecting "civilized" European mores. Since Neville and Knox utilized an Arcadia as their ideal society, neither of their chief characters struggled with moral questions as Robinson Crusoe had. Defoe's use of the Robinsonade rejected the Arcadian paradigm as ludicrous and unreal.

Although Daniel Defoe (1660–1731) spent the better part of his life before writing *Robinson Crusoe* engaged in partisan political writing, it was this, his first novel, that made him famous. The story used a crisis structure of having Crusoe accidentally stranded to show the development of individual character rather than mere survival. Also, the character of Crusoe did not possess appealing characteristics, so the story dealt with human reformation as well as survival. Although Robinson Crusoe was forced by his isolated, shipwrecked condition to fend for himself for 28 years, he obviously relied upon both the knowl-edge of civilization and its accompanying techniques, some of which he salvaged from the wreck. Thus the idyllic state of nature in which Crusoe found himself would have become a nightmare without the special knowledge gained from his education and experience. Crusoe established priorities including provisions of food and security as well as maintaining the hope of rescue. He ultimately learned to trust in God and his own ingenuity.

Defoe's Robinsonade, therefore, was distinct from the noble savage utopia as well as from Arcadia because it presupposed a practical rather than a primitive approach to survival. Among the elements that distinguished it was its attitude toward work; Crusoe was forced to labor for survival, whereas most early modern utopias provided a limited role for work. The format did, however, allow certain critical jabs at features of contemporary eighteenth-century society such as class consciousness. Crusoe and his manservant Friday, the true noble savage, would not have formed such an alliance in contemporary society since they were from different backgrounds. The setting of the novel also allowed the utopia to take shape without benefit of the trappings of church or state, institutions that invariably complicated human lives.

Although Defoe penned two sequels to *Robinson Crusoe*, there was no displacing the original as the new prototype of the practical utopia. Penelope Aubin's *The Noble Slaves* (1722) was one of the earliest imitations of *Robinson Crusoe*, although her story dealt with a group of survivors instead of an individual. When Jean-Jacques Rousseau included a prominent reference to Robinson Crusoe in his educational tract *Émile* in 1761, Defoe was given immense notice as well as credibility. The story of Robinson Crusoe strongly appealed to the romantic nationalist German writers in the late eighteenth and early nineteenth centuries. Johann von Goethe was the first *Volksbuch* writer to publicize the Robinsonade, pace *Émile*, as a method of instruction for children. In

1779, Joachim Heinrich Campe published an imitation, *Robinson der Jüngere* (Robinson the Younger), which placed the story in the context of children's literature. Some of Campe's methods were adopted by the Swiss pastor Johann David Wyss in his manuscript written to help educate his four sons. Later in 1812 one of those sons, Johann Rudolph Wyss, edited and published the work under the title *Der Schweizerische Robinson*. Oddly, the story became more popular in England, where it was translated and published in 1814 as *Swiss Family Robinson*. The tale followed a whole family, including children, who, after a shipwreck on a deserted island, labored to produce their own society. In England, Captain Frederick Marryat's *Masterman Ready* (1841) and Robert Michael Ballantyne's *Coral Island* (1858) copied Defoe's formula, although they tended to feature a more benevolent natural environment. Other Robinsonades appeared in stories, especially during the romantic era, published in France, Austria, Hungary, and even the Pacific islands. There was also a story about a female Robinson.

Although some imitators, such as Robert Louis Stevenson in *Kidnapped*, tried to inject more realism and less fantasy into the story, the fantasy formula was given even more of a boost with the publication of J. M. Barrie's *Peter Pan* in 1904. Never-Never Land was a benevolent island, even though Peter Pan and the Lost Boys had to ward off pirates and savages. Barrie made the Robinsonade purely romantic escapism by removing the story from the context of time. Another more famous allusion to the Robinsonade can be detected in Voltaire's *Candide* (1754), which utilized a utopian setting for the moral development of the principal character, in particular testing the commonplace notion of optimism. Voltaire takes Candide and his party to the real utopia of the eighteenth-century Jesuits in Paraguay as well as the fictitious utopias of Oreillon and El Dorado. There are similarities to *Candide* in Samuel Johnson's *Rasselas* (1759). Like Voltaire, Johnson was a child of the Age of Reason who disdained fantasy and clung to reality. His character Prince Rasselas could not accept his comfortable existence in the idyllic land of Happy Valley and longed for the equivocations of the real world. William Morris's *News from Nowhere* (1890) used a pastoral utopia as a method of highlighting the evils of capitalism. Indeed, there were so many imitations and adumbrations in the nineteenth century that Herman Ullrich published an elaborate bibliography of *Robinsonaden* in 1898. The Ahlstrand Collection in the Royal Library of Stockholm, Sweden, contains 130 Robinsonades in 15 languages.

In the twentieth century, important variations on Defoe's model appeared. William Golding's *Pincher Martin* (1956) injected irony into a story of survival on a deserted island. The chief character faced a treacherous rather than a purely benevolent nature. Moreover, the ingenuity of the survivor does not guarantee survival. Michel Tournier's Robinsonade, *Friday* (1967), also modified the original Defoe formula to offer a nonrational approach to the natural environment. The character Friday was not moved by Robinson's demonstrated skills of survival because Friday was not dependent upon material or technical qualities. Structure, order, and work are not crucial to a free spirit such as Friday. Oddly, when rescue comes, it was Robinson who decided to remain on the island and Friday who returned to civilization. Even television got caught up in the Robinsonade with 1960s programs like *Gilligan's Island* and *Lost in Space*. Thus Defoe's formula of the practical utopia stirred interest and imitations on a very broad scale over more than two centuries.

*Reference* Sullivan, Tom R. "The Uses of a Fictional Formula: The Selkirk Mother Lode" (1974).

## Rousseau, Jean-Jacques

*See* Arcadia; *The Social Contract*.

## R.U.R.: Rossum's Universal Robots (1920)

The curious science fiction play, *R.U.R.*, written by the Czech author Karel Capek (1890–1938), mixes humor with drama in its utopian projection of the clash of machines and humans. Updating Mary Shelley's *Frankenstein*, Capek's notion of an artificial man, a robot, was biological rather than mechanical and looked perfectly human, unlike Shelley's semihuman creation. Obviously fascinated by H. G. Wells's futuristic writing—especially *The Island of Dr. Moreau* (1896)—Capek may have been inspired to write his play after reading E. M. Forster's anti-Wellsian essay "The Machine Stops" (1909). Capek coined the word "robot" from a Czech word meaning forced labor. The three-act play first appeared on the Czech stage in 1921, in New York in 1922, and in London in 1923. Lacking an ideological orientation, Capek refused to tout either capitalism or a collectivist society as potential solutions to human problems. Responding to reviews of his play, Capek described *R.U.R.* as a comedy of science.

The story of *R.U.R.* focuses upon the robot's atheist inventor, Old Dr. Rossum (derived from the Czech word for reason), who wanted to show that humans do not need a deity to be solely responsible for creation. Rossum had arrived on an Atlantic island prior to Act I and developed the science that led to the creation of the artificial humanoids. Old Dr. Rossum dies, and his work is carried on by his son. Although Old Rossum's interest in the robots was purely scientific, Young Rossum views the robots more pragmatically, and they are mass-produced to serve humans in a variety of work environments. The Rossums' world is presented to Helena Glory, a female visitor representing the Humanity League, by the industry's business manager, Harry Domin (possibly representing H. G. Wells), who introduces two of the pilot robots, Marius and Sulla. Helena learns that the robots are not always controlled by their human creators and receive punishment. She seeks to humanize the robots and marries Domin. The robots continue to assume more human qualities and plan a takeover of the world from humans, which is accomplished at the end of Act III. In the epilogue, the robots have even perfected the re-creation of the human soul, offering a slight glimmer of hopefulness at the conclusion. Capek wants to leave the reader with the idea that the desire for survival can overcome destructive tendencies.

Capek's play reflected the post–World War I pessimism among intellectuals that resulted in the loss of confidence in the role of science and technology as promoters of progress. *R.U.R.* also became part of the growing catalog of twentieth-century dystopias that represented a fearful rather than hopeful attitude about the future. Certain elements of the play retained the framework of early modern utopias, including the isolated island setting of the robot factory and authoritarian control by the inventor-manufacturer. Yet given its humorous side, *R.U.R.* does not portray the future with the foreboding starkness of later dystopias such as *We* or *Brave New World*. One important omission in *R.U.R.* compared with later dystopias is the all-powerful repressive state. Still, Capek seemed almost frightened by the prospect of a continuous advance of science and technology that might overwhelm mankind. He certainly believed that the human desire for an enhanced material existence combined with the profit motive of capitalism might lead to fearful results. Science and technology were making humans more like machines, which meant that people treated their fellow humans like machines. Yet Capek would not give up hope for the preservation of the human spirit, the will to live, and the existence of the soul.

Capek's 1936 novel *War with the Newts* showed many parallels with *R.U.R.*, except that the advance of totalitarianism and the effects of the Great Depression offered even more convincing evidence about the dim prospects of the future. *War with the Newts* was set in the present rather than the future, and the Newts already existed and did not have to be created, as had the robots in his earlier work. The novel offered the familiar tension between the prospects for happiness and tragedy. Capek wanted desperately to view humanity as virtuous and capable of improvement, but not perfectibility. Warnings similar to those in Capek's writing would be repeated by other twentieth-century dystopian writers, including Aldous Huxley, Ayn Rand, George Orwell, and Margaret Atwood.

**Reference** Naughton, James D. "Futurology and Robots: Karel Capek's *R.U.R.*" (1984).

**Saint-Simon, Henri Comte de**
*See* Utopian Socialism.

## Science Fiction Anti-Utopias

For a long period after the application of the seventeenth century's "new science" to utopian constructions, the influence of science was almost entirely seen as positive. The potentially dark side of science did not appear in utopias until the late nineteenth century. Hints at the possible derangement were evident in the writings of both Jules Verne and H. G. Wells, although their concerns related more to the human than the scientific element. Edward Bulwer-Lytton's Vril in *The Coming Race* (1871) showed ambivalent potentials for both good and evil. By the time atomic bombs exploded over Japan at the end of World War II, the ominous implications of scientific technology began to be explored by numerous intellectuals. Although technology enhanced the nightmare scenarios of major dystopias such as Aldous Huxley's *Brave New World* (1932) and George Orwell's *1984* (1949), such works dealt more with the human than the technological aspects of totalitarianism. The full development of the genre of science fiction anti-utopias emerged in the 1950s with Kurt Vonnegut's *Player Piano* and Ray Bradbury's *Fahrenheit 451*. Other significant works followed in the 1960s: Anthony Burgess's *Clockwork Orange*, Frank Herbert's *Dune*, and Arthur C. Clarke's film in collaboration with Stanley Kubrick, *2001: A Space Odyssey.* In more recent years, the trend has been best represented by Michael Crichton in a number of novels and by Terry Gilliam's films. Because of science fiction's popular appeal, many of the modern works have been produced as motion pictures, furthering public awareness of the print ideas. Thus science fiction served to reinforce the negative view of utopias in the twentieth century, whereas it had in earlier decades positively supported utopias.

By the 1950s the Science and Society movement launched by J. D. Bernal in the 1920s had failed to sustain the previous hopeful attitude toward science. Despite the heroic attempt of C. P. Snow to restore science's prestige and credibility in *The Two Cultures and the Scientific Revolution* (1959) and Nell Eurich's optimistic appraisal of science as a benefit to utopias in *Science in Utopia* (1967), the trend toward questioning the viability of science as a harbinger of progress accelerated. In the tradition of Huxley and Orwell, most post–World War II utopian authors increasingly viewed science as a problem rather than a solution to the human condition. Indeed, the 1950s work with the most influence on utopists was Jacques Ellul's foreboding *The Technological Society* (1954), which had been anticipated by Aldous Huxley two decades earlier. Thus when dystopian works by Ray Bradbury and Kurt Vonnegut appeared in the early 1950s using science as a negative prop, the pattern of the science fiction anti-utopia had been set. Because they admired the potential positive contributions of science and technology, it is inaccurate to classify these writers as latter-day Luddites. However, they were concerned about the possible human misuse of such powers.

In one of his earliest forays into science fiction, Ray Bradbury (b. 1920) portrayed a near-future technologically advanced society whose peculiar repression included the banning and burning of books. As George Orwell had shown in *1984* with Newspeak and the Thought Police, a totalitarian regime cannot permit unauthorized ideas to be circulated. *Fahrenheit 451* (1953) was more than just a science fiction story since it depicted a dystopia

*Scene from the 1966 film version of Ray Bradbury's* Fahrenheit 451, *directed by François Truffaut and starring Oskar Werner*

with plausible realism involving the individual against the system. Although Bradbury's story focuses more upon the character of Guy Montag, a "fireman" whose task is to burn illegally stashed books, it shows how science and technology can advance the techniques of social repression and control that tend to eliminate individual identity as well as freedom. Even as he gains recognition and promotion, Montag struggles with his own curiosity about the content of books until he defies the system by reading hoarded books. Later he flees to join a group of rebels determined to preserve the heritage of classic books literally by memorizing them verbatim. Writing in the era of Cold War paranoia about Communist subversion highlighted by Senator Joseph McCarthy's conspiracy theories, Bradbury reflected a determination to protect free expression popular with the intelligentsia of the early 1950s. By making it easier to maintain a repressive system instead of being used for positive human benefit, technology—especially through mass media brainwashing—in *Fahrenheit 451* was perverted to malevolent ends.

Another post–World War II intellectual concern emanated from the international proliferation of nuclear weapons. The possibility of a nuclear holocaust ensured an audience for Kurt Vonnegut

(b. 1922) in his prophetic utopia, *Player Piano* (1952). The story's setting is post–World War III, and the United States is the sole superpower in the world, so international conflicts have been eliminated. With a vision inspired by his work at General Electric (1947–1950), Vonnegut describes a third industrial revolution led by computers following the war. A giant computer, EPICAC XIV, makes all the necessary decisions for life, setting industrial, social, and educational policy. Government as it had been traditionally known does not exist; only technocratic administrators are needed to make the system function smoothly. Virtually all production facilities have been automated and are run by computers rather than humans, creating systemic technological unemployment. Since ordinary humans are not needed for normal productive capacities, they serve in the military or perform perfunctory tasks such as road repairs as part of the Reconstruction and Reclamation Corps (nicknamed Reeks and Wrecks). Despite the material benefits of an advanced technology, ordinary humans lose their self-respect and dignity, so they come to despise the system. When the principal character, a high-ranking technocrat named Dr. Paul Proteus, becomes disenchanted with the lifestyle under the automated system, he is joined by other technocrats critical of the system who form an underground subversive group, the Ghost Shirt Society. The ensuing rebellion led by Proteus and his friends fails to overturn the powerful system. The scenario of repression, despair, and rebellion in *Player Piano* is a replica of most twentieth-century dystopias. In Vonnegut's piece, unlike in other twentieth-century dystopias, the nightmare results more from the power of science and technology rather than from a phenomenon such as totalitarianism.

Added to the nuclear fears of the 1950s, the 1960s produced a great deal of fearful anticipation about overpopulation outstripping food supplies, partially diminished by pollution. Anthony Burgess's *The*

*Wanting Seed* (1962) portrayed an over-populated world already engaged in infanticide, limiting births and encouraging homosexuality to reduce population growth. When a food crisis occurs, desperate survivalists resort to cannibalism. The famine causes massive upheavals, political realignments, and even rumors of false wars intended to further diminish population growth. John Brunner's futuristic *Stand on Zanzibar* (1968) outlines a society desperate for food that has expanded the reasons for abortion and birth control by the state. Prophetically anticipating policy in present-day China, Brunner's dystopian society punishes families that produce more than the allotted two children.

Fascinated by Olaf Stapledon's transformation of humanity through a cosmic expansion of space and time in *Last and First Men* (1930), Arthur C. Clarke (b. 1917) used an updated application of Vonnegut's computer technology in a favorite science fiction stage, outer space. *2001: A Space Odyssey* (1968) also draws upon other literary genres such as adventurous voyages and the utopian quest for perfection. Ultimately Clarke's story, brilliantly translated into a motion picture by Clarke and Stanley Kubrick, revolves around a contest between man and machine, in this case the astronaut Dave and the supercomputer HAL. The notion that computers could be more than just efficient adjuncts of human effort, that they could actually develop a mind and intent of their own, showed not so much Clarke's fear that technology was dehumanizing but his concern that manifestations of technology were not always carefully considered. Humanity rather than machines was the dilemma. Again with Clarke, science fiction did not just open up a frightening scenario for literary effect; it suggested that science and technology were advancing so fast that the implications for humanity were not always clear and were certainly not guaranteed to be entirely positive.

The use of computers in an anti-utopian framework was continued by the Japanese writer Kobo Abe in his *Inter Ice Age 4* (1970), reflecting a Cold War mentality. A Japanese computer expert named Katsumi invents a new computer that can predict the future, while Soviet scientists develop the identical technology for purposes of spreading international communism. The Japanese select a random individual to become a guinea pig in the project, but he is murdered, which leads to a search for the killer. Meanwhile, the dead subject's mind is analyzed by computer simulation, which reveals the prospect of world disaster from earthquakes and floods. Based upon this prediction, the Japanese concentrate on producing a hybrid human complete with gills to allow survival underwater. Abe argued that even if science could predict the future, humans could not comprehend its meaning. Thus, as in chaos theory, there can be no meaningful connection between present and future, and the future will remain unpredictable.

The dystopian elements of a futuristic space society become starkly apparent in the serial epic *Dune* and its sequels, by Frank Herbert (1920–1986), beginning in 1965. Herbert's experience as an ecology reporter in San Francisco and his interest in comparative religions provided an interesting mix for his science fiction. The popularity of the *Dune* series resulted in a film version in 1984. On Herbert's fictional planet Arrakis, various power groups struggle for control of a fountain-of-youth drug, melange, produced by a giant sandworm. The symbolism of the desert as the story's setting becomes a powerful prophecy of what the future may hold in an advanced technological existence, which could include intergalactic travel and colonization. In 1969, within a few years of *Dune*'s initial appearance, astronauts were walking on the moon, removing much of the "fiction" from "science." On the ecologically regressive planet, the Fremen rebels, led by mythical heroes Duke Paul Atreides and the Great Mother Lady Jessica, must concentrate all of their energies to secure an adequate supply of water and save the planet from ecological disaster. Something as basic yet necessary as water thus symbolized liberation in *Dune* and became the essence of the utopian ideal.

The utter dreariness, not to mention repression, of the totalitarian system sparked several illustrations of anti-utopias from behind the Iron Curtain. Tibor Dery's *Mr. G.A. in X* (1964) was published in Hungary, a nation that rebelled unsuccessfully against totalitarian authority in 1956. Dery's story featured a visitor from pre–World War II Hungary, G.A., to the supposed future utopia in the model city of X. G.A. quickly rejects the totalitarian methods of social engineering while becoming attached briefly to the society through a romance with a resident, Elizabeth. The native of X ironically becomes infatuated with G.A.'s description of Hungary, which she romanticizes as the true ideal society despite its imperfections. Elizabeth's grandfather, who apparently alone remembers the pre-utopian past, has resisted the imposed system of thought, especially the quasi-religious death cult that operates as the state ideology. Dery utilized the "last man" construct to offer an individual challenge to the totalitarian system reminiscent of characters in *Brave New World*, *1984*, and other dystopias. Representing the desire to escape from the self-contained and controlled environment, G.A. introduces emotions and develops personal relationships that are absent in totalitarianism. Disillusioned by the absence of freedom and the cult of death in X, G.A. returns to his native Hungary, which by then seems a better place in comparison to X. Dery thus suggests that utopias invariably become dystopias and that though humans can never be perfect, happiness also cannot be found in an arbitrary society that denies freedom of choice.

England's Anthony Burgess (1917–1993), noted above for his *The Wanting Seed*, created a greater controversy with his science fiction dystopia, *A Clockwork Orange* (1962). Burgess reflected a growing awareness and fear in the 1960s West about youth gangs and random violence as well as the popularity of B. F. Skinner's behavioral conditioning. Also effectively and powerfully translated into a motion picture by Stanley Kubrick (1971), the near-future technologically advanced age in *Clockwork* had developed methods of dealing with violent recidivism among youthful criminals. The chief character, youthful offender Alex, is subjected to technological mind alteration that mimics behaviorist psychology therapy, euphemistically known as brainwashing. Yet Burgess implied that social conditioning with advanced technology occurs in both totalitarian and welfare state regimes, thus blurring their distinctions. Technology simply gives the established authority the means to enforce uniformity and cull out the rebellious Nadsat jargon of Alex and his violent companions.

Following the initial entries in the science fiction anti-utopia genre in the 1950s–1960s, even more sophisticated expositions appeared. Chief among the current crop is the work of medically trained novelist Michael Crichton (b. 1942), whose first effort, *The Andromeda Strain* (1969), combined space research and ecological science fiction to concoct a global near-disaster by suggesting that despite scientific confidence in controlled experiments, the best laid plans sometimes go awry. That theme was continued in Crichton's *Terminal Man* (1972), which featured behavior modification through supposedly managed technology running amok. More recently, in *Jurassic Park* (1990) and *The Lost World* (1995), Crichton has mixed geological time frames with gene cloning to produce a biological retrogression—dinosaurs—into the present to illustrate the potential for scientific miscalculation, especially when driven by the profit motive. Crichton at once both marvels at the exploration of scientific frontiers and shudders at human factors leading to loss of control over such knowledge and power.

Film director Terry Gilliam has applied his talents and ideas to several dystopian film projects since the 1980s. The U.S.-born Gilliam began his career as a cartoonist, working for the *Mad Magazine* product called *Help!* He moved into motion picture production as an associate of the Monty Python comedy troupe in England and produced his first film, *Time Bandits*, in 1981 before moving more directly into dystopian projects. *Brazil* (1985) is set in a near-future metropolis and reflects the deep pessimism found in all the major dystopian literary works. Gilliam mixes Orwell's use of totalitarian fear in *1984* with Huxley's gimmicky distractions from reality in *Brave New World*. The chief character, Sam Lowry, is a typical bureaucrat working in the Orwellian Ministry of Information, a domestic spy agency and propaganda mill. The technology in *Brazil* relies upon computers, but the computer used is actually an antiquated version, even by mid-1980s standards. Even the bureaucracy in *Brazil* seems ineffectual compared to the cold efficiency of Orwell's agencies. Gilliam leaves no doubt that the totalitarian propaganda spiel cannot hide the dreary reality of life in this dystopia, including the escapist entertainment. Lowry reflects Gilliam's bleak dichotomy between illusion and reality, yet Lowry's ability to project a vision of happiness leads to a critical appraisal of society's condition and misadventures with a dissident female character and an antiregime terrorist. Gilliam's most recent film, *12 Monkeys* (1996), again mingles science fiction with time travel for the story line. The chief character, a survivor from a horrendous plague that killed five billion people by the twenty-first century, travels back in time to the 1990s to discover the origins of the disease. After spewing forth the forthcoming tragic scenario, including stories about the army of the 12 monkeys that supposedly spread the plague, the character is placed in a mental hospital. Gilliam touches upon several other themes in addition to the apocalyptic centerpiece: overpopulation, poor treatment of mentally ill, the adverse impact of television.

Hence, Gilliam's science fiction anti-utopias dwell upon pessimism and fail to offer happy endings.

*References* Boyd, Katrina G. "Pastiche and Postmodernism in Brazil" (1990); Clarke, I. F. *The Pattern of Expectation, 1644–2001* (1979); Gorra, Michael. "The World of *A Clockwork Orange*" (1990); Parkinson, Robert C. "*Dune*: An Unfinished Tetralogy" (1971); Sargent, Lyman Tower. "Utopia and Dystopia in Contemporary Science Fiction" (1972); Segal, Howard P. "Vonnegut's *Player Piano*: An Ambiguous Technological Dystopia," in Rabkin, Eric S., Martin H. Greenburg, and Joseph D. Olander, eds. *No Place Else* (1983); Stupple, A. James. "The Past, the Future, and Ray Bradbury," in Clareson, Thomas D., ed. *Voices for the Future* (1976).

## Science and Society Movement

Despite the post–World War I collapse of the liberal system with its scientific underpinning as represented in Aldous Huxley's *Brave New World* (1932), positivist worshipers of science continued their fanciful social engineering. The Science and Society movement's most important contributor in the 1920s was John Desmond Bernal and his *The World, the Flesh, and the Devil* (1929). Bernal tried to show that science could conquer mankind's scourges: physical nature, human passions, and superstition. The Science and Society movement was revived after World War II by science advocates such as C. P. Snow and Daniel Bell, and thence evolved into futurology with popular writers such as Alvin Toffler.

Science had played a major role in utopian thinking from Francis Bacon's *New Atlantis* in the seventeenth century to its heights in the positivism of Auguste Comte in the late nineteenth century. After a tenure with the Royal Air Force in World War I, young British scientist John Desmond Bernal (1901–1971) outlined a vision of the future dominated by science in his 1929 publication *The World, the Flesh, and the Devil: An Enquiry into the Future of the Three Enemies of the Rational Soul*. Bernal believed that science was the key to overcoming human incapacity to act upon knowledge. He suggested that although humans recognize the desirability of improvement, they actually resist change because they fear the unknown outcomes. Science can help humans come to grips with their fear of change involving their physical environment. Yet the application of such scientific advances presumed a control by an elite—physicists, biologists, and psychologists. Bernal predicted that science would overcome obstacles that prevented mankind from enjoying more leisure and security. The main obstacle to such progress would be politicians and humanists. Charlotte Franken Haldane, with her husband J. B. S. Haldane, true believers like Bernal in his optimism about scientific advances, wrote in *Man's World* (1926) that politicians and humanists would be displaced by the scientific elites.

Such concepts were discussed with a wide audience, including several Soviet scientists, at the 1931 Second International Conference of the History of Science and Technology meeting in London. Shortly, Bernal was touting the Soviet version of dialectical materialism as the appropriate model for British scientists. The exploration of practical applications was later recounted in Bernal's *The Freedom of Necessity* (1949). Yet Bernal remained doubtful of ultimate success. His 1935 essay "Science and Industry," in a collection entitled *The Frustration of Science*, examined the past misuse of scientific knowledge through manipulation either for profit or for military uses. All the more reason, according to Bernal, to embrace scientific socialism as a "new master" of humanity because socialist regimes such as the Soviet Union were willing to fund scientific research at the level necessary for proper usefulness. Bernal's position proved very popular with science publicists, including Haldane in his *The Marxist Philosophy and the Sciences* (1939). The British Association of Scientific Workers adopted a Marxist philosophy in 1932, and Bernal served on the body's executive committee in 1934.

Bernal argued that science would promote a rapid evolution of human physiology that would include a host of artificial limbs and organs, producing a type of half-human, half-robot. Bernal did not consider the changes to the human body to be inhuman even though his mechanical man would become godlike at the end of the new evolutionary development. Science would also assist the conquest of the devil by constructing a new psychology that would initially envelop a select elite of true believers, who in turn would spread the philosophy to others. Ethical questions of right and wrong, good and evil, would be reduced to scientific and nonscientific.

Bernal's utopia would promote a science not limited to the traditional modification of the physical universe but extended to humanity itself. This scientifically modified existence would replace nature's evolution and be virtually artificial, from the new fabrics to the new man. Energy would come primarily from the sun, and production of food would be transferred from the soil to the scientist's laboratory. In certain respects, Bernal hoped to achieve the idyllic freedom from want dreamed of by the utopian socialists of the early nineteenth century. The ultimate escape from dependence upon the earth for human sustenance was Bernal's concept of space colonies, including space rockets, orbiting space stations, and landings on other planets. As an elitist, however, Bernal reasoned that few would be able to seize the opportunity to depart the bounds of earth to partake of an extraterrestrial utopia. Thus those ordinary humans left behind on earth would have to content themselves with pursuing the old-fashioned, world-based utopias. Indeed, Bernal used the term "human zoo" in reference to the resident population remaining on earth following the elite's departure.

Because of external events such as totalitarianism, economic depression, and World War II's destructiveness, Bernal's scientism did not stand up well to critics. However, beginning in the 1950s, C. P. Snow, in *The Two Cultures and the Scientific Revolution* (1959), sought to rehabilitate the scientific community battered by the 1950s reaction against nuclear weapons. Snow agreed with Bernal that the future rested on the shoulders of scientists, who were not the amoral creatures depicted by literary intelligentsia. Rather, scientists were the potential rescuers of a progressive technological society from regressive, reactionary forces that had become postmodern Luddites. World problems of pollution, disease, and death could only be solved by the application of scientific knowledge. Herman Kahn of the Hudson Institute and Daniel Bell's *The Coming of Post-Industrial Society* (1973) touted scientists as the only leaders of society who could manage the complexities of social and economic problems. Kahn's 1960–1965 trilogy (*The Resourceful Earth*, *Thinking about the Unthinkable*, *The Coming Boom*) considered ways to mitigate possible thermonuclear war by proposing that scientists draft elaborate possible scenarios so that catastrophe could be averted. As a scientist, Kahn portrayed political leaders as incapable of solving such global issues. He also predicted that technology would pave the way for what he called "superindustry" and space colonies. Bell appeared to be a latter-day positivist who predicted the evolution of a growing service economy led by a scientific-technological bureaucracy. He assumed that such an elite would implement a meritocracy and a future orientation to economic planning.

Freeman J. Dyson's Third Bernal Lecture in 1972 argued that the scientific future should be placed in the hands of molecular biologists and astronomers. Specifically, Dyson projected that genetically altered humans would flee in spaceships to inhabit comets as part of a new frontier. The latter-day spokesmen—including groups like the World Council of Churches—of the Science and Society movement (sometimes called "futurology" by the 1960s) sought to put a positive twist upon a postindustrial world increasingly beset with seemingly unmanageable crises. Based upon essentially positive outlooks, futurology sought to move away from ideology to concentrate upon necessary practical scientific planning for the future. Futurologists utilized nonfictional rather than fictional formats, speaking more in terms of what would be rather than what might be wished.

A current author who represents the futurology trend as well as any other is Alvin Toffler (b. 1928), whose works since *Future Shock* (1970) have projected a dramatic impact of changes, primarily technological innovation, on the future of Western civilization. Toffler does not espouse an agenda as previous advocates of science did, but he is nonetheless a believer in the positive benefits of the applications of scientific and technological knowledge. In *Future Shock*, Toffler examined the impact of rapidly changing technological advances upon society. He predicted the advent of a "social futurism" in which democracy would triumph over elitism and the profit motive would be eliminated from social planning in order to anticipate future changes. In *The Third Wave* (1980), Toffler constructed a third revolutionary economic system to follow agriculture and the Industrial Revolution. Actually embodying several small-scale revolutions, the third wave began in the mid-1950s, according to Toffler, and will evolve to maturity over following decades. Toffler described the new economy in terms of a "practopia" in which work becomes increasingly domesticated, occurring in the home rather than in offices and factories. Such a change would be made possible mainly by the technological uses of computers. Toffler also predicted the increased popularity of cults and religious fundamentalism and favored greater reliance upon eugenics. In 1990, Toffler's *Powershift* argued that the scramble for advantage in the computer information era would lead to "wars" for control of knowledge sources that would affect virtually all institutions. Other contemporary writers have offered variations on Toffler's futurology, including John Naisbitt's *Megatrends* (1982) and Jeremy Rifkin's *The End of Work* (1995).

*References*   Kumar, Krishan. *Prophecy and Progress: The Sociology of Industrial and Post-Industrial Society* (1978); McGucken, William. *Scientists, Society, and State: The Social Relations of the Science Movement in Great Britain, 1931–47* (1984.

## Scientology
*See* New Age Cults.

## Sforzinda
*See* Renaissance City-State Utopias.

### *Sinapia* (1682)

Written by an anonymous late-seventeenth-century Spanish author (but attributed to the count of Campomanes), the *Sinapia* manuscript dated 1682 was only discovered in 1975; it has been edited by Miguel Aviles. Incorporating a rather poor literary style, *Sinapia* borrowed heavily from Thomas More's *Utopia* to offer a critique of Spanish society by describing a utopia dramatically unlike seventeenth-century Spain. Set in a peninsula remarkably similar to Iberia, *Sinapia* put forth a detailed system of government and society that reflected an elitist orientation by the author. The influence of Erasmus, More's humanist friend, is also apparent in the reform agenda of *Sinapia*. The author obviously believed that contemporary Europe had become decadent and virtually anti-Christian. Soon after the manuscript's publication, Fernando Savater composed a play based upon the utopia, *Vente a Sinapia*, presented at the National Theater in Madrid.

Except for certain elements in Cervantes's *Don Quixote*, Spain did not foster utopian schemes in the Iberian peninsula. Modern literary references reveal that Spanish writers had a wholly negative attitude toward utopias. Thus the *Sinapia* remains distinctive. Instead, Spain focused its utopian energies via its early contact with the New World to invite a new genre of utopias often called noble savage utopias. These perfect native societies were described by explorers beginning with Christopher Columbus. Peter Martyr, in his treatise on the New World, believed that it was a door back to a golden age. The removal of values such as the profit motive and money itself in the native societies combined with their reverence for nature and lack of class consciousness. Bartolomé de Las Casas wrote that the natives even exhibited a kind of primitive, innocent form of Christianity. He proposed to create in the American virgin lands the conditions for a European utopia, a new beginning. Whereas other Spaniards concentrated their utopian efforts in the New World, the author of the *Sinapia* focused attention upon Spain and Europe.

The story of *Sinapia* supposedly was based on the adventures of a Dutch navigator, Abel Tasman, who landed on the peninsula and described it. It is set in an imaginary country that reminds the reader of Spain. Originally called Bireia (derived from Iberia), the country was renamed for a Persian Prince Sinap who conquered and ruled Sinapia (a corruption of Hispania). The author's selection of a non-Spanish and non-European ruler suggests a distaste for seventeenth-century European rulers. Reversing the geography of Spain meant that the Pyrenees mountains were located to the south of Sinapia, and the country was surrounded by the Gauls and the Germans. Prince Sinap and his patriarch, Bishop Codabend, were Christians driven from their native Persia to China and then Bireia in search of religious freedom. The cosmopolitan population of Sinapia included Malaysians, Chinese, and Peruvians. Like More's Utopia, Sinapia had its own language. Sinapia elected its rulers, who must be qualified by training and experience, from nominees selected by subordinate classes. Officeholders, whether religious, political, or military, must be qualified by training and experience to be elected. Hence, the primary emphasis in Sinapia's society was upon education, especially Christian learning.

As was typical of other early modern utopias, the property system in Sinapia was communal, with no private ownership. The society was organized around the family in a patriarchal fashion, so women could not hold office or vote. The moral code in Sinapia was rigidly enforced. The author stresses that social injustice and economic inefficiencies have been eliminated in Sinapia. Following More's Utopia, the Sinapians were a pacific people who opposed war and violence. Unlike More's secular Utopia, Sinapia was a Christian commonwealth where political reforms would be based on Christian ethics as opposed to the secular methods of seventeenth-century European princes. The author suggests that not only had Europe allowed decadence to envelop their society but rulers had discarded the Christian principles of government. *Sinapia* is an exceptional illustration of Spanish utopian thought, which appeared only in the sixteenth and seventeenth centuries.

*Reference* Cro, Stelio. "The New World in Spanish Utopianism" (1979).

**Skinner, B. F.**
*See Walden Two.*

*The Social Contract* (1762)

Although considered more of a reformer than a utopian, Jean-Jacques Rousseau enumerated various utopian elements in his famous treatise about how to form a perfect government and society, *The Social Contract or Principles of Political Right*. Rousseau regarded utopia as fantasy, but he did not dismiss it as other Enlightenment philosophers did. Beginning with a theory of social history based upon the development of inequality, Rousseau devised a secular quest for perfectibility that has impacted the modern era as much as any other principle. Rousseau's preliminary work, *The Discourse on Inequality* (1755), contrasted the ideal of equality in the state of nature (more real than theoretical to Rousseau) with the reality of inequality in human society. The quest of human culture, according to Rousseau, is

*Jean-Jacques Rousseau*

to achieve perfectibility, but the quest most often results in corruptibility instead. Thus history has been a series of peaks and valleys, periods of progress punctuated by eras of decay and decline. More than the other philosophers of the Enlightenment pursuing the ideal society, Rousseau sought to balance the uses of reason with the role of human emotion and will. He recognized the inherent conflict between the individual and society, yet sought a system in which the two could be compatible.

Rousseau's distinctive philosophy was shaped as much by his life experience as by education. He was orphaned at an early age, so he missed the love and nurture of parents. Indeed, Rousseau penned a famous treatise (*Émile*) on education, yet failed to train effectively his own children. Confused about his own faith, Rousseau tried both Catholic and Protestant versions of Christianity before adopting a religion of his own design that resembled Socinianism. He was notably unsuccessful throughout most of his career making a living from writing, and though he knew the major philosophes, such as Voltaire and Diderot, Rousseau did not embrace reason as the paramount solution to human issues. In particular, he challenged the conventional wisdom of the eighteenth century involving the social contract theory of government as outlined by John Locke and endorsed by the French philosophes. Locke's theory of social contract assumed that reason would be the sole guide in constructing a system of ordered government that respected limited natural rights while guaranteeing equal application of the law. Yet Rousseau argued that it was patently unreasonable for humans to give up any of their absolute natural rights in order to form a government. Hence, government and society must be organized around a principle other than reason, the general will.

In the *Discourse on Inequality* Rousseau was not dogmatic about the ideal state of nature being historical, but in any event he recognized the impossibility of recovering that utopian condition. Yet in the *Social Contract* Rousseau vigorously pursued the unlikely goal of creating an ideal society. Rousseau's definition of liberty primarily meant not being subject to another's will, living according to one's conscience. He first set up a contrast with the present, corrupt society (an anti-utopia) in order to demonstrate how far away from the Arcadian state of nature society had moved. The utopian elements in all of Rousseau's writings remained fragmentary since he did not compose a comprehensive utopia. The *Social Contract* was not designed for a metropolitan society because Rousseau argued that urban cultures encouraged the worst elements of humanity. Instead, Rousseau chose the pastoral island of Corsica, albeit an imagined island rather than the real Corsica, as the intended object of his constitution. Enlightenment philosophers had been fascinated by the efforts of Pascal Paoli to establish a republic on Corsica, and Rousseau likened his ideal state to that living attempt. Further, the fact that Rousseau grew up in the small, self-contained canton of Geneva explains

the scale of utopian construction along the city-state model. By filtering out the corrosive external influences, small states had a greater capacity for shaping moral and emotional qualities than did unwieldy megastates, an important consideration for Rousseau.

Rather than framing his ideal society according to the dictates of human reason, Rousseau relied upon a eupsychian technique—learning to subsume the self in the greater good of the community—of presenting the ideal psyche in the state of nature, which incorporated feelings as well as intellect. It was the human-created social mechanisms that instituted inequality and exploitation throughout history, thereby reorienting the psyche toward fear rather than hope. Forced to conform to society's conventions, the individual could not express or even comprehend the existential meaning of existence much less achieve the instinctual quest for life, liberty, and happiness. Thus Rousseau sought a social framework that would approach the ideal eupsychia of nature. Rousseau favored the maturation of the conscience as a method of perfecting human desires, leading to contentment with adequate needs rather than extravagant wants. Believing that altering the psychological environment would in turn produce a positive, caring relationship among humans, Rousseau embraced a genuine utopian approach to change.

The human will, the essence of being to Rousseau, has been shaped historically by society to avoid fulfillment in order to survive—safe but sorry. Society posed so many obstacles to the satisfaction of desires that the will simply surrendered to their suffocating reality rather than fought against them. Rousseau suggested that the result of social accommodation of the will changes self-love, a positive natural trait, into pride or self-esteem, a less satisfying artificial condition that encourages covetousness. Social beings have thus changed direction from pursuing self-satisfaction to seeking to deprive others of satisfaction. Hence Rousseau sought in his utopia to reclaim the love of self, which in fact nurtures a genuine sense of justice absent from existing society. Because self-love sanctifies the passions and seeks to harm no one, it becomes the basis of promoting virtue in an emotional struggle against evil. Rousseau's ideal person would not pursue phony values such as wealth, status, or fame since none of those pursuits would promote self-love. Thus in terms of creating an ideal society, Rousseau advocated recognizing the individual will as the key instrument in designing a constitution. People would never be satisfied with a government grounded upon abstract reason, that is, law, since it was not reasonable to constrain their natural rights. Yet the individual will seeks compatibility, not rivalry, with other wills, so it could agree to surrender or limit natural rights for the good of the community. The merging of individual wills into the general will of the nation would guarantee that laws and institutions would sanction not reason per se but the opportunity to recapture self-love.

Because Rousseau essentially proposed to force humanity to be free, he fits into the typical utopian methodology of authoritarianism, for which he has been roundly criticized by scholars such as J. L. Talmon. Yet the subtlety of Rousseau's system envisions acts based on consent, so he does not see a contradiction between legitimate authority and liberty. For Rousseau the conversion of liberty or independence of action in the state of nature into moral-political freedom in the social contract simply reflects the application of the general will, which allows the free play of reason and the conscience. In reality, Rousseau simply assumed that the individual would voluntarily surrender sovereignty to the state. The real problem in Rousseau's social contract is not the question of authority but the replacement of religion as the standard for moral actions with a secular rule. No such standard was successfully articulated either by Rousseau or other Enlightenment philosophers. Rousseau argued that the general will, the true law, should be substituted for existing laws because the general will required the individual to accept and be bound by the majority's interpretation of the general will, which becomes the moral authority. Rousseau also elaborated a civil religion, controlled by the state, as the voice of moral instruction. Yet in other writings, Rousseau insisted that the individual conscience was the final arbiter of actions. Unquestionably, the French Revolution–era utopists—Babeuf, Restif, Condorcet et al.—relied upon their understanding of Rousseau to guide their utopian constructions.

*References* Fabre, Jean. "Realité et utopie dans la pensée politique de Rousseau" (1959–1962); Venturi, Franco. *Utopia and Reform in the Enlightenment* (1971).

## Spirit Fruit Society

Strongly influenced by the Transcendentalists, Jacob Beilhart founded the Spirit Fruit Society in an effort to blend spiritual objectives with anarchism in a utopian experiment that lasted from 1899 to 1905 in Ohio before moving to Illinois. The society seemed to thrive there until Beilhart's death in 1908 but then declined until its end in 1929. Although the Spirit Fruit Society became sensational because of Beilhart's tolerance of sexual freedom, it proved to be a unique utopian experiment. The Spirit Fruit Society coincided with other 1890s spiritually oriented communes, including the Theosophist colony at Point Loma, California. However, these anachronistic perfectionist utopian groups seemed more aligned with the early-nineteenth-century trends than the more pragmatic late-nineteenth-century schemes.

Instilled with a strong religious tradition, Jacob Beilhart (1867–1908) grew up in Ohio with his nine siblings and had a limited education. His father, who died when Beilhart was six years old, was a Lutheran and his mother, who became a strong single parent, was a Mennonite. Beilhart retained the influences of his religious upbringing throughout his life and added the outlook of Transcendentalist writers Ralph Waldo Emerson and Walt Whitman. He left the family farm at age 17 to make an independent living, initially working in his brother-in-law's harness shop. He later moved to Kansas, where he worked for a Seventh-Day Adventist family of sheep farmers who converted Beilhart from his formal Lutheran membership. Beilhart married in 1893 and had two children. Before long, Beilhart became a full-time church worker selling literature and moved to Colorado. After attending classes at an Adventist college, Beilhart began preaching in Ohio and Kansas but left the calling after only two years to attend an Adventist nursing school in Battle Creek, Michigan. Upon completion of his nursing program, Beilhart took a position at a sanatorium operated by Dr. Harvey Kellogg, a spokesman for natural health remedies in Battle Creek. Beilhart continued to pursue religious studies, but he eventually broke with the Adventist church—which advocated a vegetarian diet—because he decided that illness could be cured with prayer alone. Thereafter, Beilhart engaged in faith healing and through his acquaintance with another cereal manufacturer, C. W. Post, became a follower of the Christian Science movement. Beilhart soon tired of the newfound religion and studied other spiritual ideas including Theosophy, but found none wholly satisfying.

Ultimately, Beilhart developed his own unique religious movement called "Universal Life," which incorporated various elements from almost all of the religious movements he had followed at one time or another. He added socialist views, including the criticism of competition, private property rights, and materialism, while remaining aloof from politics. Due largely to his mother's influence, Beilhart also advocated freeing women from society's bonds. By 1899, Beilhart had determined that starting his own community was the best way to implement his principles. He began publicizing his plans in a magazine, *Spirit Fruit*, and chose a five-acre site outside of Lisbon, Ohio, for the colony. The location was quite close to the place where Beilhart had grown up, and the surrounding area seemed to be a haven for various spiritualists who might be recruited to join the colony. However, the few immigrants to the Spirit Fruit colony mostly came from outside Ohio, the largest portion from Chicago. Two important converts were labor leader Robert G. Wall and industrialist Irwin E. Rockwell, who provided much of the needed financial support. Ultimately, the Spirit Fruit Society was incorporated as a religious organization, but virtually all governing decisions were made by Beilhart without participation by the members.

Within two years after the small settlement began, it became controversial in the neighboring town of Lisbon due to rumors of illicit sexual relations and free love. Newspaper reporters from Chicago came to the colony in 1901 seeking information about a supposed abduction of a Chicago physician's wife. After considerable legal maneuvering, the doctor finally persuaded his wife to leave the settlement, but not before unwanted attention had been brought to Beilhart's utopia. In 1904 a Chicago newspaper sent reporters again to Ohio to write an account of the Spirit Fruit Society. While some positive attributes were cited, overall the story painted the society as a bunch of fanatics and suggested that Beilhart claimed to be the Messiah. An Ohio paper followed with a story describing an event, similar to the 1901 incident, involving a young woman from Chicago who had taken up with Beilhart's commune and was rescued by family members. During these incidents, Beilhart exhibited a pronounced pacifism, refusing to use force against the interlopers. When local residents threatened to invade the community to tar and feather its residents, Beilhart became alarmed and left for Illinois to locate a new site for the colony.

While dismantling the Ohio settlement during 1904–1905, Beilhart purchased 90 acres for a new colony at Wooster Lake near Ingleside, Illinois, 20 miles northwest of Chicago. Eventually, the colony's holdings totaled about 300 acres. Only 13 settlers started the Illinois colony, which based its economy on dairy farming. A large community house known as "Spirit Temple" was built in 1906. The Illinois experiment seemed to be moving along quite well before Beilhart's appendix ruptured and he died in 1908. Although the colony never really recovered from the loss of its leader, it continued to operate along lines determined by its leader for another 21 years. The advent of the Great Depression caused the remaining residents, less than a dozen, to terminate the colony. Although the Spirit Fruit Society depended upon a single charismatic leader and never grew to a respectable size, it illustrated the marginal interest of certain spiritual groups in utopian ideals. Beilhart also seemed unique as a communal leader in that he never resorted to intimidation or force to achieve his following. In his own peculiar anti-egoist fashion, Beilhart tried to remodel human nature to produce a selfless and loving attitude toward others. He was a forerunner of the libertarian movement, which condemned legal and institutional restraints upon human freedom. Beilhart also anticipated a much freer social and sexual ethic in the twentieth century.

*Reference* Fogarty, Robert S., and H. Roger Grant. "Free Love in Ohio: Jacob Beilhart and the Spirit Fruit Society" (1980).

**Swift, Jonathan**
*See Gulliver's Travels.*

**Swiss Family Robinson**
*See* Robinsonades.

**Taiping Rebellion**
*See* Millennialism.

**Tarde, Gabriel**
*See Underground Man*.

**Theosophy**
Theosophy, a religious philosophy that combined various elements of ancient Oriental religions and philosophical thought, began as an organized movement in the United States in 1875. The term "theosophy," or divine wisdom, derived from the Greek words *theos*, meaning God, and *sophia*, meaning wisdom. The movement attracted a variety of Westerners including its Ukrainian founder, Helena Petrovna Blavatsky, Irish-born William Q. Judge, and Annie Wood Besant of England. Though there were diverse elements within theosophy, the basic belief shared a concept of uniting humanity spiritually into a universal brotherhood. Many of the theosophists adopted aspects of Hinduism and Buddhism, including belief in a universal oversoul and in reincarnation. The movement in the United States resulted in the establishment of a few experimental communities that extended into the twentieth century.

Theosophy began as an esoteric form of Christianity, although links with the Jewish Kabala and Islamic Sufism can be demonstrated. Theosophy's first appearance dates to the mysticism of the late Reformation thinker Jakob Boehme (1575–1624), who stressed the inner illumination of the soul. God is the First Cause of physical creation, which originates in the black hole of *Urgrund*. Humanity must experience a spiritual rebirth before acquiring a genuine knowledge of God. Boehme's most direct influence was upon the Society of Friends (Quakers) in England.

Later, in the eighteenth-century Enlightenment, freethinkers such as Richard Payne Knight (1751–1824) added to theosophy elements from various Oriental natural philosophies. In turn, romantic writers of the early nineteenth century, including Charles Dupuis (1742–1809), Constantin de Volney (1757–1820), and Sir William Drummond (1770–1828), blended fascination with the Oriental occult and a growing skepticism toward Christianity and the church, a skepticism nurtured by the Enlightenment. The transformation of the movement from esoteric Christianity into esoteric Buddhism or "modern spiritualism" has been identified with the three Fox sisters' (Leah, Kate, Margaretta) mediumistic communication with the dead at Hydesville, New York, in 1848. From the beginnings of the 1848 phenomena, modern spiritualism came to England in the 1850s through the efforts of a U.S. psychic, Mrs. Hayden. She and her colleagues converted prominent English utopists to spiritualism, including Robert Owen and Edward Bulwer-Lytton. Meanwhile, Emma Britten's *Modern American Spiritualism* (1870) further prepared the way for the Theosophical Society. The society was founded in the United States in 1875, and its leading influence was Helena Blavatsky.

Helena Petrovna Blavatsky (1831–1891) was born in the Ukraine into a Greek Orthodox family and became fascinated with the occult. Soon after arriving in the United States in 1873, Blavatsky and a small group of 17, including William Q. Judge (1851–1896) and Henry S. Olcott (1832–1907), established the Theosophical Society in New York City in 1875. Captivated by mysticism from his youth, before arriving in the United States, Judge had been a member of the Dublin society that included the poet William Butler Yeats.

*Helen Petrovna Blavatsky*

Olcott, a lawyer and journalist, was elected president of the society. As secretary of the society, Blavatsky became editor of the journal *The Theosophist* and specified that theosophy could not be easily defined since it was a dynamic process of mystical truth seeking. She did suggest that the objective of theosophy was to blend the divine and human elements that were both part of mankind. Theosophists preached toleration, charity, and kindness toward others and strove for perfect justice. Thus, in practical terms, theosophy supported movements that sought to alleviate the injustices of the world. The three tenets of theosophy became to create a universal brotherhood of humanity, to study the ancient wisdom literature, and to investigate the laws of nature and human potential. Blavatsky detailed the philosophy of theosophy in several works, including her first book, *Isis Unveiled* (2 vols., 1877), and the influential *The Secret Doctrine: The Synthesis of Science, Religion, and Philosophy* (2 vols., 1888).

Within four years of the founding of the U.S. society, Blavatsky and Olcott traveled to India to establish a branch of the society at Adyar near Madras. Soon branches of the Theosophical Society existed in major European cities. The Indian organization attracted the attention of many Hindu nationalist leaders, including Mohandas Gandhi. One of Blavatsky's most important disciples, Annie Wood Besant (1847–1933), joined the Theosophic Society in 1889. In a short time, Besant traveled to India to become affiliated with the branch of the society there, and she eventually became its leader. She helped found a Hindu college in Benares in 1898 and became a loyal follower of Gandhi in the Indian National Congress, which lobbied for Indian independence from Great Britain. Indeed, Besant was elected president of the Congress in 1917.

Meanwhile, back in the United States, by participating in the World Congress of Religions that met during the Chicago World's Fair in 1893, the Theosophical Society gained a measure of respectability. The movement's popularity continued to grow under Blavatsky's successor as head of the Theosophical Society, Katherine Tingley (1847–1929). Influenced by the utopian scheme Edward Bellamy outlined in *Equality* (1897), Tingley had been recruited into the society by Judge. Tingley had immersed herself in various reform causes after three failed marriages. She founded a theosophic experimental community on 330 acres at Point Loma, California, near San Diego in 1898. Tingley became interested in the community at Point Loma in large part because of a desire to establish a school. The children recruited for the Raja-Yoga school came from wealthy families, who paid tuition. Tingley often mentioned that she felt the school could create a unique type of spiritually sensitive human. Although the population at Point Loma grew to several hundred, the emphasis on education overshadowed the cooperative aspects—such as the communal house—and few residents were from the working classes. Many settlers came from outside the United States, the largest contingent from Cuba, and by 1910 the population had grown to 500. The community's buildings included a domed temple and a Greek amphitheater. Upon the death of Tingley in 1929, the community leadership fell to Gottfried de Prucker, but the depression years forced the settlement to move to Covina in 1942, and many of what communal features there originally were disappeared.

Theosophists were also involved in the founding of the Cooperative Brotherhood at Burley, Washington, in 1898. Organized as a stockholding corporation, the brotherhood's economy featured logging and a sawmill. Families lived together, although single members resided in a communal dormitory. Burley reflected the communitarian socialism present in many U.S. settlements of the time, and it was specifically inspired by the Ruskin colony in Tennessee. But the chief spokesman at Burley, Cyrus Willard, was a theosophist, and his presence led to other theosophist settlers moving to Burley. The population at Burley grew to more than a hundred in the first few years, but it never expanded beyond its moderately auspicious beginnings. When the colony broke up in 1908, most of the theosophists at Burley moved to Point Loma.

The Theosophical Society has continued to function through the twentieth century in the United States, and its 5,000 members operate a printing press in Wheaton, Illinois. The society claims to be "dedicated to the promotion of the unity of humanity and the encouragement of the study of religion, philosophy, and science, to the end that we may better understand ourselves and our place in the universe." The society's international operations remain centered at Adyar, India, where it also runs a press. Possibly the leading contemporary theorist is Steve Hagen, a teacher of Buddhism and Zen, whose ideas are found in *How the World Can Be the Way It Is: An Inquiry for the New Millennium into Science, Philosophy, and Perception* (1995). The Theosophical Society did more than any other organization to popularize Eastern philosophy and religion in the United States, and it has been a major influence upon the avant-garde New Age movements.

*See also* New Age Cults.

*References* Cranston, Sylvia, *HPB: The Extraordinary Life and Influence of Helena Blavatsky, Founder of the Modern Theosophical Movement* (1993); Godwin, Joscelyn. *The Theosophical Enlightenment* (1994); Greenwalt, Emmett A. *California Utopia, Point Loma: 1897–1942* (1978).

## "Tlön, Uqbar, Orbis Tertius" (1940)

The Latin American writer Jorge Luis Borges composed a curious short story in 1940 that incorporated a chronological survey from ancient times to the future of utopian elements from the "esoteric tradition." Utilizing a style sometimes called magic realism, Borges sought to link the historical past with the present in the development of the tradition in order to show its vital élan.

Jorge Luis Borges (1899–1986) was born in Argentina. His father was a half-English lawyer who inspired Borges's interest in English literature during his early education at home. Later, during World War I, Borges attended schools in Switzerland, where he came under the influence of the pessimistic philosopher Arthur Schopenhauer. Borges traveled across Spain in 1919–1921 before returning to Argentina, where he published his first book of poetry in 1923. Yet as a writer Borges was best known for his short stories and essays. He was a founder of the literary school of Ultraismo in Latin America, espousing a nationalistic view that attempted to create a distinctive Latin American tradition divorced from European influences. Ultraismo was considered avant garde because of its view that, although philosophy and science were useful to solve practical problems, they had no objective reality. Ultraismo clearly played upon the existentialist view that nothing in the universe is certain and that mankind should only be concerned with individual existence. Borges delighted in using literary deceits such as allusions and puzzles in his writing, and he preferred to concentrate on plots rather than character development. Borges unabashedly stated his belief that authors were merely readers of humanity rather than creators. He attempted to remain nonideological and to avoid politics.

The essay "Tlön, Uqbar, Orbis Tertius" is composed of three clear sections that form a historical and chronological analysis of the esoteric tradition. The narrator, presumably Borges, discusses the prospect of writing a novel in the first person with his assistant. In the process the discussion becomes focused upon the historical development of the esoteric tradition, a form of utopian thought. The first part focuses upon Uqbar, or the mystery of life and its origins in ancient philosophies such as the Kabala and Oriental mysticism. This section traces the development of the tradition to the seventeenth century. Borges suggested the origins of Uqbar in the "heresiarchs," or Gnostics of Hellenistic Greece. In addition to revering knowledge, as their name suggests, the Gnostics decreed that the physical universe was an illusion, that it does not really exist. Borges argued that the Gnostics had incorporated several ancient Near East mystical teachings, especially Persian Manichaeanism, a pseudo-religion that portrayed the universe in spiritual rather than material terms. Tracing the evolution of Uqbar into the early modern era, Borges says the tradition incorporated the pseudo-science of Paracelsus, Hermeticism, and the Rosicrucians. Even in its modern dress, Uqbar never deals with reality; instead, it deals only with the imagination and the conception of the ideal. Hence its utopian character, derived from the notion of an imagined ideal society. An example of an Uqbarian institution would be the eighteenth-century Freemason society.

In the second part Borges introduces Tlön by way of the discovery of an old encyclopedia that explains the esoteric tradition. In Borges's terminology "Tlön" means idealism about the world and involves transforming mental concepts into tangible objects, the theoretical into reality. In part two he discusses a seventeenth-century secret society founded to promoted a formal tradition through a nation and eventually the world. The knowledge of the society is revealed through the discovery of the Tlön encyclopedia in 1944, which acts like a mirror reflecting the tenets of established society. Borges wanted to convince the reader that an ordinary encyclopedia, while supposedly being a reflection of the real world, is itself a fiction since reality is always invented and foisted upon society. Yet Borges's invention of the encyclopedia of Tlön was intended to represent true reality since the esoteric tradition had existed almost throughout human history. Tlön is a product of Uqbar because modern philosophy and science are products of the esoteric tradition that reaches back to the Gnostics. The tradition continued in the Renaissance through thinkers such as Giordano Bruno and into the seventeenth and eighteenth centuries through contributors such as Gottfried Wilhelm Leibniz and David Hume. It climaxed in the twentieth-century writings of Bertrand Russell, just before Borges wrote the essay. Along the way, the esoteric tradition also borrowed from ancient Oriental philosophies such as Buddhism. The view of Tlön about reality is expressed directly in the encyclopedia: "A system is nothing more than the subordination of all aspects of the universe to some one of them." Materialism thus repels Tlön, and Borges contrasted nineteenth-century German idealism (part of the esoteric tradition) and the philosophical materialism enshrined by the Enlightenment tradition. A similar contrast occurred during the Middle Ages in the philosophical debates between the realists and the nominalists, who were in turn merely repeating the conflict between Plato (ideas have a real, independent existence) and Aristotle (knowledge only derives from experience in the physical world through the senses).

The third section of Borges's essay concludes by predicting in the near future the merger of Uqbar and Tlön into the Orbis Tertius, or third realm, which actually involves accepting illusion as reality. Thus Borges turned from a mere chronicler of an idea to a utopian predicting and hoping for the emergence of an ideal world. He did not suggest that the ideal would be produced by a single organized movement such as the Rosicrucians, Freemasons, or theosophists; rather, it would come simply through a coalescing of thought around the esoteric principles. In short, rather than requiring a forced implementation of utopia, Borges believed that it would simply evolve naturally as it had in the past. The difference in the future would be that it would move from the periphery to the center of human activity and be embraced by the majority. Borges described the achievement of the Orbis Tertius as the ability to understand the real world—whether "banal" or "horrible" or both—hidden by the adherence to the everyday illusions of life. The influence of Borges's emphasis upon the esoteric tradition since the 1960s has been important. The emergence of a variety of New Age cults suggests that Borges was correct about the renewed interest in ancient mystical teachings—philosophical, religious, and social theories. Marilyn Ferguson's *The Aquarian Conspiracy* (1980) suggested that the merging of various related movements might mean the effective existence of a secret society of which the movements themselves were unaware. In other words, the application of the esoteric tradition in Borges's definition could mean that people would become more attached to illusions than to reality. Borges described the achievement of the Orbis Tertius as the culmination of Schopenhauer's advice to accept illusion as reality.

*See also* New Age Cults; Theosophy.

*Reference* Jaen, Didier T. "The Esoteric Tradition in Borges' 'Tlön, Uqbar, Orbis Tertius'" (1984).

## Toffler, Alvin

*See* Science and Society Movement.

## Topolobampo Bay Colony

Included as part of an ambitious railroad project in the 1880s, the utopian experiment at Topolobampo Bay, Mexico, was the brainchild of Albert Kimsey Owen. Drawing on his knowledge of well-known community idealists, including the Mormons, Zoarites, and socialists, Owen believed that careful integration of capital investment, labor, and urban planning could eliminate the sordid aspects of modern cities. A unique blend of idealism and practicality (that is, cooperative and corporation), the Topolobampo colony was planted in 1886 and lasted until 1894.

Albert Kimsey Owen (1847–1916) was born at Chester, Pennsylvania, into a prosperous Quaker family. Following graduation from Jefferson College in 1867 with a degree in civil engineering, Owen became deeply involved in western railroad expansion. Owen worked for Denver and Rio Grande Railroad owner William J. Palmer, who inspired Owen's utopian thinking with ideas about creating new urban centers complete with planned economies, architectural guidelines, and even moral systems. Because Palmer dreamed of extending the Denver and Rio Grande line into Mexico, he sent Owen to survey the projected route in 1872. On one of his side tours, Owen discovered the pristine Topolobampo Bay area on the Gulf of California, which he determined would be an excellent endpoint for the rail line extension. He also became acquainted with several Mexican political leaders. After returning to the United States, Owen began seeking political and financial support for a railroad project, which he said would link the northeast coast of the United States with the Pacific coast of Mexico. After failing to obtain federal backing for his plan in the United States, Owen turned to his Mexican friends for assistance. President Porfirio Díaz showed serious interest in Owen's project, which began to take shape with surveys and plans to purchase a right-of-way across northern Mexico to Texas in the early 1880s.

In 1885, Owen founded the Credit Foncier Company to build settlements along the route of the proposed rail line, to be called the Texas, Topolobampo, and Pacific Railroad. Investors would be given rights to lease residences built by the company along the route and at the endpoint at Topolobampo Bay on the future site of Owen's "Pacific City." The planned city would encompass 29 square miles and would be laid out in a formal grid pattern with wide streets and sidewalks. The utopian settlement would contain community parks and recreation facilities interspersed throughout the neighborhoods. Moorish architecture would shape community structures such as a library, restaurants, and a hotel, and aesthetic beauty would be preserved by measures such as electric cars and buried utility lines. Owen wanted to emphasize the individual's responsibility to community, instill public confidence in the planners, and establish equality between the sexes. Rules that Owen hoped to apply to Pacific City included prohibiting advertising and saloons as well as lawyers and prostitutes. Marriage and traditional family relations would be encouraged, along with dress codes. Cooperative credit arrangements would promote entrepreneurship along with the absence of taxation. Owen publicized the future attraction in his *Integral Cooperation* (1885), which served as a prospectus, albeit romantically idealized.

Owen found backing from other utopian idealists, including Marie Howland (1836–1921), who had experimented with cooperative ventures in New York City since the 1850s and penned a utopian romance in 1874. Howland had read about French industrialist-socialist Jean-Baptiste Godin's communal workers' residence, called a *familistère* (started in 1859) at Guise, France, and she lived there during 1864 with her husband. Godin's *familistère* featured cooperative industry and stores, schools, profit sharing, and social security for its workers. The Howlands agreed to publish in New Jersey the biweekly *Credit Foncier of Sinaloa* during 1885 to promote interest in the colony at Topolobampo Bay. Other publicity derived from articles in newspapers such as *The American* in New York City. Owen also received publicity assistance from New York publisher John Lovell, a one-time follower of theosophy. Within a year, more than 2,500 investors had advanced capital for the project, including utopian enthusiasts such as Horace Greeley, Peter Good, and Isaac Rumford. Always seeking intellectual approval and insights, Owen corresponded with other U.S. communalists, including Isaac Broome of Ruskin in Tennessee and J. W. Gaskine of the Kaweah colony in California, which also involved railroads.

By the summer of 1886 more than 1,400 colonists representing diverse backgrounds (but no clerics) had arrived in Mexico to launch Owen's experiment. They signed a pledge to follow 37 principles established by Owen. Each colonist would be guaranteed both a job and a house. Colony members must work for 30 years before retirement but would have insurance against accident, illness, old age, and death. At the same time, the Mexican government granted permission for the construction of the Texas, Topolobampo, Pacific Railroad, requiring the Credit Foncier Company to place 500 settlers within two years and to provide free transport to the colony. The early arrivals at Topolobampo Bay started building at four sites but found the harbor unsuitable, fresh water inadequate, and diseases such as malaria rampant. By 1887, when internal problems threatened the project with collapse, Kansas millionaire businessman Christian B. Hoffman offered cash and personal support for the colony. Hoffman visited Mexico often and became romantically involved with Mrs. Howland (Edward Howland died in 1890), but his Kansas emigrants caused internal divisions and Hoffman eventually withdrew support in 1893 to pursue other interests back in Kansas. In 1890, Owen traveled to England to solicit fresh financial backing, which he received along with the prospect of additional immigrants to Pacific City. He even considered reconstituting Pacific City on the lines of Theodor Hertzka's *Freeland*. Yet Owen eventually succumbed to the reality of the failure of his dream and left Topolobampo Bay permanently in 1893, though he tried unsuccessfully to sell the site to another utopian, Thomas Lake Harris of the Fountain Grove, California, colony. Marie Howland also left in 1893 to join the single-tax colony at Fairhope, Alabama, modeled on the theories of Henry George. Other colonists gradually withdrew, and Topolobampo Bay was vacated by almost all the settlers in 1894. Owen's dream of a great commercial railroad project with its utopian port city was never realized.

*Reference* Reynolds, Ray P. *Cat's Paw Utopia* (1972).

## Transcendentalism

The U.S. response to European romanticism in the first half of the nineteenth century included a movement known as Transcendentalism that was popular with New England cultural elites. The chief inspiration behind the movement was poet Ralph Waldo Emerson, who formulated his ideas while a minister at a Unitarian church in Boston. Emerson and his colleagues sought to combine their religious philosophy with modern science and Oriental mysticism to create practical social reforms. The basic idea of Transcendentalism involved the concept of a higher metaphysical truth that transcended human physical senses. The philosophy inspired many practical reforms and cooperative experiments in the period before the Civil War, most notably the Brook Farm community. Indeed, Emerson wrote in the 1840s that virtually every well-read person "has a draft of a new community in his waistcoat pocket."

Ralph Waldo Emerson (1803–1882) argued that the universe was first and foremost spiritual, with God represented as an "oversoul" who transmitted his essence into both man and nature. Thus the Tran-

*Brook Farm, West Roxbury, Massachusetts*

scendentalists viewed humanity and nature more in spiritual than physical terms. Though humans had the capacity to transcend their senses and thought, they were capable of perfection since they possessed the spark of the divine. Yet no institution such as government should coerce an individual to make choices incompatible with his or her conscience. The Transcendentalists campaigned for social justice and various reform projects, including the abolition of slavery and gender equality. The founding group of Transcendentalists met at Unitarian minister George Ripley's Boston home and included, besides Emerson, Henry David Thoreau, Bronson Alcott, Nathaniel Hawthorne, and Margaret Fuller. Thoreau's experiment in living close to nature, *Walden* (1854), demonstrated best the Transcendentalists' goal of proving the capacities of self-reliance and independence. The movement's ideas were reflected in the works of other writers, such as in Walt Whitman's *Leaves of Grass* (1855), with its promotion of romantic nationalism.

Taking their cue from the utopian socialist communitarian experiments modeled after the ideas of Charles Fourier and Robert Owen, the Transcendentalists embarked upon some communist experiments of their own. The most famous was Brook Farm, begun in 1841 by George Ripley on 200 acres at West Roxbury, Massachusetts, near Boston. It lasted about six years and attracted a little more than 100 communalists, including Transcendental enthusiasts such as Nathaniel Hawthorne, Margaret Fuller, and Charles Dana. Actually, most of the Transcendentalists did not show great enthusiasm for Ripley's experiment. The group raised money for Brook Farm by selling stock. The experiment was intended to be an agricultural commune, but its urban residents lacked adequate experience in the vagaries of farming. Hawthorne, finding the manual labor utterly exhausting and lacking in fulfillment, left Brook Farm in less than a year. He later used his Brook Farm experience, "an unnatural and unreal one," as the fictional setting for *The Blithedale Romance* (1852), a utopia full of artifice yet lacking substance. All Brook Farm property was held in common, including the cultural collections, and no class distinctions existed. Workers were paid wages and used money to pay for necessities and lodgings, but no one lacked support if they needed it. Brook Farm maintained a variety of social and cultural activities, including recreation, games, and a theater. Most noteworthy was the school at Brook Farm, which graduated some talented pupils. By 1845 the floundering community had been transformed into a Fourierist phalanstery. A newspaper, the *Harbinger*, was published during the last two years of Brook Farm's existence. Following a severe fire in 1846, the small group determined to give up the settlement, and it disbanded in 1847.

A direct outgrowth of Brook Farm was a Transcendentalist experimental society called Fruitlands, founded in 1843 by Bronson Alcott (1799–1888), the father of Louisa May Alcott. It was established on 100 acres at Harvard, Massachusetts, with financial backing from Charles Lane, a radical English follower of Alcott. The idea of Fruitlands was to strictly avoid any action that might cause harm to anyone or anything. Thus not only did the Fruitlanders not eat animal flesh, they would not use animals to help them pull carriages or plow fields. They would not wear cotton clothing since it came from slave labor. The residents began their day with a cold bath, a music lesson, and a natural breakfast of grains, nuts, and fruits. Work of some sort ensued for the remainder of the morning, followed by a vegetarian midday meal. The communal meal allowed residents to engage in stimulating conversation. The afternoon was spent working, and the day concluded with an evening meal and further enlightened discussions. The absence of structure, especially an economic basis for livelihood, led to the collapse of the colony after a few months. The Transcendentalist conviction of social responsibility proved to be incompatible with unencumbered individualism. Alcott's dreams ran afoul of practical reality, and Fruitlands was abandoned in 1845.

Another Emerson disciple, Sylvester Judd (1813–1853), penned a utopian novel, *Margaret*, in 1845 that embodied rather specifically the Unitarian version of Transcendentalism. Judd argued that a transformation of earth into heaven could not take place until people recognized their own self-worth, which had been taught by Christ. Such a shift in practice required that the vision of God as punisher of sin and evil be abandoned. The novel's chief character, Margaret, was born poor and unknowing, yet she obtained by intuition the necessary knowledge of love to lead her community of Livingston toward the utopian society. A knowledge and practice of love would allow mankind to make the proper decisions for organizing and operating society. Judd's utopia does not include man-made laws produced by human institutions. Judd reflects the common U.S. attitude that the nation was chosen by God for a special purpose, in this case to become the perfect society. *Margaret*'s effusive optimism and belief in progress fit neatly into the mid-nineteenth-century belief that the future held great promise. Livingston applies the best knowledge of farming, science, and technology to make life easier and more comfortable for its residents.

The closest practical application of Judd's religious communitarianism came with the founding of the Fraternal Community in Mendon, Massachusetts, in 1840 by Universalist minister Adin Ballou (1803–1890). Almost 200 workers and farmers joined the community, which moved to Milford in 1841 to occupy 600 acres and took the name "Hopedale." Ballou believed that the test of true Christianity was the promotion of social justice, though residents were free to decide how to pursue the noble goals. The community promoted chastity, sobriety, charity, and equality. It opposed oaths, slavery, and violence, including war. As a joint stock company, Hopedale eventually came under the control of George and Ebenezer Draper, who sought capitalist profits and caused its dissolution in 1856. A small remnant of the community moved to Union Grove, Minnesota, but only survived three years there. A secular version of Hopedale was the Skaneateles community founded on 300 acres at Mottville, New York, by antislavery leader John Collins. The 150 members at Skaneateles embraced principles of communal property, anarchism, monogamy, and vegetarianism. Collins published a paper, the *Communitist*, that expressed the philosophy of Skaneateles.

Though the community prospered for three years, Collins abruptly decided the experiment was impractical and left Skaneateles, whereupon the other residents decided to dissolve the community in 1846.

For the Transcendentalists, spiritual progress was a prerequisite to material progress because material well-being must be ensured for all and not just the few. The reform of morals must precede the application of knowledge—the conscience rules and disciplines reason. The Transcendentalists feared that the worship of reason alone would eclipse the importance of the individual and the right of free and independent action. However, their utopian ideals proved difficult to translate into practice.

*See also* Utopian Socialism.

*Reference* Francis, Richard. *Transcendental Utopia: Individual and Community at Brook Farm, Fruitlands, and Walden* (1997).

## Twain, Mark

*See A Connecticut Yankee in King Arthur's Court.*

## Underground Man (1904)

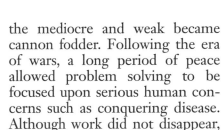

Because of his firsthand understanding of social conditions, the French sociologist-criminologist Gabriel de Tarde could envision detailed means of constructing a future utopia with the aid of science and technology. His *Fragment d'histoire future* (1896) was translated into English as the *Underground Man* in 1904. His utopia was sweeping in its comprehension of the entire world and all cultures. Tarde mirrored other late-nineteenth-century utopias, especially those of H. G. Wells, in viewing the future of mankind in a unified world condition. Science would allow humanity many options for survival, but it could not guarantee the discarding of selfish proclivities.

A French judge and criminologist, Gabriel de Tarde (1843–1904) produced a varied corpus of writings including poetry, plays, novels, and nonfiction writings on criminology. Despite the popularity of biological evolution in his time, Tarde rejected Darwin's theory and argued that humans fell into two categories: They were either inventor-producers or imitator-users. After serving an apprenticeship in the provinces, he spent most of his career as head of the criminal statistics bureau in the French Ministry of Justice, where he viewed a variety of social phenomena from quantified standards. Upon retirement from his Ministry of Justice post, Tarde served as professor of philosophy at the Collège de France. As a sociologist, his reputation rivaled that of Auguste Comte and Max Weber. His utopian fragment reflected a great deal of his sociology.

In the *Underground Man*, the world experienced a long era of warfare in the twentieth century which reshaped society, since the brightest young men were exempted from military service, whereas the mediocre and weak became cannon fodder. Following the era of wars, a long period of peace allowed problem solving to be focused upon serious human concerns such as conquering disease.

Although work did not disappear, it was essentially optional and resembled the elective cooperatives of the utopian socialists. Pace H. G. Wells, Tarde unveils a one-world, Greek-speaking confederacy, with its capital, called Nebuchadnesor, at New Babylon. The splendid world capital was connected by advanced railroads to all parts of the globe. Energy was derived from electricity, water, and wind. Everything in the era of peace was directed by reason and efficient technologies. The people, both male and female, simulated pleasant bourgeois values in their physical appearance, dress, and demeanor. Yet this time of peace and plenty did not last forever. In the year 2409 scientists discovered that the sun was losing its energy and power to stimulate life on earth. With the sun's demise, albeit with a disarming beauty, the earth became steadily colder until ice covered every land mass. Many people simply froze to death, and survivors gathered around New Babylon for protection. A second major human winnowing thus took place.

Meanwhile, a small group led by Miltiades, a primitive troglodyte, and his romantic interest Lydia has gone underground to create a new existence. Tarde literally turned the world inside out. Beneath the earth human civilization (without any other life-forms) reemerges, with cities producing energy and light to sustain a sense of community cohesion and happiness. But due to limited resources new births are restricted greatly. Tarde emphasized that his underground utopia is sustained by cerebral rather than material exchanges. Society's existence revolves around common interests and free expression rather than either a goal of justice or commerce. Yet the underground civilization allows the sciences (except chemistry and psychology) to become religion, and scientists have changed to clerics. The advent of a form of ancient nature religion creates some disunity among the populace. Then the main underground society meets a Chinese, that is, overpopulated, counterpart that has resorted to cannibalism in order to survive. After arguing about how to respond to the outsiders, the civilized constituency tries but fails to cultivate and teach the uncivilized Chinese. The Chinese will eventually return to the earth's surface when the sun reappears, forcing the civilized remnant to remain underground. Tarde thus concluded that "among the stars as among mankind, the most brilliant are not the best," so that "in the heavens as on the earth true happiness lives concealed."

Tarde reflected both the realism and optimism of his times in arguing that human ingenuity and creativity often emerge from conditions of storm and stress. The chances of creating an ideal society resembled the Renaissance belief in *fortuna*; the acceptance of an innovative idea depended on the spirit of the times more than the attractiveness of the concept. Thus, though the odds of a utopia being established might be small, it is often during periods of crisis for civilization that the germ of the future resides. Tarde, like H. G. Wells, was one of the last optimistic utopians who thought in universal terms of a single world system. Thereafter, the dystopia would largely overwhelm the optimism of the French sociologist.

*Reference* Barnes, Harry Elmer. "The Philosophy of the State in the Writings of Gabriel Tarde" (1919).

## *Utopia* (1516)

When Thomas More published his *Utopia* in 1516, he could not have envisioned the impact his work would have over the centuries that followed. More spent little more than a year contemplating and writing *Utopia*, during which time he traveled to the Netherlands as part of a diplomatic mission from Henry VIII to the future Holy Roman Emperor Charles V. Although many modern scholars have offered different motives and meanings for *Utopia*, contemporaries had no trouble analyzing its meaning. *Utopia* reflects both the Renaissance's and More's own predilections for reform projects often framed in the form of handbooks or guides. More was above all a social reformer, and *Utopia* embodied many of his thoughts about changing his own society and institutions.

Thomas More (1478–1535) was a leader in the English Renaissance, a noted Christian humanist who served the monarch Henry VIII in the highest political office of lord chancellor, and a martyred defender of the Catholic faith. After studying at Oxford, More was trained in the law and tutored by the early humanist John Colet. Though he amassed a comfortable fortune in his law practice and later won a reputation as an officeholder, More always considered himself a scholar rather than a lawyer or politician. Christian humanists such as More desired to produce practical schemes to reform society, schemes that would be drawn from both virtuous classical models and the life of Christ. More wrote the second part of *Utopia* first while in the Netherlands on his diplomatic mission in 1515, where he conceived of the need for an ideal state. The first part was written upon his return to England during 1516, when he was concerned about the sources of ideas for governing. More had discussed the composition and publication of *Utopia* with his longtime friend, Desiderius Erasmus. Indeed, Erasmus wrote his own treatise, *The Education of a Christian Prince* (dedicated to the future Charles V), in 1516, so they most likely compared notes on their respective projects. *Utopia* was published in Latin at Louvain in 1516 with Erasmus's assistance, but it was not translated into English until 1551, by Ralph Robinson. A second English translation appeared in 1684 by the divine Gilbert Burnet, and the next not until 1923 by G. C. Richard. *Utopia* was also translated eventually into all other modern languages, including Japanese and Chinese. The form of utopia chosen by More undoubtedly resulted from his reading of the classics, including especially Plato's *Republic*. Plato was the most stylish Greek author studied by contemporaries during More's time. The classical utopias not only were imaginary societies but also were isolated from the real world, as was More's island. More deliberately coined the word "utopia" from two Greek words with contrasting meanings—"outopos" or no place, and "eutopos" or ideal place.

Books I and II of *Utopia* were deliberate contrasts between the real world of an imperfect Christian Europe and the ideal world of Utopia, where reason alone rules human actions. In Book I, readers meet More in the company of Peter Giles, a magistrate in Antwerp and a student of Erasmus. Giles introduces More to the fictional Raphael Hythloday (from the Greek word meaning a storyteller), a world traveler from Portugal who describes his journey to the island of Utopia. Most of Book I concentrates on More's diplomatic mission and his growing awareness of a multitude of social problems, including crime, abuse of peasants, and the power of the wealthy. Utopia was mentioned only once in Book I and in the context of three other ideal societies visited by Hythloday. Book I provided the contrast in the real world to the imagined world presented in the second part. More sought to create a society wherein mankind lived peacefully and productively. He determined that the authorities of law, public opinion, and the Christian conscience must work in a complementary fashion. The guidelines obviously were not working satisfactorily in contemporary Europe. Even conscience, represented in *Utopia* by Hythloday, needed discipline and could not actually be free. Hythloday tells More and Giles that

*Thomas More, from an engraving by Grignion.*

princes will ignore precepts of both reason and conscience in determining their policies. Thus Hythloday's argument about counsel, which coincides with Plato's position, that intellectuals should not serve in government, is ultimately rejected by More, who decided he had a moral duty to serve his king and country.

Book II recounts Hythloday's narrative of Utopia, an island 200 miles wide and 500 miles long, similar, not surprisingly, to the island of Britain. The island, formerly called Abraxis, was conquered hundreds of years earlier by King Utopos, who had created the ideal society Hythloday discovered. More did not believe that mankind left to its own devices would ever develop a utopian system; it had to be imposed by a single authority. Because of its geographical isolation, Utopia had less to fear from external aggression, thereby improving the likelihood of a peaceful society. Still, it remained in a constant state of preparation for war against potential aggressors. Since More sought to portray war as irrational and ineffectual, it

*Plan of Utopia, from a woodcut illustration in the first Basle edition of Thomas More's* Utopia.

must still be present in his story. The island of Utopia contained 54 cities, all uniform in their design and each divided into four sectors. Each city maintained 6,000 households, and every 30 households elected a representative phylarch each year. A protophylarch was elected for every ten phylarchs. In turn, the 200 phylarchs elected a city governor, who held power for life unless he resorted to tyranny. The cities' administrative body, a senate, was composed of the governor, the protophylarchs, and two phylarchs. A central council representing the 54 cities governed Utopia, but self-government in the cities was more important than the central authority.

The social organization of Utopia revolved around the family unit, which was an extended family based on kinship. Families in the cities were smaller than those in the rural parts of Utopia. The economy of Utopia was based upon a diverse system of agriculture, trade, and manufacture; all residents were taught skills of farming and a particular craft. Since all residents worked, the workday only required six hours to complete the tasks, a very limited time to More's contemporaries. Hence work became more pleasurable and less arduous. Free time for the Utopians was spent in recreation and study, the higher pleasures. The purpose of work, moreover, was not the capitalistic profit motive since the Utopians practiced communism, which virtually eliminated the lust for materialism and possessions. More concluded that the primary failure of his own society's laws was traceable to pride resulting from the ownership of and lust for possessions. Hythloday espoused More's position on the corrupting nature of property. Utopians did not even place special value on precious metals such as gold and silver; gold was used for the bracelets of criminals and for toilets. Children were given precious stones as play toys.

The regimentation of the society was evident in almost every area, including the proscriptions for marriage—women could not marry before age 18 and men at age 22. The Utopians frowned upon antisocial behavior, and vices such as adultery were severely punished. There were no crimes of violence since property was communal. Utopian law relied upon shaming lawbreakers, a technique common in More's England. Punishment for criminals and conquered peoples might result in condemnation into slavery, but slave labor was not a major factor in the Utopian economy. More assured his readers that the focus was on moral pleasures and he provided programs such as euthanasia to deal with pain. Although the Utopians recognized a creator-god, they were guaranteed freedom of religion. The priestly class, not a powerful group, was limited to 13 members in each city. Their main function was to accompany the military into battle and pray for protection. Utopians did not know about Christianity until Hythloday arrived, yet they seemed to practice its tenets without express knowledge of the absolute truth. The Utopians had an advanced society compared to More's England and Europe, yet it was not paradise.

The fact that More resorted to wit and satire in *Utopia* only reflects his conviction that literature must entertain before it can instruct. His technique of turning contemporary traditions such as property and money upside down was designed to critique his society rather than to propose such a turn of events. He probably conceived his exercise as presenting an incentive rather than a blueprint for reform. It is impossible to divorce More's *Utopia* from either its classical or its Renaissance influences, although his Utopia lacked any ingredients from the Arcadia, golden age, or Land of Cockaygne fantasies of earlier eras. In terms of political philosophy, More was acquainted with both the Renaissance humanist tradition that derived from Hellenistic Stoicism and the late medieval scholastic tradition grounded in Aristotle's writings. In Book I, More suggests through Hythloday that a humanist philosopher cannot possibly become a politician since politics requires expedient and even immoral acts. The scholastic tradition, which relied upon reason to solve problems, resisted the intrusion of the imagination to conceive of the ideal society and government. Hence More not only mirrored the influence of the classics and Renaissance humanism but also examined those same traditions in his experimental ideal society. Moreover, as a Christian philosopher, More desired reform of the church and clergy more than any other area of life. His vision of Christianity in *Utopia* advocated a simple imitation of the earthly ministry of Christ—expressions of love and compassion for one's fellow man—which was characteristic of all Christian humanists in the early sixteenth century.

From the early letters of commendation by contemporaries attached to sixteenth-century editions up through the works of twentieth-century analysts, More's work has been subjected to extensive and widely varying interpretations. The coeditors of the most authoritative twentieth-century translation of *Utopia*, J. H. Hexter and Edward L. Surtz, agreed about the general intent and meaning of More's treatise. They pointed out that More's humanist friends—Erasmus, Giles, Cuthbert Tunstall, Guillaume Budé, Ulrich von Hutten et al.—to whom the *Utopia* was directed took the piece to represent a humanist creation of an ideal society complete with appropriate conduct. To these colleagues, *Utopia* was a particular type of handbook that should not be taken literally as a whole but that could inspire those in authority to contemplate reforms that might produce a more virtuous society. Hexter and Surtz have suggested that tendencies to take More either too literally or too playfully by seizing upon episodes or specific language miss the mark by not placing the *Utopia* as a whole in its proper context. Admittedly, there are some distinctions in the details of Hexter's and Surtz's interpretations. Hexter preferred to view More's critique aimed at two constituencies, the religious society of pre-Reformation Europe and the Christian humanists themselves. Hexter believed that More thought the humanist reform agenda was impractical in many respects since it relied upon human reason taking action when it became enlightened. More realized that reform required radical, forced structural change in order to achieve the just society. Surtz preferred to focus upon the fundamentally medieval and backward-looking framework of More's mind. More served several years in a monastery, and his Utopia is replete with examples of monastic asceticism—uniform dress codes, the work ethic, disciplined study, contempt for material possessions, and communal property and means. Thus Surtz thought that More felt reform would have to rely upon a combination of reason and revelation reminiscent of Thomas Aquinas's approach to achieve success.

Other interpreters have stressed particular aspects of *Utopia* rather than trying to see it as a whole. Thus More's ideal society was seized upon by the nineteenth-century Marxist socialists because of its attack upon private property. It had also been viewed as a plan for imperialism by the new colonialists of the nineteenth century. Some scholars have been led to dismiss all serious intentions by More because he used satire and irony. Because of More's knowledge of the recent voyages of discovery to the New World and the specific link of Hythloday to the explorer Amerigo Vespucci, some scholars believe that More's Utopia was modeled after an actual native society in the New World, such as the Mayans or Incas. These arguments are based upon the coincidence of More's physical descriptions of Utopia with places in the New World as well as attempts to link the Utopian alphabet to Native American languages.

Few would argue that More did not create an authoritarian system that became the pattern for virtually all modern utopias. Since utopias are made and controlled by mankind, they must be highly disciplined in order to work as they are intended. More was not an idealist in regard to human nature and did not believe that the free play of either reason or conscience would lead humans toward a peaceful and stable society. The only way to change human behavior, according to More, was to alter the human environment and arbitrarily coordinate the forces of laws, public opinion, and conscience. Hence More's prescription for utopia would require the surrender of most freedoms in order to create a well-ordered society. Though other utopian writers after More would often be troubled by the consequences to human freedom of enlightened, if arbitrary, reforms embodied in the perfect society schemes, the only other alternative was to leave it all to God. Thus Thomas More was unique in that he rejected both the humanist naïveté that radical social reforms could be achieved by relying upon reason alone and the classical admonition by Plato that intellectuals should not enter public service because they would be corrupted like the politicians. Progress could only result from a dialogue between the real and the ideal. For More, utopia was neither an easy nor

certain solution to society's ills, but contemplation of it would keep hope for the future alive. All modern utopias owe their nature and existence, to one extent or another, to More's *Utopia*.

*References* Bradshaw, Brendan. "More on Utopia" (1981); Hexter, J. H. *More's Utopia: The Biography of an Idea* (1952); Logan, George M. *The Meaning of More's "Utopia"* (1983).

## Utopian Socialism

Post-Napoleonic France witnessed the birth of the most profound utopian movement since Thomas More's *Utopia*. Utopian socialism was the first of three phases of socialist thought that developed during the nineteenth century. Socialism traced its utopian heritage to twin sources, More's egalitarian communalism and Francis Bacon's idea of harnessing science to benefit the human condition. Socialism also became the first testing ground of the Enlightenment's idea of progress, although it insisted upon individual deference to the more important ideal of the community. Utopian socialism was led by French thinkers Henri Comte de Saint-Simon, Charles Fourier, Etienne Cabet, and Louis Blanc, but it also included British industrialist Robert Owen and Russian writer Nikolay Chernyshevsky. Socialist thought derived from the impact of both the Industrial Revolution and the French Revolution upon the social and economic order. The utopian socialists were the first group both to recognize the social implications of industrialism and to offer a solution. That purported solution failed to stop the advance of industrialization, but it demonstrated that socialism would become an influential force in thought and action for decades to follow. Indeed, other competing ideologies in the nineteenth century—liberalism, conservatism, nationalism, social Darwinism—all discovered socialism to have the most profound external influence upon their own philosophies.

All French thinkers of the nineteenth century started their analysis of contemporary problems with their interpretation of the French Revolution of 1789. They believed that while the revolution had succeeded in enunciating lofty ideals, it had failed as a model of how to reconstruct society. As a by-product of the revolution, capitalism had begun with a flawed motive of competition that both demeaned humanity and exploited human labor. The utopian socialists wanted to replace ruinous competition with cooperation, which meant altering the profit motive. Importantly, they did not propose the abolition of private property as did the later scientific socialists and anarchists. The utopian socialists believed that capitalism was flawed, not that it was irredeemable. The means to achieving their goal led to a variety of experiments that were rarely in agreement. The utopian socialists owed much to the emergence of liberalism and science, but they eschewed the romantic avoidance of grappling with the new social issues. Certainly, they were more attracted to social and economic matters than to politics and religion.

Henri Comte de Saint-Simon (1760–1825) was undoubtedly the father of the new movement, although he was not properly speaking a utopian socialist himself. Although from an aristocratic background, he joined the revolutionaries of 1789 and renounced his birthright. Saint-Simon's philosophy of history was cyclic: Periods of stability would be followed by increasing instability, then chaos followed by reconstruction. The period following the Napoleonic wars was one of reconstruction for France and Europe. Unlike the Romantics, Saint-Simon recognized that society's economic foundation was now industrial rather than agricultural. Hence the new leaders of society, replacing the old orders of nobility and clergy, were the businessmen, scientists, and engineers. Saint-Simon's ideal society, detailed in *The Industrial System* (1821), would be organized into three divisions, which he called chambers. The engineers, writers, and artists would design both the goals and methods of achieving the goals through a program of public agencies and work. A second chamber of scientists would then design a system of education to instruct citizens about their roles in achieving the goals. A third chamber made up of representative legislators would enact laws to implement the aims and means outlined by the other two chambers as well as the tax revenues to pay for the projects. Saint-Simon, therefore, operated much like the early modern utopists in creating an authoritarian means of implementing his utopia. Just as in More's first utopia, the benefits of such selfless authority would accrue to all citizens, especially women. Saint-Simon and his followers stumbled upon the recognition that women had been suppressed by society and should be liberated. An important difference between More and Saint-Simon, which resulted from the secular impact of the Enlightenment, was that a secular morality would replace Christianity in the socialist system. Moreover, scientific knowledge would become the social cement for society. Saint-Simon's elitist socialism did not produce a following among the new working classes, nor did he convince the French parliament to enact his somewhat vague solutions.

Charles Fourier (1772–1837) agreed with Saint-Simon's analysis of the social and economic problems but offered rather different solutions, primarily in *The New Industrial World* (1829). Fourier came from a bourgeois background and became enthralled at the prospect of reforming capitalism. For that purpose, he designed the first utopian community institution, known as the phalanstery. His dream of a utopian society included some rather bizarre notions: people living to the age of 150, the sea becoming lemonade, an aurora borealis to heat the North and South Poles, four new moons appearing, animals taking music lessons, and wars replaced by cake-eating contests. Taking his cue from Jean-Jacques Rousseau, Fourier argued that the individual and society were inherently incompatible. Unlike Thomas Hobbes, Fourier believed that the passions could not be regulated satisfactorily simply by laws and force. Instead, the environment should be changed to become compatible with human passions. The phalanstery was a social unit of 5,000 residents in an essentially agrarian setting. Work teams would be formed from volunteers so that each resident would engage in a preferred form of labor. All members would share equally in the work and likewise in the fruits of their labors. Gradations would only arise because some might contribute more work because of their skills and must be proportionally rewarded. In Fourier's system, more than in Saint-Simon's, cooperation would effectively replace competition and the society would be contented and productive. Though Fourier publicized his ideas in a journal on industrial reform, there was no effort to create a phalanstery.

Several Fourier-type phalansteries were started in the United States, however. The most successful was the North American Phalanx planted at Monmouth County, New Jersey, in 1843 after moving from Albany, New York. The settlement of over 100 was led by Albert Brisbane, a wealthy disciple of Fourier, who edited a journal during the early years of the experiment. Brisbane received financial backing for the phalanx from Horace Greeley, editor and publisher of the New York *Tribune*, who had a very large national audience. Warren Chase founded the second most successful Fourierist community, the Wisconsin Phalanx, which functioned from 1844 to 1850 at Ripon with about 180 participants. Other Fourierist phalanxes operated briefly in New York, Pennsylvania, Ohio, Indiana, Illinois, Michigan, and Iowa.

The stubborn and sincere Robert Owen (1771–1858) began a successful cotton textile operation at age 19 during the takeoff period for industry in Great Britain after 1790. Yet he saw firsthand the social evils of the factory system and desired to experiment with methods to ameliorate those bad results without resorting to class warfare or revolution. From the end of the Napoleonic wars until his death, Owen wrote numerous

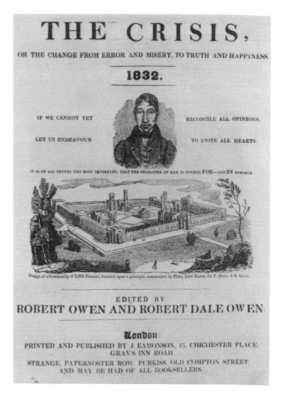

*Title page of Robert Owen's* The Crisis, or the Change from Error and Misery, to Truth and Happiness *(1832) showing a portrait of Owen and the New Harmony Community in Indiana.*

pamphlets, lectured, and founded a variety of reform organizations all aimed at assisting the working poor to adjust to the new industrial economy. He tried to improve the working conditions in his own factories by raising wages, making the workplace safer, and refusing to hire very young children. He also developed programs to reduce alcoholism among workers and even established schools for the children of the working classes.

Owen's first utopian scheme, outlined in 1817, foresaw the organization of cooperative communities in all economic realms from agriculture to industry. He proposed forming small village communities with populations of between 500 and 3,000. He did not foresee the growth of industry beyond the small units that he owned. Similar to ideas of later behavioral psychologists, Owen believed that the workers' character might be shaped by reforming their environment. Owen deeded to the workers one of his factory units at New Lanark, Scotland, which allowed his experiment to be put into practice. As owners, the workers would decide democratically how to manage the factory and share the profits. One result was that the wage system disappeared. Yet Owen ignored the problems that would result from turning management over to those ill-prepared for such tasks. Owen then traveled to the United States in 1824 to launch a cooperative agricultural community on the frontier at New Harmony, Indiana, though it disbanded in 1827. The Owenite movement spawned an exuberant era of utopianism that lasted for two decades in the United States. Brief Owenite settlements appeared at Yellow Springs and Kendal in Ohio; Haverstraw and Coxsackie in New York; Goose Pond, Promisewell, and Valley Forge in Pennsylvania; Blue Springs, Indiana; Nashoba, Tennessee; and Waukesha, Wisconsin. All of the utopian communities failed, in part because of their unrealistic economic schemes, but also because of the working of human nature among the participants. Utopian socialists such as Fourier and Owen failed to account for natural tendencies such as greed or sloth, and there was no totalitarian authority to prevent corruption as existed in the earlier literary utopias. Owen's later creation of the Grand National Trades Union (1831) unifying all workers' unions also failed to effectively promote worker cooperatives.

Etienne Cabet (1788–1856), influenced by both Fourier and Owen, founded the Icarian communities in the United States. Trained in the law, Cabet was often involved in secret societies and intrigue, including the Revolution of 1830 that resulted in Louis Philippe becoming France's king. As a reward, Louis made Cabet state's attorney in Corsica, but Cabet's antimonarchical writings had forced him into exile in England by 1833. While in England for several years, Cabet became familiar with English utopian projectors from Thomas More's to Robert Owen's. The year after returning to France in 1839, Cabet published a fictional utopia, *Un Voyage en Icarie* (Journey to Icaria), which attracted a wide audience. *Icarie* surveyed communal theories as well as the unjust social system in Europe and outlined a method of implementing a utopian community by focusing upon the fictional Mediterranean republic of Icaria. The utopia was carefully planned, utilizing the best scientific and technological knowledge complete with a circular capital city reminiscent of More's Utopia. A benevolent dictatorship provided for all the physical needs of the Icarians but did not permit individuality.

Over the next several years, Cabet spent much time editing a newspaper, *Le Populaire*, which advocated reforms along the lines of his utopia and served to increase further his fame. Although Cabet had not originally envisioned creating an actual experiment like the one described in *Icarie*, he was pressed by his followers to do so. Thus he departed France on Owen's advice for the Texas frontier along the Red River in 1848 to establish a utopian community. Almost totally unprepared to face the vagaries of the frontier and inflicted with a fever, the Texas settlement failed just as Cabet arrived on the scene with additional settlers. So Cabet traveled to Nauvoo, Illinois, with fewer than 300 survivors to resurrect a settlement vacated by the Mormons. Cabet insisted upon applying Fourier's population limits of 1,800, and so he soon lost his standing with residents, who removed him from office in 1856. Cabet then moved with a remnant of utopians to St. Louis, where he died. The Nauvoo settlers migrated in 1857 to Corning, Iowa, where the movement remained intact until 1878. Another Icarian group founded the Speranza colony at Cloverdale, California, on 900 acres, where they remained from 1881 to 1886.

By the 1840s in France, utopian socialism was being challenged from various quarters. Yet there was one more practical attempt to apply its principles during the revolutions of 1848. Louis Blanc (1811–

1882) began to doubt that socialism could be achieved without the abolition of property rights. Yet his blend of past and future socialism resulted in an intriguing experiment known as the "social workshop" outlined in *The Organization of Work* (1834). Blanc concluded that even if factory owners such as Owen donated their possessions to the workers, such enterprises were doomed to fail since the workers did not have the proper training to run a business. If the government would set up "social workshops" as schools to teach the workers all aspects of business and industry, from bookkeeping to machine maintenance, they might be able to launch such ventures themselves and succeed. During the Revolution of 1848, the provisional government actually agreed briefly to set up the workshops, but they did not last long enough to allow a judgment on their potential. Blanc used the concept of all socialists, that each worker would contribute work according to his ability and would receive benefits to satisfy his needs, although Blanc spoke only of material needs whereas Fourier had included social needs as well. Some of Blanc's slogans were later co-opted by both Marxist and anarchist socialists.

Typically trailing the rest of Europe in the realm of new ideas, utopian socialism did not appear in Russia until the long-imprisoned Nikolay Chernyshevsky (1828–1889) authored *What Is to Be Done?* in 1863. Even though czarist censorship caused it to remain in manuscript form until publication during the 1905 revolution, it was widely circulated and had an enormous influence in late-nineteenth-century Russia. Not only did Chernyshevsky criticize Russia's political autocracy, but he also heaped scorn upon emerging capitalism. Instead, Chernyshevsky showed partiality to the cooperative commune model of the utopian socialists as the ideal society. The primary need was to free labor from constraints, which in turn would allow the advancement of enlightenment for all citizens. *What Is to Be Done?* was especially attractive to women since Chernyshevsky advocated greater freedoms for females. Using several dream scenarios and a female narrator, the novel described a "new woman," or equality, living in a socialist utopia in which property was communally owned and work shared equally. The centerpiece of the agrarian commune was a gigantic crystal palace (modeled after the real Crystal Palace at the 1851 London Exhibition) that provided housing, shops, and cultural centers in an effortless blending of the public and private aspects of life. Writing from a czarist prison, Chernyshevsky dreamed of an ideal society that particularly would ameliorate the plight of the working classes and women.

As for the rest of Europe, following the failures in the revolutions of 1848, the utopian socialists were quickly eclipsed by Karl Marx and Friedrich Engels. The Saint-Simonians eventually rejoined the traditional capitalists, while the Owenites and Fourierists splintered into insignificant sects. It is probably fair to say that utopian socialism was a necessary stage in the development of socialism, even though their ideas and work did not completely disappear with the advent of scientific and anarchist socialism. More than any previous utopian movement, the utopian socialists subjected their ideas to practice in a fascinating and noble experiment. When literary utopias reappeared toward the end of the nineteenth century, almost all began with a socialist premise, and the anti-utopias of the next century largely existed as a weapon to oppose the socialist utopia. Although the naive idealism of utopian socialism retained significant elements of early modern utopias, the primary difference from earlier utopias was the socialists' overt application of utopian thought in existing society.

***References*** Beecher, Jonathan, and Richard Bienvenu, eds. *The Utopian Vision of Charles Fourier* (1972); Harrison, John F. C. *Quest for the New Moral World: Robert Owen and the Owenites in Britain and America* (1969); Johnson, Christopher. *Utopian Communism in France: Cabet and the Icarians* (1974); Manuel, Frank E. *The New World of Henri Saint-Simon* (1956).

**Vairasse, Denis**
*See* Huguenot Utopias.

**Vico, Giambattista**
*See The New Science.*

**Vonnegut, Kurt**
*See* Science Fiction Anti-Utopias.

## *A Voyage to Arcturus* (1920)

Scotsman David Lindsay's utopia, *A Voyage to Arcturus*, has been characterized by some critics as a fantasy on the level of Lewis Carroll's Alice books, highlighting the contest between light and darkness in both the macrocosmic universal level and the microcosmic human dimension. *A Voyage* has also been identified as science fiction, but it utilizes such bizarre creations (for example, the artificial creation and destruction of organs) that it has almost no apparent relation to the science and technology that existed in Lindsay's era. It illustrates well the affinity between utopian and fantasy literature. Indeed, Lindsay forced the reader to become terribly anxious about outcomes in the fantastic journey because the story was overlaid with a utopian veneer and not mere escapism. Lindsay confronted serious questions about how mankind can achieve worthy objectives while coming to grips with humanity itself, in particular the ego. In short, as the great dystopian writers of the twentieth century argued, nightmares or fantasies can be real.

Born in England, David Lindsay (1876–1945) was reserved and awkward both in his youth and as an adult. Lindsay served in the army during World War I and tried to become a full-time writer following the conflict. Yet he was never financially successful during his lifetime in the half-dozen novels he published. Only after his death did his work gain a measure of acclaim. Lindsay was strongly influenced by the British aesthetic literary movement of the late nineteenth century, led by writers such as Oscar Wilde and William Butler Yeats. The aesthetics blended traditions of the past such as Romanticism and Hellenistic philosophy to create mystical imagery in their poetry and novels. Among the Romantics, Lindsay was especially influenced by and imitative of the poet William Blake, historian Thomas Carlyle, and Mary Shelley, creator of the fantastic tale (forerunner of modern science fiction).

*A Voyage to Arcturus* accepts the philosophical school of the Hellenes, which argued that the only important considerations in life were pleasure, representing good, and pain, symbolizing evil. Lindsay argues that humanity is bound up in its pursuit of pleasure, which keeps humans entwined in ill-defined worldly goals such as happiness. Thus in the end the pursuit of pleasure is in fact evil since it breeds illusions. Lindsay borrowed many of the literal images of the aesthetics in creating his fantastic utopia full of emotional tensions while largely devoid of intellectual contemplation. He also invokes Eastern mysticism, especially Buddhism, in the process of rejecting the world and reality, holding that this world is an illusion and another world is the true reality. Further, like most writers of his time, Lindsay became enthralled by Sigmund Freud's exploration of the workings of the mind. Colin Wilson has argued that Lindsay was rebelling against the modern, superficial reality of the "communal life-world" that makes individual expression and thought difficult.

The story begins with a séance in contemporary England in which Maskull, the giant hero; Nightspore, Maskull's alter ego; and Krag, an evil power representing pain, make their appearance and initiate the conflict. *A Voyage* visits the mystical realm of Tormance, the planet of the double star Arcturus, where the central issue is how to achieve pleasure and avoid pain in a world of sensation. Lindsay relates a titanic contest between Crystalman (corresponding to Freud's superego), representing a poetic sensitivity (equated with Epicurean pleasure), and Krag (representing the ego), who has the power to remove pain. Caught in the middle of this struggle is the central figure of Maskull, manipulated by the godlike powers. Everything on the planet Tormance is created by Krag, although Maskull only discovers this fact gradually. Concentrating on the means of achieving freedom, albeit limited to the aesthetic, Lindsay illustrates the tension between the appeal of physical bondage (pain) and the ideal of metaphysical free expression (pleasure).

The Promethean earth figure Maskull (fulfilling the libido in Freud's terminology) awakens in the land of Tormance, ruled by King Arcturus, to discover the Sublime, a kind of Darwinian nature that exudes suffering. Maskull makes a quest-like journey from the southern part of Tormance to find the source of fire in the city of Muspel, but he dies at the gates of the city and is only able to enter in the spiritual form of Nightspore (representing Freud's id). Nightspore had been Maskull's acquaintance on earth but cannot come into existence on Tormance except through Maskull's death. Lindsay suggests in Maskull's Promethean-like quest a form of destructive narcissism that causes the tension between the desire for absolute freedom and the fear of determinism, that humans have no control over their destiny. Maskull discovers too late,

like Alice in Wonderland, that his search for fire external from himself was foolish since the source was all the while within rather than without him.

On his journey to Muspel, the lost traveler Maskull encounters a variety of obstacles, representing pleasure, that threaten to divert Maskull's quest. Thus Lindsay suggests that although humans may have noble dreams and goals, distractions constantly appear in the form of appealing pleasures. But he goes farther to offer an unsettling conclusion, that the quest itself becomes a form of pleasure and thus in reality is ignoble. Maskull is not simply trying to hurdle specific obstacles; rather, he is himself the greatest obstacle to a successful quest, since the fire was not actually at Muspel but within himself. The sexual encounters in *A Voyage* suggest Lindsay's view that the male sex drive was like a hunger of the will that needed to absorb the female. The reader becomes increasingly uncomfortable in the realization that Lindsay is not just providing an escapist story but is challenging human sensibilities by pursuing the self-destructive element. The reader has chosen to be immersed in Lindsay's work partly as an act of pleasure and expects to be rewarded with a pleasurable outcome. Yet the author has created some formidable obstacles in the path; the reader thus becomes Maskull. Even when mankind embarks upon noble quests such as freedom, he is buffeted by the external forces of light and dark, good and evil, which ultimately are also part of a fatally deterministic human nature. By thinking in utopian terms and assailing humanity's narcissistic nature, Lindsay managed to make the normally fluffy fantasy harsh and all too real.

***Reference*** Bloom, Harold. "Clinamen: Toward a Theory of Fantasy," in Slusser, George E., Eric S. Rabkin, and Robert Scholes, eds., *Bridges to Fantasy*, (1982), 1–20.

## Walden Two (1948)

Composed just at the end of World War II by the founder of modern behavioral psychology, B. F. Skinner, *Walden Two* attempted to restore the glory days of optimistic utopias. By resurrecting the image of Henry David Thoreau's ideal experiment of a century earlier, Skinner sought to reduce the scope of utopias to a smaller, more manageable scale. Much in *Walden Two* can claim a utopian lineage back to Thomas More and Robert Owen, only with a greater sophistication relying upon psychological behaviorism. Psychological elements had already become a vital aspect of early dystopias such as Aldous Huxley's *Brave New World*, and Skinner added the formula to twentieth-century utopias, though *Walden Two* was preceded by H. G. Wells's *Men Like Gods* (1923) in giving psychological authority to utopias.

The product of a small-town, middle-class upbringing, Burrhus Frederic Skinner (1904–1990) helped to bury Freudian psychoanalysis with his notion that the brain was too complicated to be dissected. Rather, the results of irrational thought, unsocial behavior, must simply be modified to make it acceptable without attempting to "cure" the patient. The primary influence upon Skinner's education was Ivan Pavlov's study of conditioning in animals. Skinner's first major publication, *The Behavior of Organisms* (1938), outlined his psychological behaviorism. Skinner's philosophy, as opposed to his psychology, had no truck with liberal humanitarian themes such as human freedom and dignity, as is suggested by the title of his most famous 1971 summary of his labors, *Beyond Freedom and Dignity*. Liberalism, by creating the goals of freedom and responsibility, must rely upon a threat of punishment to achieve its goals, which Skinner saw as its major flaw. Skin-

ner hoped to abolish liberalism's "autonomous man" by denying the whole concept of freedom. By the end of World War II when the world had seen enough of antifreedom totalitarian "utopias" in Germany and Russia, Skinner was appalled at the seeming abandonment by intellectuals of the idea of progress and the perfectibility of man. Thus he sought to experiment with behavior modification as a vehicle for reforming education and treating the whole person from the earliest impressionable years of life. The result was *Walden Two*.

The setting for *Walden Two* is the end of World War II with two young veterans returning home. Rogers and Jamnik learn about an experimental commune in the agricultural Midwest run by a man named Frazier. They travel with their girlfriends, a psychology professor named Burris, and a professor of philosophy, Castle, to visit the working utopia. Skinner shows in his utopia great respect for the work ethic, including education, and middle-class values, including leisure and recreation time. Frazier and a small group of social engineers have created a society completely compatible with Skinner's behavioral psychology, which offers positive reinforcement for acceptable behavior. Far from being a primitive society, the utopia embraces the best knowledge of science and technology to ensure its success and the residents' happiness. Work schedules for residents are staggered so that work goes on continuously. A variety of labor-saving devices, especially benefiting household chores, are introduced to show the importance of relying upon science and technology. The real molding of the new society centers in the child-rearing and educational features of Walden—children are cared for and trained by "professionals" rather than their biological parents. Children are promised "rewards" for conforming to proper behavior and developing self-discipline. Adolescent girls are allowed sexual freedom and the freedom to make decisions about childbearing whether or not they marry, although marriage is certainly the norm at Walden. Skinner's "operant conditioning" at Walden was intended to make people more productive, cooperative, honest, unbiased, and compassionate by teaching them the proper way to satisfy their needs. The reinforcement for the approved behavior derives from the positive environment in Walden. The Skinnerian system proposed not to create automatons but to develop character in the old-fashioned sense but without the method of punishment.

Skinner employed the old-fashioned Lucian dialogue to engage the visitors with Frazier in a lengthy debate about the merits of his ideal society. Ultimately, the debate contrasts the utopian ideals of Frazier with the humanist concerns of Professor Castle about regimentation. One group of visitors determine that Frazier's system is superior to the real world and join the commune, including Burris who initially leaves but returns to Walden. It is clear from Frazier's defense of his experiment that Skinner believed that the survival of a culture depended not upon social or economic organization but, rather, upon the solution of psychological problems. Frazier also refuses to employ political action to achieve these goals, since that would require controls and Walden is at bottom a voluntary society. The only important function of government is in planning and management. Yet Skinner falls prey to other utopian dilemmas in the problematic notion that an ill-defined, selfless elite will establish the control mechanisms in Walden. Unlike other utopias that visualized an ideal result, Skinner's utopia focused almost entirely upon the means to the end. Previous utopists had either ignored the problem of reforming human behavior to suit the utopian norm or simply removed freedom of choice for the individual. Skinner believed he was the first utopist to grapple with the need to modify behavior of the utopians. He was convinced that by adopting his technique of behavior modification, the idea of utopia could finally be fulfilled in reality. Since a perfect utopia could not be created full-blown, it must evolve from experiments with the technique. One result of such research and experiment was the conclusion that small communities work better than large conglomerates.

Given the antitraditional framework of Walden's society, it was not surprising that the work was received in 1948 without much acclaim. Further, the skillful contempt that Skinner demonstrated for the liberal philosophy of freedom could not win him many converts among the establishment.

One critic comparing *Walden Two* to classics such as Thomas More's *Utopia* described Skinner's creation as an ignoble utopia. Another bristled at the idea of placing humanity on a plane with pigeons. Some critics even suggested that Skinner was lampooning his own ideas by creating a parody of utopia. *Walden Two* did not prove to be a financial success, as readers greeted it with either hostility or boredom. Nonetheless, there were some actual experiments based upon *Walden Two*. In 1967, Kathleen Kinkade founded a Skinnerian utopia grounded upon positive reinforcement, and not negative punishment, at Twin Oaks, Virginia, and later recounted its history in print. A spinoff from Twin Oaks was East Wind, Missouri, which stressed craft production for the main economic livelihood of residents. Skinner not only pinpointed the negative controls of liberalism but also its lack of positive reinforcements to good behavior, which created the "happy slave." Was it rational to pay farmers not to plant crops and thereby make them dependent upon the government subsidies ("deferred aversive consequence") instead of their own labor? In his critique of liberalism Skinner appeared to be a fellow traveler with the Frankfurt school of modern Marxists.

Whatever might be said positively about Skinner's system, it left open the great problem of allowing human creativity and ingenuity the freedom to experiment with new ideas.

References Nye, Robert D. *What Is B. F. Skinner Really Saying?* (1979); Puligandla, R. *Fact and Fiction in B. F. Skinner's Science and Utopia* (1974).

**Wang Yuan**
*See Pingshu.*

**Wayland, Julius A.**
*See* Marxism.

## *We* (1921)

The Russian Yevgeny Zamyatin's post–World War I dystopian novel influenced other more noted twentieth-century anti-utopian works, including Aldous Huxley's *Brave New World* (1932) and George Orwell's *1984* (1949). Zamyatin's *We* reflected a uniquely Russian perspective on the problems of society and their potential solutions. Thus Zamyatin can easily be placed in the tradition of Russia's antiliberal writer Fyodor Dostoyevsky and anarchist leader Mikhail Bakunin. Much of the twentieth century's dystopian attitude can be summed up in Zamyatin's suggestion that mankind cannot cope with too much individual freedom. Thus the citizens of *We*'s "United State" relish rather than fret over their absence of freedom.

Born in the Ukrainian wheat-farming region, Yevgeny Zamyatin (1884–1937) was the son of a Russian Orthodox priest. From an early age through his education as an engineer, Zamyatin reveled in the Russian literature of Nikolay Gogol and Dostoyevsky. In his early adult years, he developed an anticzarist outlook that was typical of many youth in that era. Further, after a sojourn in England before World War I, Zamyatin became suspicious of Western attitudes despite an interest in English writers including H. G. Wells. Although he initially supported the Bol-shevik revolution, Zamyatin retained his independence and eventually criticized Lenin's totalitarian regime. His fascination with utopian subjects was evident as early as 1921 before he composed *We*. In 1931 a disillusioned Zamyatin left Russia and lived his remaining years in France.

*We* reflects Zamyatin's reading both of anarchists such as Bakunin and of Frederick W. Taylor, whose *Principles of Scientific Management* (1911) favored reorganization of industry based on science. The novel also shows the influence upon Zamyatin of the utopian writings of H. G. Wells. Zamyatin's philosophy followed the science of quantum physics, seeing the universe as an ever-expanding, virtually infinite realm incapable of being known. History moves in a dialectical cycle but in an ever-progressive direction. Therefore, Zamyatin's world does not have any real meaning, and it vacillates between entropy and upheaval. Likewise, people are divided into two types: the pragmatic majority who seek only selfish ends and a small minority of visionary rebels who challenge traditions and willingly risk their security. These opposites are represented in *We* by D-503 and I-330.

In the United State—a condition of entropy—humans have become veritable robots living under the benevolent despotism of the all-powerful Well-Doer, clearly based upon Dostoyevsky's Grand Inquisitor and anticipating Orwell's Big Brother. The utopia of the United State must be authoritarian because humans cannot and do not want to deal with their freedom. The primary concern of humans in the United State is security. The chief character in *We* is D-503, an engineer who accepts the regimented conditions in the United State without question. Yet he meets and falls in love with I-330, a fanatical female who is a member of a group of rebels known as the Mephi (short for Mephistopheles); they represent Zamyatin's second type, the visionary, and seek to restore a simple, anarchistic society that promotes human freedom. I-330 convinces D-503 to join the Mephi, who need

D-503's help to commandeer a space rocket, the Integral. The rebels in *We* do not seek a pleasure-oriented Land of Cockaygne or hedonistic lifestyle found in classical utopias but would be content to live in a primitive agrarian environment that provided only basic necessities. The great symbol of loss of freedom in the novel is the Green Wall that separates the paternalistic United State from the wilderness of the natural world of freedom beyond the Wall. The Mephi thus seek to become free from the technocratic authority of the Well-Doer and the stifling bureaucracy in order to build their own ideal society. They are trying to end the power of collectivism over the individual. Zamyatin makes the reader think about the choices between happiness and freedom, for he does not believe that the two are compatible. The Mephi cannot succeed in their plan, yet they and others after them are compelled to carry forth the struggle. As for D-503, he is captured and endures a surgical procedure known as "fantasierctomy," which eliminates his desire for change.

Although it is impossible not to see in Zamyatin's *We* specific opposition to the Bolshevik totalitarian state being developed at the time by Lenin, like Dostoyevsky, Zamyatin was thinking more broadly about the condition of humanity everywhere. In many respects Zamyatin anticipated the chilling 1950s treatise by Jacques Ellul about the dangers of sophisticated machines dehumanizing and ultimately controlling mankind. Such a Luddite mentality was not new to the industrial age, yet Zamyatin's warning about how technology could be used by totalitarian regimes to terrorize their own people did not have to await Orwell's *1984*. Adolf Hitler's Nazi concentration camps and Josef Stalin's Soviet gulag prisons both made fact what had appeared in Zamyatin's fiction by instituting mass genocide with a barbaric technological efficiency.

Although Zamyatin's vision in *We* suggests that there is no end to the dialectical cycle, it also suggests that totalitarian regimes such as the United State will always be challenged by rebels and by the coexistence of a dynamic society beyond the Green Wall. Moreover, even dyed-in-the-wool "dead-alive" figures, like the mathematician D-503, who accept the static, unfree conditions of the United State, can be transformed into heretic rebels. Zamyatin seemed ambivalent toward his goals; he did not like the primitive instinctual results of absolute freedom, and yet he also could not accept the seemingly necessary sacrifice of freedoms required by collectivist societies. Like Dostoyevsky, Zamyatin could not accept the consequences of irrational man, but unlike Dostoyevsky, Zamyatin did not believe that there is any solution to the clash of the rational and the irrational. In the end, Zamyatin only seemed to consider the extremes and was unable to conceive of any middle ground much less a solution for society other than chaos and nihilism. Perhaps if Zamyatin had been able to see the end result of totalitarianism in the Holocaust and the gulags, he might have drawn more certain conclusions.

*References* Beauchamp, Gorman. "Zamiatin's *We*," in Rabkin, Eric S., Martin H. Greenberg, and Joseph D. Olander, eds. *No Place Else* (1983); Collins, Christopher. *Evgenji Zamjatin: An Interpretative Study* (1973).

## Welfare State

More than any single historical event, the advent of the welfare state in the late nineteenth century demonstrated the fact that utopia or dystopia was possible. Thus the welfare state, and later totalitarianism, caused many to argue that the era of utopia was over since the imagined world had become reality. Although its elements were anticipated by utopias such as Robert Burton's *Anatomy of Melancholy* (1621) and Morelly's *Code of Nature* (1754), the welfare state did not result from a utopian treatise. Thus the design of the welfare state first originated not in a utopist's dreaming of a better society but in the search by a politician, Otto von Bismarck, for a program to strengthen his political grip on Germany. Other nations that have adopted welfare-state methods, often slowly and haphazardly in the twentieth century, also followed a political rather than a utopian blueprint. Nonetheless, the welfare state definitely possesses powerful utopian elements in its claim that the state will assume the roles of parent, teacher, provider, and protector from the cradle to the grave for each citizen. By the end of the twentieth century, scholarly analysts were comparing the welfare state to a non-repressive form of totalitarianism. One of the earliest literary equations was Ayn Rand's *Atlas Shrugged* (1957). Indeed, the welfare state has come under intense assault for its failures either to achieve or to make affordable the massive state regulation of so many aspects of life.

The emergence of early-nineteenth-century classical liberalism, which advocated limited government and protection of private property and individual liberty, began to become dominant politically soon after the failed revolutions of 1848–1849. Yet no sooner had liberalism seemingly triumphed over the old conservatism than it was faced with new rivals, including socialism and neoconservatism. These emerging isms promoted the very programs that were antithetical to liberalism, including political democracy and state restrictions upon laissez-faire economics. The twin forces of labor and big business proved superior to the limited government advocates among the liberals. Soon enough, the liberals were forced to reshape their political agenda to survive and succumbed to the growth of both the size of government and the expansion of political participation. At first, there was no intentional manipulation of the state from laissez-faire to welfare state, yet it seemed almost inevitable. By the time of World War I, classical liberals had joined either the socialists or the conservatives, both wanting to enlarge the powers of the state for different reasons.

A staunch member of the feudal *Junker* class in Prussia, Otto von Bismarck (1815–1898) was as far removed from utopian thought as one could get. As the neoconservative chancellor first of Prussia (1862–1871) and then of the Second German Reich (1871–1890), Bismarck had achieved the foremost objective of the German liberals, German unification. Thereafter he was engaged in a political game of protecting his power base and outdueling his political enemies, chiefly the liberals and socialists. Dealing with the liberals proved easy, since they split evenly over the issue of unification and were too divided to threaten Bismarck. However, with the awarding of adult male suffrage in the Constitution of 1871, Bismarck had to contend with a new and powerful working-class constituency naturally inclined to support the socialists. Initially the socialists were divided between two major parties, but when they merged in 1875 as the Social Democratic Party, they became a formidable political foe to Bismarck. His calculated strategy for frustrating the socialists involved co-opting much of their program, which was easier to embrace than ideological differences might suggest since Bismarck, like the socialists, was no friend of laissez-faire liberal economics. Hence Bismarck pushed through a series of measures starting in 1883 to establish state programs for unemployment insurance and job searches, workers' compensation for job injuries, national health insurance for workers, and old-age pensions. Shrewdly, Bismarck conceived that if citizens (subjects to him) were obligated to or dependent upon the state for vital services, they could never afford to support reductions of state powers. State paternalism was the perfect model in an age of political democracy to achieve controls resembling those of the absolute monarchs of the seventeenth century. As it happened, Bismarck's social program did not destroy the political power of the socialists, but it did inaugurate the model for the democratic welfare state that would spread throughout the twentieth century.

Great Britain and France enacted limited social welfare programs just before

World War I. The British Liberal Party (1906–1914) sponsored measures, including old-age pensions, workmen's compensation, and health insurance, that required hefty tax hikes upon the wealthy and big business to pay for the benefits. Ironically, the binding of the lower social classes to dependency upon the government not only represented a position philosophically at odds with classical liberalism but also helped the emerging Labour Party rapidly displace the Liberals as the second major parliamentary power. A coalition French socialist government enacted an old-age pension bill in 1910. The fledgling welfare initiatives in Britain and France were the beginnings of larger state welfare programs that followed the war. Also following Germany's lead were smaller nations in Europe, such as Belgium, which initiated old-age pensions in 1900.

After World War I, state welfare programs appeared in authoritarian guise in fascist Italy, Nazi Germany, and Soviet Russia, further demonstrating the political appeal of such methods. Meanwhile, the British economist John Maynard Keynes (1883–1946) provided a powerful rationale for the existence of the democratic welfare state. Keynes argued that the government was responsible for stimulating the economy through borrowing to finance state-run programs. Actually, the British government had pursued a similar policy at the end of the seventeenth century and on into the eighteenth century, but it lacked a philosophical foundation at the time since mercantilism was crumbling. The advent of the Great Depression in the 1930s created near-perfect economic conditions to apply Keynes's theories, which spurred further development of social welfare programs. The great period of expansion of the democratic welfare state thus occurred between 1930 and 1975.

The United States became the last major democratic nation to succumb to the welfare state. Actually, the process of increasing state powers had been emerging since the late-nineteenth-century attacks upon laissez-faire consequences of big business's freedom from state regulation. The Progressive era before World War I resulted in a number of federal regulatory bureaucracies being created to protect the consumer from monopolistic practices of big business. Thus it was actually easy for the Democratic administration of Franklin D. Roosevelt to install programs of workmen's compensation, unemployment insurance, and old-age pensions as well as additional regulatory bureaucracies. Hence it was the Democratic Party that stumbled into the realization that making citizens dependent upon the state would facilitate greater expansion of government authority and thus political power for the majority party controlling Congress and the presidency. Yet in practice the U.S. welfare state, like those in Europe, became the agency for expansion of power for appointed bureaucracies rather than elected legislatures. The unwieldy, inefficient parliaments and Congress found it expedient to delegate authority for managing the vast state programs to nonelected agencies, which came to possess the real power.

The welfare state's concentration of power in the hands of a bureaucratic central government also benefited from World War II because even more authority moved into the executive branch due to the emergency conditions. The postwar continuation of international tensions during the Cold War era postponed any recasting of the welfare state while advancing the phenomenon of the industrial-military complex, which also affected the economy. Indeed, in the United States, President Lyndon Johnson's Great Society program of the mid-1960s featured additional major expansions of social programs. The advent of hyperinflation in Western countries throughout the 1970s, spurred by a spike in energy costs, threw a huge monkey wrench into the welfare-state machinery. By the time of the end of the Cold War in the late 1980s, the costs of maintaining the welfare state through Keynesian deficit financing forced the Western democracies to consider limiting programs that required continuous tax increases.

A revitalized neoconservative movement, previously complicit in the expansion of the welfare state, seized an opportunity to propose scaling back the expensive bureaucracies and legal regulations. The tax burden of the middle classes had become onerous, reaching to more than 40 percent in the United States and to more than 50 percent in many European welfare states. Yet the public's expectations of receiving benefits combined with their reluctance to grant more taxes caused frustration and political upheavals, jerking states like France, Great Britain, and the United States in sharply different directions. Defenders of the welfare states pursued varied responses to the 1970s crisis. True believers, the Old Left, argued that the welfare system was irreversible and played upon the fears of the masses who received benefits and did not pay taxes. Some states, such as Sweden and Austria, sought compromises, chiefly the emergence of "social corporatism," which favored mixing capitalism and socialism in formulating economic policy. In Great Britain and the United States, welfare-state defenders (the Labour Party and the Democratic Party) relied upon class warfare tactics to stave off reductions in welfare programs or bureaucracies. Other measures included shifting from central to local governments the burden of financing welfare programs, so-called unfunded mandates. Yet even though the defenses were well constructed, the future of the welfare state remained questionable. The deliberate creation of the welfare state for political reasons by Bismarck and its continuation on the same basis by other liberal-socialist political parties gradually changed utopia into a nightmare of excessive state regulation, reduced individual liberties, and higher taxes as the twenty-first century approached. Some modifications of the welfare state seem inevitable, although political survival for those in office may mean its essence will remain intact for the foreseeable future. The welfare state reprises the aphorism: Be careful what you wish for because you might get it.

*See also* Anatomy of Melancholy; Code of Nature; A Modern Utopia

*References* Katsaros, Thomas. *The Development of the Welfare State in the Western World* (1995); Mishra, Ramesh. *The Welfare State in Capitalist Society* (1990).

## Wells, H. G.
*See A Modern Utopia.*

## Winstanley, Gerrard
*See* Diggers.

## *Wolfaria* (1521)

Though not regarded by many literary critics as a utopia because it did not imitate Thomas More's model, Johan Eberlin von Gunzburg's brief Protestant utopia *Wolfaria* nonetheless portrayed an ideal Christian community shaped by the Reformation teachings of Martin Luther. Though there is no direct evidence that Gunzburg read More's *Utopia*, he had ample opportunity to do so. Gunzburg was caught up emotionally in the Lutheran movement, and his passion ranged from attacking the Catholic church to suggesting an ideal society modeled largely on Luther's precepts. *Wolfaria* illustrates what life should be like in the new order outside the influence of the universal church and state of the German Middle Ages.

Johan Eberlin von Gunzburg (ca. 1460–1533) was born in the German duchy of Swabia and studied theology at several major universities in Germany and Switzerland, including the universities of Ingoldstadt and Basel. He entered church service as a Franciscan friar but broke with his order and the Catholic church in 1521 to follow Martin Luther. Gunzburg also began producing numerous pamphlets defending the Lutheran cause and had the opportunity to become more intimately acquainted with Luther while serving on the faculty at the University of Wittenberg during 1522. The 20-page *Wolfaria* was written in two consecutive pamphlets during this time of intense propaganda on behalf of his newfound faith. In the years following the publication of Gunzburg's utopia, his thinking became more tolerant and less belligerent than in the 1521 work. Gunzburg became a court pastor to the count of Wertheim. Throughout his life and career, Gunzburg exhibited a sincere empathy for peasants, a humanism of the people that in some respects was distinct from the intellectual humanism reflected in Luther.

Wolfaria was an imaginary state that strongly resembled Reformation Germany. The work details the new statutes passed to govern Wolfaria. In the first section, reformed laws dealt with the spiritual areas of life: the priesthood, the sacraments, and so on. Each law in this part reflected the doctrinal positions of Martin Luther and thus contrasted sharply with Catholic doctrine. On occasion Gunzburg went further than Luther's positions, as in the case of his proposal to abolish the friars and to allow more liberal divorce laws. Gunzburg not only offered a program of laws for the ideal society but also detailed the means for replacing the old system with the new. The second section of laws concerned the secular realm. The most remarkable feature of the government in Wolfaria was the election of magistrates and their payment by salaries rather than fees, both modern notions.

Gunzburg was not writing a philosophical piece for intellectuals to debate, as Thomas More did in his *Utopia*. For one thing, *Wolfaria* was written in the vernacular German rather than Latin. Rather, the author sought to implore ordinary Germans to throw off the yoke of the traditional church and state. Gunzburg wanted not merely religious reform but social and economic reforms that would turn the feudal society upside down. Indeed, *Wolfaria* literally incorporated a major portion of the Twelve Articles (1524) articulated by peasant spokesmen prior to the bloody German Peasants' Revolt (1524–1525). These included the election of priests;

abolition of forced tithing; hunting, fishing, and forest rights for peasants; abolition of serfdom; and equal justice under the law. Gunzburg outlined a new society complete with attention to economic conditions and trades; to the education, health, and welfare of citizens; and to education. The religious reforms not only would have simplified the liturgy, recast the sacraments, and reduced the number of holy days but also dictated vigorous assaults on monasticism, especially on begging friars. Monks and nuns would be encouraged to leave their orders but would be allowed to remain until death if they chose. Gunzburg would use the dismantled monasteries as schools, poor houses, or orphanages. The clergy would be elected by the parishioners instead of being appointed by the church, and they would have to dress in the same clothes as the lay population rather than using a distinctive attire. The clergy could marry but could not hold political office and were subject to the secular laws like any civilian. Their sole function would be to teach and preach the word of God. Priests also could leave their calling to become laymen without bearing any social or legal stigma.

The political system in Wolfaria appears to be an early version of the social welfare state. Political officeholders would be elected and paid salaries. The government would maintain state hospitals for the sick as well as public bath houses. Schools would be tax supported, and attendance for both boys and girls was mandatory from ages three to eight. Gunzburg advocated early marriage, but laws made divorce easier (he was thus at odds with Luther) while strongly condemning adultery. The state would ensure that towns were carefully planned with wide streets. Taxes could not be assessed for the military except during wars. Armies must be led by elected officials rather than professional officers, an ingenious method by Gunzburg to give assurance that wars would be entered reluctantly and seriously. The minting of coins would be carefully regulated to prevent counterfeiting. The state would also carefully regulate the economy, primarily seeking to avoid waste. Professions such as bankers, lawyers, and merchants would be discouraged but could operate with a government license. Goods produced in foreign territories could not be imported into Wolfaria so as to protect the market of local producers. Though that view was antithetical to modern laissez-faire capitalism, it would become the prevailing view the next century in the political economy of mercantilism. Wolfaria showed prejudice in favor of agriculture, but again the state would regulate prices for commodities. It also would set policy for hunting, fishing, and cutting timber. Masters were to treat servants humanely and pay them decent wages. The rich were required by law to be charitable toward the poor, and clothing was kept simple to avoid class consciousness.

*Wolfaria* did not influence other Protestant German utopists such as Gasparus Stiblinus, author of *The Eudaemonian Republic* (1553), or Johann Valentin Andreae, author of *Christianopolis* (1619). They exhibited a humanism more typical of the Renaissance and thus of More's *Utopia*. However, Gunzburg accurately mirrored the new age that Germany and Europe entered as a result of the events of the Protestant Reformation. Moreover, because he spoke more from an emotional than an intellectual perspective, Gunzburg, better than most intellectuals of the era, including Luther, anticipated the unrest of the German peasants. That upheaval emanated from economic dislocation caused by the shift from manorialism to capitalism as well as from the dissatisfaction with the Catholic church.

It is understandable that Gunzburg's rulers in Wolfaria were from the noble class. Because the Holy Roman Emperor and the pope were allied against the Protestants, the princes and the nobles became bulwarks to ensure the success of the Reformation. Moreover, their place was also a reflection of Gunzburg's own dependence upon noble rulers for his income. Further, Gunzburg did not see any natural conflict between noble and peasant; only the system—church, state, economy—was at fault for creating unbearable conditions crying out for reform. Perhaps his peasant background prevented him from demonstrating any sympathy or understanding of capitalist occupations such as that of merchant. Thus for all his desire for reform, Gunzburg mirrored the medieval mental frame of reference, trying to come to grips with the gradual implosion of feudal systems—political, social, economic, and religious.

*Reference* Bell, Susan G. "Johan Eberlin von Gunzburg's *Wolfaria*: The First Protestant Utopia" (1967).

## Wright, Austin
*See* Islandia.

## Wright, Frank Lloyd
*See* Broadacre City.

## Wu Chih-hui
*See* Anarchism.

**Zamyatin, Yevgeny**
*See We*.

**Zola, Émile**
*See Germinal*.

**Zionism**
*See* Kibbutzim.

# Chronology

| | | | | |
|---|---|---|---|---|
| **1621** | Robert Burton's *Anatomy of Melancholy* | | **1699** | Fenelon's *Adventures of Telemachus* |

**1621** Robert Burton's *Anatomy of Melancholy*

**1627** Francis Bacon's *New Atlantis*

**1638** Francis Godwin's *Man in the Moone*

**1641** Gabriel Plattes's pansophic *Macaria*

Johann Comenius visits England to promote "invisible college."

**1648** Samuel Gott's *Nova Solyma*

Abiezer Coppe, Laurence Clarkson, and Jacob Bauthumley lead Ranters in England.

**1650** Jacob Bauthumley's Ranter treatise *The Light and Dark Side of God*

**1652** Gerrard Winstanley's *Law of Freedom in a Platform* based on the Digger movement

**1656** James Harrington's *The Commonwealth of Oceana*

**1657** Cyrano de Bergerac's *Voyage to the Moon*

First millennialist Fifth Monarchy rebellion in England

**1659** John Eliot's *The Christian Commonwealth*

**1662** Huang Tsung-hsi's neo-Confucian *A Plan for the Prince* in China

**1668** Henry Neville's *Isle of Pines*

**1675** Denis Vairasse d'Allais's *History of the Sevarambians*

**1676** Gabriel de Foigny's *Australian Land Discovered*

**1682** The anonymous *Sinapia*

**1690** The anonymous *Free State of Noland*

**1694** Woman in the Wilderness millenarian sect started in Pennsylvania by Johannes Kelpius.

**1695** Gottfried Wilhelm Leibniz's pansophic *Monadology*

**1699** Fenelon's *Adventures of Telemachus*

**1708** Wang Yuan's *Pingshu* in China

**1719** Daniel Defoe's *Robinson Crusoe*

**1725** Giambattista Vico's *The New Science*

**1726** Jonathan Swift's Gulliver's Travels

**1731** Abbé Prévost's *Cleveland*

**1750** Robert Turgot's *Sorboniques* lectures

**1754** Morelly's *Code of Nature*

Voltaire's *Candide*

**1755** Jean-Jacques Rousseau's *Discourse on the Origin of Inequality*

**1759** Samuel Johnson's *Rasselas*

**1762** Jean-Jacques Rousseau's *The Social Contract*

Sarah Scott all-female utopia, *A Description of Millenium Hall*

**1763** The anonymous *The Reign of George VI*

Hiraga Gennai's *Furyu Shidoken den* in Japan

**1771** Louis Sebastien Mercier's *The Year 2440*

**1774** Ann Lee founds the first American Shaker settlement in New York.

**1775** *Shizen Shin'eido* attacks caste system in Japan.

**1776** Restif de la Bretonne's *The Perverted Peasant*

**1780** Abbé Raynal's *A Philosophical History of the Two Indies*

**1781** Restif de la Bretonne's *The Discovery of Australia*

**1793** William Godwin's *Enquiry Concerning Political Justice*

1794    Marquis de Condorcet's "Essay on the History of Progress"

Joanna Southcott leads millennialist movement in England.

1795    Marquis de Sade's *Aline et Valcour*

1796    Gracchus Babeuf's *Manifesto of the Equals*

Denis Diderot's *Supplement to Bougainville's Voyage*

1805    George Rapp launches Harmony Society in Pennsylvania.

1811    Shawnee Prophet Tenskwatawa preaches deliverance for Native Americans.

1814    Johann Rudoph Wyss's *Swiss Family Robinson*

1817    Joseph Bimeler's Separatists of Zoar settle in Ohio.

1821    Henri Comte de Saint-Simon's *The Industrial System*

1824    Robert Owen launches New Harmony utopian community in Indiana.

1826    Frances Wright starts feminist settlement at Nashoba, Tennessee.

Mary Shelley's *The Last Man*

1829    Charles Fourier's *The New Industrial World*

1830    Auguste Comte publishes first volume outlining positivism in France.

1839    Etienne Cabet's *Journey to Icaria*

Louis Blanc's *Organization of Work* outlines social workshops.

1840    John Humphrey Noyes establishes Putney Association in Vermont; moves to Oneida, New York, in 1848.

Joseph Proudhon's *What Is Property?*

Vladimir Odoevsky completes *Year 4338*.

1841    Brook Farm Transcendental community founded by George Ripley in Massachusetts.

Adin Ballou's Hopedale Community founded in Massachusetts.

1842    Christian Metz starts Ebenezer Society in New York; moves to Amana, Iowa, in 1853.

1843    Fruitlands Transcendental community founded by Bronson Alcott in Massachusetts.

Albert Brisbane's North American Phalanx Fourierist community founded in New Jersey.

1844    William Miller gathers millennial following expecting Second Coming of Christ in New York.

1845    Sylvester Judd's *Margaret*

1846    Herman Melville's *Typee*

1848    Karl Marx and Friedrich Engels publish *The Communist Manifesto*

Icarian community started on Red River in Texas.

1850    Taiping rebellion led by Hung Hsiu-ch'uan begins in China.

1852    Nathaniel Hawthorne's *Blithedale Romance*

1853    Henry Edger establishes positivist community at Modern Times, New York.

1863    Nikolay Chernyshevsky's *What Is to Be Done?*

1864    First International founded by Marx; dissolves in 1872 when anarchists split with Marxists.

| | |
|---|---|
| **1864** (cont.) | Fyodor Dostoyevsky's *Notes from the Underground* |
| | Martha McWhirter starts Woman's Commonwealth in Texas. |
| **1867** | Gabino Barreda launches positivist education reform in Mexico. |
| **1868** | William Frey founds Cedar Vale, Kansas, positivist settlement. |
| **1871** | Edward Bulwer-Lytton's *The Coming Race* |
| **1872** | Samuel Butler's *Erewhon* |
| **1880** | Fyodor Dostoyevsky's "Grand Inquisitor" |
| **1881** | Muhammad Ahmad 'Abd Allah claims to be the Mahdi in the Sudan. |
| **1882** | Friedrich Engels's *Socialism: Utopian and Scientific* |
| **1883** | Fabian Society founded in England. |
| | Otto von Bismarck begins legislation to launch the welfare state in Germany. |
| **1884** | Edward Bellamy's *Looking Backward* and Nationalist Clubs |
| **1885** | Alfred Kimsey Owen outlines Topolobampo Bay utopia in *Integral Cooperation*. |
| | Kaweah Colony started in California. |
| | Sudanese "madhi" dies after leading popular revolt. |
| | Émile Zola's *Germinal* |
| **1887** | W. H. Hudson's *A Crystal Age* |
| **1888** | Paiute shaman Wovoka preaches Ghost Dance movement among Native American tribes. |
| | Helena Petrovna Blavatsky outlines Theosophy in *The Secret Doctrine*. |
| **1889** | Mark Twain's *A Connecticut Yankee in King Arthur's Court* |
| **1890** | Theodor Hertzka's *Freeland* |
| | William Morris's *News from Nowhere* |
| **1891** | Ignatius Donnelly's *Caesar's Column* |
| **1894** | Julius Wayland founds Marxist Ruskin Cooperative in Tennessee. |
| | William Dean Howells's *Altruria* |
| | Ernest B. Gaston launches Fairhope colony. |
| **1898** | Ebenezer Howard's *Tomorrow: A Peaceful Path to Reform*, basis of Garden City movement |
| | Katherine Tingley launches theosophical community at Point Loma, California. |
| | Cooperative Brotherhood community founded at Burley, Washington. |
| **1899** | Petr Kropotkin's *Fields, Factories, and Workshops* |
| | Jacob Beilhart founds Spirit Fruit Society in Ohio. |
| **1901** | Alcanoan Grigsby's *Nequa* |
| | H. G. Wells's *First Men in the Moon* |
| **1902** | Theodor Herzl's *Altneuland* |
| | K'ang Yu-wei's *The Great Equality* |
| **1904** | Gabriel Tarde's *Underground Man* |
| | G. K. Chesterson's *The Napoleon of Notting Hill* |
| **1905** | H. G. Wells's *A Modern Utopia* |
| **1906** | Georges Sorel's *Reflections on Violence* |
| **1907** | William Dean Howells's *Through the Eye of the Needle* |
| | Wu Chih-hui founds first Chinese anarchist society. |
| | Mohandas K. Gandhi inaugurates *satyagraha* in South Africa. |
| **1908** | Jack London's *The Iron Heel* |

Anatole France's *Penguin Island*

Filippo Marinetti's *Futurist Manifesto*

E. M. Forster's *The Machine Stops*

**1913** Earliest Jewish kibbutzim started in Palestine.

Job Harriman founds Llano colony in California.

**1915** Mohandas K. Gandhi begins work on nationalist utopia in India.

Charlotte Perkins Gilman's *Herland*

**1917** Bolshevik Revolution in Russia

**1918** Ernst Bloch's *Spirit of Utopia*

**1920** Bruno Taut's expressionist *The Dissolution of the Cities*

Karel capek's *R.U.R.: Rossum's Universal Robots*

David Lindsay's *A Voyage to Arcturus*

**1921** Yevgeny Zamyatin's *We*

George Bernard Shaw's play *Back to Methuselah*

Simon Kimbangu launches messianic movement in central Africa.

**1923** H. G. Wells's *Men Like Gods*

**1924** Frankfurt Institute opens in Germany.

**1925** Gerhart Hauptmann's *Island of the Great Mother*

**1926** Muana Lesa, founder of Kitawala millennial movement in Nyasaland, executed.

**1927** Fritz Lang's expressionist motion picture *Metropolis* shown in Germany.

**1929** John Desmond Bernal's *The World, the Flesh, and the Devil*

Karl Mannheim's *Ideology and Utopia*

**1930** Olaf Stapledon's *Last and First Men*

**1932** Aldous Huxley's *Brave New World*

Frank Lloyd Wright outlines Broadacre City.

**1935** Le Corbusier's *Radiant City*

K'ang Yu-wei's *The Great Equality*

**1937** Ayn Rand's *Anthem*

**1940** Erich Fromm's *Escape from Freedom*

Jorge Luis Borges's "Tlön, Uqbar, Orbis Tertius"

**1943** Hermann Hesse's *The Glass Bead Game*

**1946** George Orwell's *Animal Farm*

Vladimir Nabokov's *Bend Sinister*

**1948** B. F. Skinner's *Walden Two*

**1949** George Orwell's *1984*

**1951** Merger of Israeli kibbutzim in Ichud Hakvutzot Vehakibbutzim.

**1952** Kurt Vonnegut's *Player Piano*

**1953** Ray Bradbury's *Fahrenheit 451*

Arthur C. Clarke's *Childhood's End*

**1954** William Golding's *The Lord of the Flies*

Jacques Ellul's *The Technological Society*

L. Ron Hubbard founds the Scientology movement.

**1955** Herbert Marcuse's *Eros and Civilization*

**1956** William Golding's *Pincher Martin*

**1958** Mao Ze-dong launches the Great Leap Forward in China.

**1959** Teilhard de Chardin's *The Future of Man*

| | | | |
|---|---|---|---|
| **1959**<br>*(cont.)* | Ernst Bloch's *Principle of Hope* details his "concrete utopia." | **1975** | Ernest Callenbach's *Ecotopia* |
| **1960** | Paul Goodman's *Communitas* | **1976** | Marge Piercy's *Woman on the Edge of Time* |
| **1961** | Robert Heinlein's *Stranger in a Strange Land* | **1977** | Samuel R. Delany's *Triton* |

**1959**
*(cont.)*  Ernst Bloch's *Principle of Hope* details his "concrete utopia."

**1960**  Paul Goodman's *Communitas*

**1961**  Robert Heinlein's *Stranger in a Strange Land*

**1962**  Aldous Huxley's *Island*

Anthony Burgess's *A Clockwork Orange*

**1964**  Tibor Dery's *Mr. G.A. in X*

Herbert Marcuse's *One Dimensional Man*

**1965**  Mao Ze-dong launches the "Great Proletarian Cultural Revolution" in China.

Findhorn commune in Scotland begins revival of communal societies.

Frank Herbert's *Dune*

**1967**  Herbert Marcuse's *The End of Utopia*

Kathleen Kinkade founds Twin Oaks, Virginia, commune based on *Walden Two.*

**1968**  Arthur C. Clarke's *2001: A Space Odyssey*

Monique Wittig's *Les Guerillères*

**1970**  Kobo Abe's *Inter Ice Age 4*

**1972**  Michael Crichton's *Terminal Man*

Theodore Roszak's antiscience ecotopia *Where the Wasteland Ends*

**1974**  Robert Nozick's *Anarchy, State and Utopia*

Ursula Le Guin's *The Dispossesed*

**1975**  Ernest Callenbach's *Ecotopia*

**1976**  Marge Piercy's *Woman on the Edge of Time*

**1977**  Samuel R. Delany's *Triton*

**1978**  Jonestown, Guyana, mass cult suicide of 900 people

**1979**  Ruhallah Al-Musari Al-Khomeini seizes power in Iran as new *Mahdi.*

**1980**  Ecotopian Murray Bookchin's *Toward an Ecological Society*

Alvin Toffler's *The Third Wave*

**1981**  Residential utopia at Seaside, Florida, begins

**1985**  Margaret Atwood's *The Handmaid's Tale*

Terry Gilliam's motion picture *Brazil*

**1991**  Michael Crichton's *Jurassic Park*

Murray Bookchin's *Remaking Society*

**1993**  Branch Davidian cult compound burned near Waco, Texas.

Order of the Solar Temple mass suicides in Canada and Switzerland

**1996**  Terry Gilliam's film *12 Monkeys*

**1997**  Heaven's Gate cult suicides at San Diego

# Bibliography

## I. Bibliographies and Reference Sources

Albertson, Ralph. "A Survey of Mutualistic Communities in America." *Iowa Journal of History and Politics* 34 (1936): 375–444.

Beauchamp, Gorman. "Themes and Uses of Fictional Utopias: A Bibliography of Secondary Works in English." *Science Fiction Studies* 4 (1977): 55–63.

Booker, M. Keith. *Dystopian Literature: A Theory and Research Guide*. Westport, CT: Greenwood Press, 1994.

Cioranescu, Alexandre. *L'Avenir du passe: Utopie et litterature*. Paris: Gallimard, 1972.

Clarke, I. F. *The Tale of the Future from the Beginning to the Present Day: An Annotated Bibliography*. New York: Library Association, 1972.

Dare, Philip N. *American Communes to 1860: A Bibliography*. New York: Garland Press, 1990.

Fogarty, Robert S. *Dictionary of American Communal and Utopian History*. Westport, CT: Greenwood Press, 1980.

Haschak, Paul G. *Utopian/Dystopian Literature: A Bibliography of Literary Criticism*. Metuchen, NJ: Scarecrow Press, 1994.

Leeming, David A., and Kathleen M. Drowne, *Encyclopedia of Allegorical Literature*. Santa Barbara, CA: ABC-CLIO Press, 1996.

*Macmillan Encyclopedia of Architects*. 4 vols. New York: Macmillan, 1982.

Miller, Timothy. *American Communes, 1860–1960: A Bibliography*. New York: Garland Press, 1990.

Negley, Glenn. *Utopian Literature: A Bibliography with a Supplementary Listing of Works Influential in Utopian Thought*. Lawrence: University of Kansas Press, 1977.

Sargent, Lyman Tower. *British and American Utopian Literature, 1516–1985: An Annotated Chronological Bibliography*. New York: Garland Press, 1988.

Snodgrass, Mary Ellen. *Encyclopedia of Utopian Literature*. Santa Barbara, CA: ABC-CLIO Press, 1995.

## II. Anthologies

*Communal Societies in America*. 160 vols. New York: Ames, 1975.

Disch, Thomas M., ed. *The New Improved Sun: An Anthology of Utopian Science Fiction*. New York: Harper and Row, 1975.

# Bibliography

Fogarty, Robert S., ed. *American Utopianism*. Itasca, IL: Peacock, 1972.

Johnson, J. W., ed. *Utopian Literature: A Selection*. New York: Modern Library, 1968.

Lewis, Arthur O., ed. *Utopian Literature*. New York: Arno Press, 1971.

Manuel, Frank E., and Fritzie P. Manuel, eds. *French Utopias: An Anthology of Ideal Societies*. New York: Free Press, 1966.

Negley, Glenn, and J. Max Patrick, eds. *The Quest for Utopia: An Anthology of Imaginary Societies*. New York: Henry Schuman, 1952.

## III. Secondary Sources

Abash, Merritt. "Utopia Subverted: Unstated Messages in *Childhood's End*." *Extrapolation* 30 (1989): 372–379.

Alexander, Peter, and Roger Gill, eds. *Utopias*. LaSalle, IL: Open Court Publishing Co., 1984.

Allain, Mathe, ed. *France and North America: Utopias and Utopians*. Lafayette: Center for Louisiana Studies, 1978.

Anderson, Fulton H. *Francis Bacon: His Career and His Thought*. Los Angeles: University of Southern California Press, 1962.

Armytage, W. H. G. *Heavens Below: Utopian Experiments in England, 1560–1960*. London: Routledge & Kegan Paul, 1961.

———. Armytage, W. H. G. *Yesterday's Tomorrows: A Historical Survey of Future Societies*. Toronto: University of Toronto Press, 1968.

"Aspects of Utopian Fiction." *Studies in the Literary Imagination* 6, no. 2 (1973).

Avineri, Shlomo. *The Making of Modern Zionism: The Intellectual Origins of the Jewish State*. New York: Basic Books, 1981.

Baker-Smith, Dominic, and C. C. Barfoot, eds. *Between Dream and Nature: Essays on Utopia and Dystopia*. Amsterdam: Rodopi, 1987.

Barnes, Harry Elmer. "The Philosophy of the State in the Writings of Gabriel Tarde." *Philosophical Studies* 28 (1919): 248–279.

Barr, Marleen, and Nicholas D. Smith, eds. *Women and Utopia: Critical Interpretations*. Lanham, MD: University Press of America, 1983.

Barthel, Diane L. *Amana: From Pietist Sect to American Community*. Lincoln: University of Nebraska Press, 1984.

Bartkkowski, Frances. *Feminist Utopias*. Lincoln: University of Nebraska Press, 1989.

Bauer, Wolfgang. *China and the Search for Happiness: Recurring Themes in Four Thousand Years of Chinese Cultural History*. Translated by Michael Shaw. New York: Seabury Press, 1976.

Beauchamp, Gorman. "Melville and the Tradition of Primitive Utopia." *Journal of General Education* 33 (1981): 6–14.

———. "*1984*: Oceania as an Ideal State." *College Literature* 11 (1984): 1–12.

Becker, George J. "Edward Bellamy." *Antioch Review* 14 (1954): 181–194.

Beecher, Jonathan, and Richard Bienvenu, eds. *The Utopian Vision of Charles Fourier*. Boston: Beacon Press, 1972.

Bell, Susan G. "Johan Eberlin von Gunzburg's *Wolfaria*: The First Protestant Utopia." *Church History* 36 (1967): 122–139.

Bennett, George N. *The Realism of William Dean Howells, 1889–1920*. Nashville, TN: Vanderbilt University Press, 1973.

Benson, Timothy O. *Expressionist Utopias: Paradise, Metropolis, Architectural Fantasy*. Seattle: University of Washington Press, 1993.

Berghahn, Klaus L., and Reinhold Grimm, eds. *Utopian Vision, Technological Innovation and Poetic Imagination*. Heidelbérg: Carl Winter, 1990.

Berneri, Marie Louise. *Journey through Utopia*. New York: Schocken Books, 1971.

Bierman, Judah. "Science and Society in the *New Atlantis* and Other Renaissance Utopias." *Publications of the Modern Language Association* 78 (1963): 492–500.

Blitzer, Charles. *An Immortal Commonwealth: The Political Thought of James Harrington*. New Haven, CT: Yale University Press, 1960.

Bloom, Harold. "Clinamen: Toward a Theory of Fantasy." In *Bridges to Fantasy*. Edited by George E. Slusser, Eric S. Rabkin, and Robert Scholes. Carbondale: Southern Illinois University Press, 1982.

Boguslaw, Robert. *The New Utopians: A Study of System Design and Social Change*. Englewood Cliffs, NJ: Prentice-Hall, 1965.

Bookchin, Murray. *Toward an Ecological Society*. Buffalo, NY: University of Toronto Press, 1980.

Bowman, Sylvia E. *The Year 2000: A Critical Biography of Edward Bellamy*. New York: Bookman Associates, 1958.

Boyd, Katrina G. "Pastiche and Postmodernism in Brazil." *Cinefocus* 1 (1990): 33–42.

Bradley, Ian C. *William Morris and His World*. New York: Scribner, 1978.

Bradshaw, Brendan. "More on Utopia." *Historical Journal* 24 (1981): 1–27.

Bronner, Stephen E., and Douglas Kellner, eds. *Passion and Rebellion: The Expressionist Heritage*. New York: J. F. Bergin, 1983.

Brosio, Richard A. *The Frankfurt School: An Analysis of the Contradictions and Crises of Liberal Capitalist Societies*. Muncie, IN: Ball State University, 1980.

Campbell, Carlos C. *New Towns: Another Way to Live*. Reston, VA: Reston, 1976.

Carden, Maren Lockwood. *Oneida: Utopian Community to Modern Corporation*.

Baltimore, MD: Johns Hopkins University Press, 1969.

Champion, Larry S. "Gulliver's Voyages: The Framing Events as a Guide to Interpretation." *Texas Studies in Literature and Language* 10 (1969): 529–536.

Chesneaux, Jean. "Egalitarian and Utopian Traditions in the East." *Diogenes* 62 (1968): 76–102.

Chung, Carson. *The Development of Neo-Confucian Thought*. 2 vols. New York: Bookman Associates, 1957–1962.

Clareson, Thomas D., ed. *Voices for the Future: Essays on Major Science Fiction Writers*. Bowling Green, OH: Bowling Green University Press, 1976.

Clarke, I. F. *The Pattern of Expectation, 1644–2001*. New York: Basic Books, 1979.

Clough, Rosa Trillo. *Futurism, the Story of a Modern Art Movement: A New Appraisal*. New York: Philosophical Library, 1961.

Coe, Richard N. *Morelly: Ein Rationalist auf dem Wege zum Sozialismus*. Berlin: Rutten and Loening, 1961.

Coleman, Janet. "The Continuity of Utopian Thought in the Middle Ages: A Reassessment." *Vivarium* 20 (1982): 1–23.

Coleman, Stephen, and Paddy O'Sullivan. *William Morris and News from Nowhere: A Vision of Our Time*. Devon, Eng.: Green Books, 1990.

Collins, Christopher. *Evgenji Zamjatin: An Interpretative Study*. The Hague: Mouton, 1973.

Collins, George R. "Broadacre City: Wright's Utopia Reconsidered." In *Four Great Makers of Modern Architecture*. New York: DeaCapo Press, 1970.

Conkin, Paul. *Two Paths to Utopia: The Hutterites and the Llano Colony*. Lincoln: University of Nebraska Press, 1964.

Cranston, Sylvia. *HPB: The Extraordinary Life and Influence of Helena Blavatsky, Founder of the Modern Theosophical Movement*. New York: G. P. Putnam's Sons, 1993.

Creese, Walter L. *The Search for Environment: The Garden City Before and After*. New Haven, CT: Yale University Press, 1966.

Cro, Stelio. "The New World in Spanish Utopianism." *Alternative Futures: The Journal of Utopian Studies* 2 (1979): 39–53.

Davis, J. C. *Fear, Myth and History: The Ranters and the Historians*. New York: Cambridge University Press, 1986.

———. *Utopia and the Ideal Society: A Study of English Utopian Writing, 1516–1700*. New York: Cambridge University Press, 1981.

Davis, Walter R., and Richard A. Lanham. *Sidney's Arcadia*. New Haven, CT: Yale University Press, 1965.

De Vos, Luk, ed. *Just the Other Day: Essays on the Suture of the Future*. Antwerp: EXA, 1985.

Dunstan, Helen. "Wang Yuan's *Pingshu*: A Late Seventeenth Century Utopia." *Papers on Far Eastern History* 35 (1987): 31–78.

Duval, Edwin M. *The Design of Rabelais's* Pantagruel. New Haven, CT: Yale University Press, 1991.

Edmunds, R. David. *The Shawnee Prophet*. Lincoln: University of Nebraska Press, 1983.

Elliott, Robert C. *The Shape of Utopia: Studies in a Literary Genre*. Chicago: University of Chicago Press, 1970.

Erlich, Richard D., and Thomas P. Dunn, eds. *Clockwork Worlds: Mechanized Environments in SF*. Westport, CT: Greenwood Press, 1983.

Eurich, Nell. *Science in Utopia: A Mighty Design*. Cambridge: Harvard University Press, 1967.

Faber, M. D. *New Age Thinking: A Psychoanalytic Critique*. Ottawa: University of Ottawa Press, 1996.

Fabre, Jean. "Realité et utopie dans la pensée politique de Rousseau." *Annales J. J. Rousseau* 35 (1959–1962): 181–221.

Fairbank, John K., ed. *Chinese Thought and Institutions*. Chicago: University of Chicago Press, 1957.

Favre, Pierre. *Sade, utopiste: Sexualité, pouvoir et L'Etat dans le roman Aline et Valcour*. Paris: University of Paris, 1967.

Fekete, John. "*The Dispossessed* and *Triton*: Act and System in Utopian Science Fiction." *Science-Fiction Studies* 6 (1979): 129–143.

Fiedler, Leslie A. *Olaf Stapledon: A Man Divided*. New York: Oxford University Press, 1983.

Finley, M. I. "Utopianism Ancient and Modern." In *The Use and Abuse of History*. New York: Viking Press, 1975.

Firchow, Peter Edgerly. *The End of Utopia: A Study of Aldous Huxley's* Brave New World. Cranbury, NJ: Associated University Presses, 1984.

Firpo, Luigi. "Il processo di Giordano Bruno." *Revista storica italiana* 60 (1948): 542–597.

Fishman, Robert. *Urban Utopias in the Twentieth Century: Ebenezer Howard, Frank Lloyd Wright, and Le Corbusier*. New York: Basic Books, 1977.

Fogarty, Robert S. *All Things New: American Communes and Utopian Movements, 1860–1914*. Chicago: University of Chicago Press, 1990.

Fogarty, Robert S., and H. Roger Grant. "Free Love in Ohio: Jacob Beilhart and the Spirit Fruit Society." *Ohio History* 89 (1980): 206–221.

Foster, Lawrence. *Women, Family and Utopia: Communal Experiments of the Shakers, the Oneida Community, and the Mormons*. Syracuse, NY: Syracuse University Press, 1991.

Fox, Richard G. *Gandhian Utopia: Experiments with Culture*. Boston: Beacon Press, 1989.

Francis, Richard. *Transcendental Utopia: Individual and Community at Brook Farm, Fruitlands and Walden*. Ithaca, NY: Cornell University Press, 1997.

Frank, Joseph. "Nihilism and *Notes from the Underground*." *Sewanee Review* 69 (1961): 1–33.

Friedman, Jerome. *Blasphemy, Immortality and Anarchy: The Ranters and the English Revolution*. Athens: Ohio University Press, 1987.

Garreau, Joel. *Edge City: Life on the New Frontier*. New York: Doubleday, 1991.

Gaston, Paul B. *Man and Mission: E. B. Gaston and the Origins of the Fairhope Single Tax Colony*. Montgomery, AL: Black Belt Press, 1993.

Geoghegan, Vincent. *Utopianism and Marxism*. London: Methuen, 1987.

Godwin, Joscelyn. *The Theosophical Enlightenment*. Albany: State University Press of New York, 1994.

Gorra, Michael. "The World of *A Clockwork Orange*." *Gettysburg Review* 3 (1990): 630–643.

Greenwalt, Emmett A. *California Utopia, Point Loma: 1897–1942*. San Diego: Point Loma Publications, 1978.

Grendler, Paul F. "Utopia in Renaissance Italy: Doni's New World." *Journal of the History of Ideas* 26 (1965): 479–494.

Grimm, Reinhold, and Jost Herman, eds. *From the Greeks to the Greens: Images of the Simple Life*. Madison: University of Wisconsin Press, 1989.

Hall, A. Rupert. "Science, Technology and Utopia in the Seventeenth Century." In *Science and Society, 1600–1900*, edited by Peter Mathias. New York: Cambridge University Press, 1972.

Hansot, Elizabeth. *Perfection and Progress: Two Modes of Utopian Thought*. Cambridge: MIT Press, 1974.

Harp, Gillis J. *Positivist Republic: Auguste Comte and the Reconstruction of American Liberalism, 1865–1920*. University Park: Pennsylvania State University Press, 1995.

Harrison, John F. C. *Quest for the New Moral World: Robert Owen and the Owenites in Britain and America*. New York: Scribner, 1969.

———. *The Second Coming: Popular Millenarianism, 1780–1850*. London: Routledge, & Kegan Paul, 1979.

Harth, Erica. *Cyrano de Bergerac and the Polemics of Modernity*. New York: Columbia University Press, 1970.

Hertzler, Joyce O. *History of Utopian Thought*. New York: Cooper Square, 1923.

Hexter, J. H. *More's Utopia: The Biography of an Idea*. Princeton: Princeton University Press, 1952.

Hillegas, Mark R. *The Future as Nightmare: H. G. Wells and the Anti-utopians*. New York: Oxford University Press, 1967.

Holloway, Mark. *Heavens on Earth: Utopian Communities in America, 1680–1880*. 2nd ed. New York: Dover Publications, 1966.

Holstun, James. *A Rational Millennium: Puritan Utopias of Seventeenth-Century England and America*. New York: Oxford University Press, 1987.

Holt, Peter M. *The Mahdist State in the Sudan, 1881–1898: A Study of Its Origins, Development and Overthrow*. 2nd ed. Oxford: Clarendon Press, 1970.

Hsiao Kung-chuan. "In and Out of Utopia: K'ang Yu-wei's Social Thought." *The Chung Chi Journal* 7 (1967): 1–18, 101–149; 8 (1968): 1–52.

Jaen, Didier T. "The Esoteric Tradition in Borges' 'Tlön, Uqbar, Orbis Tertius' " *Studies in Short Fiction* 21 (1984): 25–39.

Johnpoll, Bernard K., and Lillian Johnpoll. *The Impossible Dream*. Westport, CT: Greenwood Press, 1981.

# Bibliography

Johnson, Christopher. *Utopian Communism in France: Cabet and the Icarians, 1839–1851.* Ithaca, NY: Cornell University Press, 1974.

Jones, J. D. F. *Freeland.* London: Sinclair-Stevenson, 1994.

Jones, James T. "A Middle Class Utopia: Lewis's *It Can't Happen Here.*" In *Sinclair Lewis at 100: Papers Presented at a Centennial Conference,* edited by Richard M. Connaughton. St. Cloud, MN: St. Cloud State University, 1985.

Kateb, George. *Utopia and Its Enemies.* 2nd ed. New York: Schocken Books, 1972.

Katsaros, Thomas. *The Development of the Welfare State in the Western World.* New York: University Press of America, 1995.

Kellner, Douglas, and Harry O'Hara. "Utopia and Marxism in Ernst Bloch." *New German Critique* 9 (1976): 11–35.

Kershner, R. B. "Degeneration: The Explanatory Nightmare." *Georgia Review* 40 (1986): 416–444.

Ketterer, David. "Margaret Atwood's *The Handmaid's Tale.*" *Science-Fiction Studies* 16 (1989): 209–217.

Kolnai, Aurel. *The Utopian Mind and Other Papers.* London: Athlone Press, 1995.

Krause, Charles A. *Guyana Massacre: The Eyewitness Account.* New York: Berkley Publishing, 1978.

Kumar, Krishan. *Prophecy and Progress: The Sociology of Industrial and Post-Industrial Society.* New York: Penguin, 1978.

———. *Utopia and Anti-Utopia in Modern Times.* Oxford: Basil Blackwell, 1987.

Lanternari, Vittorio. *The Religions of the Oppressed: A Study of Modern Messianic Cults.* Translated by Lisa Sergio. New York: Knopf, 1963.

Levaillant, Jean. *Les Aventures du scepticisme: Essai sur l'evolution intellectuelle d'Anatole France.* Paris: Colin, 1965.

Levitas, Ruth. "Marxism, Romanticism and Utopia: Ernst Bloch and William Morris." *Radical Philosophy* 18 (1989): 27–36.

Logan, George M. *The Meaning of More's "Utopia.".* Princeton, NJ: Princeton University Press, 1983.

Lugon, Clovis. *La République Communiste Chrétienne des Guaranis, 1610–1778.* Paris: Editions Ouvrières, 1949.

McClelland, James. "Utopianism versus Revolutionary Heroism in Bolshevik Policy: The Proletarian Culture Debate." *Slavic Review* 39 (1980): 403–425.

McGucken, William. *Scientists, Society, and State: The Social Relations of the Science Movement in Great Britain, 1931–47.* Columbus: Ohio State University Press, 1984.

Malak, Amin. "Margaret Atwood's *The Handmaid's Tale* and the Dystopian Tradition." *Canadian Literature* 112 (1987): 9–16.

Mannheim, Karl. *Ideology and Utopia: An Introduction to the Sociology of Knowledge.* Translated by Louis Wirth and Edward Shils. New York: Harcourt, Brace, 1936.

Manuel, Frank E. *The New World of Henri Saint-Simon.* Cambridge: Harvard University Press, 1956.

———. "Pansophia: A Seventeenth-Century Dream of Science." In his *Freedom from History and Other Untimely Essays.* New York: New York University Press, 1971.

———. *The Prophets of Paris.* Cambridge: Harvard University Press, 1962.

———, ed. *Utopias and Utopian Thought.* Boston: Houghton Mifflin, 1966.

Manuel, Frank E., and Fritzie P. Manuel. *Utopian Thought in the Western World.* Cambridge: Harvard University Press, 1979.

Maravall, Jose Antonio. *Utopia and Counterutopia in the "Quixote."* Translated by Robert W. Felkel. Detroit: Wayne State University Press, 1991.

Martin, Marianne W. *Futurist Art and Theory, 1909–1915*. Oxford: Clarendon Press, 1968.

Meisner, Maurice. "Utopian Goals and Ascetic Values in Chinese Communist Ideology." *Journal of Asian Studies* 28 (1968): 101–110.

Melton, J. Gordon, Jerome Clark, and Aidan A. Kelly. *New Age Almanac*. New York: Visible Ink, 1991.

Mishra, Ramesh. *The Welfare State in Capitalist Society*. New York: Basic Books, 1990.

Mitchell, Charles. "The *Lord of the Flies* and the Escape from Freedom." *Arizona Quarterly* 22 (1966): 27–40.

Montgomery, John Warwick. *Cross and Crucible: Johann Valentin Andreae (1586–1654), Phoenix of the Theologians*. 2 vols. The Hague: Martinus Nijhoff, 1973.

Mooney, James. *The Ghost-Dance Religion and Wounded Knee*. New York: Dover, 1976 (1896).

Morton, Arthur Leslie. *The English Utopia*. London: Lawrence & Wishart, 1952.

Moylan, Tom. *Demand the Impossible: Science Fiction and the Utopian Imagination*. New York: Methuen, 1986.

Mumford, Lewis. *The Story of Utopias*. New York: Viking Press, 1962 (1922).

Naughton, James D. "Futurology and Robots: Karel Capek's *R. U. R.*" *Renaissance and Modern Studies* 28 (1984): 72–86.

Nye, Robert D. *What Is B. F. Skinner Really Saying?* Englewood Cliffs, NJ: Prentice-Hall, 1979.

Parkinson, Robert C. "*Dune*: An Unfinished Tetralogy." *Extrapolation* 13 (1971): 16–24.

Patrick, J. Max. "The Free State of Noland: A Neglected Utopia from the Age of Queen Anne." *Philological Quarterly* 25 (1946): 79–88.

———. "Robert Burton's Utopianism." *Philological Quarterly* 27 (1948): 345–358.

———. "*Nova Solyma*: Samuel Gott's Puritan Utopia." *Studies in the Literary Imagination* 10, no. 2 (1977): 43–55.

Pavlyshyn, Marko. "Games with Utopia: Herman Hesse's *Das Glasperlenspiel*." In *Just the Other Day: Essays on the Suture of the Future*, edited by Luk de Vos. Antwerp: EXA, 1985.

Pfaelzer, Jean. *The Utopian Novel in America, 1886–1896: The Politics of Form*. Pittsburgh: University of Pittsburgh Press, 1984.

Plath, David W., ed. *Aware of Utopia*. Urbana: University of Illinois Press, 1971.

Pocock, J. G. A. "James Harrington and the Good Old Cause: A Study of the Ideological Context of His Writings." *Journal of British Studies* 10 (1970): 30–48.

Popkin, Richard H. "Jewish Messianism and Christian Millenarianism." In *Culture and Politics from Puritanism to the Enlightenment*, edited by Perez Zagorin. Berkeley: University of California Press, 1980.

Poster, Mark. *The Utopian Thought of Restif de la Bretonne*. New York: New York University Press, 1971.

Puligandla, R. *Fact and Fiction in B. F. Skinner's Science and Utopia*. St. Louis, MO: W. H. Green, 1974.

Quinn, Joseph A. "Eden and New Jerusalem: A Study of *The Napoleon of Notting Hill*." *Chesterton Review* 3 (1977): 230–239.

Rabkin, Eric S., Martin H. Greenburg, and Joseph D. Olander, eds. *No Place Else: Explorations in Utopian and Dystopian Fiction*. Carbondale: Southern Illinois Press, 1983.

Rawson, Claude. *Gulliver and the Gentle Reader: Studies in Swift and Our Time*. London: Routledge, 1973.

Reynolds, Ray P. *Cat's Paw Utopia*. El Cajon, CA: Ray P. Reynolds, 1972.

Ricoeur, Paul. *Lectures on Ideology and Utopia.* Edited by George H. Taylor. New York: Columbia University Press, 1986.

Roemer, Kenneth M., ed. *America as Utopia.* New York: Burt Franklin, 1981.

Rohrlich, Ruby, and Elaine H. Baruch, eds. *Women in Search of Utopia: Mavericks and Mythmakers.* New York: Shocken Books, 1984.

Rose, R. B. *Gracchus Babeuf: The First Revolutionary Communist.* Stanford, CA: Stanford University Press, 1978.

Rose, Steven. "The Fear of Utopia." *Essays in Criticism* 24 (1974): 55–70.

Rosenau, Helen. *The Ideal City: Its Architectural Evolution in Europe.* New York: Methuen, 1983.

Ruether, Rosemary Radford. *The Radical Kingdom: The Western Experience of Messianic Hope.* New York: Harper and Row, 1970.

Saalman, Howard. "Early Renaissance Architectural Theory and Practice in Antonio Filarete's Trattato di Architettura." *Art Bulletin* 41 (1959): 89–106.

Sadler, Elizabeth. "One Book's Influence: Edward Bellamy's 'Looking Backward.'" *New England Quarterly* 17 (1944): 530–555.

Sargent, Lyman T. "Utopia and Dystopia in Contemporary Science Fiction." *The Futurist* 6 (1972): 93–98.

Schram, Stuart R. "To Utopia and Back: A Cycle in the History of the Chinese Communist Party." *China Quarterly* 87 (1981): 407–439.

Sciabarra, Chris Matthew. *Ayn Rand: The Russian Radical.* University Park: Pennsylvania State University Press, 1995.

Seligman, Adam B., ed. *Order and Transcendence: The Role of Utopias and the Dynamics of Civilizations.* Leiden: E. J. Brill, 1989.

Sewell, David R. "Hank Morgan and the Colonization of Utopia." *American Transcendental Quarterly* 3 (1989): 27–44.

Sexton, Richard. *Parallel Utopias: Sea Ranch, California and Seaside, Florida.* San Francisco: Chronicle Books, 1995.

Sharma, G. N. "Butler's *Erewhon*: The Machine as Object and Symbol." *Samuel Butler Newsletter* 3 (1980): 3–12.

Simon, Walter Michael. *European Positivism in the Nineteenth Century: An Essay in Intellectual History.* Ithaca, NY: Cornell University Press, 1963.

Soleri, Paolo. *Arcology: The City in the Image of Man.* Cambridge: MIT Press, 1969.

Sonn, Richard D. *Anarchism.* New York: Twayne, 1992.

Spiro, Melford E. *Kibbutz: Venture in Utopia.* Cambridge: Harvard University Press, 1956.

Stansky, Peter S. *On Nineteen Eighty-four.* New York: W.H. Freeman, 1983.

Steiner, Page. *Escape into Aesthetics: The Art of Vladimir Nabokov.* New York: William Morrow, 1966.

Sterrenburg, Lee. "*The Last Man:* Anatomy of Failed Revolutions." *Nineteenth-Century Fiction* 33 (1978): 324–347.

Stewart, Philip. "Utopias That Self-Destruct." *Studies in Eighteenth Century Culture* 9 (1979): 15–24.

Stites, Richard. *Revolutionary Dreams: Utopian Vision and Experimental Life in the Russian Revolution.* New York: Oxford University Press, 1989.

Sullivan, E. D. S., ed. *The Utopian Vision: Seven Essays on the Quincentennial of Sir Thomas More.* San Diego: San Diego State University Press, 1983.

Sullivan, Tom R. "The Uses of a Fictional Formula: The Selkirk Mother Lode." *Journal of Popular Culture* 8 (1974): 35–52.

Suvin, Darko. "Defining the Literary Genre of Utopia." *Studies in the Literary Imagination* 6, no. 2 (1973): 121–145.

———. "The Utopian Tradition of Russian Science Fiction." *Modern Language Review* 66 (1971): 139–159.

Talmon, Jacob L. *Political Messianism: The Romantic Phase*. New York: Praeger, 1960.

Tanzy, Eugene. "Contrasting Views of Man and the Evolutionary Process: *Back to Methuselah* and *Childhood's End*." In *Arthur C. Clarke*, edited by Joseph D. Olander and Martin H. Greenberg. New York: Taplinger Publishing Co., 1977, 172–195.

Thrupp, Sylvia L., ed. *Millennial Dreams in Action: Studies in Revolutionary Religious Movement*. New York: Schocken Books, 1970.

Tod, Ian, and Michael Wheeler. *Utopia*. New York: Harmony Books, 1978.

Tuveson, Ernest Lee. *Millennium and Utopia: A Study in the Background of the Idea of Progress*. New York: Harper & Row, 1964.

"Utopias and Utopians." *Transactions of the Fifth International Congress on the Enlightenment* 2 (1980): 609–742.

Venturi, Franco. *Utopia and Reform in the Enlightenment*. New York: Cambridge University Press, 1971.

Wagar, W. Warren. *The City of Man: Prophecies of a World Civilization in Twentieth-Century Thought*. Boston: Houghton Mifflin, 1963.

———. *H. G. Wells and the World State*. New Haven, CT: Yale University Press, 1961.

Wagner, Geoffrey. "A Forgotten Satire: Bulwer-Lytton's *The Coming Race*." *Nineteenth Century Fiction* 19 (1965): 379–385.

Walker, Philip. *Germinal and Zola's Philosophical and Religious Thought*. Philadelphia: John Benjamins Publishing, 1984.

Wands, John M. "Antipodal Imperfection: Hall's *Mundus Alter et Idem* and Its Debt to More's *Utopia*." *Moreana* 18, no. 69 (1981): 85–100.

Weaver, Dusk, and Willow. *Sunburst: A People, a Path, a Purpose*. San Diego: Avant Books, 1982.

Webster, Charles. "The Authorship and Significance of *Macuria*." *Past and Present* 56 (1972): 34–48.

Weller, Allen Stuart. *Francesco di Giorgio, 1439–1501*. Chicago: University of Chicago Press, 1943.

Westfall, Carroll William. *In This Most Perfect Paradise: Alberti, Nicholas V, and the Invention of Conscious Urban Planning in Rome, 1447–55*. University Park: Pennsylvania State University Press, 1974.

Worsley, Peter. *The Trumpet Shall Sound: A Study of "Cargo" Cults in Melanesia*. New York: Schocken Books, 1968.

Yates, Frances A. *Giordano Bruno and the Hermetic Tradition*. Chicago: University of Chicago Press, 1964.

Zavala, Silvio. *Sir Thomas More in New Spain: A Utopian Adventure of the Renaissance*. N.p., 1955.

# Illustration Credits

# Index

Page numbers in bold refer to main entries

# Index